SEPTEMBER 1999–

MW01241235

# TARBELL'S

# KJV & NRSV
# Lesson
# Commentary

BASED ON THE INTERNATIONAL SUNDAY SCHOOL LESSONS

DR. WILLIAM P. BARKER

DAVID C. COOK CHURCH MINISTRIES CURRICULUM
COLORADO SPRINGS, COLORADO/PARIS, ONTARIO

Edited by Dan Lioy

ISBN: 0-7814-5484-0

# CONTENTS

■

## SEPTEMBER, OCTOBER, NOVEMBER 1999
## FROM SLAVERY TO PROMISED LAND

### UNIT I: LIBERATION AND COVENANT

### UNIT II: WILDERNESS WANDERINGS

### UNIT III: ENTERING THE PROMISED LAND

■

## DECEMBER 1999, JANUARY, FEBRUARY 2000
## STUDIES IN MATTHEW

### UNIT I: BEGINNINGS: BIRTH AND MINISTRY

### UNIT II: JESUS' TEACHINGS AND MINISTRY

### UNIT III: FULFILLMENT OF JESUS' MISSION

# CONTENTS

■

## MARCH, APRIL, MAY 2000
## CONTINUING JESUS' WORK

■

## JUNE, JULY, AUGUST 2000
## NEW LIFE IN CHRIST

The youngest of our seven grandchildren is now a first grader. When I asked Blair what her favorite subject was at school, I was expecting her to tell me it was gym or art, as her older brothers had always replied. Instead, she promptly answered, "Computers!"

Computers? For a 7-year-old? For a child in first grade? I had not realized how the computer has become so much part of our children's daily lives.

Some people, in fact, insist that the computer age will mean the end of the traditional Sunday school class and the Sunday church school teacher. After all, they point out Bible software now exists which means that electronic study may be done anytime, anywhere by anyone without the need of a class or teacher. These computer wizards insist that some digital tools offer programs that can eliminate traditional forms of Christian education. They tell us that Bible reference CD-ROMs, Internet religious discussion groups, and hundreds of web sites dealing with spiritual matters can replace the traditional teacher. Over 40 companies now have electronic concordance products on the market. One leading theological seminary conducts graduate courses solely on the Internet. The professor told me that he never will see any of his students but will communicate with them only through the computer.

Does all this glitzy gadgetry mean that Sunday church schools will soon die out? Does the coming of the computer mean that the teacher will be as obsolete as the lamplighter and the iceman?

No! You as a church school teacher are more important than ever. No electronic device can replace the presence of a live human guiding a group of live humans on the quest for a Christ-filled existence. No microchip can fill the role of a person exemplifying the power and presence of Jesus in a local setting. No computer-based tool can know the hurts and needs of persons struggling to serve as Christ's community. Only you as a teacher can!

Use the computer as an implement to assist in learning when suitable. But don't be intimidated by the claims of those who insist that you as a teacher are redundant and unnecessary. Rather, recognize the unique calling you have from the Lord! Carry out the task of weekly classroom leadership that is never outdated!

Most of all, rely on the promise of Christ's goodness and nearness as you present each lesson!

Your colleague always in His ministry,
William P. Barker

## A Note of Appreciation

*A special word of appreciation to Mrs. Ellen Meier and Dr. John Barker who have helped prepare this volume and whose ministry means so much!*

Sunday school materials from the following denominations and publishers follow the International Sunday School Lesson outlines (sometimes known as the Uniform Series). Because *Tarbell's KJV & NRSV Lesson Commentary* follows the same ISSL outlines, you can use *Tarbell's* as an excellent teacher resource to supplement the materials from these publishing houses.

**Denominational:**
Advent Christian General Conference—*Adult*
American Baptist (Judson Press)—*Adult*
Church of God in Christ (Church of God in Christ Publishing House)—*Adult*
Church of Christ Holiness—*Adult*
Church of God (Warner Press)—*Adult*
Church of God by Faith—*Adult*
National Baptist Convention of America (Boyd)—*All ages*
National Primitive Baptist Convention—*Adult*
Progressive National Baptist Convention—*Adult*
Presbyterian Church (U.S.A.) (Bible Discovery Series—Presbyterian Publishing House or P.R.E.M.)—*Adult*
Southern Baptist (Baptist Sunday School Board)—*All ages*
Union Gospel Press—*All ages*
United Holy Church of America—*Adult*
United Methodist Church (Cokesbury)—*All ages*

**Nondenominational:**
David C. Cook Church Ministries—*Adult*
Echoes Sunday School Literature—*Adult*
Standard Publishing—*Adult*
Urban Ministries—*All ages*

# FROM SLAVERY TO PROMISED LAND

# GOD CALLS MOSES

**BACKGROUND SCRIPTURE:** Exodus 3.
**DEVOTIONAL READING:** Exodus 6:2-8

**KEY VERSE:** God said to Moses, "I AM WHO I AM." . . . "Thus you shall say to the Israelites, 'I AM has sent me to you.' " Exodus 3:14.

*KING JAMES VERSION*

EXODUS 3:1 Now Moses kept the flock of Jethro his father in law, the priest of Midian: and he led the flock to the backside of the desert, and came to the mountain of God, even to Horeb.

2 And the angel of the LORD appeared unto him in a flame of fire out of the midst of a bush: and he looked, and, behold, the bush burned with fire, and the bush was not consumed.

3 And Moses said, I will now turn aside, and see this great sight, why the bush is not burnt.

4 And when the LORD saw that he turned aside to see, God called unto him out of the midst of the bush, and said, Moses, Moses. And he said, Here am I.

5 And he said, Draw not nigh hither: put off thy shoes from off thy feet, for the place whereon thou standest is holy ground.

6 Moreover he said, I am the God of thy father, the God of Abraham, the God of Isaac, and the God of Jacob. And Moses hid his face; for he was afraid to look upon God.

7 And the LORD said, I have surely seen the affliction of my people which are in Egypt, and have heard their cry by reason of their taskmasters; for I know their sorrows;

8 And I am come down to deliver them out of the hand of the Egyptians, and to bring them up out of that land unto a good land and a large, unto a land flowing with milk and honey; unto the place of the Canaanites, and the Hittites, and the Amorites, and the Perizzites, and the Hivites, and the Jebusites.

9 Now therefore, behold, the cry of the children of Israel is come unto me: and I have also seen the oppression wherewith the Egyptians oppress them.

10 Come now therefore, and I will send thee unto Pharaoh, that thou mayest bring forth my people the children of Israel out of Egypt.

11 And Moses said unto God, Who am I, that I should go unto Pharaoh, and that I should bring forth the children of Israel out of Egypt?

12 And he said, Certainly I will be with thee; and this shall be a token unto thee, that I have sent thee: When thou hast brought forth the people out of Egypt, ye shall serve God upon this mountain.

*NEW REVISED STANDARD VERSION*

EXODUS 3:1 Moses was keeping the flock of his father-in-law Jethro, the priest of Midian; he led his flock beyond the wilderness, and came to Horeb, the mountain of God. 2 There the angel of the LORD appeared to him in a flame of fire out of a bush; he looked, and the bush was blazing, yet it was not consumed. 3 Then Moses said, "I must turn aside and look at this great sight, and see why the bush is not burned up." 4 When the LORD saw that he had turned aside to see, God called to him out of the bush, "Moses, Moses!" And he said, "Here I am." 5 Then he said, "Come no closer! Remove the sandals from your feet, for the place on which you are standing is holy ground." 6 He said further, "I am the God of your father, the God of Abraham, the God of Isaac, and the God of Jacob." And Moses hid his face, for he was afraid to look at God.

7 Then the LORD said, "I have observed the misery of my people who are in Egypt; I have heard their cry on account of their taskmasters. Indeed, I know their sufferings, 8 and I have come down to deliver them from the Egyptians, and to bring them up out of that land to a good and broad land, a land flowing with milk and honey, to the country of the Canaanites, the Hittites, the Amorites, the Perizzites, the Hivites, and the Jebusites. 9 The cry of the Israelites has now come to me; I have also seen how the Egyptians oppress them. 10 So come, I will send you to Pharaoh to bring my people, the Israelites, out of Egypt." 11 But Moses said to God, "Who am I that I should go to Pharaoh, and bring the Israelites out of Egypt?" 12 He said, "I will be with you; and this shall be the sign for you that it is I who sent you: when you have brought the people out of Egypt, you shall worship God on this mountain."

| | | |
|---|---|---|
| *Monday, Aug. 30* | Exodus 2:1-10 | *Birth and Youth of Moses* |
| *Tuesday, Aug. 31* | Exodus 2:11-15 | *Moses Flees to Midian* |
| *Wednesday, Sept. 1* | Exodus 2:16-25 | *Moses Settles in Midian* |
| *Thursday, Sept. 2* | Exodus 3:1-12 | *Moses at the Burning Bush* |
| *Friday, Sept. 3* | Exodus 3:13-22 | *Moses Called to Deliver Israel* |
| *Saturday, Sept. 4* | Exodus 4:1-9 | *Moses Empowered by God* |
| *Sunday, Sept. 5* | Exodus 4:10-20 | *Moses Responds to God's Call* |

## BACKGROUND

In this quarter's lessons, we will study the account of God's people from their departure from Egypt through their entry into the promised land. We will focus on God's rescuing Israel from slavery, including His establishment of the Mosaic covenant and His giving the people the land of promise.

Jacob and his family settled in Egypt around 1876 B.C. At this time, his son Joseph was the prime minister of Egypt, being the second-in-command next to Pharaoh (Gen. 41:41-43). Jacob died in 1859 B.C., and Joseph died in 1805 B.C. For the next four centuries, the Israelites lived in Egypt (Exod. 12:40). But by the time Moses was born in 1526 B.C., a new king had come to the throne, and he knew nothing about Joseph or what he had done (1:8). This ruler was possibly Ahmose, who founded the 18th dynasty and expelled a group of foreigners named the Hyksos from the land.

The next pharaoh, Thutmose III, told his people that the large number of Israelites living in Egypt were becoming a threat to the nation. He therefore ordered that they be enslaved and placed into labor gangs under harsh Egyptian taskmasters (1:9-11). Moses, who by now had become a prominent member of Pharaoh's court (Acts 7:22), reacted angrily at the cruelty of an Egyptian brutally beating an Israelite laborer, and he thus murdered the Egyptian. Moses then fled for his life and sought asylum among the Midianite people (Exod. 2:11-15).

Moses married Zipporah (the daughter of a Midianite priest named Reuel), started a family, and spent the next 40 years as a sheepherder (2:16-22). During this time, Thutmose III died and was succeeded by his son, Amunhotep II. Meanwhile, the Israelites groaned beneath their burden of slavery, and God responded to their cries for help (2:23-25). He did so by revealing Himself to Moses and commanding him to return to Egypt to lead the Israelites to freedom (3:1-10).

## NOTES ON THE PRINTED TEXT

One day Moses was tending the flock of his father-in-law and led the animals deep into the wilderness of the Sinai Peninsula. He eventually came to Horeb, which is called *the mountain of God* (3:1). This was either a different name for Mount Sinai or another mountain in the same general area.

*There the angel of the LORD appeared to him in a flame of fire out of a bush* (3:2). Moses' attention was riveted to a bush engulfed in flames. Strangely, the bush did not burn up. This made Moses curious, and so he investigated. He was aware of God's presence. Forget the varied natural explanations, such as flaming volcanic gases escaping from a fissure in the earth or the sun striking the whirling sand particles of a mini cyclone. Moses understood that he was in the presence of God.

The Lord personally summoned the sheepherder with the cry, *"Moses, Moses!"* (3:4). Moses' response indicated his willingness to listen and obey. The Lord told Moses not to come any closer to the burning bush and to remove his sandals, for the ground on which he stood was sacred due to the divine presence (3:5). Moses' actions showed his respect for and reverence of God.

The Lord declared that He was the God of Moses' ancestors. *"I am the God of your father, the God of Abraham, the God of Isaac, and the God of Jacob"* (3:6). Moses, who was perhaps feeling overwhelmed and afraid, hid his face, rather than risk death by looking at the Lord's glorious presence.

God announced that He had seen the misery of His people in Egypt and had heard their cries for deliverance from their harsh taskmaskers (3:7). Unlike the idols of Egypt, the Lord was not uncaring, aloof, or powerless. He would rescue the Israelites from their cruel overlords, lead them out of Egypt, and bring them into their own good and spacious land. It was a fertile region of bounteous provision, as the phrase *flowing with milk and honey* (3:8) suggests.

The Lord was serious about rescuing His people from their oppressive condition (3:9). And He wanted to use Moses to lead the Israelites to freedom. God chose him to be the human instrument to confront Pharaoh. That's why the Lord said to Moses, *"I will send you to Pharaoh to bring my people, the Israelites, out of Egypt"* (3:10).

Moses felt reluctant to do the job. It was natural for him to feel inadequate, for no one could do God's will apart from His power. But Moses wouldn't be working alone, for the Lord would be with him every step of the way. Nevertheless, Moses made excuses as to why he shouldn't go. For example, he protested that he was an insignificant nobody. *"Who am I that I should go to Pharaoh, and bring the Israelites out of Egypt?"* (3:11).

In response, God simply said, *"I will be with you"* (3:12). As proof that Moses represented the Lord, God said, *"when you have brought the people out of Egypt, you shall worship God on this mountain."*

## SUGGESTIONS TO TEACHERS

Anyone becoming a naturalized citizen of the United States is required to learn the basic history of the nation. Citizenship means knowing and appreciating the events that brought the U.S. into existence. The same is true with our faith. To be members of God's family, we must understand the account of

His dealings with His people. For example, Israel's departure from Egypt was a pivotal event. Although we will be discussing Moses as the key human leader in this great drama, we should remember that God was the central character.

**1. INEXPLICABLE REVELATION.** Moses' encounter with the Lord through the burning bush cannot be explained away by stating that it was a species of brilliant thornbush found in Sinai or the reflection of the sunlight on the bush. No, Moses had met the living God, and His holy presence defied explanation. Ask your students to share why they think God's presence in their lives sometimes is beyond explanation.

**2. UNEXPECTED ROLE.** God said that He was sending Moses to Pharaoh to lead the Israelites out of Egypt. This suggests that God's encounters with us usually include a call to serve. The tasks that He gives us to do sometimes are not what we might expect or desire. Discuss with the class members some of the unexpected jobs God has had them do in the past.

**3. UNDERSTANDABLE RELUCTANCE.** Moses had no wish to go back to Egypt, where he was a wanted fugitive for murdering an Egyptian official. At times, we might drag our feet or plead that we are unable to carry out what the Lord wants us to do. But God sweeps aside our excuses!

**4. UNMISTAKABLE REALIZATION.** When Moses balked at appearing before Pharaoh, the Lord reassured him that he would not be alone. Regardless of how difficult or unpleasant the situation might get, God would give him success. Let the students know that God continues to help believers to do His will. With His strength and companionship, they can serve Him with confidence!

**FOR ADULTS** ■ TOPIC: Called to Obedience

■ QUESTIONS: 1. How did God make His presence known to Moses, and what was unusual about it? 2. In what way did Moses' initial response show that he wanted to hear and heed the Lord? 3. Why do you think Moses felt inadequate when God directed him to appear before Pharaoh and liberate the Israelites? 4. What are some things God has called you to do, and how have you typically responded? 5. How can the promise of God encourage you to do tasks for Him that seem too difficult to handle?

■ **ILLUSTRATIONS:**

**Unexpected Call.** A few years ago in Atlanta, a young businessman named Jack Stephens got a call from a friend heading a local boys' club. The man asked Jack to drive a youngster and his mother to the hospital. Jack agreed, and met the mother and her boy at their house, which was not far from his home. (Jack learned that the boy had leukemia and that the disease was in its final stages.) Early the next day as the three rode to the hospital, the boy was stretched out on his mother's lap, and his feet extended over to Jack. Jack glanced down at the child, and their eyes met.

"Are you God?" the boy asked. Though startled by the question, Jack answered, "No, son. Why do you ask?" The boy responded, "My mother said that God would come and take me away with Him." Jack was shaken by the reply. Even more distressing was the fact that a week later, the boy went home to be with the Lord.

Despite the sadness of the boy's death, Jack Stephens found himself drawn to God in a way that he had not expected. The question, "Are you God?" was like a voice from the "burning bush" in Jack's life. He realized that he had to do more for the Lord with his life. Eventually, Jack became the Director of the Joseph B. Whitehead Memorial Boys' Club in Atlanta, Georgia.

Perhaps the voice of God is calling from the "burning bush" in your life. The Lord might be summoning you to do more than just enjoy a life of ease with other believers in your church. God might be calling you to be His representative to those in this world who are suffering and spiritually lost. Perhaps the Lord wants you to be His agent among the helpless and forgotten, whom He remembers.

Do you feel overwhelmed by such a prospect? You don't need to be, for God will remain with you every step of the way.

**God's Name.** In Exodus 3:14, God revealed Himself as *"I AM WHO I AM."* This could also be rendered, "I AM WHO I AM" or "I WILL BE WHAT I WILL BE." Scholars struggle over the precise meaning of the Hebrew phrase. Some say this name for God points to His self-existence and eternality. Albert Van Den Heuvel offers another interpretation. He says that the original should be translated, "I WILL BE WHO I WAS" and that God intended this phrase to instill hope in His people down through the ages. For example, the Lord was saying to Moses, "I will be to you who I was to Abraham." Jesus was saying to Peter, "I will be to you who I was to Abraham and Moses." And today this same Lord is declaring to us, "I will be to you who I was to Peter and those Galilean fisherman, and to Moses and to Abraham and to the prophets, as well as to Paul and Silas, to Matthew and Mark and Luke and John, to Luther, to Calvin, to Wesley, and to all the host of the family of faith."

**Burning but Not Consumed.** Many of our Protestant forebears in Europe identified closely with God's call to Moses to serve Him obediently. In fact, many in the Reformed tradition—such as the Scots, the Irish, the Huguenots, and the Magyars—depict a burning bush on their church's official seal or insignia. It often has the Latin inscription, *Nec Tamen Consumebatur.* This means, in effect, "burning but not consumed." The phrase refers to the Lord's mysterious call to His people and His holy, indescribable presence among them. God's fire was understood to burn on without end, and continued to confront them. As Hebrews 12:29 says, *"our God is a consuming fire."*

■ TOPIC: Who Me?

■ QUESTIONS: 1. In what ways do you think Moses' experience as a shepherd in the wilderness humbled him? 2. How would you have responded if God revealed Himself to you in a burning bush? 3. What difficult tasks has God called you to do, and how have you responded? 4. What do you think it means to serve God obediently? 5. What are some ways that God cares for believers today?

■ ILLUSTRATIONS:

**Sense of Call.** When Laura Hannant was four years old, she went to Nepal and met Mother Teresa. Now twelve, Laura stood before an assembly of juniors and seniors at Pittsburgh's Baldwin High School and spoke about the evils of child labor.

Laura said that she was the daughter of a Canadian television newsman. She noted seeing firsthand in India children living in virtual slavery. Laura related that at four, she accidentally wandered into a sweatshop in India. She recalled her and her father watching the children run and hide as the owner screamed at them. Laura told the audience that she later heard about a child who had tried to escape the 14-hour work days and the regular beatings, only to be caught and killed in front of the other children as a warning. Laura said that some of the children she saw in India had the skin on their fingers split open from working on carpet looms while chained by their ankles to the machinery.

Laura explained that her experiences in India prompted her to become active in "Free the Children," which is an organization that campaigns against the exploitation of child labor. (The poised and confident speaker does not consider herself too young to support the eradication of child labor around the globe.) When someone in the audience asked why she felt called to do this job, she said, "Standing up for people's rights was something that my parents once did, and now it's something that students must do."

Laura felt called to speak for the children of the world as much as Moses felt called by the Lord to speak for Him and the Israelites. At some point, you too will sense God's call and claim on your life to serve Him.

**Sacred Ground?** Tourists pass at a rate of 1200 people per hour. Often they leave flowers or teddy bears and—much to the chagrin of the caretakers—even peel the bark off of nearby trees where they write messages in red ink. The spot is the bronze plaque marking Elvis Presley's grave at Graceland. Karen Christ of Canton, Ohio, called the ground "sacred." Fay Mathany of Richmond, Virginia, feels close to Elvis at this spot.

When Moses stood before the burning bush, he was filled with awe, but not because he was near the spot where a dead person had been buried. Rather, he knew that he was in the presence of the holy and living God. The ground was sacred because God had made His presence known there. At different times in your life you will sense God's holy presence. In those moments, you should show Him respect, sincerity, and reverence.

**Special Spot.** The Air Force wanted to build a 50-foot dark aluminum star to honor the war dead from the youngest service branch of the United States. The dedication was supposed to take place on September 18, 1997, which was just in time for a fiftieth anniversary celebration.

Oddly enough, the largest foe of the memorial was the Marine Corps. Why? Because, the spot the Air Force had chosen was just downhill from the 78-foot high Marine Corps Memorial, which features the images of the five marines and one sailor raising the American flag on Mount Suribachi, Iwo Jima, during World War II. The Marines countered that a second memorial was too much for the two-acre park. Former Marine and now New York Representative Gerald Solomon spoke for many when he declared that the area was sacred ground.

In contrast, note the attitude of Moses concerning the spot where *"the angel of the LORD appeared to him in a flame of fire out of a bush"* (Exod. 3:2). Moses never set aside this area as special, and he never built any shrine to mark the spot. Why? Because he knew that the ground was sacred, or special, due to God's presence there. Holy ground may be found in a church building, at a church camp, in a funeral home, or many places. It will be special to you because you sense God's presence there and His call on your life to serve Him.

# CROSSING THE RED SEA

**BACKGROUND SCRIPTURE:** Exodus 13:17—14:31
**DEVOTIONAL READING:** Psalm 106:1-12

**KEY VERSE:** Do not be afraid, stand firm, and see the deliverance that the LORD will accomplish for you today. Exodus 14:13a.

---

*KING JAMES VERSION*

EXODUS 13:17 And it came to pass, when Pharaoh had let the people go, that God led them not through the way of the land of the Philistines, although that was near; for God said, Lest peradventure the people repent when they see war, and they return to Egypt:

18 But God led the people about, through the way of the wilderness of the Red sea: and the children of Israel went up harnessed out of the land of Egypt.

19 And Moses took the bones of Joseph with him: for he had straitly sworn the children of Israel, saying, God will surely visit you; and ye shall carry up my bones away hence with you.

20 And they took their journey from Succoth, and encamped in Etham, in the edge of the wilderness.

21 And the LORD went before them by day in a pillar of a cloud, to lead them the way; and by night in a pillar of fire, to give them light; to go by day and night:

22 He took not away the pillar of the cloud by day, nor the pillar of fire by night, from before the people. . . .

14:26 And the LORD said unto Moses, Stretch out thine hand over the sea, that the waters may come again upon the Egyptians, upon their chariots, and upon their horsemen.

27 And Moses stretched forth his hand over the sea, and the sea returned to his strength when the morning appeared; and the Egyptians fled against it; and the LORD overthrew the Egyptians in the midst of the sea.

28 And the waters returned, and covered the chariots, and the horsemen, and all the host of Pharaoh that came into the sea after them; there remained not so much as one of them.

29 But the children of Israel walked upon dry land in the midst of the sea; and the waters were a wall unto them on their right hand, and on their left.

30 Thus the LORD saved Israel that day out of the hand of the Egyptians; and Israel saw the Egyptians dead upon the sea shore.

31 And Israel saw that great work which the LORD did upon the Egyptians: and the people feared the LORD, and believed the LORD, and his servant Moses.

*NEW REVISED STANDARD VERSION*

EXODUS 13:17 When Pharaoh let the people go, God did not lead them by way of the land of the Philistines, although that was nearer; for God thought, "If the people face war, they may change their minds and return to Egypt." 18 So God led the people by the roundabout way of the wilderness toward the Red Sea. The Israelites went up out of the land of Egypt prepared for battle. 19 And Moses took with him the bones of Joseph who had required a solemn oath of the Israelites, saying, "God will surely take notice of you, and then you must carry my bones with you from here." 20 They set out from Succoth, and camped at Etham, on the edge of the wilderness. 21 The LORD went in front of them in a pillar of cloud by day, to lead them along the way, and in a pillar of fire by night, to give them light, so that they might travel by day and by night. 22 Neither the pillar of cloud by day nor the pillar of fire by night left its place in front of the people. . . .

14:26 Then the LORD said to Moses, "Stretch out your hand over the sea, so that the water may come back upon the Egyptians, upon their chariots and chariot drivers." 27 So Moses stretched out his hand over the sea, and at dawn the sea returned to its normal depth. As the Egyptians fled before it, the LORD tossed the Egyptians into the sea. 28 The waters returned and covered the chariots and the chariot drivers, the entire army of Pharaoh that had followed them into the sea; not one of them remained. 29 But the Israelites walked on dry ground through the sea, the waters forming a wall for them on their right and on their left.

30 Thus the LORD saved Israel that day from the Egyptians; and Israel saw the Egyptians dead on the seashore. 31 Israel saw the great work that the LORD did against the Egyptians. So the people feared the LORD and believed in the LORD and in his servant Moses.

## BACKGROUND

Exodus describes the central historical event for the Israelites—their deliverance from slavery in Egypt. The date of the Exodus has been the subject of considerable debate. Biblical chronology says the event occurred 480 years before the reign of Solomon (1 Kings 6:1). This would place the Exodus at about 1446 B.C., which was during the 18th-dynasty rule of an Egyptian pharaoh named Amunhotep II.

This early date is consistent with Judges 11:26, which declares that 300 years had elapsed since Israel entered Canaan. The 1446 B.C. date is also supported by Exodus 12:40-41, where the text says that 430 years was the duration of Israel's stay in Egypt.

Advocates of a later date appeal to the name *Rameses* (Gen. 47:11) as one of the *supply cities* (Exod. 1:11) the Egyptians built with Israelite labor. Rameses II (1304–1236 B.C.) is said to be the Pharaoh of the Exodus, and the approximate date of the event is set at 1290 B.C. This is claimed to be more consistent with the archaeology of the cities destroyed in Palestine and with the lack of evidence showing any settlement of Israelites in the Transjordan before this time. (The Transjordan is the region east of the Jordan River and the Dead Sea.) However, recent discoveries in the Transjordan and a new evaluation of the destruction of Jericho have weakened the case for the later date of the Exodus. When all the evidence is considered, the earlier date (1446 B.C.) seems more likely.

God caused a series of 10 plagues to strike Egypt, and each demonstrated the power of the Lord over a particular idol worshiped by the Egyptians. The final plague—the death of the firstborn—signified that mighty Pharaoh could no longer pose as divine, for not even his own son was spared. However, God intervened so that the deadly plague "passed over" the Hebrews' blood-protected families, which spared them.

Although Pharaoh agreed to let the captives leave, he quickly changed his mind and sent his imperial troops to herd Moses and the Israelites back to the slave camps. The people found themselves trapped between the waters of the Red Sea and the approaching chariots. As we will learn in this week's lesson, God delivered His people by opening a path through the waters to safety.

The most direct route from Egypt to Canaan would have been the road that ran through Philistine territory. However, the Israelites were not psychologically ready to fight the Philistines. Such an encounter would so unsettle God's people that they would want to *return to Egypt* (13:17).

Thus, God led His people along a route through *the wilderness toward the Red Sea* (13:18). The Hebrew literally means "Sea of Reeds," and refers to an area of water east of Egypt. There are a variety of views concerning the exact location of the Red Sea crossing. However, the most likely spot would have been the Bitter Lakes region.

The text says that the Israelites were *prepared for battle* (13:18). This perhaps means they had various weapons of war (for example, slings, bows, and so forth). Though they were militarily equipped, they were not mentally ready to fight, and would quickly lose their resolve if they engaged an opponent in combat.

Centuries earlier as Joseph neared death, he made the Israelites swear that they would take his remains with them to Canaan (Gen. 50:24-25). In honor of that promise, Moses had the Israelites carry Joseph's coffin with them (Exod. 13:19). After the years of wilderness wandering, Joseph's remains would reach their final resting place in Shechem (Josh. 24:32).

The departure from Egypt began with the Israelites traveling from Succoth to Etham, which was *on the edge of the wilderness* (Exod. 13:20). (Most likely, this campsite bordered on the desert area to the east of Egypt.) God led His people by using a single column, which was a cloud by day and fire by night (13:21). This symbolized the Lord's continued presence among His people, and must have given them reassurance (13:22).

It did not take long for Pharaoh to change his mind about letting the Israelites go. He assembled his imperial troops and led them in hot pursuit of God's people. As the Egyptian army drew closer, the Israelites could see them in the distance. The people began to panic and cried out to the Lord for help. Moses encouraged them not to fear, for God would rescue them from the enemy (14:5-14).

At God's command, Moses raised his shepherd's staff and hand over the sea, and the Lord opened a path through the water with a strong east wind (14:21). The Israelites walked through on dry ground, and safely reached the other side (14:22, 29). Then the imperial Egyptian troops followed them across the bottom of the sea. The Lord caused the wheels of their chariots to become clogged with the sand and mud, and this threw the enemy into a panic (14:23-25).

Again at God's command, Moses raised his shepherd's staff and hand over the sea, and the waters came crashing down on the Egyptian forces (14:26-28). Not one person survived the ordeal (14:28). In fact, the Israelites could see the Egyptians dead on the seashore (14:30).

The dead bodies were evidence of God's great power. The Israelites responded by revering the Lord. They put their faith in His power as well as in the leadership abilities of Moses (14:31). The Lord's act of deliverance would form the basis of the Mosaic covenant He would later make with His people. In fact, the Exodus is the event upon which all subsequent Old Testament history is built.

## SUGGESTIONS TO TEACHERS

In the Passover celebration each spring, the Jewish people remember the events of God's leading the Israelites out of Egypt. You might consider talking to a local rabbi to gain insights on how significant the Exodus event has been to the Jewish people.

It is helpful to remember that the Lord Jesus Christ celebrated the Passover, and that Christians have traditionally looked upon the Good Friday-Easter event as God's mighty Exodus-like deliverance for all humankind. Just as the Lord rescued His people from slavery in Egypt, so too He can save people from slavery to sin when they put their trust in Christ. It's no wonder that God's mighty act of delivering the Israelites from Egypt has been celebrated through the centuries by believers.

Do not try to rationalize or explain away the remarkable escape the Israelites had from their Egyptian taskmasters. The Bible makes it clear that God had acted decisively to save His people and destroy the enemy.

**1. SURVIVING AND SEASONING.** The deliverance from Egypt was God's way of continuing His work. His providential care continues to be with His people, namely, those of us who have trusted in Christ for salvation.

**2. SHINING AND SHOWING.** The Lord went before the camp of Israelites to disclose the way. The pillar of cloud by day and the pillar of fire by night signified His presence and guidance. Through faith in Christ, we know that God is always by our side throughout our life journey. He is also with the church, the body of Christ, in its pilgrimage through history.

**3. SCARING AND SHOCKING.** The appearance of the Egyptian imperial forces terrified the Israelites. Nevertheless, Moses ordered them to walk through the Red Sea on dry ground. At times doing God's will might seem either scary or shocking to us. But we can step out in faith, for we know that our sovereign Lord will watch over us, as Hebrews 13:5 makes clear. Consider also the promise that is recorded in 13:6, *"The Lord is my helper; I will not be afraid. What can anyone do to me?"*

**4. SAVING AND PRAISING.** God brought the Israelites safely through the waters. Just as God intervened on their behalf, so too now He continues to act on behalf of the faith community. Ask the class members to recall instances in which the Lord has intervened for them or others.

**5. SAVORING.** Miriam's triumphant song (Exod. 15:20-21) praised God for His mighty deed of delivering His people. Ask the students to discuss how Christians use the imagery of the Exodus account to describe what the resurrection of Jesus means to them.

■ TOPIC: Called to Deliverance
■ QUESTIONS: 1. How is God's boundless love evident in His deliverance of His people from Egypt? 2. How is God's power evident in His overthrow of the Egyptian army? 3. What connection does the Exodus have with the Easter account? 4. What is the significance of the Exodus for people of faith today? 5. What is the significance of the Exodus for oppressed peoples today?

■ ILLUSTRATIONS:

**Into the Waters.** Ancient Jewish writings tell about the time when Moses and the Israelites came to the Red Sea. Behind them in the distance they could see the dust from the columns of Egyptian troops moving to capture them and return them to the slave camps or massacre them if they resisted. Ahead of the Israelites lay the terrifying waters of the Red Sea. God told Moses that He would part the waters so that the Israelites could be delivered. But how could the people hope to survive if they ventured into those deep waters? The situation looked hopeless, and fear set in.

According to an ancient rabbinic tradition, a man named Nahshon, son of Amminadab, stepped into the water and started to move out, confident that the Lord would bring His promised deliverance. Other Israelites finally followed Nahshon. The water came up to their knees, but they plunged onward. They found the waters up to their waists, yet they plowed on. The waters came higher, to their armpits, their shoulders, and their chins. Finally, when the waters lapped at their nostrils, the sea parted (Midrash on Exodus, *Rabbah* 21.10, and Midrash on Numbers, *Rabbah* 13.9).

That story captures what faith is all about! Isn't it time that you took some risks for the Lord?

**Empty Boasting.** The evidence suggests that Amunhotep II of the 18th dynasty was the Pharaoh of Egypt at the time of the Israelites' departure. He not only defied Moses but also the God of Israel. Amunhotep II arrogantly thought that he and his nation's idols could defeat the sovereign Lord and conquer His people. But Scripture reveals that not one of the Egyptians who chased after the Israelites survived the ordeal.

The poet Shelley wrote how an antique traveler, who came across the remains of a colossal statue of Amunhotep II, proclaimed the following:

Two vast and trunkless legs of stone
Stand in the desert.
And on the pedestal these words appear:
"Look on my works, ye mighty and despair!
Nothing beside remains round the decay.

Of that colossal wreck, boundless and bare,
The lone and level sands stretch far away."
(Shelley, *Ozymandias*)

**Carrying Us.** There once was a minister's child who had been born with a severe deformity in her legs and feet. Severely crippled, the youngster hobbled painfully with crutches and braces. Though everything medically possible was done, the lovely little girl could only drag her virtually useless legs.

Near Christmas one day, the minister came in with a poinsettia for his wife, who was upstairs in bed recovering from an illness. The crippled daughter was delighted to see her father and the lovely plant. She said, "Oh, daddy! Let me carry it up to mommy!" The man looked at the youngster and sighed. Trying to suppress his own weariness and sadness, he said, "Honey, I wish you could. I'd give anything to have you do it. But you know you can't." The little one gleefully replied, "Oh, but I can, daddy! I'll carry the plant and you'll carry me!"

You may feel burdened with problems. But the Lord of life can bear you up and carry you through your most difficult experiences.

---

| | |
|---|---|
| **FOR YOUTH** | ■ **TOPIC:** Hope out of Despair<br>■ **QUESTIONS:** 1. How did God show His care and concern for His people? |

people? 2. How is God's wisdom evident in the way in which He led His people? 3. What are some ways that God has led you through difficult circumstances? 4. How has God demonstrated His power in your life? 5. In what ways has God responded to your prayers for deliverance?

■ **ILLUSTRATIONS:**

**Overcame Obstacle.** Young Pam Ford was a little over five feet tall, weighed 210 pounds, and wore size 22 clothing. She had tried reducing her eating and even went on a cabbage soup diet. But losing weight seemed impossible. Finally, with God's help, Pam enrolled herself in a weight loss program and over a year lost 33 pounds. The University of Pittsburgh's Obesity and Nutrition Research Center enabled her to slim down another 49 pounds, and she has continued her own diet and exercise program.

Obesity is just one of the obstacles that Christian youth face. Others might be teen violence, sex, and drugs. Like Pam, they cannot overcome these difficulties in their lives on their own. They need the Lord and His people to help them. Ultimately only God can bring true deliverance in the lives of young people.

**Sense of Hope.** It was the dark early days of World War II. Battles were raging across Europe. German forces had triumphed and pushed the last British forces from Dunkirk, France. The United States remained isolationist and opposed to any intervention. England's situation was desperate. There was little hope coming from the nation's leadership.

But then Winston Churchill became Prime Minister. He offered his unshakable confidence in the Allied cause, as well as his fierce determination to win the war. On May 13, 1940, he said the following to the House of Commons:

"I would say to the House, as I said to those who have joined this Government: 'I have nothing to offer but blood, toil, tears, and sweat.' We have before us an ordeal of the most grievous kind. We have before us many, many long months of struggle and suffering. You ask: What is our aim? I can answer in one word: 'Victory!' Victory at all costs, victory in spite of all terror, victory, however long and hard the road may be; for without victory there is no survival."

In spite of all the problems raging at the time, Churchill gave his nation a sense of hope that lifted them out of despair. Moses offered his people the same kind of hope. Despite the possibility of defeat at the hands of the Egyptians, Moses assured the Israelites of victory, that is, God's victory!

**Faced the Enemy.** "Am I going to die?" The question was posed by six-year-old Alex Myers of Oakmont, Pennsylvania. Alex's story had begun only two days earlier. He seemed tired, and his parents wondered whether he needed vitamins. At a routine checkup in July, 1997, they asked his physician for a blood test.

After the blood test, the family went for a river cruise, and then to Alex's soccer game, where he played for almost two hours. A dinner at a fast food restaurant concluded the day. When the family arrived at home, the pediatrician's voice message on the telephone answering machine told the parents to take Alex immediately to Pittsburgh's Children's Hospital.

The physician's diagnosis was acute lymphoblastic leukemia, which is a cancer that affects the blood and bone marrow. Alex's red blood cell and platelet count were dangerously low. He was taken to the operating room, where a plastic device was inserted in his vein in his upper chest for blood transfusions. He also began chemotherapy.

During the treatment, Alex asked his father whether he would live. While the next three years would be hard, his father reassured him that he would live. A ninety percent success rate bolstered Alex's spirits. Though there would be obstacles in those years, his parents assured him that he could trust the medical experts to help him.

Consider the Israelites' situation. Moses reminded them of the power of God. They could trust Him to be with them and to lead them through their ordeal. He would enable them to face their enemy and triumph.

# THE COVENANT

**BACKGROUND SCRIPTURE:** Exodus 19:1—20:21
**DEVOTIONAL READING:** Deuteronomy 4:32-40

**3**

**KEY VERSE:** If you obey my voice and keep my covenant, you shall be my treasured possession out of all the peoples. Exodus 19:5.

*KING JAMES VERSION*

EXODUS 19:3 And Moses went up unto God, and the LORD called unto him out of the mountain, saying, Thus shalt thou say to the house of Jacob, and tell the children of Israel;

4 Ye have seen what I did unto the Egyptians, and how I bare you on eagles' wings, and brought you unto myself.

5 Now therefore, if ye will obey my voice indeed, and keep my covenant, then ye shall be a peculiar treasure unto me above all people: for all the earth is mine:

6 And ye shall be unto me a kingdom of priests, and an holy nation. These are the words which thou shalt speak unto the children of Israel. . . .

20:2 I am the LORD thy God, which have brought thee out of the land of Egypt, out of the house of bondage.

3 Thou shalt have no other gods before me.

4 Thou shalt not make unto thee any graven image, or any likeness of any thing that is in heaven above, or that is in the earth beneath, or that is in the water under the earth: . . .

7 Thou shalt not take the name of the LORD thy God in vain; for the LORD will not hold him guiltless that taketh his name in vain.

8 Remember the sabbath day, to keep it holy. . . .

12 Honour thy father and thy mother: that thy days may be long upon the land which the LORD thy God giveth thee.

13 Thou shalt not kill.

14 Thou shalt not commit adultery.

15 Thou shalt not steal.

16 Thou shalt not bear false witness against thy neighbour.

17 Thou shalt not covet thy neighbour's house, thou shalt not covet thy neighbour's wife, nor his manservant, nor his maidservant, nor his ox, nor his ass, nor any thing that is thy neighbour's.

*NEW REVISED STANDARD VERSION*

EXODUS 19:3 Then Moses went up to God; the LORD called to him from the mountain, saying, "Thus you shall say to the house of Jacob, and tell the Israelites: 4 You have seen what I did to the Egyptians, and how I bore you on eagles' wings and brought you to myself. 5 Now therefore, if you obey my voice and keep my covenant, you shall be my treasured possession out of all the peoples. Indeed, the whole earth is mine, 6 but you shall be for me a priestly kingdom and a holy nation. These are the words that you shall speak to the Israelites." . . .

20:2 I am the LORD your God, who brought you out of the land of Egypt, out of the house of slavery; 3 you shall have no other gods before me.

4 You shall not make for yourself an idol, whether in the form of anything that is in heaven above, or that is on the earth beneath, or that is in the water under the earth. . . .

7 You shall not make wrongful use of the name of the LORD your God, for the LORD will not acquit anyone who misuses his name.

8 Remember the sabbath day, and keep it holy. . . .

12 Honor you father and your mother, so that your days may be long in the land that the LORD your God is giving you.

13 You shall not murder.

14 You shall not commit adultery.

15 You shall not steal.

16 You shall not bear false witness against your neighbor.

17 You shall not covet your neighbor's house; you shall not covet your neighbor's wife, or male or female slave, or ox, or donkey, or anything that belongs to your neighbor.

## BACKGROUND

The Bible never hides the fact that the group led by Moses was a timid and undisciplined collection of "nobodies." Regarded as the dregs of society by the powerful and important people in that age, the Israelites who reluctantly followed Moses appeared to be the least-promising material for God to mold into a nation. And their descendants acknowledged that the rag-tag crew of escapees from Egypt's labor camps could never make any claims of being stronger, cleverer, or wiser than any other community. The one distinguishing feature about this group of people was that God had claimed them as His own. He had rescued them from the slave gangs, brought them safely across the Red Sea, and called them to be a nation that would serve Him.

To establish that special relationship with this party of weary ex-slaves, God set them apart in a solemn pact or covenant. After the Israelites had escaped into the wilderness, the Lord commanded Moses to assemble them at Mount Sinai. Though scholars debate the exact location of this mountain, the experience in that forbidding terrain where God covenanted with Moses and the Israelites is recalled to this day.

In the sacred agreement, God reminded the people that He had delivered them and intended them to serve only Him. The exclusive allegiance between God and His people included instruction in the law. The Ten Commandments, or the Decalogue, are the ethical directives that God gave to Moses by voice and by writing on two stone tablets at Mount Sinai. One tablet revealed humankind's duty toward God, while the other tablet revealed humankind's duty toward their neighbor. Archaeological discoveries indicate that the Ten Commandments are patterned after the prevailing international political treaties used in that day.

## NOTES ON THE PRINTED TEXT

As the Israelites moved deeper into the wilderness of the Sinai Peninsula, the valleys became more spectacular and the ravines widened. Stark granite hills sparkled in the sun. These gave way to the plain beyond in which a red granite mountain rose thousands of feet above the plateau. This was Mount Sinai (also called Mount Horeb). It was located north of the southernmost end of the peninsula. It was here that the Israelites encamped. And this was where God spoke with Moses. *Then Moses went up to God; the Lord called to him from the mountain* (19:3).

Moses was to reiterate what God had done for Israel. For example, He had delivered His people from Egypt. Using the image of a mother eagle that cared for its vulnerable young, God described the way in which He cared for and protected the Israelites. (The female golden eagle would nudge the young from the nest to get them to try their wings, and, when necessary, the mother would swoop below them and carry them on her outspread wings.) *"Thus you shall say to the house of Jacob, and tell the Israelites: You have seen what I did to the Egyptians, and how I bore you on eagles' wings and brought you to myself"* (19:3-4).

Given His care, the Lord expected obedience from the Israelites. *"Now therefore, if you obey my voice and keep my covenant, you shall be my treasured possession out of all the peoples"* (19:5). In other words, if the people kept His commandments, they would enjoy God's special blessings. He could make and keep this promise, for all the earth belonged to Him. *"You shall be for me a priestly kingdom and a holy nation"* (19:6). The people were to be wholly consecrated to God's service. Both as individuals and as a nation they were to do His will and make it known to others. The Hebrew word rendered *holy* implies that God had set apart the Israelites from the other nations for this specific purpose.

Like many other ancient royal covenants, the ten commandments that God communicated to Moses at Mount Sinai began with a preamble in which the great King identified Himself. The Lord did not define Himself abstractly. Rather, He made Himself known by what He had done, particularly in the redemption of His people from Egypt. This saving act was the basis for His demand that the Israelites be exclusive in their devotion to Him. *I am the LORD your God, who brought you out of the land of Egypt, out of the house of slavery; you shall have no other gods before me* (20:2-3).

God's claim of ownership on the Israelites was so encompassing that He forbade them to make idols of any kind, whether in the shape of birds, animals, or fish (20:4). The Lord would permit no rivals—whether real or imagined—in His presence, for such would create a hostile dynamic—one that would go against God and His relationship with His people.

God barred the use of His name for false worship, for incantations or divination, and for speaking blasphemy (20:7). The Lord regarded the knowledge of His name to be a privilege, for it meant that the Israelites did not revere an anonymous far away deity, but rather someone whose personal name was known. Another form of reverence was the dedication of the Sabbath, or the seventh day of the week, to the Lord (20:8). This time of rest from work enabled the people to celebrate God's presence and to love Him through worship.

The Israelites' love for God was to be demonstrated in their love for other people. For example, children were to honor their parents (20:12), people were not to murder each other (20:13), sexual intimacy was to be expressed between a male and a female only in the context of marriage (20:14), stealing was forbidden (20:15), giving false testimony was barred (20:16), and coveting what others had was prohibited (20:17).

## SUGGESTIONS TO TEACHERS

A minister related that in the course of going over wedding vows with prospective brides and grooms who are planning their marriage ceremonies, he tells them that the word "covenant" appears in the liturgy. But in asking them what the word means, he almost always gets a confused look or a vague reply. Few can give a definition that reflects the Bible's understanding of "covenant." You may want to kick off your lesson by asking the members of your class to relate what "covenant" means to them. (Don't be too dismayed at the ignorance of the Bible that some might show!)

**1. REMINDER OF THE DIVINE DELIVERANCE.** God established the covenant at Mount Sinai after He reminded the people of how He had redeemed them from slavery in Egypt. Our covenanted relationship with the Lord stems from His gracious acts on our behalf, particularly His sacrificial love through Christ. We should respond by exclusively worshiping and serving the Lord.

**2. REITERATION OF THE DIVINE DECISION.** God called the Israelites to be a kingdom of priests and a holy nation. Have your students explain what these words should mean to God's people today (see 1 Pet. 2:9-10).

**3. RESPONSE TO THE DIVINE DICTATES.** Devote time to plumb the intent and message of the Lord in each of the Ten Commandments.

**4. RESPECT FOR THE DIVINE DEMANDS.** Jesus said that loving God was the first commandment, and that the second was loving other people (Mark 12:29-31). Have your class members consider where their relationships with others might be frayed and what they can do to bring reconciliation.

**FOR ADULTS**

■ TOPIC: Called to Covenant

■ QUESTIONS: 1. How was God's protective care of His people demonstrated? 2. Why was obedience important to God? 3. In what areas of life do you find it hardest to obey God ? 4. In what ways do you find it hardest to love others? 5. Why do you worship God?

■ **ILLUSTRATIONS:**

**Sermon in a Carving.** While in a quaint old church outside Winchester, England, a visitor was studying a Bible resting on an old carved oak lectern. He had noticed that in nearly all old English churches, the lectern was shaped like an eagle. The pulpit in this sanctuary was also shaped like a huge eagle, except that the bird had the beak of a parrot. While examining the odd beak on the eagle, the visitor moreover noticed that a small heart was carved on the head of the eagle. The perplexed tourist asked the attendant why the lectern had the parrot's beak and the little carved heart.

"You must understand," stated the attendant, "that this ancient eagle was carved this way to remind everyone who reads the holy Word to us not to do so mechanically like a parrot, but fervently from the heart." This reminds us that when we study God's covenant to His people, we must not merely mouth the words in parrot-like fashion, but read them from the heart!

**Mistaken Understanding.** Tim Robbins, the film director who has produced several acclaimed movies, was interviewed at the Berlin Film Festival in 1996 about his motion picture entitled *Dead Man Walking*. When asked about the place of God and faith, this director mumbled, "I believe in . . . er . . . that there are people who live highly enlightened lives and who achieve a certain level of spirituality in connection with a force of goodness. And because these people have walked the earth, I believe that they have created God."

Nothing could be farther from what the Bible teaches! Scripture reveals that God created the universe and humankind, not the other way around. This means that He is the sovereign Lord and that people exist to worship and serve Him. They show their love for Him by obeying His Word and loving others. They can do so only in His power and wisdom. Their motivation is not to exalt themselves but rather to glorify the Lord.

**Regulations for Our Own Safety and Survival.** Tom Johnston flies his own airplane. He stressed that it was important for him to follow the regulations of the Federal Aviation Administration. He also believes that Christians must heed what Jesus commanded in Scripture.

"I have become aware of how much the air traffic control system is like God's presence with us. I do a good deal of my synod travel flying my own plane. So it is not surprising that I am thinking about flight safety!

"Whenever I make a flight, I have to prepare carefully. My preparation begins by checking my currency logs: that I have had my required periodic flight check and physical, that I have flown sufficient recent instrument approaches and flight hours without outside reference, and that my airplane and instruments have all had the required Federal Aviation Administration checks. Next, I prepare and file a flight plan of where I would like to go. Then I get a detailed weather briefing and do a careful preflight inspection of the plane. Sometimes this preparation to fly can take as much time as the flight itself!

"The air traffic control system itself is awesome. My aircraft is tracked all the way to my destination by a gigantic computer with the help of radar. A host of highly trained air traffic controllers direct my flight, warn me of other traffic, vector me around thunderstorms, alert me if I deviate from my assigned heading or altitude, and provide me with a sector of safe airspace. I am in constant radio contact with these controllers, and sometimes I talk with as many as 20 or 30 of them during the course of a trip. It is reassuring to have someone there to help me when I need it!

"All of my flights and the activity of the air traffic controllers are precisely and extensively codified by the Federal Aviation Administration. Rather than resent these regulations, I have come to value them. Each regulation has been carefully researched, tested, and evaluated for its primary purpose: to provide aircraft with a safe and reliable flying environment. I know that these regulations are also strictly enforced, and that if I fail to follow them, I am not only endangering my own safety and that of others, but I can be punished for the violation" (Thomas Johnston, *The Trinitarian*, Synod of the Trinity Newsletter, Dec. 1996).

When we heed God's Word, we are ensuring our own spiritual safety and survival. However, when we spurn God's commands, we flirt with spiritual disaster.

■ TOPIC: What Are the Limits?
■ QUESTIONS: 1. Why was it proper for God to expect His people to obey Him? 2. In what ways would the Israelites serve God as a kingdom of priests and a holy nation? 3. What promises has God made in Scripture to you? 4. Why should you obey the Lord? 5. What is your motivation for worshiping and serving God?

■ ILLUSTRATIONS:

**Medium or the Message?** In Cecil B. deMille's movie entitled *The Ten Commandments,* an arrow of fire circles and then strikes the rock beside Moses, searing ancient Hebrew letters into the stone. The fire gouges out the rock and carves it onto two slabs. Old Moses marches down the mountain carrying the two tablets in his hands, ready to share God's law with the Israelites.

Archaeologists continue to debate the exact shape and size of the stone tablets. Some think they were no more than 12 inches high, while others claim they were small clay slabs similar to those excavated throughout many Near Eastern sites. A few maintain that the tablets were stone slates on which the laws were scratched with a sharp tool.

More important than the material on which the Ten Commandments were inscribed is the message of God they contained. We learn that He wants us to love Him with our entire heart and that He wants us to love others unconditionally and sacrificially. When we do these things, our lives and those of others will be transformed in profound ways.

**No-No's.** Remember when you were a small child and headed for the stove? You were fascinated with the brilliant orange coils of the hot electric range. You wanted to pick up those coils, but your mother quickly thrust your hand away from the hot object. In your mind touching the stove became a "No! No!" That was the law of the family. There was no room for experimentation. The restriction was made to keep you from potential third-degree burning. Similarly, God has established His laws to keep you from experiencing potential spiritual tragedy.

**Divine Wisdom.** "No law, no heaven" is an old Chinese way of describing lawlessness. For centuries, people have implemented laws and legal systems. This reflects divine wisdom, which teaches that people need rules and regulations to maintain order and prevent chaos in society.

**Standards.** Judith Martin (who is otherwise known as Miss Manners) receives lots of mail from young people. An eighth grader's letter was typical. The teenage girl asked for Judith's opinion on what is "socially acceptable" on and off school grounds. Martin wrote that the issue was not a question of manners but morals. There are standards of life, and these should be taught by parents.

Long before Judith Martin wrote about proper conduct, God gave Moses a set of moral standards for people to follow in life. Even today the principles embodied in the Ten Commandments are worth studying and heeding.

# THE TABERNACLE AND OBEDIENCE

**BACKGROUND SCRIPTURE:** Exodus 40:1-33; Leviticus 26
**DEVOTIONAL READING:** Psalm 84

**KEY VERSE:** You shall keep my sabbaths and reverence my sanctuary: I am the LORD. Leviticus 26:2.

4

*KING JAMES VERSION*

EXODUS 40:1 And the LORD spake unto Moses, saying,

2 On the first day of the first month shalt thou set up the tabernacle of the tent of the congregation.

3 And thou shalt put therein the ark of the testimony, and cover the ark with the vail.

4 And thou shalt bring in the table, and set in order the things that are to be set in order upon it; and thou shalt bring in the candlestick, and light the lamps thereof.

5 And thou shalt set the altar of gold for the incense before the ark of the testimony, and put the hanging of the door to the tabernacle.

6 And thou shalt set the altar of the burnt offering before the door of the tabernacle of the tent of the congregation.

7 And thou shalt set the laver between the tent of the congregation and the altar, and shalt put water therein.

8 And thou shalt set up the court round about, and hang up the hanging at the court gate.

9 And thou shalt take the anointing oil, and anoint the tabernacle, and all that is therein, and shalt hallow it, and all the vessels thereof: and it shall be holy. . . .

LEVITICUS 26:2 Ye shall keep my sabbaths, and reverence my sanctuary: I am the LORD.

3 If ye walk in my statutes, and keep my commandments, and do them;

4 Then I will give you rain in due season, and the land shall yield her increase, and the trees of the field shall yield their fruit.

5 And your threshing shall reach unto the vintage, and the vintage shall reach unto the sowing time: and ye shall eat your bread to the full, and dwell in your land safely.

6 And I will give peace in the land, and ye shall lie down, and none shall make you afraid: . . .

11 And I will set my tabernacle among you: and my soul shall not abhor you.

12 And I will walk among you, and will be your God, and ye shall be my people.

13 I am the LORD your God, which brought you forth out of the land of Egypt, that ye should not be their bondmen; and I have broken the bands of your yoke, and made you go upright.

*NEW REVISED STANDARD VERSION*

EXODUS 40:1 The LORD spoke to Moses: 2 On the first day of the first month you shall set up the tabernacle of the tent of meeting. 3 You shall put in it the ark of the covenant, and you shall screen the ark with the curtain. 4 You shall bring in the table, and arrange its setting; and you shall bring in the lampstand, and set up its lamps. 5 You shall put the golden altar for incense before the ark of the covenant, and set up the screen for the entrance of the tabernacle. 6 You shall set the altar of burnt offering before the entrance of the tabernacle of the tent of meeting, 7 and place the basin between the tent of meeting and the altar, and put water in it. 8 You shall set up the court all around, and hang up the screen for the gate of the court. 9 Then you shall take the anointing oil, and anoint the tabernacle and all that is in it, and consecrate it and all its furniture, so that it shall become holy. . . .

LEVITICUS 26:2 You shall keep my sabbaths and reverence my sanctuary: I am the LORD.

3 If you follow my statutes and keep my commandments and observe them faithfully, 4 I will give you your rains in their season, and the land shall yield its produce, and the trees of the field shall yield their fruit. 5 Your threshing shall overtake the vintage, and the vintage shall overtake the sowing; you shall eat your bread to the full, and live securely in your land. 6 And I will grant peace in the land, and you shall lie down, and no one shall make you afraid; . . .

11 I will place my dwelling in your midst, and I shall not abhor you. 12 And I will walk among you, and will be your God, and you shall be my people. 13 I am the LORD your God who brought you out of the land of Egypt, to be their slaves no more; I have broken the bars of your yoke and made you walk erect.

| | | |
|---|---|---|
| *Monday, Sept. 20* | Exodus 40:1-15 | *God's Command Regarding Tabernacle and Priests* |
| *Tuesday, Sept. 21* | Exodus 40:16-23 | *Building the Tabernacle* |
| *Wednesday, Sept. 22* | Exodus 40:24-33 | *Equipping the Tabernacle* |
| *Thursday, Sept. 23* | Leviticus 26:1-13 | *Rewards for Obedience* |
| *Friday, Sept. 24* | Leviticus 26:14-22 | *Consequences of Disobedience* |
| *Saturday, Sept. 25* | Leviticus 26:27-39 | *War and Exile* |
| *Sunday, Sept. 26* | Leviticus 26:40-46 | *Confession Will Bring Renewal* |

## BACKGROUND

The tabernacle was a portable, tent-like structure that could be carried around by the Israelites on their wilderness wanderings. The northern, western, and southern sides of the tabernacle were constructed on a wooden framework to give it greater stability and security than ordinary tent poles could provide. Only the eastern side, or front, of the structure was essentially a linen screen. The entire tabernacle was covered by a tent, and over the tent were additional coverings.

The total structure consisted of three parts. First, there was the outer court, which was enclosed by curtains placed over its top and which hung down on each side. The entire structure was supported on pillars and was oblong in shape. On the eastern side was the entrance.

Second, within the courtyard and facing the entrance was the bronze altar of burnt offerings. Behind it, toward the west, was the bronze laver, or basin, for the priests.

Third, in the western portion of the court was the sanctuary proper. This was divided by a veil, or hanging curtain, into two chambers. The first of these was the Holy Place, which only the priests could enter. It contained the table of show-bread, the golden lampstand, and the altar of incense. The second of the chambers was called the Holy of Holies, or the Most Holy Place. It contained the ark of the covenant (a portable rectangular chest made out of acacia wood).

The tabernacle teaches us that the Lord desires to meet regularly with His people; that He desires to display His glorious presence consistently in the lives of His people; that the presence of sin restricts our open fellowship with God; that it is necessary to approach God through the provision of an acceptable atoning sacrifice; that it is vital to worship God in a proper and reverent manner; that only God is to be given our devotion and service; that moral purity is essential in our relationship with God; and that God is absolutely sovereign in all acts of worship.

This week's lesson will focus on both the tabernacle and the blessings associated with the Mosaic covenant. This is a balanced emphasis, for the proper worship of God cannot be separated from obedience to His commands. In fact, exclusively worshiping and serving the Lord is the key to enjoying His blessings.

# NOTES ON THE PRINTED TEXT

*T*he Lord spoke to Moses: On the first day of the first month you shall set up the tabernacle of the tent of meeting* (40:1-2). God gave Moses some final commands regarding the tabernacle and its furnishings. This desert tent shrine was not peculiar to Israel. Even the shape and structure of the tabernacle were similar to that used by other ancient Near Eastern peoples. The materials that the Israelites used were all obtained in the area where they wandered.

For weeks the people had worked to construct the shrine. They wove yards of fine linen and goat hair. They used acacia wood to make tent poles and hammered gold, silver, and bronze into utensils. When the tabernacle was completed, they brought its parts to Moses, he inspected them, and approved them (39:32-43).

*You shall put in it the ark of the covenant, and you shall screen the ark with the curtain* (40:3). The ark was made out of a dark, hard, and durable wood called acacia. The chest was entirely covered with pure gold (namely, with all of its alloys and impurities removed) and carried on poles inserted in rings in the four lower corners (25:10-15).

The various items deposited within the ark were the two stone tablets on which were inscribed the Ten Commandments (25:16, 21), Aaron's rod which budded (Num. 17:10), and a golden jar holding the wilderness manna (Exod. 16:32; Heb. 9:4). The various items placed on top of the ark included a pure gold lid (namely, the mercy seat, atonement cover, or place where divine satisfaction was made; Exod. 25:16-17; Lev. 16:15-17) and a pair of winged creatures called cherubim (Exod. 25:18-20). The ark served as the place where the Lord met with the Israelites and provided them with guidance (25:22).

The construction of the tabernacle was a massive act of obedience (40:4-8). When the shrine was set up, the priests were to take *the anointing oil* (40:9) and sprinkle it on the tabernacle and all its furnishings to set these things apart for God's exclusive service.

The Israelites' obedience was also evident in their willingness to heed the various decrees of the Mosaic covenant. For example, Leviticus reveals that if the people obeyed the Lord's commands, He would bless their stay in Canaan. However, if they rebelled against Him, He would severely discipline them.

Because the Lord was the God of Israel, the people were to observe His sabbath days of rest and show reverence for His sanctuary (Lev. 26:2). If they kept all His laws, the Lord would send seasonal rains, the land would yield its crops, and the trees would produce their fruit (26:3-4). And if the Israelites carefully obeyed God's commands, He would extend their threshing season until the time of the grape harvest, and their grape harvest would last until it was time again to plant grain (26:5).

Abundance and peace would be the divine reward for obedience. The Israelites would eat their fill, live securely in the land, and sleep without fear (26:6). The Lord would manifest His holy presence among them (26:11). He would be their

God, and they would be His people (26:12). They would no longer be slaves, as they were in Egypt, for the Lord had lifted the yoke of bondage from their necks so that they could walk free with their heads held high (26:13).

## SUGGESTIONS TO TEACHERS

At first glance, the biblical material in this week's lesson might seem irrelevant to the lives of Christians. But don't get hung up on what might appear to be trivial details about the furniture, decorations, and rituals of the tabernacle described in the Scripture text. The Lord was teaching His people (and us) about the importance of properly worshiping Him and obeying His Word. These are the basis for experiencing a joyous relationship with Him.

**1. SACRED WARRANT.** The detailed instructions about the tabernacle should be regarded as a solemn call to revere God as the sovereign Lord. The concept of divine sovereignty is not heard much in circles that promote the egotistic concern for self, which is so widespread in our society. Take time to discuss not only the meaning of the theological concept of God's sovereignty but also its implications for your church, community, and nation. For example, there's no need to fear the unknown, because God is in control of it.

**2. SOLEMN WORSHIP.** The passages in this week's lesson offer specific instructions for regular and orderly forms of worship. Until God is the sole object of our adoration and praise, life will be hopelessly chaotic and destructive. Our reverence for Him must not be left to our moods or whims. Rather, we must worship Him *"in spirit and truth"* (John 4:24).

**3. SANCTIFIED WISDOM.** When God is the center of our life, we will enjoy spiritual abundance and peace. God's wisdom will fill our minds and guide us down the path of uprightness.

**4. SOMBER WARNINGS.** Obedience to God means taking Him with the utmost seriousness. It also means heeding the teachings of His Word. There is no trifling with God!

**FOR ADULTS**

■ TOPIC: Called to Obedience

■ QUESTIONS: 1. What did the tabernacle and its furnishings signify to Moses and the Israelites? 2. Where do you turn for spiritual guidance? 3. How does the Bible help you to handle life's problems? 4. What daily discipline do you follow to help you worship God? 5. How has the Lord spiritually blessed you for obeying His Word?

■ ILLUSTRATIONS:

**Trivializing God.** We are not the first generation that has attempted to trivialize God into a more manageable deity. However, because we live in a century notable for its loss of awe, its impatience with God's silence, and its rampant individualism, we have perhaps failed in this way more than others from bygone eras. We have fashioned gods to fit the contours of our desires, and then bowed before them with religious abandon. The god of my cause, the god of my understanding, the god of my experience, the god of my comfort, the god of my nation, and the god of my success have been our particular favorites.

Our malady suggests a good stiff dose of agnosticism toward these so-called "gods." We must recognize that on our own, we cannot scale spiritual heights to discover the true nature of God. Sin has distorted our perspective, and thus we remain imprisoned in ignorance. Our only hope is to listen attentively to the self-revelation God has graciously given us in Christ.

When we do, we will discover a God who is fundamentally different from any deity we might have created for ourselves. We learn that the Lord is holy, righteous, all-knowing, all-powerful, loving, gracious, and kind. Most of all, we realize that He is worthy of our obedience and worship (Donald W. McCullough, *The Trivialization of God: The Dangerous Delusion of a Manageable Deity*, NavPress, 1995, p. 9).

**Lesson from AA.** Friends in Alcoholics Anonymous tell us about how they sometimes feel the urge to take a drink. But they also know that practicing the Twelve-Step program helps them to maintain sobriety. This means attending weekly AA meetings. And it also means daily attention to their spiritual lives in a serious, disciplined way.

Every member of Alcoholics Anonymous realizes that they are constantly apt to "slip." Though a member of AA might have been sober for 20 years, he or she always refers to himself or herself as a "recovering alcoholic." Note that the term is "recovering," not "recovered." The person giving the "lead," or testimony, in any AA meeting always opens with the statement, "I *am* an alcoholic," not "I *was* an alcoholic."

These recovering alcoholics know from personal experience that the wiles and snares of destruction in the form of temptations to take a drink are present. But with help from the Lord's strengthening hand of grace, these recovering alcoholics also know that they can make it for another 24 hours. Further, they realize that they are called to obedience.

We in the church, borrowing a term from AA, should refer to ourselves as "recovering sinners." We have not yet arrived, but rather continue to press on in our spiritual growth and development. We are always aware of our need to trust and obey the Lord.

**Speaking of *How,* It's Funny Isn't It . . .**

How $20 looks so large at church, and how it looks so small at the grocery store?

How long an hour is while attending a Sunday school class, and how short it is when watching television?

How tough it is to read a chapter in the Bible, and how easy it is to read several chapters in a best-selling novel?

How we claim we don't know what to say when we pray, and how we can talk for hours on the phone with a friend?

How we just can't fit in a church-related event (though it has been announced long in advance), and how we can always fit in a last minute party invitation?

Funny, isn't it? Or is it?

---

| **FOR YOUTH** | ■ TOPIC: A Point of Contact<br>■ QUESTIONS: 1. Why did God place such a strong emphasis on His people worshiping Him in a particular way? 2. Why did God |

make such a big deal about obeying Him? 3. When was the last time you spent a few quiet moments alone with God to worship Him? 4. Can people tell by your life that you follow the Lord? 5. How has God spiritually enriched you for faithfully following Him?

■ ILLUSTRATIONS:

**Symbols.** Rabbi Sara Rae Perman ushered the children into a synagogue lounge. Dozens of dreidels were spread on each table. (A dreidel is a 4-sided toy marked with Hebrew letters and spun like a top in a game of chance.) The rabbi of Greensburg, Pennsylvania's Emmanuel Israel Congregation has one of the best collections of the traditional Hanukkah tops in the world, and it has taken her 30 years to collect them.

The rabbi spent some time explaining to the children the significance of the spinning tops. "The dreidel is used in the eight-day commemoration of the successful Jewish revolt against the Syrian oppressors in 165 B.C. The toy's origins might lie with those who engaged in the forbidden study of the Torah under the Syrians. Often these individuals would disguise their gatherings as a gambling party. Or perhaps the story was only created to legitimize a German custom that tried to limit gambling to two holidays, Hanukkah and Purim.

"A dreidel has four sides, and each side has a different Hebrew letter. These stand for the great miracle that happened in the temple in Jerusalem. We are reminded of how a single day's supply of oil burned for the eight days necessary to rededicate the sanctuary, after Judas Maccabeus and his fellow Jews had liberated the temple in December, 165 B.C."

Perman's listeners came to appreciate the symbolism of the small religious objects. They joined with their ancestors in understanding how God can be remembered through various items and rituals.

In this week's lesson, we learn that God through Moses instructed the Israelites to build the tabernacle and fill it with various items. Each had a symbolic meaning that the people came to appreciate. And they used each item to help them worship God properly.

**A Special Place.** Old Miss Snell was as mean as she was aged, according to the kids. True, the old woman had a sharp tongue for children she felt were misbehaving in the church. Many a young child was rebuked for running or wearing what she thought was inappropriate clothing, or speaking too loudly, or not paying attention, or eating outside the lounge or the fellowship hall, or committing a host of other transgressions known only to Miss Snell. More than one youngster heard her lecture that the church was God's home, and that it was to be treated with respect.

While most of the children listened grudgingly, they also came to respect Miss Snell's opinion. They learned from her that just as the tabernacle was used as a special place to worship God, so too the church could be a special place for the children and for all Christians to gather together and revere the Lord.

**Special Place for Special Memories.** The creators of Disneyland and Disney World strive to create a place and an atmosphere that is conducive to creating special memories. The idea is that everyone will have so much fun in the make-believe worlds that every visitor will want to bring their children and grandchildren to the theme parks.

Israel had a special place that had brought them cherished memories. And the church can also be a special place where Christians create wonderful memories of fellowship as they join together in giving praise to God for His goodness in their lives.

# THE CLOUD AND THE FIRE

**BACKGROUND SCRIPTURE:** Exodus 40:34-38, Numbers 9:15-23
**DEVOTIONAL READING:** Psalm 107:1-9

**KEY VERSE:** The cloud of the LORD was on the tabernacle by day, and fire was in the cloud by night, before the eyes of all the house of Israel at each stage of their journey. Exodus 40:38.

*KING JAMES VERSION*

EXODUS 40:34 Then a cloud covered the tent of the congregation, and the glory of the LORD filled the tabernacle.

35 And Moses was not able to enter into the tent of the congregation, because the cloud abode thereon, and the glory of the LORD filled the tabernacle.

36 And when the cloud was taken up from over the tabernacle, the children of Israel went onward in all their journeys:

37 But if the cloud were not taken up, then they journeyed not till the day that it was taken up.

38 For the cloud of the LORD was upon the tabernacle by day, and fire was on it by night, in the sight of all the house of Israel, throughout all their journeys. . . .

NUMBERS 9:15 And on the day that the tabernacle was reared up the cloud covered the tabernacle, namely, the tent of the testimony: and at even there was upon the tabernacle as it were the appearance of fire, until the morning.

16 So it was alway: the cloud covered it by day, and the appearance of fire by night.

17 And when the cloud was taken up from the tabernacle, then after that the children of Israel journeyed: and in the place where the cloud abode, there the children of Israel pitched their tents.

18 At the commandment of the LORD the children of Israel journeyed, and at the commandment of the LORD they pitched: as long as the cloud abode upon the tabernacle they rested in their tents.

19 And when the cloud tarried long upon the tabernacle many days, then the children of Israel kept the charge of the LORD, and journeyed not. . . .

22 Or whether it were two days, or a month, or a year, that the cloud tarried upon the tabernacle, remaining thereon, the children of Israel abode in their tents, and journeyed not: but when it was taken up, they journeyed.

23 At the commandment of the LORD they rested in the tents, and at the commandment of the LORD they journeyed: they kept the charge of the LORD, at the commandment of the LORD by the hand of Moses.

*NEW REVISED STANDARD VERSION*

EXODUS 40:34 Then the cloud covered the tent of meeting, and the glory of the LORD filled the tabernacle. 35 Moses was not able to enter the tent of meeting because the cloud settled upon it, and the glory of the LORD filled the tabernacle. 36 Whenever the cloud was taken up from the tabernacle, the Israelites would set out on each stage of their journey; 37 but if the cloud was not taken up, then they did not set out until the day that it was taken up. 38 For the cloud of the LORD was on the tabernacle by day, and fire was in the cloud by night, before the eyes of all the house of Israel at each stage of their journey. . . .

NUMBERS 9:15 On the day the tabernacle was set up, the cloud covered the tabernacle, the tent of the covenant; and from evening until morning it was over the tabernacle, having the appearance of fire. 16 It was always so: the cloud covered it by day and the appearance of fire by night. 17 Whenever the cloud lifted from over the tent, then the Israelites would set out; and in the place where the cloud settled down, there the Israelites would camp. 18 At the command of the LORD the Israelites would set out, and at the command of the Lord they would camp. As long as the cloud rested over the tabernacle, they would remain in camp. 19 Even when the cloud continued over the tabernacle many days, the Israelites would keep the charge of the LORD, and would not set out. . . .

22 Whether it was two days, or a month, or a longer time, that the cloud continued over the tabernacle, resting upon it, the Israelites would remain in camp and would not set out; but when it lifted they would set out. 23 At the command of the LORD they would camp, and at the command of the LORD they would set out. They kept the charge of the LORD, at the command of the LORD by Moses.

| Monday, Sept. 27 | Exodus 40:34-38 | *God's Glory Fills the Tabernacle* |
| Tuesday, Sept. 28 | Numbers 9:15-23 | *Led by God's Cloud and Fire* |
| Wednesday, Sept. 29 | Numbers 10:29-36 | *Journeying away from Mount Sinai* |
| Thursday, Sept. 30 | Psalm 105:1-15 | *God Keeps Covenant Forever* |
| Friday, Oct. 1 | Psalm 105:16-25 | *God Provided for Israel in Egypt* |
| Saturday, Oct. 2 | Psalm 105:26-36 | *God Sent Plagues upon Egypt* |
| Sunday, Oct. 3 | Psalm 105:37-45 | *God Delivered Israel from Egypt* |

## BACKGROUND

God had commanded Moses to tell the Israelites: *"And have them make me a sanctuary, so that I may dwell among them"* (Exodus 25:8). The people obeyed, and constructed the tabernacle. God then fulfilled His promise to abide in their midst. The descent of a cloud on the sanctuary indicated to the community that the Lord was truly present among them.

In our modern scientific age, we regard clouds as being simply masses of water vapor suspended in the air. But in Old Testament times, God's people looked upon clouds as bringers of life-giving rains in a desert region thirsty for water (Isa. 18:4). And in Exodus 40:34-38, the cloud covering the tabernacle was understood to be a manifestation of the divine presence. This same perspective is also evident in the New Testament. For example, during Jesus' transfiguration, God's voice came from a cloud (Matt. 17:5; Mark 9:7; Luke 9:34-35). Similarly, as Jesus ascended into heaven, He disappeared into a cloud (Acts 1:9).

In Bible times, the darkness of night seemed mysterious and uninviting to people. But even after the sun went down, the Israelites wandering in the wilderness were not alone, for God manifested His presence over the tabernacle in a cloud *having the appearance of fire* (Num. 9:15). This reassured the covenant community that the Lord would remain with them and guide them even in the darkness of night. The pillar of fire also served as a reminder that God is not to be trifled with, for He is *a devouring fire* (Deut. 4:24; see Heb. 12:29).

During the initial phase of the Israelites' travels in the wilderness, they obediently followed the cloud of God's glory. When the cloud remained over the tabernacle for a time, the people encamped at the spot they had reached. And when the cloud lifted up from the tabernacle and moved, the people followed it. As long as the Israelites obediently followed the pillar of cloud by day and the pillar of fire by night, they journeyed where God desired.

## NOTES ON THE PRINTED TEXT

After many weeks of hard work, the Israelites had finished making the tabernacle. Yet it remained unoccupied. The completed sanctuary awaited the presence of the Lord. The manifestation of His glory would be an indication of His approval on the work the people had done.

*Then the cloud covered the tent of meeting, and the glory of the LORD filled the tabernacle* (40:34). At the divinely appointed time, a cloud surrounded the tabernacle and a bright light, God's glory, appeared in the sanctuary. The Lord's holy presence was now dwelling with Israel.

Numbers 9:15-16 relates a similar incident: *On the day the tabernacle was set up, the cloud covered the tabernacle, the tent of the covenant; and from evening until morning it was over the tabernacle, having the appearance of fire. It was always so: the cloud covered it by day and the appearance of fire by night.* Nothing profane could come near the sanctuary during these times. *Moses was not able to enter the tent of meeting because the cloud settled upon it, and the glory of the LORD filled the tabernacle* (Exod. 40:35).

Through the presence of the cloud over the tabernacle, God signaled when the Israelites were to break camp and when they were to stop traveling. All encampments and all journeys were marked by the ascent and descent of the pillar of cloud by day and the pillar of fire by night.

Under the Lord's sovereign guidance, whenever the cloud moved from the desert sanctuary, the people pulled up their tent stakes and journeyed on. *Whenever the cloud was taken up from the tabernacle, the Israelites would set out on each stage of their journey; but if the cloud was not taken up, then they did not set out until the day that it was taken up* (40:36-37). This same phenomenon is recorded in Numbers 9:17-18: *Whenever the cloud lifted from over the tent, then the Israelites would set out; and in the place where the cloud settled down, there the Israelites would camp. . . . As long as the cloud rested over the tabernacle, they would remain in camp.*

God used the cloud to govern Israel's travels. Patiently the people awaited the Lord's marching orders. Whether it was a night or longer than a month, the people would remain encamped until God directed them to resume their travels (9:19). *Whether it was two days, or a month, or a longer time, that the cloud continued over the tabernacle, resting upon it, the Israelites would remain in camp and would not set out; . . . At the command of the Lord they would camp, and at the command of the LORD they would set out* (9:22-23).

As the covenant community journeyed through the wilderness, they obeyed only the command of the Lord that was spoken to them by Moses, for *the people feared the LORD and believed in the LORD and in his servant Moses* (Exod. 14:31). The cloud of glory was a constant reminder that God was present among the Israelites. *For the cloud of the LORD was on the tabernacle by day, and fire was in the cloud by night, before the eyes of all the house of Israel at each stage of their journey* (40:38).

The Book of Exodus began in gloom and ended in glory. The Lord had freed His people from slavery in Egypt so that they could know the joy that comes from serving Him. As the redeemed of God, they would end their pilgrimage by living with Him forever. What a glorious future they had awaiting them!

# SUGGESTIONS TO TEACHERS

Few newspapers in North America fail to feature a daily horoscope. Occasionally, an editor will decide that the space used to print the horoscope should be filled with something other than the 12 signs of the zodiac and their "clues" for daily living. But the uproar of protesting readers will keep the horoscope running, for millions of Americans seek guidance from astrology (as well as other ungodly sources). This week's lesson reminds us that true guidance for living only comes from God and His Word.

**1. COMPANIONSHIP IN THE CLOUD.** God's holy presence, which was symbolized in the cloud, assured the Israelites that they were not alone. The promise of the constant companionship of Christ through the Holy Spirit also assures us that we are not alone in the universe. This means that we do not have to turn for guidance to astrological charts, crystal power objects, tarot cards, New Age teachers, magic, witchcraft, or any occult source. Truly God is sufficient!

**2. COMMAND OF THE CREATOR.** God continues to give us guidance for daily living. Here is a good opportunity to discuss the place of prayer. Remind your class members that prayer entails listening to God.

**3. CONTINUING IN THE CAMP.** The Israelites were told not to proceed until the cloud had moved on ahead. Tragically, we often refuse to wait for God's guidance. And just as sadly, we want to move on ahead without Him. But Christian living always means obedience. This often calls for waiting and watching for the right time in God's sovereign plan to take action.

**4. CONTROL OF THE COMMUNITY.** The Israelites recognized that they belonged to God. They also knew that the Lord was in sovereign control of their lives. God is also in charge of our faith community, the church. Day by day He offers His counsel and help. We are truly blessed when we heed His guidance.

**FOR ADULTS**

■ TOPIC: Follow Day by Day

■ QUESTIONS: What challenges did the people face in the wilderness? 2. How could God's guidance help them meet those challenges? 3. What are some difficulties right now in your life? 4. How can God's guidance help you to overcome those problems? 5. How can your dependence on the Lord encourage others to trust in Him?

■ ILLUSTRATIONS:

**Steady Habit of Following.** David Livingstone was one of the great missionaries of history. He literally opened the continent of Africa to Christianity. (Incidentally, Africa is where Christianity is growing fastest today. This remains true despite the presence of so much turmoil throughout the continent.) When Livingstone was young, his Sunday school teacher greatly influenced his thinking. One day the teacher said to him: "David, make Christianity the steady habit of your life, not a thing of fits and starts!"

"The steady habit of your life" is what it takes to be a godly and productive Christian. There's no better way to spiritually grow and mature in the faith.

**Never Discouraged!** A Little League baseball game was being played one Saturday when a visitor stopped to watch. Walking up along the first baseline, he asked the boy playing nearby whether he knew the score.

"We're behind 13 to nothing," the boy replied. "Thirteen to nothing!" the visitor bellowed with a jolt. "Hey, you don't seem very discouraged about it." "Naw," answered the youngster. "Why should I? We haven't been up to bat yet!"

That kind of attitude is the outlook Christians should have as they follow the Lord each and every day!

**Winner's Attitude.** Daley Thompson of England, who was a gold medalist in the 1980 and 1984 decathlon, once said, "If to win a gold medal in the 1980 Olympic games, I had to die in 1981, I'd do it!" For many there is no discipline too severe and no sacrifice too great to win an Olympic gold medal. We Christians need to remind ourselves that the eternal glory awaiting us in heaven is more precious than an Olympic gold medal. Whatever discipline and sacrifice God might require of us in this life is well worth it, for we know that *in the Lord [our] labor is not in vain* (1 Cor. 15:58).

---

| | |
|---|---|
| **For Youth** | ■ TOPIC: Following Faithfully |
| | ■ QUESTIONS: 1. Why was it important for God to manifest His presence among the Israelites? 2. How would God's people have |

been reassured by His continual presence in their midst? 3. In what ways is God's continual presence in your life an encouraging truth? 4. In what ways is God's continual presence in your life a sobering truth? 5. What can you do to remain a faithful follower of the Lord?

■ **ILLUSTRATIONS:**

**Signs.** In October, 1997, employees at Datacom Systems in San Rafael, California, demanded that city officials remove a tree in front of the building. Manager Colman Chan explained that the tree was sapping all of the good energy from his business and the employees. Workers believed that the tree's presence violated the Chinese principle of *fengshui,* or harmonious living with the environment. They also felt that a foreboding spirit hung over them. City officials, however, refused to comply with their request. Instead, the city suggested that Datacom hang wind chimes and crystals in the tree limbs.

As Christians, we do not believe in *fengshui.* Nevertheless, the story shows that many are fascinated with and see signs of the supernatural in their lives. The Israelites were sensitive to signs of God's guidance in their life. And their belief that the cloud signified the glorious presence of the Lord was based on truth, not superstition.

**Assurance.** David Geoffrey Moore of Berkeley, California, was nineteen and just out of high school when he joined a cult named Heaven's Gate. On March 22, 1997, he was one of 39 members who committed suicide in Rancho Santa Fe, California. The members hoped to link up with the Hale-Bopp Comet and ride for eternity with the Creator. Their faith was based on a mixture of science fiction, the Bible, and New Age superstition.

David was only one of many seeking meaning in the cult. He and his peers fit the typical psychological profile of those who join cults. For example, any individual with an unsatisfied spiritual longing is a prime candidate.

In contrast to such people as David, the Israelites did not have to look to the pagan beliefs of the world to satisfy their deepest spiritual longings. The presence of the cloud was their assurance that their Creator was always with them. Today, the indwelling Holy Spirit is our assurance that the Lord is present in our lives.

**Guidance.** Today there are 10,000 registered astrologers in the United States. It's no wonder that over three-quarters of the daily newspapers publish a horoscope. Scripture makes it clear that God, not the stars, governs our life. In Old Testament times, He faithfully led the Israelites as they wandered through the wilderness. Believers today can also look to Him for guidance. Unlike reading a horoscope, the Lord will never lead us astray.

# THE PEOPLE REBEL

**BACKGROUND SCRIPTURE: NUMBERS 12:1—14:25**
**DEVOTIONAL READING: NUMBERS 14:5-19**

---

**KEY VERSE:** If the LORD is pleased with us, he will bring us into this land and give it to us, a land that flows with milk and honey. Only, do not rebel against the LORD. Numbers 14:8-9.

*KING JAMES VERSION*

NUMBERS 13:1 And the LORD spake unto Moses, saying,

2 Send thou men, that they may search the land of Canaan, which I give unto the children of Israel: of every tribe of their fathers shall ye send a man, every one a ruler among them.

3 And Moses by the commandment of the LORD sent them from the wilderness of Paran: all those men were heads of the children of Israel. . . .

32 And they brought up an evil report of the land which they had searched unto the children of Israel, saying, The land, through which we have gone to search it, is a land that eateth up the inhabitants thereof; and all the people that we saw in it are men of a great stature.

33 And there we saw the giants, the sons of Anak, which come of the giants: and we were in our own sight as grasshoppers, and so we were in their sight.

14:1 And all the congregation lifted up their voice, and cried; and the people wept that night.

2 And all the children of Israel murmured against Moses and against Aaron: and the whole congregation said unto them, Would God that we had died in the land of Egypt! or would God we had died in this wilderness!

3 And wherefore hath the LORD brought us unto this land, to fall by the sword, that our wives and our children should be a prey? were it not better for us to return into Egypt?

4 And they said one to another, Let us make a captain, and let us return into Egypt. . . .

20 And the LORD said, I have pardoned according to thy word:

21 But as truly as I live, all the earth shall be filled with the glory of the LORD.

22 Because all those men which have seen my glory, and my miracles, which I did in Egypt and in the wilderness, and have tempted me now these ten times, and have not hearkened to my voice;

23 Surely they shall not see the land which I sware unto their fathers, neither shall any of them that provoked me see it:

24 But my servant Caleb, because he had another spirit with him, and hath followed me fully, him will I bring into the land whereinto he went; and his seed shall possess it.

*NEW REVISED STANDARD VERSION*

NUMBERS 13:1 The LORD said to Moses, 2 "Send men to spy out the land of the Canaan, which I am giving to the Israelites; from each of their ancestral tribes you shall send a man, every one a leader among them." 3 So Moses sent them from the wilderness of Paran, according to the command of the LORD, all of them leading men among the Israelites. . . .

32 So they brought to the Israelites an unfavorable report of the land that they had spied out, saying, "The land that we have gone through as spies is a land that devours its inhabitants; and all the people that we saw in it are of great size. 33 There we saw the Nephilim (the Anakites come from the Nephilim); and to ourselves we seemed as grasshoppers, and so we seemed to them."

14:1 Then all the congregation raised a loud cry, and the people wept that night. 2 And all the Israelites complained against Moses and Aaron; the whole congregation said to them, "Would that we had died in the land of Egypt! Or would that we had died in this wilderness! 3 Why is the LORD bringing us into this land to fall by the sword? Our wives and our little ones will become booty; would it not be better for us to go back to Egypt?" 4 so they said to one another, "Let us choose a captain, and go back to Egypt." . . .

20 Then the LORD said, "I do forgive, just as you have asked; 21 nevertheless—as I live, and as all the earth shall be filled with the glory of the LORD— 22 none of the people who have seen my glory and the signs that I did in Egypt and in the wilderness, and yet have tested me these ten times and have not obeyed my voice, 23 shall see the land that I swore to give to their ancestors; none of those who despised me shall see it. 24 But my servant Caleb, because he has a different spirit and has followed me wholeheartedly, I will bring into the land into which he went, and his descendants shall possess it."

## BACKGROUND

Jealousies and complaints, timidity and criticism surfaced among the Israelites. All the petty nastiness that humans still seem capable of showing threatened to tear apart God's community during the wilderness sojourn.

Most of the Israelites were not hero-quality material. After having been beaten down physically and psychologically by years of servitude in Pharaoh's slave labor compounds, the Israelites who originally accompanied Moses often seemed to whine. Sometimes, when conditions on the long march through the Sinai desert proved arduous, they looked back longingly on Egypt. After all, they thought, even slavery offered some security.

Although God had covenanted with the Israelites and promised them an inheritance in Canaan, they still grumbled. For example, many had bitterly complained about the food that God provided. And even Moses' own brother and sister had criticized his leadership. Implicit in all the carping was an underlying attitude of insubordination against God.

The rebellion against the Lord flared at various times during the 40 years' wandering in the wilderness. One of the most notable episodes was when Moses sent 12 men to spy out the land of Canaan. The 12 were representatives from each of the tribes and looked upon as leaders.

Ten of the 12 returned with a disheartening report. The majority were intimidated by the people in Canaan and claimed that it would be impossible to conquer the land that God had promised to give to Israel. Only Caleb and Joshua had enough trust in the Lord to present a favorable word. Sadly, the Israelites listened only to the negative news of the other scouts and clamored to return to Egypt. Only Moses' intercession with God saved the community from being wiped out by a plague.

## NOTES ON THE PRINTED TEXT

After spending some time at Mount Sinai and traveling in the desert, the Israelites arrived at an oasis named Kadesh-Barnea in the wilderness of Paran (an ill-defined area of desert to the southwest of Palestine; 13:26). From Kadesh-Barnea, the people looked northward to Canaan, the land which the Lord had promised to give to them.

*The Lord said to Moses, "Send men to spy out the land of Canaan, which I am giving to the Israelites; from each of their ancestral tribes you shall send a man, every one a leader among them"* (13:1-2). Moses obeyed God's command by choosing 12 men, all of whom were tribal leaders (13:3). This intelligence-gathering group was to survey the fertility of the land, probe its defenses, and ascertain the strengths and weaknesses of its inhabitants. Such information would be useful to the Israelites as they made preparations to conquer the land.

After 40 days of traversing the land, the 12 returned (13:25). They had good news. They described an extremely fertile and fruitful land. To support their description, they brought back some pomegranates, figs, and bunches of grapes so massive that they had to be carried on poles between two men (13:23-24).

However, 10 of the 12 scouts also brought back disheartening news. They exclaimed that the residents were powerful, war-like, and lived in fortified cities (13:27-29). *So they brought to the Israelites an unfavorable report of the land that they had spied out, saying, "The land that we have gone through as spies is a land that devours its inhabitants; and all the people that we saw in it are of great size. There we saw the Nephilim (the Anakites come from Nephilim); and to ourselves we seemed like grasshoppers, and so we seemed to them"* (13:32-33).

One group, the descendants of Anak, were especially large warriors. The unbelieving majority of spies claimed that the Anakites were related to a group of strong men called *Nephilim* (Gen. 6:4), who had lived on the earth before the Flood. The descendants of Anak were compared to these giants, which led the spies to view themselves as grasshoppers before them.

Aside from Joshua and Caleb, the spies said that any military action would be dangerous, foolish, and hopeless. It's no wonder that the Israelites were frightened and disheartened by the spies' report. The people complained against Moses, Aaron, and God! They disregarded the Lord's mighty acts of deliverance and wished that they were dead. Using their women and children as an excuse, the leaders reasoned that it would be better for them to return to Egypt than to die by the sword in the heat of battle (Num. 14:1-3). They then began to plot among themselves, *"Let us choose a captain, and go back to Egypt"* (14:4).

Moses and Aaron responded by falling face down on the ground before the Israelites (14:5). Then Joshua and Caleb urged the people to trust God and not be afraid of the inhabitants of Canaan (14:6-9). Only God's intervention kept the people from stoning the two (14:10).

The Lord announced to Moses that He would destroy Israel with a plague. But Moses interceded on behalf of the people by claiming that God's reputation was at stake. Moses reasoned that other nations would conclude that the Lord was not able to bring the people into the promised land. Moses thus asked God to forgive the Israelites (14:12-19).

The Lord agreed to pardon the offenders (14:20). He also declared that as surely as He lived and as surely as the earth was filled with His glory, none of the rebels would enter Canaan (14:21-23). After all, the people had seen His glorious presence and the miraculous signs He had performed both in Egypt and in the wilderness. Yet the Israelites repeatedly tested the Lord by refusing to heed His commands (14:22).

The rebels had wished they had died in the desert (14:2), and so the Lord would grant their request (14:29). The spies had taken 40 days to explore Canaan, and so that generation of Israelites would wander for 40 years in the wilderness (14:34). Each day they would suffer the consequences of treating God with contempt, and none of them would enter the promised land (14:23). Only Caleb, who had remained loyal to the Lord, would be allowed to enter Canaan (14:24).

## SUGGESTIONS TO TEACHERS

A lovely young woman in our community one day took her own life. She had apparently endured a loss of her job and a long bout with Lyme disease. At her memorial service, her closest friend stated how the deceased had been suffering from the "what if's."

All of us live with some "what if's." The memories of missed opportunities in our past haunt us. This week's lesson reminds us to depend on God for the strength we need to tackle the challenges of life.

**1. RESENTFUL SIBLINGS.** Moses had to face unjustified criticism from his own sister and brother (see 12:1-3). Many family members fail to show care and appreciation for one another. Perhaps some in your class are missing the opportunities to be loving and supportive to others in their own families.

**2. RELUCTANT SPIES.** The majority of the spies reported that it would be impossible to conquer Canaan. This created fear in the Israelites and it prompted them to doubt, rather than trust, God. Sadly, Christians often fail to avail themselves of opportunities to serve God because they are afraid of criticism or failure!

**3. REBELLIOUS SENTIMENTS.** It's amazing that the Israelites clamored to return to Egypt. Apparently the risk of following the Lord was too great for them. Remind your class members that faith often means risk-taking!

**4. REJECTED SINNERS.** God was ready to disinherit His rebellious people (see 14:12). But thankfully Moses successfully interceded on their behalf. Let your students know that missed opportunities can have unpleasant consequences!

| FOR ADULTS | ■ TOPIC: A Missed Opportunity |
|---|---|

■ QUESTIONS: 1. In what ways had God been gracious toward the Israelites? 2. In what ways had the people shown contempt for the Lord? 3. What are some of the ways that the Lord has immensely blessed you? 4. How have things gone for you when you failed to trust God wholeheartedly? 5. What are some opportunities for Christian service that God might want you to perform, despite the possible risks involved?

**Missing the Tide.** In the days before modern harbors, a ship had to wait for the flood time before it could make it to port. The term for this situation in Latin was *ob portu,* which literally means "toward port" or "toward harbor." It referred to a ship standing over against a port and waiting for the right moment when it could ride the turn of the tide into harbor. The English word *opportunity* is derived from this original meaning. Shakespeare used the history of this word to help him write one of his most famous passages:

> *There is a tide in the affairs of men,*
> *Which, taken at the flood, leads on to fortune;*
> *Omitted, all the voyage of their life*
> *Is bound in shallows and in miseries.*
> *On such a full sea are we now afloat;*
> *And we must take the current when it serves,*
> *Or lose our ventures.*

**A Life of Could-Have-Beens.** Sallam Omron's life was full of missed chances and unfortunate incidents, but the biggest "could-have-been" was that he had the opportunity to be a concert pianist. More than 30 years earlier, he studied with Richard Neubert, and he'd read off scores for Chopin, Beethoven, Mozart, Strauss, just as if he were reading a newspaper.

But then came World War II. This was followed by marriage, children, a bitter divorce, a second marriage, more children, a second divorce, and a line of jobs that ranged from spray-painting auto bodies in Detroit to peddling ice cream on the street. The piano-playing became something just to pass the time. It was little more than a memory when Omron relinquished his last piano to the taxman in 1963.

But the "could-have-beens" disappeared when Omron sat down to play the piano. In those serene moments, he thought of himself as the concert pianist he had once wanted to become. Sometimes tears rolled down his cheeks, as they did one day when he played at Allentown's Symphony Hall. He just walked in off the street and began playing, as he sometimes did when he played at thrift shops.

The hall was empty, except for a few shoppers picking through racks of clothes strung across the stage for the annual flea market. Omron the piano player was dressed in a heavy winter coat and hat. He played like someone who once knew the music well. Though he had forgotten some of the notes, he still remembered the motions. Ormon's music was full of delicate arabesques, crescendos, and crashing 10-fingered chords. He played the classical music he had put to memory years ago.

Ormon now lives as a loner in a room at the Hotel Lafayette in Easton, Pennsylvania. His checks from the federal government don't allow for much more than that. In his shopping bag he keeps a thermos and some food, and his emergency fire equipment—a long rope and a flashlight—in case there is a fire in the hotel. He won't leave these items in his room lest they be stolen.

Omron talks about evaluations and transcriptions. A jazz pianist would call it improvisation. Twenty years without sheet music and sometimes months without a piano have made Omron a fearless improviser. And that has made the music he plays distinctively his own. The man who says he was "a whiz at chromatics," that is, at working the black keys, has transformed Beethoven and Strauss and Chopin into an eerily discordant sound that perhaps reflects some of the uncertainties of his own life.

---

| **For Youth** | ■ TOPIC: Hitting the Panic Button<br>■ QUESTIONS: 1. What was the basis for the Israelites' complaints? |
|---|---|

2. In what way was the heart of the people filled with ingratitude? 3. Why is God grieved when you rebel against Him and fail to trust Him? 4. What does God do when you seek His forgiveness? 5. What can you do to avoid panicking in a crisis situation?

■ **ILLUSTRATIONS:**

**Went Along.** The three students of Penn Hills High School of Pittsburgh handed the lunch room cashier a five dollar bill to pay for their tray of sandwiches and drinks. Flipping the bill over, the woman noticed that it was blank on the back. Police were summoned. The police also brought in the U.S. Secret Service to investigate the counterfeiting.

The youth, one 17 and two who were 15, ran the five-dollar bill through a color computer printer, neglecting to print the reverse side. Although one had voiced his concern that their actions were likely to get them into trouble, he went along with the other two. He failed to stand up for what was right. All were suspended for three days and were charged with conspiracy, forgery, and theft.

Despite Joshua and Caleb's pleas that their fellow Israelites not doubt God, the people sided with the majority of spies, much like the one student who went along with the felonious plan of his peers. The nation had failed to stand up for God. As a result, an entire generation suffered.

**Sins of the Fathers.** The packages are occasionally found at various political parties' annual conferences or at Britain's Chemical Defense Establishment at Porton Down in Wiltshire. Usually they are galvanized metal buckets with earth inside, and are sometimes wrapped in plastic. The packages are part of a clever and curious campaign by young environmentalists protesting slow governmental action.

In 1941, British scientists from Porton Down conducted a series of bacteriological research experiments on a bleak uninhabited one-mile island 600 yards off the west coast of northern Scotland. Anthrax bacilli were released in a bomb on Guinard Island. After the war, scientists realized that the spores were difficult to destroy and might live for decades. The government posted warning signs to keep people off of the island. Apparently, everyone forgot about the island until the London *Sunday Times* published a story on the experiments.

Strange protests were begun by a group who called their campaign Operation Dark Harvest. The group demanded that the government solve the island's contamination by burying the bacilli under thick layers of reinforced concrete, or by removing soil, or by soaking the island in potassium permanganate.

Students from two universities claimed that they had landed on the island and taken 300 pounds of soil. Over a 12 month period, this soil would be deposited at different points around the country to end the government's indifference. That same day, the package at Porton Down labs arrived and analysis showed that it contained the anthrax bacillus.

The group of vengeful protesters apparently is angry at inheriting a previous generation's problem and mistake. Because of the sins of their parents, many in Israel would suffer for a time. An entire generation learned that sin can have far-reaching consequences.


**Feels Challenged.** Richard Stoops was born blind. Being sightless, he relies on his ears and other senses as well as friends for help. More than anything, though, the Thomas Jefferson High School (Jefferson Boro, PA) junior wanted to be like his father, who lettered all four years at the same academic institution and won a football scholarship to North Carolina's Davidson College. Many youth would see the disability as an impossibility to overcome. Few would ever try to play football, let alone dream of succeeding at the sport.

Stoops started playing football on the junior varsity team. He worked out on the weight machines. He also went through the training, the drills, and the practice sessions, all for a few occasional plays. Rich never felt overwhelmed by the problem of being blind. And he never gave up his dream. Despite the enormity of the obstacle facing him, he rose to the challenge and strove to succeed.

Sadly, Israel never rose to the challenge before them. Despite God's presence, the nation cowered fearfully, convinced that they could not possibly succeed. Because the people gave up, they suffered the consequences of their faithlessness.

# THE DESERT YEARS

**BACKGROUND SCRIPTURE:** Deuteronomy 1:41—2:25
**DEVOTIONAL READING:** Isaiah 35

**KEY VERSE:** Surely the LORD your God has blessed you in all your undertakings; he knows your going through this great wilderness. These forty years the LORD your God has been with you; you have lacked nothing. Deuteronomy 2:7.

*KING JAMES VERSION*

DEUTERONOMY 1:41 Then ye answered and said unto me, We have sinned against the LORD, we will go up and fight, according to all that the LORD our God commanded us. And when ye had girded on every man his weapons of war, ye were ready to go up into the hill.

42 And the LORD said unto me, Say unto them, Go not up, neither fight; for I am not among you; lest ye be smitten before your enemies.

43 So I spake unto you; and ye would not hear, but rebelled against the commandment of the LORD, and went presumptuously up into the hill.

44 And the Amorites, which dwelt in that mountain, came out against you, and chased you, as bees do, and destroyed you in Seir, even unto Hormah.

45 And ye returned and wept before the LORD, but the LORD would not hearken to your voice, nor give ear unto you.

46 So ye abode in Kadesh many days, according unto the days that ye abode there.

2:1 Then we turned, and took our journey into the wilderness by the way of the Red sea, as the LORD spake unto me: and we compassed mount Seir many days.

2 And the LORD spake unto me, saying,

3 Ye have compassed this mountain long enough: turn you northward.

4 And command thou the people, saying, Ye are to pass through the coast of your brethren the children of Esau, which dwell in Seir; and they shall be afraid of you: take ye good heed unto yourselves therefore:

5 Meddle not with them; for I will not give you of their land, no, not so much as a foot breadth; because I have given mount Seir unto Esau for a possession.

6 Ye shall buy meat of them for money, that ye may eat; and ye shall also buy water of them for money, that ye may drink.

7 For the LORD thy God hath blessed thee in all the works of thy hand: he knoweth thy walking through this great wilderness: these forty years the LORD thy God hath been with thee; thou hast lacked nothing.

8 And when we passed by from our brethren the children of Esau, which dwelt in Seir.

*NEW REVISED STANDARD VERSION*

DEUTERONOMY 1:41 You answered me, "We have sinned against the LORD! We are ready to go up and fight, just as the LORD our God commanded us." So all of you strapped on your battle gear, and thought it easy to go up into the hill country. 42 The LORD said to me, "Say to them, 'Do not go up and do not fight, for I am not in the midst of you; otherwise you will be defeated by your enemies.' " 43 Although I told you, you would not listen. You rebelled against the command of the LORD and presumptuously went up into the hill country. 44 The Amorites who lived in that hill country then came out against you and chased you as bees do. They beat you down in Seir as far as Hormah. 45 When you returned and wept before the LORD, the LORD would neither heed your voice nor pay you any attention.

46 After you had stayed at Kadesh as many days as you did, 2:1 we journeyed back into the wilderness, in the direction of the Red Sea, as the LORD had told me and skirted Mount Seir for many days. 2 Then the LORD said to me: 3 "You have been skirting this hill country long enough. Head north, 4 and charge the people as follows: You are about to pass through the territory of your kindred, the descendants of Esau, who live in Seir. They will be afraid of you, so, be very careful 5 not to engage in battle with them, for I will not give you even so much as a foot's length of their land, since I have given Mount Seir to Esau as a possession. 6 You shall purchase food from them for money, so that you may eat; and you shall also buy water from them for money, so that you may drink. 7 Surely the LORD you God has blessed you in all your undertakings; he knows your going through this great wilderness. These forty years the LORD your God has been with you; you have lacked nothing." 8 So we passed by our kin, the descendants of Esau who live in Seir.

7

## HOME BIBLE READINGS

## BACKGROUND

Learning to obey orders is imperative in any military operation. Unhappily, the Israelites often resisted the orders that the Lord gave through Moses. When God made the covenant at Mount Sinai, the people seemed willing and determined to obey its stipulations. Yet when the circumstances got difficult, they frequently murmured and protested. Though they resented the leadership of Moses, God was the real target of their dissatisfaction. Their yammering was a tacit refusal to trust and obey the Lord.

Disobedience in any campaign almost always proves to be costly. It thus should come as no surprise that the insubordination of the Israelites on various occasions always ended in disaster for them. On one such occasion, some impetuous leaders convinced their peers to mount an ill-conceived assault on the inhabitants of the promised land. Despite God's command to the contrary, His people went through with the attack. The campaign came to a sudden, inglorious halt when the powerful Amorites chased the would-be invaders back into the Sinai Desert.

The Israelites' attempt to take matters into their own hands without obtaining God's approval and guidance was a tragic but necessary lesson. Through Moses, the Lord made it clear that His chosen community still had lessons in obedience to learn. Only after many more years of learning some hard lessons in the wilderness on the importance of obedience would the Israelites be forged into a disciplined people who were ready to enter and conquer Canaan.

## NOTES ON THE PRINTED TEXT

The Israelites encamped at Kadesh-Barnea for almost 38 years before journeying to Moab on Canaan's eastern border and before entering the promised land (see 2:14). At the central rift valley to the east of the Jordan River (1:1), Moses repeated the stipulations of the covenant to a new generation of Israelites. He reminded them about the spies' mission and the disloyalty of the previous generation. He also spoke about God's anger and about the Lord's punishment of that ill-fated age group.

Though Moses was speaking to a new generation of Israelites, he addressed them as if they were the ones who had rebelled against the Lord. Moses' intent was to stress their continuity with the previous generation of Israelites, the ones who had defied the Lord's will on many occasions (see 1:26-28).

God directed that previous generation of malcontents to turn around and go back through the wilderness toward the Red Sea (1:40). The Israelites responded with the confession, *"We have sinned against the Lord!"* (1:41). However, despite their acknowledgement of sin, the people were plotting a sinful course of action.

The Israelites declared that they would go into Canaan and fight for it, *just as the LORD our God commanded us* (1:41). But God had not told them to do this. They deliberately rebelled against Him by strapping on their weapons. And they were wrong to think that it would be easy for them to conquer the hill country.

God could have wiped out this rebellious group. Yet He dealt patiently with them by directing Moses to issue a warning. The Lord declared that He would not go with His people into battle. If they insisted on fighting anyway, they would be crushed by their enemies (1:42).

This warning was ignored, and the people arrogantly went into the hill country to fight. The Israelites thought they were doing God's will, but instead they were merely churning out their own rebellious desires (1:43). When they encountered the Amorites, the enemy chased the Israelites all the way from Seir as far as Hormah, which was a town about 55 miles northeast of Kadesh-Barnea (1:44).

When the routed Israelite soldiers returned to camp, the entire community wept before the Lord at the tabernacle. God showed His displeasure by not sympathizing with their defeat (1:45). In fact, for that generation there was no escape from death in the desert during the next 38 years (1:46).

In accordance with the Lord's instructions, the Israelites wandered around Mount Seir for a long time (2:1). After that generation had died and a new generation had been born, the Lord directed His people to turn northward in the direction of the promised land (2:2-3). At God's command, Moses told the Israelites that they would be passing through the region belonging to their distant relatives, the Edomites. These people were the descendants of Esau and lived in Seir (2:4).

The Lord warned His people that the Edomites would feel threatened by their presence. Thus the Israelites were not to start a fight. Instead, they were to respect the Edomites' territory and to pay for whatever they used. In other words, God wanted His people to deal justly with their neighbors (2:5-6).

Since the Lord had granted Mount Seir as an inheritance to the Edomites, it was off-limits to the Israelites. They need not be bothered by this, for God intended to bless His people with something far better. They could trust Him to do so, for He had been with them throughout their wilderness wanderings. During that 40-year period, He had faithfully provided for their every need so that they *lacked nothing* (2:7).

The Israelites obeyed God's command. They went around the border of the Edomites (2:8). In other words, the Israelites traveled to the east of the Edomite territory.

## SUGGESTIONS TO TEACHERS

At the beginning of the American Revolution, George Washington's Continental Army was a motley collection of untrained, inexperienced, and poorly armed farmers and laborers. After being driven from New York in a series of disastrous defeats, Washington's rag-tag force retreated to the winter snows at Valley Forge, Pennsylvania. Gradually, through the patience and genius of Washington's leadership, what had been not much more than an armed rabble became welded into a lean and effective fighting force.

**1. DISOBEDIENT AND DEFEATED.** The Israelites also had to endure the pain of being forged into a cohesive and obedient strike force. Without consulting God, some impetuously took matters into their own hands and tried to mount an assault on the Canaanites. Their ill-planned act of disobedience brought total defeat. The Israelites had to submit to God's chastening. They needed to learn to be dutiful before the Lord. Let the class members know that God's people are called to serve in His spiritual army. Our term of enlistment is for life. As Christians, we should be prepared to go through God's "basic training" and constantly keep ourselves ready as the Lord's frontline defense against evil.

**2. DIRECTED AND DUTIFUL.** In accordance with God's leading, a new generation of Israelites respected the rights of their distant kinfolk, Esau's descendants, when they skirted Edomite territory. As Christians, we too should act justly toward others and respect their rights.

**3. DISCIPLINED AND DETERMINED.** Gradually the Israelites were welded by God into a dedicated and disciplined fighting force. And eventually, the critics and complainers died off. The new generation of God's chosen people were hardy and ready to heed His commands. Take this opportunity to discuss with the students how their congregation can become a trained and dedicated group of believers who are ready to fight against the forces of darkness.

---

**FOR ADULTS**

■ TOPIC: In the Wilderness

■ QUESTIONS. 1. In what way had the rebellious generation acted presumptuously? 2. In what ways did the new generation of Israelites contrast with the previous one? 3. How has God responded to you when you acted presumptuously? 4. What areas of life has God said are "off-limits" to you? 5. What are some ways you can respect the rights of others?

■ ILLUSTRATIONS:

**Impetuous Steel Producing.** During World War II, the famous Liberty ships were produced hurriedly to replace the enormous number of merchant ships lost to enemy action. The standardized 10,000-ton ships were produced at an average rate of one every 42 days. But for some reason, these ships tended to break in two when they first set sail. A number, complete with their cargoes, broke apart like glass, with a crack running instantaneously around their hull. Along the water-fronts and in the union halls, old timers tried to avoid shipping on the Liberties, and passed on scuttlebutt about early ones that were never heard from after sailing on their maiden voyages.

Engineers suspected that the method of fabrication or the use of welding could cause these ships to break apart suddenly. It took the research of Dr. Constance Tipper, a British metallurgist and mechanical engineer at Cambridge University, to find the cause of the problem. She discovered that the material used in the hulls became dangerously brittle under certain conditions. Her name is now known everywhere as the creator of the "Tipper Test" for determining brittleness in steel.

In their haste and carelessness to fabricate materials for these early Liberty ships, the steel producers caused sailors and the Allies to pay a heavy price before their errors were corrected. Likewise, haste and carelessness led the Israelites on an impetuous attack. Imagine how different things would have been if they had heeded God's directive!

**Making Our Earth a Wilderness.** In an essay entitled "What Is Education," Professor David Orr of Oberlin College wrote the following: "If today is a typical day on planet earth, we will lose 116 square miles of rain forest, or about an acre a second. We will lose another 72 square miles to encroaching deserts, the results of human mismanagement and overpopulation. We will lose 40 to 250 species, and no one knows whether the number is 40 or 250. Today the human population will increase by 250,000. And today we will add 2,700 tons of chlorofluorocarbons and 15 million tons of carbon dioxide to the atmosphere. Tonight the earth will be a little hotter, its waters more acidic, and the fabric of life more threadbare. By the year's end the numbers are staggering. The total loss of rain forest will equal an area the size of the state of Washington; expanding deserts will equal an area the size of the state of West Virginia; and the global population will have risen by more than 90,000,000. By the year 2000 perhaps as much as 20 percent of the life forms extant on the planet in the year 1900 will be extinct."

Sometimes we in the Christian community have been slow to acknowledge the threat imposed by unbridled economic growth, environmental carelessness, and human greed. Our ambivalence represents a reckless and defiant attitude toward the One who created this world. Tragically, the ecological crisis is causing our planet to be turned into a wasteland.

**Critical of God.** Like the Israelites, we sometimes become impatient and critical of God. Our inclination to think that we know better is reminiscent of the story about a farmer named Nasr-ed-Din Hodja, who lived in the Near East. One day Hodja sat irritably in the sun under a walnut tree while looking at his pumpkin vines. Perhaps the heat had disrupted his thinking when he said to himself, "How foolish God is! He has made such silly mistakes. Here He puts a great big heavy pumpkin on a tiny vine without strength enough to do anything but lie on the ground. And He puts tiny walnuts on a big tree whose branches could hold the weight of a man. If I were God, I could do better than that!"

Just then, a breeze dislocated a walnut in the tree, and it fell on the head of skeptical Nasr-ed-Din Hodja, who rubbed his head, now a sadder and a wiser man. "Suppose," he mused, "there had been a pumpkin up there, instead of a walnut. Never again will I try to plan the world for God. From here on, I will thank God that He has done so well!"

---

| **FOR YOUTH** | ■ **TOPIC:** Paying the Price<br>■ **QUESTIONS:** 1. Why was loyalty to God so important for Israel? 2. What did the Lord promise to do for His people, if they remained |

faithful to Him? 3. What are some ways you can show your loyalty to God? 4. What can you do to ensure that you don't act foolishly or rashly in any given situation? 5. What are some ways you can show respect for the rights of others?

■ **ILLUSTRATIONS:**

**Impulsive Action.** In high school, I had a teacher that repeatedly urged my class to read through the test before starting to answer the questions. Her hope was that we would see what questions or sections of the test we would need to place particular emphasis upon, or to notice whether certain essays at the end carried more value or points. Following her advice would enable us to devote more time to those questions and less time on the true and false or multiple choice questions.

I remember one particular day when our teacher passed out an exam. Every member of the class immediately began to answer the questions, failing, as always, to read through the test. It was not until we arrived at the next to the last question that we read, "Do Not Write Anything On This Test!"

Like the Israelites, we had acted impulsively and failed to listen to our teacher's directions. Fortunately, it did not carry the same consequences that followed Israel's rash action.

**No Direction.** On Tuesday, December 23, 1997, actor-comedian Chris Farley died. The gifted comic had a successful five-year career with *Saturday Night Live* before moving to movies and completing such films as *Tommy Boy, Black Sheep,* and *Beverly Hills Ninja.*

Despite wealth and popularity, Farley seemed to lack direction. He regularly attended church and had practically every creature comfort anyone could want. But he seemed to have a void in life that he yearned to fill. In his attempt to do so, he succumbed to drugs, alcohol, gluttony, and anxiety. Farley aimlessly wandered through the vast desert of his life searching for contentment and meaning.

It's tragic that Farley failed to trust God for leadership, wisdom, and joy. His life reminds us that apart from God there can be no true meaning or satisfaction. It is only when we read and heed His Word that life will have real direction and purpose for us.

**Long-Term Consequence.** The police stopped young Craig's car. It was initially a routine Friday night traffic stop. However, the law enforcement officers discovered that Craig had been drinking. They thus charged him with driving under the influence of alcohol and underage drinking. Craig was convicted, and he lost his driver's license until he was 21.

An action committed early can have long-term negative consequences. The Israelites learned this hard lesson, and it prevented an entire generation from entering the promised land. When we are unfaithful to God, it might adversely affect our life for years to come. It's always better to follow God's will than to recklessly move forward with our sinful plans.

# THE GREAT COMMANDMENT

**BACKGROUND SCRIPTURE:** Deuteronomy 6
**DEVOTIONAL READING:** Deuteronomy 30:11-20

**KEY VERSE:** Hear, O Israel: The LORD is our God, the LORD alone. You shall love the LORD your God with all your heart, and with all your soul, and with all your might. Deuteronomy 6:4-5.

*KING JAMES VERSION*

DEUTERONOMY 6:1 Now these are the commandments, the statutes, and the judgments, which the LORD your God commanded to teach you, that ye might do them in the land whither ye go to possess it:

2 That thou mightest fear the LORD thy God, to keep all his statutes and his commandments, which I command thee, thou, and thy son, and thy son's son, all the days of thy life; and that thy days may be prolonged.

3 Hear therefore, O Israel, and observe to do it; that it may be well with thee, and that ye may increase mightily, as the LORD God of thy fathers hath promised thee, in the land that floweth with milk and honey.

4 Hear, O Israel: The LORD our God is one LORD:

5 And thou shalt love the LORD thy God with all thine heart, and with all thy soul, and with all thy might.

6 And these words, which I command thee this day, shall be in thine heart:

7 And thou shalt teach them diligently unto thy children, and shalt talk of them when thou sittest in thine house, and when thou walkest by the way, and when thou liest down, and when thou risest up.

8 And thou shalt bind them for a sign upon thine hand, and they shall be as frontlets between thine eyes.

9 And thou shalt write them upon the posts of thy house, and on thy gates. . . .

20 And when thy son asketh thee in time to come, saying, What mean the testimonies, and the statutes, and the judgments, which the LORD our God hath commanded you?

21 Then thou shalt say unto thy son, We were Pharaoh's bondmen in Egypt; and the LORD brought us out of Egypt with a mighty hand:

22 And the LORD shewed signs and wonders, great and sore, upon Egypt, upon Pharaoh, and upon all his household, before our eyes:

23 And he brought us out from thence, that he might bring us in, to give us the land which he sware unto our fathers.

24 And the LORD commanded us to do all these statutes, to fear the LORD our God, for our good always, that he might preserve us alive, as it is at this day.

*NEW REVISED STANDARD VERSION*

DEUTERONOMY 6:1 Now this is the commandment—the statutes and the ordinances—that the LORD your God charged me to teach you to observe in the land that you are about to cross into and occupy, 2 so that you and your children and your children's children may fear the LORD your God all the days of your life, and keep all his decrees and his commandments that I am commanding you, so that your days may be long. 3 Hear therefore, O Israel, and observe them diligently, so that it may go well with you, and so that you may multiply greatly in a land flowing with milk and honey, as the LORD, the God of your ancestors, has promised you.

4 Hear, O Israel: The LORD is our God, the LORD alone. 5 You shall love the LORD your God with all your heart, and with all your soul, and with all your might. 6 Keep these words that I am commanding you today in your heart. 7 Recite them to your children and talk about them when you are at home and when you are away, when you lie down and when you rise. 8 Bind them as a sign on your hand, fix them as an emblem on your forehead, 9 and write them on the doorposts of your house and on your gates. . . .

20 When your children ask you in time to come, "What is the meaning of the decrees and the statutes and the ordinances that the LORD our God has commanded you?" 21 then you shall say to your children, "We were Pharaoh's slaves in Egypt, but the LORD brought us out of Egypt with a mighty hand. 22 The LORD displayed before our eyes great and awesome signs and wonders against Egypt, against Pharaoh and all his household. 23 He brought us out from there in order to brings us in, to give us the land that he promised on oath to our ancestors. 24 Then the LORD commanded us to observe all these statutes, to fear the LORD our God, for our lasting good, so as to keep us alive, as is now the case.

## HOME BIBLE READINGS

| | | |
|---|---|---|
| Monday, Oct. 18 | Deuteronomy 6:1-9 | *God's Great Commandment to Israel* |
| Tuesday, Oct. 19 | Deuteronomy 6:10-15 | *Do Not Follow Other Gods!* |
| Wednesday, Oct. 20 | Deuteronomy 6:16-25 | *Tell about God's Mighty Acts!* |
| Thursday, Oct. 21 | Deuteronomy 7:7-11 | *Chosen by God's Love and Grace* |
| Friday, Oct. 22 | Deuteronomy 10:12-22 | *Blessing of Obedience* |
| Saturday, Oct. 23 | Deuteronomy 11:8-12 | *A Land of Milk and Honey* |
| Sunday, Oct. 24 | Deuteronomy 11:13-21 | *Love God and Teach Your Children* |

## BACKGROUND

Imagine a foreigner asking the Israelites to choose the foremost commandment of the Mosaic covenant. Which one would it be? Perhaps they would select an ordinance about a sacrificial offering, or about paying a tithe, or about keeping the sabbath, or about not stealing from one's neighbor. As important as these injunctions might have been, they were eclipsed by one supreme command—the Shema (shuh-MAH).

*Shema* is a Hebrew verb that is rendered *Hear* in Deuteronomy 6:4. This term became the watchword of Israel's faith. It was not so much a prayer as it was a declaration of God's oneness and uniqueness. The practice of reciting the Shema daily is clearly established in the Mishnah (a collection of mostly Jewish legal traditions compiled around A.D. 200). And there is also evidence to suggest that the Shema was an integral part of the Jewish faith before and during the New Testament era. For example, every morning and evening temple priests would recite the Shema, which came to include Deuteronomy 6:4-9; 11:13-21; and Numbers 15:37-41.

In traditional Jewish practice, the Shema is written in the phylacteries (square leather boxes containing slips of Scripture and worn on the head and left arm) and the mezuzah [muh-ZOO-suh] (a small parchment scroll placed in a case and fixed to a doorpost). Each passage of the Shema declares an important truth of the Jewish faith. Deuteronomy 6:4-9 proclaims God's oneness and directs Israel to love Him and obey His commandments. In 11:13-21, the rewards for obeying these commandments and the punishments for disobeying them are detailed. And in Numbers 15:37-41, the law concerning tassels on garments are set forth as a reminder to the people to heed all the Lord's decrees.

In ancient times, women, children, and slaves were not required to recite the Shema. In contrast, as soon as boys could speak, they were taught the first verse of the creed (Deut. 6:4). Jewish tradition says that martyrs being led to death would recite the Shema, as would those who were on their death-bed. The idea is that faithful Jews—namely, those who truly loved the Lord—would have His name on their lips from early childhood to death. Incidentally, this emphasis on being supremely devoted to God is in harmony with the teaching of Christ (see Matt. 22:34-40; Mark 12:28-34).

# NOTES ON THE PRINTED TEXT

**D**euteronomy has been dubbed "the second law," for it represents a restatement of the Mosaic covenant. A generation of Israelites had died in the wilderness due to their rebellion against God. A new generation had been born, and the Lord wanted them to enter and take possession of Canaan.

Moses, who was now 120, would soon die. Before his departure, he wanted to ensure that the new generation understood the law and were committed to following its decrees. Thus, Deuteronomy is a set of farewell speeches in which Moses urged the people to trust in the Lord and obey His covenant made at Mount Sinai.

Deuteronomy reflects the pattern of ancient treaties that existed between a master and his vassals. Note the following correspondences: a preamble or introduction (1:1-5); a review of the past relationship between the parties (1:6—4:49); basic stipulations that ensured fidelity to the treaty (5:1—26:19); sanctions in the form of blessings and curses (27:1—30:20); witnesses to the treaty (32:1); and a provision for the storage and reading of the treaty (31:1—34:12).

The Scripture text for this week's lesson is part of the basic stipulations of the Mosaic covenant. If the Israelites hoped to prosper in Canaan, which they were about to cross and occupy (6:1), they needed to learn and obey the statutes and ordinances of the law, which God told Moses to teach them.

The intent was not merely to help the people achieve a rote understanding of the covenant. More importantly, the Lord wanted the Israelites—both the present and future generations—to revere and obey Him. Only then would they enjoy a long and successful life (6:2).

It was God's desire that His people did well and had many children in the land of abundance they were about to inherit. For 40 years the nation had wandered in a parched wilderness. Canaan would seem like paradise by comparison. It would have rich crops, rushing streams, gentle rains, and lush fields brimming with livestock (6:3).

In order for the blessings of the covenant to become a reality, the Israelites had to hear and heed what Moses said. Of supreme importance was their devotion to God. That's why in 6:4, Moses declared the Lord's uniqueness and unity. The people were to understand that Yahweh alone is the true and living God and thus worthy of their supreme devotion. They were to love Him with every aspect of their existence, namely, their heart, soul, and might (6:5).

Moses exhorted the Israelites to commit themselves wholeheartedly to keeping the commands he gave them that day (6:6). What he said pertained not only to them but also to their descendants. Moses urged the people to recite the decrees to their children (6:7). In addition to formal instruction, the Israelites were to use informal occasions to teach the law. This included times at home and when the family was away on a journey. It also encompassed the entire day, from the time when the family members awoke to when they went to bed.

While some interpret 6:8 literally, others understand this verse in a figurative sense. In either case the verse teaches that God's people were to continually meditate upon and be directed by the law. The stipulations of the covenant were to govern the Israelites in all realms of living, whether personal or private, spiritual or social, economic or political (6:9).

Moses urged the people to remember that God had graciously given them the land of Canaan and that He had rescued them from Egypt. They were to worship and serve Him alone. If they heeded His decrees, they would have great success in Canaan (6:10-19).

Whenever the situation arose, the Israelites were to share with their children the reason why the covenant community lived by the Mosaic law (6:20). Parents were to explain that the Lord had used His amazing power to redeem them from Egypt (6:21-22). He freed them from slavery so that they would serve Him exclusively in the promised land (6:23). Children were to learn that the foremost reason for their existence was to obey God and revere Him. In fact, this was the key to their continued prosperity and well-being in Canaan (6:24).

## SUGGESTIONS TO TEACHERS

Christian education leaders often tell audiences, "The Church is always one generation away from extinction." They remind their hearers about the necessity of instructing their children in the faith. With the appalling ignorance of the Bible and Christian doctrine and practice among church people and their offspring, believers must seriously teach and preach the Word.

**1. RESPONDING TO GOD'S CONCERN FOR THE FUTURE.** We often forget how important it is to pass on our faith and Christian heritage. It is imperative that we do so, especially when we realize how short life can be. The median age of members in many established congregations is 65. What about your church? Where will it be in a decade or two?

**2. RESPECTING GOD'S SOVEREIGNTY COMPLETELY.** Go over Deuteronomy 6:4-5 word for word, and note the meanings of each term in this passage. Let your class members know that loving God is more than a warm fuzzy "religious" feeling or a vague spirituality. To love God calls for respecting His sovereignty in every area of life, and doing everything possible to promote His interests in each of those areas.

**3. RELAYING GOD'S TEACHINGS TO OUR CHILDREN.** Discuss how teaching our children calls for more than just flashy Sunday school classes and Christian education programs. Relaying God's commandments demands a consistent example in the lifestyle of each church member. Talk with the students about the ways children learn about God's grace through Christ.

**4. REMEMBERING GOD'S ACTS IN THE PAST.** This week's Scripture text points out the perils of complacency. How might your church encourage its younger members to cherish the solid convictions of their faith community? We and they must remember what God has done in the past if we are to have a vital Christian witness in the future!

---

**FOR ADULTS**

■ TOPIC: Teach Your Children Well
■ QUESTIONS: 1. What commandments were the Israelites to observe and teach future generations of their children in the promised land? 2. How could God's people encourage future generations to love and serve the Lord wholeheartedly? 3. Why do we sometimes want to take credit for our wealth and accomplishments, rather than acknowledge that God made these things possible? 4. What can we do to keep God at the center of our lives? 5. How might we encourage others in our church to pass their faith on to their children?

■ **ILLUSTRATIONS:**

**Neglecting the Bible.** A recent survey of Presbyterians showed a distressing trend that is also believed to be true among members of other church groups. Despite the importance of regular Scripture reading to the spiritual vitality and growth of the church, the Bible reading rate among many church goers is distressingly low. Sixty-two percent of members and 56 percent of elders in a recent study reported infrequent or no Bible reading during the previous year, and 52 percent of members never read the Bible in a group devoted specifically to Scripture study. Also, family Bible reading occurs rarely in Presbyterian homes, except at Christmas and Easter. Not surprisingly the report indicates that older members (over 70) are more likely to read the Bible more frequently (at least weekly), while only 29 percent of members under age 40 do so.

Regarding the next generation, the figures are even more alarming. Most lay people (66 percent of members and 65 percent of elders) reported that they had not read the Bible to children outside of a Sunday school class. And only a few frequently read Bible stories to children outside of a Sunday school class (6 percent of members, 5 percent of elders, 20 percent of pastors, and 14 percent of specialized ministers).

**The Place of Memory.** Miguel de Unamuno (1864–1936) was an influential Spanish writer. In his classic work entitled *Tragic Sense of Life,* he wrote the following about the importance of teaching our children to remember what God has done in the past: "Memory is the basis for individual personality, just as tradition is the basis of the collective personality of a people. We live in memory and by memory, and our spiritual life is at the bottom of the effort of our memory to persist, to transform itself into hope, the effort of our past to transform itself into our future."

**Most Saluted Man in America.** Richard Stans, according to William Safire, is the most saluted man in the United States. Safire points out that millions of school children place their right hands over their hearts to pledge allegiance to the flag, and to the republic for Richard Stans. Safire also claims that he has learned that many youngsters start the famous pledge by saying, "I pledge a legion to the flag," while others begin with, "I led the pigeons to the flag." The words, "one nation, indivisible," sometimes are corrupted into "One naked individual," or "One nation in a dirigible," or "One nation and a vegetable."

While we may smile at these childish misunderstandings of the words of the Pledge of Allegiance, we should note that many of our children have just as poor an understanding of what God's Word says. We have failed to teach our children well in many areas, and must heed the warning that the generation that forgets the truths of Scripture will spiritually perish.

---

**FOR YOUTH**
- **TOPIC:** Link in the Chain
- **QUESTIONS:** 1. What were the blessings of the promised land that the Israelites were to enjoy? 2. What concerned Moses about the nation's life in the promised land? 3. Does your wealth come from God or your own effort? 4. What is the negative result of forgetting to love and serve God wholeheartedly? 5. How might you tell others about your relationship with God through Christ?

■ **ILLUSTRATIONS:**
**Sense of Heritage.** One day Walter Kolar stood in the hall of the Bulgarian-Macedonian Club in West Homestead, Pennsylvania. The aroma of pumpkin strudel and lamb served with rice and spinach stew filled the large room as bursts of his Slavic tongue rang in the background. The club was formed by Bulgarian immigrants who flocked to Pittsburgh's steel mills. They wanted to maintain close ties to their heritage and history.

Each weekend, dances, wrestling matches, and other activities were held. In fact, prior to World War II, an interest in one's heritage thrived. However, by the 1960s, the club began to dwindle as people died and others moved from the area. Younger people no longer had an interest in their history, culture, or heritage. The hall itself deteriorated as garbage piled up in various areas of the building.

Kolar dreams of a rebirth and renewal of the club. He knows that making his dream come true will not be easy. He has discovered that many young people (not only those of Bulgarian descent) are ambivalent about their traditions and heritage. They sense no tie to the past or to those who went before them.

Perhaps Moses was also concerned about the lack of interest among the youth of his day in their religious heritage and traditions. He urged the Israelites to teach future generations of children about their nation's history and faith. Moses especially urged people to remember God's involvement in their lives. After all, apart from the Lord, the covenant community had nothing to look forward to in the future.

**Unwavering Commitment.** The most famous and best-loved athlete Scotland ever produced was Eric Liddell. He was an internationally known rugby player and an Olympic gold medalist. The story of his refusal to run in the preliminary heats of the 100-meter dash on the Lord's Day at the Paris Olympics in 1924 was told in the movie entitled *Chariots of Fire*.

Liddell was a man who had an unswerving commitment to love the Lord and keep His commandments. While the race put him into a conflict with his fellow citizens, the leaders of his nation, the International Olympic Committee, his friends, and others, Liddell would not deviate from his stand.

Like Liddell, you will often be torn by conflicting allegiances to family, peers, and others. But like Liddell, you too can stand up to the world by relying on God's power. He will give you the strength to do what is right.

**Revolution Ending.** The so-called "sexual revolution" is slowing, and perhaps, even ending. Mark Judge of *Insight* magazine cites surveys (including one of 200,000 teens done by *USA Today*) that demonstrates a "decline" in sexual activity among teens. Literally thousands more young people are saying *no* to premarital sex, are waiting for marriage, and are returning to more traditional dating and courtship patterns.

A growing tide of problems, such as sexually transmitted diseases, AIDS, divorce, and a culture saturated with sex, plus a more affirmative effort by churches, has led a younger generation to adopt a different perspective on physical intimacy. As a follower of Christ, you will want to consider what the Bible teaches about this. Let your love for God and commitment to His Word be demonstrated by your efforts to remain chaste.

# A WARNING

**BACKGROUND SCRIPTURE:** Deuteronomy 8
**DEVOTIONAL READING:** Psalm 85

**KEY VERSE:** Take care that you do not forget the LORD your God, by failing to keep his commandments, his ordinances, and his statutes, which I am commanding you today.
Deuteronomy 8:11.

*KING JAMES VERSION*

DEUTERONOMY 8:7 For the LORD thy God bringeth thee into a good land, a land of brooks of water, of fountains and depths that spring out of valleys and hills;

8 A land of wheat, and barley, and vines, and fig trees, and pomegranates; a land of oil olive, and honey;

9 A land wherein thou shalt eat bread without scarceness, thou shalt not lack any thing in it; a land whose stones are iron, and out of whose hills thou mayest dig brass.

10 When thou hast eaten and art full, then thou shalt bless the LORD thy God for the good land which he hath given thee.

11 Beware that thou forget not the LORD thy God, in not keeping his commandments, and his judgments, and his statutes, which I command thee this day:

12 Lest when thou hast eaten and art full, and hast built goodly houses, and dwelt therein;

13 And when thy herds and thy flocks multiply, and thy silver and thy gold is multiplied, and all that thou hast is multiplied;

14 Then thine heart be lifted up, and thou forget the LORD thy God, which brought thee forth out of the land of Egypt, from the house of bondage;

15 Who led thee through that great and terrible wilderness, wherein were fiery serpents, and scorpions, and drought, where there was no water; who brought thee forth water out of the rock of flint;

16 Who fed thee in the wilderness with manna, which thy fathers knew not, that he might humble thee, and that he might prove thee, to do thee good at thy latter end;

17 And thou say in thine heart, My power and the might of mine hand hath gotten me this wealth.

18 But thou shalt remember the LORD thy God: for it is he that giveth thee power to get wealth, that he may establish his covenant which he sware unto thy fathers, as it is this day.

19 And it shall be, if thou do at all forget the LORD thy God, and walk after other gods, and serve them, and worship them, I testify against you this day that ye shall surely perish.

20 As the nations which the LORD destroyeth before your face, so shall ye perish; because ye would not be obedient unto the voice of the LORD your God.

*NEW REVISED STANDARD VERSION*

DEUTERONOMY 8:7 For the LORD your God is bringing you into a good land, a land with flowing streams, with springs and underground waters welling up in valleys and hills, 8 a land of wheat and barley, of vines and fig trees and pomegrantes, a land of olive trees and honey, 9 a land where you may eat bread without scarcity, where you will lack nothing, a land whose stones are iron and from whose hills you may mine copper. 10 You shall eat your fill and bless the Lord your God for the good land that he has given you.

11 Take care that you do not forget the LORD your God, by failing to keep his commandments, his ordinances, and his statutes, which I am commanding you today. 12 When you have eaten your fill and have built fine houses and live in them, 13 and when your herds and flocks have multiplied, and your silver and gold is multiplied, and all that you have is multiplied, 14 then do not exalt yourself, forgetting the LORD your God, who brought you out of the land of Egypt, out of the house of slavery, 15 who led you through the great and terrible wilderness, an arid wasteland with poisonous snakes and scorpions. He made water flow for you from flint rock, 16 and fed you in the wilderness with manna that your ancestors did not know, to humble you and to test you, and in the end to do you good. 17 Do not say to yourself, "My power and the might of my own hand have gotten me this wealth." 18 But remember the LORD your God, for it is he who gives you power to get wealth, so that he may confirm his covenant that he swore to your ancestors, as he is doing today. 19 If you do forget the LORD your God and follow other gods to serve and worship them, I solemnly warn you today that you shall surely perish. 20 Like the nations that the Lord is destroying before you, so shall you perish, because you would not obey the voice of the LORD your God.

9

| | | |
|---|---|---|
| *Monday, Oct. 25* | Deuteronomy 8:1-10 | *Don't Let Prosperity Spoil You* |
| *Tuesday, Oct. 26* | Deuteronomy 8:11-20 | *You Are Not Self-Made People* |
| *Wednesday, Oct. 27* | Deuteronomy 9:6-14 | *You Were a Stubborn Bunch* |
| *Thursday, Oct. 28* | Deuteronomy 9:15-21 | *God Heard Moses on Your Behalf* |
| *Friday, Oct. 29* | Deuteronomy 9:25-29 | *Moses Interceded for Israel Again* |
| *Saturday, Oct. 30* | Deuteronomy 13:1-5 | *Beware of False Prophets* |
| *Sunday, Oct. 31* | Deuteronomy 13:6-11 | *Purge Those Who Worship False Gods* |

## BACKGROUND

In the Bible, "remember" is a key word. In fact, it occurs in most of the books of Scripture. The term is especially prevalent in Deuteronomy, where Moses repeatedly called God's people to remember Him in worship, service, and obedience.

The first five books of the Bible are sometimes called the Torah or Pentateuch, and Deuteronomy is sometimes called "The Book of Remembering." In this body of wisdom and law, Moses warned the Israelites not to forget who God is, what He had done for them, or who they were as a people. They were to *remember*.

Moses knew the perils of forgetting God. He warned the Israelites that spiritual amnesia would lead to the end of the covenant community. His solemn warnings to keep before them daily the recollection of God and His goodness were more than just religious rhetoric. Remembering meant spiritual survival, while forgetting meant spiritual extinction.

The peril of forgetting was real. After all, the Israelites would encounter a pagan culture and religion. If God's people were not careful, they could soon find themselves adopting Canaanite beliefs and practices, which were abhorrent to the Lord.

The Israelites had lived for 40 years as a nomadic people. In the promised land, they would find an agrarian society. They would notice the skills and sophistication of those in the powerful city-states of Canaan. Most of all, as newcomers, the Israelites would discover the allure of the fertility religions. Like most poor, struggling immigrants anywhere and at anytime, the community of God's people arriving in the promised land would be made to feel inferior and would be easily persuaded to "fit in" by adopting Canaanite practices. That's why Moses enjoined the Israelites to remember God, or suffer the painful consequences of their actions.

## NOTES ON THE PRINTED TEXT

As Moses reviewed the law with the Israelites, he considered the future. He advised the people to enjoy the good land that the Lord was giving them. He described the abundant water, fertile fields, beautiful houses, lush gardens, and even the large mineral deposits. (The area below the Dead Sea was, and still is, rich in minerals.)

*For the Lord your God is bringing you into a good land, a land with flowing streams, with springs and underground waters welling up in valleys and hills, a land of wheat and barley, of vines and fig trees and pomegranates, a land of olive trees and honey, a land where you may eat bread without scarcity, where you will lack nothing, a land whose stones are iron and from whose hills you may mine copper* (8:7-9). For the Israelites, who had to endure hardships for almost four decades, inheriting Canaan would be like a dream come true. *You shall eat your fill and bless the Lord your God for the good land that he has given you* (8:10).

Moses sensed a danger in having such abundance. *Take care that you do not forget the Lord your God, by failing to keep his commandments, his ordinances, and his statutes, which I am commanding you today* (8:11). The people might forget their allegiance to God, especially while surrounded by the blessings of abundant foodstuffs, secure homes, plenty of livestock, and a generous supply of precious metals.

Moses warned that the people might forget Yahweh, who delivered them, led them, and provided for them. *When you have eaten your fill and have built fine houses and live in them, and when your herds and flocks have multiplied, and your silver and gold is multiplied, and all that you have is multiplied, then do not exalt yourself, forgetting the Lord your God, who brought you out of the land of Egypt, out of the house of slavery, who led you through the great and terrible wilderness. . . . He made water flow . . . and fed you* (8:12-16).

Prosperity could also breed self-confidence and arrogance. Moses feared the people would see themselves as masters of their own lives instead of God's treasured possession. They would take credit for their good fortune rather than giving God His due praise. Moses solemnly declared, *Do not say to yourself, "My power and the might of my own hand have gotten me this wealth"* (8:17).

Moses reminded the new generation of Israelites that God provided the power to accumulate wealth. *But remember the Lord your God, for it is he who gives you power to get wealth, so that he may confirm his covenant that he swore to your ancestors, as he is doing today* (8:18).

Moses said that forgetting God and following pagan deities was the way of destruction. Ignoring God and disobeying Him would bring calamity, like that experienced by Israel's enemies. *If you do forget the Lord your God and follow other gods to serve and worship them, I solemnly warn you today that you shall surely perish. Like the nations that the Lord is destroying before you, so shall you perish, because you would not obey the voice of the Lord your God* (8:19-20).

## SUGGESTIONS TO TEACHERS

Tonight, Halloween Night, was originally celebrated as All Hallows Eve, the evening before All Saints Day. All Saints Day, November 1st, is still observed on the liturgical calendar in many faith traditions. In some Protestant churches, October 31st has also traditionally been known as

Reformation Sunday, remembering the date when Martin Luther nailed the 95 theses on the door of the Wittenberg Chapel, thereby igniting the movement known as the Protestant Reformation.

However you and your congregation might celebrate this Sunday, you should emphasize remembering important persons and events in your church's history. And you should remind yourselves of the dangers of forgetting or growing careless in recalling God. This week's lesson is a solemn warning to remember!

**1. DANGERS OF FORGETTING GOD.** The faith community that neglects remembering its past is a prime candidate for extinction. Remembering establishes identity and brings hope for the future. During this teaching session, encourage your students to recall persons who have nurtured them in their walk with Christ. Ask them to share stories from their own lives about faith-molding experiences.

**2. DISCIPLINE OF BEING GOD'S OWN.** Deuteronomy 8:5-10 compares God's disciplining guidance to the way a caring parent works with a child. Remind the class that the intent of God's discipline is to teach, not simply to punish. The Lord's ways in our past are intended to help us as His spiritual children to learn and grow in the faith.

**3. DIRECTION FOR REMEMBERING.** God warns us that prosperity can easily lead us to say to ourselves, *"My power and the might of my own hand have gotten me this wealth"* (8:17). But there is no such thing as a "self-made person." With our comfortable lives, we are prone to assume that we are to be congratulated, and that we deserve our exceedingly luxurious existence.

**4. DETERRENT TO PERISHING.** This week's lesson holds up the example of history, where rich and powerful societies before us have become vain and disobedient. God remains in control of human affairs. Countries and cultures that put themselves at the center (instead of the Lord) bring about their own destruction. In our own century, Nazi Germany and the Soviet Union are obvious examples. But what about the evidences of willful disobedience in our nation?

---

| | |
|---|---|
| **FOR ADULTS** | ■ TOPIC: Don't Lose Perspective<br>■ QUESTIONS: 1. How was Israel to walk in God's ways? 2. How could Israel ensure that God was not forgotten? 3. What things can |

you do to revere God? 4. How has God helped you to achieve some of your dreams? 5. What can you do to remember the many good things the Lord has done for you?

■ **ILLUSTRATIONS:**

**America's Latest Fad: Modesty It's Not.** The current decade is getting on in years, but it still has no satisfying label, like the narcissistic Me Decade of the 1970s, or the acquisitive Gimme Decade of the 1980s. Here's a suggestion for the 1990s: the Look-at-Me Decade. After all, there is enough braggadocio going around to erase modesty from the roll call of virtues. Ask not what you can do for your country or what your country can do for you, but whether the country has noticed your efforts lately.

In his new book entitled *Behind the Oval Office* (published by Random House), Dick Morris, the political tactician, claims that his wisdom got President Clinton re-elected. And after the Super Bowl of 1997, Desmond Howard, who ran back a 99-yard kickoff return for a Packers' touchdown, implied by his gestures and words that he had single-handedly defeated the Patriots: He declared, "They had just scored. They had the momentum. Then we have my return, and that was basically the game." (Later in the week, he got around to thanking his teammates for clearing the path.)

Corporate America, which has spawned many a braggart in the Donald Trump mold, has recently given us Albert J. Dunlap, whose track record of laying off thousands of workers at companies like Sunbeam and Scott Paper has earned him the nickname "Chain Saw." He says that he is in the same league as Michael Jordan and Bruce Springsteen. "I'm a superstar in my field," Dunlap writes in his book entitled *Mean Business* (published by Times Business/Random House).

This chorus of boasting might just be a coincidence of recent efforts to win raises or bolster book sales. But many sociologists see a trend, though they do not agree on what seems to be creating a nation of attention-seekers (Adam Bryant, *The New York Times,* Sunday, February 9, 1997).

**Monastic Method of Being Mindful.** In the old European monasteries, one member was assigned to move throughout the abbey each day to the kitchens, the stables, the fields, the scriptorium, and every other place where members of the faith community were at work. This person was to tap each monk on the shoulder and ask, "Are you remembering God?"

Daily devotions and weekly worship are meant to do the same for us. What are you consciously doing each day to remind yourself of God in your life?

**Conspicuous Consumption.** The brash new billionaires on the West Coast are building huge, ostentatious palaces in styles variously dubbed Techno-Baronial or Cyber-Nouveau. For example, in Washington State, Charles Simonyi, the chief programmer at Microsoft, has built a bachelor's nest as big as a train terminal, with stainless-steel trusses and a bed that rotates to capture his lakeside view.

Nearby is the 45,000-square-foot home of Bill Gates, founder of Microsoft. His guests are given an electronic badge to provide a moving halo of light and customized chants as they proceed down a reception hall with 24 winking video monitors, stacked four high and six across. According to Gates, by using hand-held remotes, "you'll be able to choose from among thousands of pictures, recordings, movies, and television programs. . . . If you regularly ask for light to be unusually bright or dim, the house will assume that's how you want it. . . . If you listened to Mozart horn concertos the last time you visited, you might find them on again when you come back."

In Washington, the houses think. In Los Angeles, they overwhelm. What is said to be the biggest single-family home in California was built by Aaron Spelling, producer of "Beverly Hills 90210" and "Charlie's Angels." The Manor occupies 65,000 square feet with 130 rooms, 12 fountains, and 6 formal gardens. Another TV mogul, Merv Griffin, has acquired an entire mountaintop for his dream house, which includes a heliport, a 360-degree living room, and 40,000 square feet of marble.

Why would anybody want so much turf? An obvious motive for these mega-manses is to provoke just such questions. They are examples of what Thorstein Veblen long ago called conspicuous consumption. But history suggests that they owe at least as much to windfall wealth resulting from tax laws and monopolies.

These vast and charmless techno-villas are more likely to be seen as landmarks of bygone-era tax cuts, which lowered top brackets from 70 percent to 28 percent in seven years. "As Federal taxation eased, especially on the top brackets," writes Kevin Phillips, "disposable income soared for the rich—and with it conspicuous consumption."

---

**FOR YOUTH**

■ **TOPIC:** Don't Forget

■ **QUESTIONS:** 1. Why did Moses want the new generation of Israelites to remember God? 2. In what ways did the Lord promise to bless His people? 3. In what ways has God shown His goodness to you in the past month? 4. How has God blessed you in the past year? 5. How is your spiritual life enhanced by remembering all that the Lord has done for you?

■ **ILLUSTRATIONS:**

**Fickled Fans.** Woody Hayes, coaching great of Ohio State University, philosophized one day on the fickleness of football fans and their short memories. He said that he could come out of Buckeye Stadium an hour and a half after the game and no one would remember what happened or would even say, "Good game, Coach!"

Moses understood the fickleness of God's people. They needed a reminder of all the good things that God had done for them. Moses thus gave the Israelites a warning and an exhortation to give God His due credit.

**Attitude of Gratitude.** Maya Angelou, America's Poet Laureate, and author of such books as *I Know Why the Caged Bird Sings* and *I'm Still Flying,* spoke about a conversation that she had in her younger days with her grandmother. It describes the attitude of gratitude we should have toward God.

Many of the old woman's friends complained about bills, disappointments, frustrations, problems, crises, and failures. They constantly grumbled and fussed. Life seemed to have no joys. Noting their ungrateful hearts to her young grand-daughter, the old woman asked, "How many people went to bed and their beds became a funeral bier? How many of the bed sheets became a burial shroud? Many of those people would have given anything to have five more minutes of life about which they complained so bitterly. Life should be an occasion to offer gratitude to God."

This is the attitude that Moses was urging the Israelites to maintain. It reflects an appreciation for everything that the believer receives from God. Give thanks to the Lord for all that you enjoy from His bountiful hand.

**Thanksgiving.** The U.S. House of Representatives paused amidst their meeting in late September, 1789. Having passed a new Bill of Rights and established a Supreme Court, they now considered a motion by New Jersey Congressman, Elias Boudinot. He had introduced a resolution asking President Washington to proclaim a day in which the people would acknowledge with their grateful hearts the many blessings of almighty God. Congressman Thomas Tucker, worrying about the threat of big government, declared that no one should legislate about matters that did not concern them or about what an individual did not care to do.

Citing traditions that went back to the Berkeley Settlement near Jamestown, Virginia, in 1619, and those of the Pilgrims at Plymouth, Massachusetts, in 1621, the House acted. Boudinot's view prevailed, and the last Thursday in November was set aside as a day of giving thanks to God for tranquillity, union, and plenty.

Boudinot, a latter-day Moses of sorts, called his people to remember God and give Him thanks. Can we who are the people of God today do less?

# JOSHUA SUCCEEDS MOSES

**BACKGROUND SCRIPTURE:** Deuteronomy 31:1-8; 34
**DEVOTIONAL READING:** Numbers 27:12-23

**KEY VERSE:** It is the LORD who goes before you. He will be with you; he will not fail you or forsake you. Do not fear or be dismayed. Deuteronomy 31:8.

*KING JAMES VERSION*

DEUTERONOMY 31:1 And Moses went and spake these words unto all Israel.

2 And he said unto them, I am an hundred and twenty years old this day; I can no more go out and come in: also the LORD hath said unto me, Thou shalt not go over this Jordan.

3 The LORD thy God, he will go over before thee, and he will destroy these nations from before thee, and thou shalt possess them: and Joshua, he shall go over before thee, as the LORD hath said.

4 And the LORD shall do unto them as he did to Sihon and to Og, kings of the Amorites, and unto the land of them, whom he destroyed.

5 And the LORD shall give them up before your face, that ye may do unto them according unto all the commandments which I have commanded you.

6 Be strong and of a good courage, fear not, nor be afraid of them: for the LORD thy God, he it is that doth go with thee; he will not fail thee, nor forsake thee.

7 And Moses called unto Joshua, and said unto him in the sight of all Israel, Be strong and of a good courage: for thou must go with this people unto the land which the LORD hath sworn unto their fathers to give them; and thou shalt cause them to inherit it.

8 And the LORD, he it is that doth go before thee; he will be with thee, he will not fail thee, neither forsake thee: fear not, neither be dismayed. . . .

34:5 So Moses the servant of the LORD died there in the land of Moab, according to the word of the LORD.

6 And he buried him in a valley in the land of Moab, over against Beth-peor: but no man knoweth of his sepulchre unto this day.

7 And Moses was an hundred and twenty years old when he died: his eye was not dim, nor his natural force abated.

8 And the children of Israel wept for Moses in the plains of Moab thirty days: . . .

9 And Joshua the son of Nun was full of the spirit of wisdom; for Moses had laid his hands upon him: and the children of Israel hearkened unto him, and did as the LORD commanded Moses.

*NEW REVISED STANDARD VERSION*

DEUTERONOMY 31:1 When Moses had finished speaking all these words to all Israel, 2 he said to them: "I am now one hundred twenty years old. I am no longer able to get about, and the LORD has told me, 'You shall not cross over this Jordan.' 3 The LORD your God himself will cross over before you. He will destroy these nations before you, and you shall dispossess them. Joshua also will cross over before you, as the LORD has promised. 4 The LORD will do to them as he did to Sihon and Og, the kings of the Amorites, and to their land, when he destroyed them. 5 The LORD will give them over to you and you shall deal with them in full accord with the command that I have given to you. 6 Be strong and bold; have no fear or dread of them, because it is the LORD your God who goes with you; he will not fail you or forsake you."

7 Then Moses summoned Joshua and said to him in the sight of all Israel: "Be strong and bold, for you are the one who will go with this people into the land that the LORD has sworn to their ancestors to give them; and you will put them in possession of it. 8 It is the LORD who goes before you. He will be with you; he will not fail you or forsake you. Do not fear or be dismayed." . . .

34:5 Then Moses, the servant of the LORD, died there in the land of Moab, at the LORD's command. 6 He was buried in a valley in the land of Moab, opposite Beth-peor, but no one knows his burial place to this day. 7 Moses was one hundred twenty years old when he died; his sight was unimpaired and his vigor had not abated. 8 The Israelites wept for Moses in the plains of Moab thirty days; . . . 9 Joshua son of Nun was full of the spirit of wisdom, because Moses had laid his hands on him; and the Israelites obeyed him, doing as the LORD had commanded Moses.

## BACKGROUND

Moses had rallied the Israelite slaves in Egypt to leave. He had stood up to the haughty Pharaoh. Moses faithfully brought God's instructions to the people. The great leader served as God's agent to institute the sacred covenant, or treaty, between the Lord and the Israelites. This, in turn, became the basis for the relationship between God and His people.

Through 40 years of desert living, Moses patiently served the Lord as the leader of that community. He endured criticism and faced rebellions. He interceded on behalf of God's people. Throughout those years, he knew that God was forging the Israelites from being a rabble into a nation. Moses looked forward to God fulfilling His promise to lead that nation-to-be into the promised land.

Moses had grown to be 120 years old. With other milestones having been reached, his one final desire was to enter the promised land. When Moses realized that God would not grant him his request, the venerable leader pleaded with the Lord to be permitted to cross over the Jordan with the Israelites (see Deut. 3:23-27). But God had made it clear that he would not enter Canaan. Thus, this most cherished dream of Moses went unfulfilled.

Moses learned that God's work goes on even after we humans pass on. Moses also discovered that the leadership needs of God's people were vital to meet. Human leaders take their places and serve, and then must prepare others to take over the job of shepherding God's community. Moses was wise to groom Joshua as his replacement and thus maintain continuity and consistency in the guidance of the people.

## NOTES ON THE PRINTED TEXT

When Moses had finished speaking all these words to all Israel, he said to them: "I am now one hundred twenty years old. I am no longer able to get about, and the LORD has told me 'You shall not cross over this Jordan' " (31:1-2). Deuteronomy is Moses' farewell speech to a new generation of Israelites who were about to enter Canaan. God had already told Moses that he would not cross over the Jordan. Nevertheless, Moses told the listeners that God would go before them and ensure their success. *"The LORD your God himself will cross over before you. He will destroy these nations before you, and you shall dispossess them. Joshua also will cross over before you, as the LORD promised"* (31:3). Knowing his age and the need for a new leader, Moses appointed Joshua as his replacement. God would use Joshua to lead Israel into the promised land.

Moses reassured the people that God would give them the victory over their enemies (31:4-5). Moses offered examples of what would happen to the opposition. Sihon was an Amorite king who had refused Israel permission to pass through his territory and attacked the nation at Jahaz. The Israelites defeated him. Og was the powerful king of Bashan and someone whom the Israelites also defeated due to God's intervention (see 2:26—3:11).

Moses urged the Israelites to be courageous. He reminded them that God would not fail them. *"Be strong and bold; have no fear or dread of them, because it is the LORD your God who goes with you; he will not fail you or forsake you"* (31:6).

Then Moses charged Joshua not to fail either God or Israel. As the new leader of the nation, he was to have courage and a deep trust in God. Joshua would be the Lord's agent to enable the Israelites to take possession of Canaan. *"Be strong and bold, for you are the one who will go with this people into the land that the LORD has sworn to their ancestors to give them; and you will put them in possession of it. It is the LORD who goes before you. He will be with you; he will not fail you or forsake you. Do not fear or be dismayed"* (31:7-8).

At some point the Lord had Moses go up from the plains of Moab to Mount Nebo. He climbed to the top of Pisgah, which is across from Jericho. From there the Lord showed the aged leader the entire land of Canaan, from the south to the north, and from the east to the west (34:1-4).

After God had graciously shown Moses the promised land, the servant of the Lord died and was buried in a valley near Beth-peor in Moab; yet no one (except God) knew the exact place of Moses' burial (34:5-6). Despite his age, his eyesight was clear and he had remained relatively strong (34:7).

There, in the plains of Moab, the Israelites mourned 30 days for Moses (34:8). Thankfully, they had a new leader whom they could follow and obey. *Joshua son of Nun was full of the spirit of wisdom, because Moses had laid his hands on him; and the Israelites obeyed him, doing as the LORD had commanded Moses* (34:9).

## SUGGESTIONS TO TEACHERS

The death of a long-time or popular leader is always upsetting to those he or she has been serving. If you can remember President John F. Kennedy's assassination, you will recall the grief that the American people felt and the anxiety many in the world experienced over his end. Moses' death probably produced reactions much like those of the citizens of the United States in November of 1963. However, in the providence of God, a strong and capable leader named Joshua had already been chosen and groomed for the heavy task of leading God's people into the promised land. Continuity was maintained despite troublesome times.

**1. THE LORD ANSWERED MOSES.** Moses had led the Israelites for 40 long years, and he had dreamed of taking them across the Jordan into Canaan. But God told him that he would not do so. Though Moses pleaded with God about the matter, the Lord refused to grant his request. He had to accept this God-ordained limitation. Moses died with some personal dreams unfulfilled and some plans uncompleted. Encourage the members of your class to think about some of their personal dreams that show no possibility of being fulfilled. How should Christians respond when God seems to say *no* to their desire to do something?

**2. MOSES APPOINTED A SUCCESSOR.** Moses accepted God's order to step aside. Because he was confident of God's wise provision for the Israelites, Moses appointed Joshua. Moses was able to leave the leadership of Israel in the hands of a younger generation. How is your congregation preparing to pass on the leadership to the next generation? What specific things can you do to maintain the continuity of the faith?

**3. MOSES ASSURED THE PEOPLE.** Moses told the Israelites that God's work would not end just because there would be a change in leadership. He assured them that Joshua would continue what God had called His people to do. In the face of unsettling conditions, Moses brought hope and confidence.

**4. MOSES ACCEPTED DISAPPOINTMENT.** Moses was forced to acknowledge that God would not allow him to enter the promised land. This must have disappointed Moses. Nevertheless, God granted him a glimpse of the area beyond the Jordan where the Israelites would settle. Though we may die without realizing all we wanted to accomplish and without seeing God's kingdom fully established, the Lord graciously gives us hope for the future! We know that God through Christ will fulfill His redemptive plans.

**5. JOSHUA ASSUMED LEADERSHIP.** Joshua was a trustworthy person. He stepped into the role of leader and moved the people forward.

---

**FOR ADULTS**

■ TOPIC: Maintaining Community

■ QUESTIONS: 1. How do you think Moses got over the disappointment of not being allowed to enter Canaan? 2. In what ways did Moses encourage the Israelites to be courageous? 3. Why are some believers wary about venturing into the unknown? 4. What risks do you find in life because of your Christian faith? 5. What indications of God's presence do you find most comforting?

■ ILLUSTRATIONS:

**Death of a Community.** An important link with the past died when the last person to speak the ancient language of the Catawba Native Americans passed away in 1996. Red Thunder Cloud, who was a member of the Catawba nation, was a singer, dancer, and storyteller and the only surviving member of the tribe to know the Catawba language. He died in Worcester, Massachusetts, at the age of 76.

Red Thunder Cloud had learned Catawba as a boy from his grandfather and tribal elders, but eventually there were only two Catawba speakers left—he and a woman who had died 40 years earlier. A friend, Foxx Ayers of Columbia, South Carolina, is a Catawba, but he resisted his parents' and grandparents' efforts to teach him the language. He now wishes that he had learned to speak it. Anthropologists and language experts predict the Catawba culture and community will soon wither with the loss of the language. Foxx Ayers and other Catawbas realize that they failed to maintain their community and pass on the language and traditions others had given them.

Moses wisely maintained the community of the Israelites by training Joshua to assume the reins of leadership. We today in the community of faith have a sacred responsibility to maintain continuity by ensuring that the next generation is instructed and new leadership is prepared to take our place.

**Run Your Lap in Life's Relay Race!** Only one person has ever lived who could conclude His life by knowing that all His God-given plans were fulfilled. That person is Jesus Christ. Only He was able to say before dying, *"It is finished"* (John 19:30), which means that He had accomplished His redemptive work.

Moses learned that the tireless and immortal God remains in charge. Though Moses would soon pass off the scene of history, his successor—Joshua—would stay behind to carry on the work of the Lord.

We are members of God's covenant community through faith in Christ. It's a bit like being a member of a great relay team. One believer runs a lap and then passes on the baton to another. The runner receiving the baton is called upon to exert every effort to carry it forward for the sake of the team, and then relinquish it to another teammate. Each believer knows that it is the victory of the team that is paramount, not one's own personal glory. In God's work, each of us is responsible for our lap in God's race.

God's Word reminds us that the Lord's redemptive plans will be accomplished. Moses was granted a look at the promised land from the top of Mount Nebo and assured that the Israelites would be settled there under Joshua. The new leader would guide the people and urge them to remain faithful to the decrees of the Mosaic covenant.

Scripture reassures us that God's plan of redemption will be fulfilled. We may not live to see all the Lord's plans carried out, just as we will not live to see all our own hopes and dreams fulfilled. The most important matter is that our desires coincide with God's will for us. Our foremost goal should be to glorify the Lord through our thoughts, words, and actions. If we can say that we did this in life, then we know that we have done things of eternal significance.

**Proud Tradition to Maintain.** A British friend of mine who served in the famous regiment, The King's Own Scottish Borderers, often pointed out the sense of continuity he and others felt through enlistment in this renowned military outfit. He proudly recounted that since 1689, this regiment has existed and won countless honors, including coveted permission to parade through Edinburgh with fixed bayonets. He told about the bond he has with members who passed away generations before, and the deep sense of obligation to pass on the heritage to future Scots. One day, after a worship service, he solemnly commented that this is the way Christians should feel about maintaining community in the church.

---

| **FOR YOUTH** | ■ TOPIC: Receiving the Torch |
|---|---|

■ QUESTIONS: 1. How did Moses handle the news that he wouldn't be entering Canaan? 2. What reassurance did Moses have that God's people under Joshua's leadership would do fine? 3. What are some dreams that you might have, and how do they coincide with God's will for your life? 4. How do you think the Lord might help you fulfill your dreams? 5. What are some disappointments that you can give to the Lord in prayer?

■ **ILLUSTRATIONS:**

**Mozart's Mentor.** Like many young people, 15-year-old Joe Melichor from New Castle, Pennsylvania, takes piano lessons. The Mohawk High School sophomore, though, has been dubbed the Mozart of Mahoning Township. He started playing and writing music as a six-year-old for his teacher, Judy Bruce, even before he could read. She urged him to write down the music that he heard in his head as he slept. One of those pieces, *Wanderlust,* won him fourth place in a national contest. He has since won first and fourth places in the National Junior Composers Contest sponsored by the National Federation of Music Clubs, second place in the national Lynn Freeman Olson Composition Competition, and second place in the Pennsylvania Music Teachers Association Competition. Only those students in the private Curtis School of Music and the Peabody in Philadelphia have beaten him. Melichor, in addition to Bruce, now works with other musicians who help him hone his musical abilities and orchestral composition.

Just as Bruce has mentored Melichor, so too Moses mentored Joshua so that he could successfully assume the leadership of Israel. And just as Bruce has challenged Melichor, calling on him to use his musical talents and abilities, so too Moses challenged Joshua to use and develop his leadership abilities.

**More Mentoring.** Pittsburgh Steelers' Coach Bill Cowher has been the head athletic director for several years. He has guided the team to one Super Bowl appearance and five AFC Championship game appearances. Bill, though, did not start out immediately as a head coach.

Cowher spent several years with Marty Schottenheimer, the head coach of the Kansas City Chiefs. Bill considers Marty his close friend and especially his mentor. Marty taught him and allowed him to mature to the point where he could assume the role of a head coach himself.

In a similar manner, Moses mentored Joshua, allowing him to mature in order to assume the leadership of Israel. To whom do you look as a mentor?

**Called to Lead.** Brandon Williams, the running back for Valley High School, stood in the Bible Way Christian Fellowship Church in New Kensington, Pennsylvania, and announced that he would attend the University of Pittsburgh. The January 23, 1997, news conference ended months of recruiting for one of the nation's top 20 running backs. The college won over such finalists as Notre Dame, UCLA, Ohio State, and Syracuse.

Landing Williams was a huge victory for the University of Pittsburgh. The struggling football program had hired new coach Walt Harris in 1997. He guided the team to its first winning season and a Liberty Bowl appearance. However, the team was largely seniors. The program needed new and younger players to replace many of the departing players. Brandon wanted to be part of that new team and its leadership. That was part of the promise he received from former University of Pittsburgh great and NFL leader, Tony Dorsett, who reminded Brandon that he had been part of the rebuilding of a program years earlier.

Brandon is an example of a youth who has been called to lead a new project. Joshua was a similar example. After being chosen by God, he accepted the opportunity to lead the Israelites across the Jordan River and into the promised land.

# ISRAEL CROSSES THE JORDAN RIVER

**BACKGROUND SCRIPTURE:** Joshua 3
**DEVOTIONAL READING:** Joshua 4:15-24

**KEY VERSE:** Be strong and courageous; do not be frightened or dismayed, for the LORD your God is with you wherever you go. Joshua 1:9.

*KING JAMES VERSION*

JOSHUA 3:7 And the LORD said unto Joshua, This day will I begin to magnify thee in the sight of all Israel, that they may know that, as I was with Moses, so I will be with thee.

8 And thou shalt command the priests that bear the ark of the covenant, saying, When ye are come to the brink of the water of Jordan, ye shall stand still in Jordan.

9 And Joshua said unto the children of Israel, Come hither, and hear the words of the LORD your God.

10 And Joshua said, Hereby ye shall know that the living God is among you, and that he will without fail drive out from before you the Canaanites, and the Hittites, and the Hivites, and the Perizzites, and the Girgashites, and the Amorites, and the Jebusites.

11 Behold, the ark of the covenant of the Lord of all the earth passeth over before you into Jordan.

12 Now therefore take you twelve men out of the tribes of Israel, out of every tribe a man.

13 And it shall come to pass, as soon as the soles of the feet of the priests that bear the ark of the LORD, the Lord of all the earth, shall rest in the waters of Jordan, that the waters of Jordan shall be cut off from the waters that come down from above; and they shall stand upon an heap.

14 And it came to pass, when the people removed from their tents, to pass over Jordan, and the priests bearing the ark of the covenant before the people;

15 And as they that bare the ark were come unto Jordan, and the feet of the priests that bare the ark were dipped in the brim of the water, (for Jordan overfloweth all his banks all the time of harvest,)

16 That the waters which came down from above stood and rose up upon an heap very far from the city Adam, that is beside Zaretan: and those that came down toward the sea of the plain, even the salt sea, failed, and were cut off: and the people passed over right against Jericho.

17 And the priests that bare the ark of the covenant of the LORD stood firm on dry ground in the midst of Jordan, and all the Israelites passed over on dry ground, until all the people were passed clean over Jordan.

*NEW REVISED STANDARD VERSION*

JOSHUA 3:7 The LORD said to Joshua, "This day I will begin to exalt you in the sight of all Israel, so that they may know that I will be with you as I was with Moses. 8 You are the one who shall command the priests who bear the ark of the covenant, 'When you come to the edge of the waters of the Jordan, you shall stand still in the Jordan.' " 9 Joshua then said to the Israelites, "Draw near and hear the words of the LORD your God." 10 Joshua said, "By this you shall know that among you is the living God who without fail will drive out from before you the Canaanites, Hittites, Hivites, Perizzites, Girgashites, Amorites, and Jebusites: 11 the ark of the covenant of the Lord of all the earth is going to pass before you into the Jordan. 12 So now select twelve men from the tribes of Israel, one from each tribe. 13 When the soles of the feet of the priests who bear the ark of the LORD, the Lord of all the earth, rest in the waters of the Jordan, the waters of the Jordan flowing from above shall be cut off; they shall stand in a single heap."

14 When the people set out from their tents to cross over the Jordan, the priests bearing the ark of the covenant were in front of the people. 15 Now the Jordan overflows all its banks throughout the time of harvest. So when those who bore the ark had come to the Jordan, and the feet of the priests bearing the ark were dipped in the edge of the water, 16 the waters flowing from above stood still, rising up in a single heap far off at Adam, the city that is beside Zarethan, while those flowing toward the sea of the Arabah, the Dead Sea, were wholly cut off. Then the people crossed over opposite Jericho. 17 While all Israel were crossing over on dry ground, the priests who bore the ark of the covenant of the LORD stood on dry ground in the middle of the Jordan, until the entire nation finished crossing over the Jordan.

| | | |
|---|---|---|
| *Monday, Nov. 8* | Joshua 2:1-7 | *Spies Are Sent to Jericho* |
| *Tuesday, Nov. 9* | Joshua 2:8-14 | *Rahab Seeks Assurance of God's Protection* |
| *Wednesday, Nov. 10* | Joshua 2:15-24 | *Rahab Helps the Spies Escape* |
| *Thursday, Nov. 11* | Joshua 3:1-6 | *Israel Follows the Ark of the Covenant* |
| *Friday, Nov. 12* | Joshua 3:7-13 | *Israel at Jordan's Banks* |
| *Saturday, Nov. 13* | Joshua 3:14—4:3 | *Israel Crosses the Jordan* |
| *Sunday, Nov. 14* | Joshua 4:4-14 | *Twelve Memorial Stones Placed in Jordan* |

## BACKGROUND

Joshua the son of Nun is the person who served as Moses' aide during the 40 years of Israel's wandering in the wilderness (Exod. 24:13; Josh. 1:1). His original name was Hoshea, which may mean "salvation." But Moses later changed the name to Joshua, which means "the Lord saves." The location of Joshua's territorial inheritance, the site of his burial, and his genealogical records indicate that he was from the tribe of Ephraim (Josh. 19:49-50; 24:30; 1 Chron. 7:20, 27).

Joshua is first mentioned in Exodus 17:9-13. The passage depicts him as a mighty Israelite warrior who, under Moses' command, fought against and defeated the Amalekites. He later went with Moses onto Mount Sinai (Exod. 24:13; 32:15-18). Joshua also guarded the tent of meeting against those who might have tried to trespass this sacred location (33:11). He was one of the 12 spies who surveyed Canaan, in which only he and Caleb declared their confidence that the Lord would enable His people to succeed in conquering the promised land (Num. 13—14).

In accordance with God's instructions, Moses commissioned Joshua to be his successor (Num. 27:12-23; Deut. 3:23-28). The Book of Joshua reports how the Lord used him to faithfully carry out all that Moses had commanded. God enabled Joshua not only to lead the Israelites into Canaan but also to begin the difficult process of taking full possession of it (Josh. 21:43-45). The Lord also used Joshua to guide His people in renewing their commitment to the Mosaic covenant (24:24-27). Joshua died at the age of 110, having served the Lord, Moses, and the Israelites courageously throughout his long life (vs. 29).

This week's lesson concerns the crossing of the Jordan, which occurred when the river was at flood level. The heavy rains and the steep descent of the Jordan from the Sea of Galilee to the Dead Sea meant that the surging waters overflowed the river's banks and made a normal crossing impossible.

The local residents believed that Baal, the Canaanite fertility-god, controlled the rain, snow, hail, and floods throughout Palestine. But when the Jordan's waters were suddenly choked off, Joshua and the Israelites knew that Yahweh, not

Baal, had made this happen. They learned that God was more powerful than any local Canaanite deity. The people were convinced that the Lord had again intervened on their behalf, just as He had done when they crossed the Red Sea 40 years earlier. The Israelites knew that Baal was helpless before the holy God, just as the Egyptian deities had been powerless a generation before!

## NOTES ON THE PRINTED TEXT

The Israelites were camped on the plains of Moab, near the major ford of the Jordan River a few miles north of the Dead Sea. At this time, they were preparing to cross the river. Joshua, the nation's new leader, knew that God would establish his authority over the people. The Lord would do this by acting through Joshua just as He had done through Moses. *The LORD said to Joshua, "This day I will begin to exalt you in the sight of all Israel, so that they may know that I will be with you as I was with Moses"* (3:7).

The Lord directed Joshua to order the priests to carry the ark of the covenant into the middle of the river and stand still. (At flood stage, the river was extremely wide, deep, and treacherous.) *"You are the one who shall command the priests who bear the ark of the covenant, 'When you come to the edge of the waters of the Jordan, you shall stand still in the Jordan' "* (3:8).

Just before the river crossing, Joshua assembled the Israelites to hear the words of the Lord (3:9). The people's fording of the Jordan would be a lesson to them that the living God was among them. They would know that the all-powerful Lord would drive out the pagan peoples of the land (3:10). As the Israelites made the river crossing, the ark of the covenant, which belonged to the Lord of all the earth, would lead them to the other side (3:11).

Joshua told the Israelites to choose 12 men (one from each tribe) who would later pick up 12 stones from the riverbed to be used to make a memorial to God's faithfulness (3:12). The new leader then announced that the Jordan's waters would be divided and the river would back up. *When the soles of the feet of the priests who bear the ark of the LORD, the Lord of all the earth, rest in the waters of the Jordan, the waters of the Jordan flowing from above shall be cut off; they shall stand in a single heap"* (3:13).

The Israelites assembled at the edge of the camp and formed a long procession behind the ark of the covenant, which the priests carried ahead of them. *When the people set out from their tents to cross over the Jordan, the priests bearing the ark of the covenant were in front of the people* (3:14).

On most occasions the Jordan was not difficult to ford. However, during the harvest season, the river overflowed its banks. This was due to the spring rains and the melting snows from Mount Hermon. As soon as the feet of the priests who were carrying the ark touched the water at the river's edge, a miracle happened. The water began piling up at a town called Adam, which was upstream and near Zarethan (3:15-16). (Adam was about 18 miles north of Jericho.)

The water below that point flowed into the Dead Sea until the riverbed was dry. Then all the Israelites safely crossed over near Jericho. Meanwhile, the priests who were carrying the ark stood on dry ground in the middle of the riverbed as the people passed by them. The priests patiently waited there until everyone had crossed over to the other side (3:17). Once the miracle was completed, God permitted the waters of the Jordan to flow again (4:18).

## SUGGESTIONS TO TEACHERS

When the Tennessee Valley Authority forced a small village to relocate to a non-flooded area, the residents felt sorry for themselves and renamed their community, "Pity Me." Not surprisingly, the resettled town never flourished. Gradually the inhabitants moved away and the newly-built houses eventually fell into such disrepair that the town finally died. As this week's lesson teaches, the people of God must go forward in faith!

**1. JOSHUA INSTRUCTED THE PEOPLE.** Consider the way Joshua acted as the leader of the Israelites at a crucial juncture. In light of his example, what traits do you think should be evident in a spiritual leader?

**2. PRIESTS IMPLEMENTED JOSHUA'S ORDERS.** To cross the flooded Jordan, the people knew that they had to rely on the Lord. That's why the priests were obedient to Joshua's instructions, which he had received from God. As Christians, we must also obey the Lord. Ask the class members what the most daunting challenge is that their congregation faces at this time and how they, as a committed group of believers, can meet that challenge in God's strength.

**3. GOD INTERVENED AT THE JORDAN.** The Lord did the impossible for the Israelites by enabling them to cross the Jordan at flood stage. Have the students discuss how God has intervened in the life of their church in the past when the future looked bleak. If time permits, ask someone in the class to interview a few of the oldest members of the church to get their inspiring testimony.

**4. GOD'S PEOPLE INVADED THE PROMISED LAND.** The Israelites under Joshua's leadership went forward in faith. Likewise, remind the students that they can and should look to the future with hope because of Christ!

| FOR ADULTS | ■ TOPIC: Going Forward in Faith <br> ■ QUESTIONS: 1. How did the crossing of the Jordan River make Joshua great in the eyes of all the Israelites? 2. How did the mirac- |

ulous event signal to the chosen people that the living God was among them? 3. What are some seemingly insurmountable odds or obstacles that you are facing right now? 4. How can the Lord enable you to overcome your problems? 5. What are some amazing things that God has done recently in your life that other believers would be encouraged to know?

**Overcoming the Obstacles.** In 1903, Branch Rickey was a baseball coach at Ohio Wesleyan University. When the team traveled on a road trip to Indiana, a lone African American player was refused lodging in the hotel. Rickey finally prevailed on the clerk to allow the young player, Charles Thomas, to use a cot in Rickey's room. When coach Rickey arrived in the room, he found Thomas sitting on the cot, pulling at the skin on his hands as if he could rub away the color.

With tears coming down his face, Charles Thomas said, "Mr. Rickey, if I could just get this color off, I'd be as good as anybody else." This was a traumatic moment in Branch Rickey's life, and it led to his resolve to end segregation in big league baseball.

As general manager of the Brooklyn Dodgers in the 1940s, Rickey was aware that every other major league team would oppose him and that his reputation would be at stake concerning the issue of integration. In 1945, major league owners had voted 15 to 1 against the Dodgers on the issue. This vote also reflected the viewpoint of most current players, coaches, umpires, sportswriters, and fans.

Rickey knew that he had little support. But emboldened by his Christian convictions, he forged ahead that year and signed Jackie Robinson, a gifted African American baseball player. Together, these two great men destroyed the sport's color bar and ushered in a new era not only for the game but also for the entire nation.

**Heroic Figure.** Joshua was such a heroic figure in Israel's history that families for centuries proudly named their baby boys after him. In Hebrew, Joshua's name is *Yeshua*, while the Greek form of the name is *Iesous*. In English, the name is *Jesus*. In each case, it means "Yahweh saves." Incidentally, the name of our Savior reminds us of the truth that He is the Redeemer of the world.

Joshua emerged as a steadfast leader of the Israelites during the years of wandering in the desert. He won the respect of Moses by being confident in God's plans for the Israelites. Though Joshua was a member of the first generation of Israelites who left Egypt, he was not like so many of his peers who rebelled against the Lord and the leadership of Moses.

When Joshua was selected as one of the 12 spies to carry out a secret reconnaissance tour of the promised land, only he and Caleb returned with a favorable report. Some scholars think that Joshua might have had military experience in the Egyptian army, and had a professional soldier's viewpoint in investigating the possibility of invading Canaan. But more important than his military assessment was his trust in God's plans.

Joshua was thrust into the leadership of God's community at a crucial time. Moses, the trusted leader for 40 years, had died. The Israelites were grief stricken over the death of their long-time leader. Undoubtedly, many were fearful of the future without Moses, and perhaps some had misgivings about continuing without him to take them into the promised land. The invasion of Canaan would have seemed impossibly difficult to the fainthearted in the covenant community. Thankfully, Joshua displayed a spirit of wisdom, and the people followed him.

**Forward on Faith.** This Thanksgiving season, we will be mindful of the group of Pilgrims who landed in Plymouth on a wintry November in 1620. Earlier, members of this brave band of Christians stepped onto a barge at Leyden, Holland, and went downstream to what is now Rotterdam. They then traveled to Southampton, England, where they transferred to a leaky, old tub called the Mayflower. Only a handful—a little over a hundred of the group of Pilgrim refugees from Goole, England—persevered by traveling to the New World, determined to preserve their faith for themselves and others. What about the stay-at-homes in Leyden? Today, no one claims descent from the group of Separatist Englishmen who had taken up residence as refugees in Holland. Apparently the group failed to persevere and eventually were simply absorbed into the Dutch culture.

---

| **FOR YOUTH** | ■ **TOPIC:** Trusting Promises |
|---|---|

■ **QUESTIONS:** 1. Why was it important for the Israelites to know that God was with Joshua? 2. How did Joshua respond to the commands of God? 3. Have you ever questioned God's commands when they seem too hard to believe? 4. Why is it always best to do exactly what the Lord wants? 5. How has God preserved you during times of difficulty?

■ **ILLUSTRATIONS:**

**Believing the Promise.** Expeditions routinely now climb Mount Everest. Despite the risks, many people enjoy the challenge. Good health and climbing experience are required. Nevertheless, each individual attempting the trek arrives believing in the promise that this mountain can be conquered with enough effort.

Joshua promised the Israelites that the land of Canaan could be conquered. This was not an empty pledge but a sure hope. The people had to trust in God's presence, for it was only through His power, not their own strength, that they would succeed in occupying the land.

**Follow the Directions.** Eleven-year-old Brad joined a model building interest group at his school. The sixth grader had never before built a plastic model by himself. All previous efforts had involved his father. In addition, he had always constructed models in the two easiest skill areas.

One particular model airplane caught his attention. Though his father warned him that it was in the highest skill group, Brad insisted on buying it. He quickly discovered how difficult the kit was to finish. His father sat with him and explained how to follow the directions step by step. With encouragement, Brad completed his World War II bomber.

Anyone who has built a model, made a dress, or done some woodworking in shop class knows the value of directions. Joshua received detailed instructions from the Lord. Though the occupation of the promised land might have seemed impossible, God gave step-by-step directions so that the people would succeed.

**Loved by God.** The idea that God loves us can be hard to understand. On the one hand, we know from John 3:16 that this is true, and we are encouraged by the knowledge of it. On the other hand, we have a hard time grasping why the God of the universe, who is over all things and has so many important tasks to perform, would bother to love us.

How wonderful it is to know that the Lord took the first step. Jesus loved us so much that He died on the cross for our sins. He now invites us to accept His offer of salvation and to live with Him forever. If we say *yes* to eternal life, we will be able to bear spiritual fruit for God.

Are you ready to accept the Lord's offer of eternal life? And are you also willing to serve Him faithfully? By answering *yes* to both of these questions, you are on the road to an abundant spiritual life with God. Jesus will enable you to produce spiritual fruit that will last forever (John 15:16).

# THE DESTRUCTION OF JERICHO

**BACKGROUND SCRIPTURE:** Joshua 6
**DEVOTIONAL READING:** Psalm 47

---

**KEY VERSE:** At the seventh time, when the priests had blown the trumpets, Joshua said to the people, "Shout! For the LORD has given you the city." Joshua 6:16.

*KING JAMES VERSION*

JOSHUA 6:1 Now Jericho was straitly shut up because of the children of Israel: none went out, and none came in.

2 And the LORD said unto Joshua, See, I have given into thine hand Jericho, and the king thereof, and the mighty men of valour.

3 And ye shall compass the city, all ye men of war, and go round about the city once. Thus shalt thou do six days.

4 And seven priests shall bear before the ark seven trumpets of rams' horns: and the seventh day ye shall compass the city seven times, and the priests shall blow with the trumpets.

5 And it shall come to pass, that when they make a long blast with the ram's horn, and when ye hear the sound of the trumpet, all the people shall shout with a great shout; and the wall of the city shall fall down flat, and the people shall ascend up every man straight before him. . . .

15 And it came to pass on the seventh day, that they rose early about the dawning of the day, and compassed the city after the same manner seven times: only on that day they compassed the city seven times.

16 And it came to pass at the seventh time, when the priests blew with the trumpets, Joshua said unto the people, Shout; for the LORD hath given you the city.

17 And the city shall be accursed, even it, and all that are therein, to the LORD: only Rahab the harlot shall live, she and all that are with her in the house, because she hid the messengers that we sent.

18 And ye, in any wise keep yourselves from the accursed thing, lest ye make yourselves accursed, when ye take of the accursed thing, and make the camp of Israel a curse, and trouble it.

19 But all the silver, and gold, and vessels of brass and iron, are consecrated unto the LORD: they shall come into the treasury of the LORD.

20 So the people shouted when the priests blew with the trumpets: and it came to pass, when the people heard the sound of the trumpet, and the people shouted with a great shout, that the wall fell down flat, so that the people went up into the city, every man straight before him, and they took the city.

*NEW REVISED STANDARD VERSION*

JOSHUA 6:1 Now Jericho was shut up inside and out because of the Israelites; no one came out and no one went in. 2 The LORD said to Joshua, "See, I have handed Jericho over to you, along with its king and soldiers. 3 You shall march around the city, all the warriors circling the city once. Thus you shall do for six days, 4 with seven priests bearing seven trumpets of rams' horns before the ark. On the seventh day you shall march around the city seven times, the priests blowing the trumpets. 5 When they make a long blast with the ram's horn, as soon as you hear the sound of the trumpet, then all the people shall shout with a great shout; and the wall of the city will fall down flat, and all the people shall charge straight ahead." . . .

15 On the seventh day they rose early, at dawn, and marched around the city in the same manner seven times. It was only on that day that they marched around the city seven times. 16 And at the seventh time, when the priests had blown the trumpets, Joshua said to the people, "Shout! For the LORD has given you the city. 17 The city and all that is in it shall be devoted to the LORD for destruction. Only Rahab the prostitute and all who are with her in her house shall live because she hid the messengers we sent. 18 As for you, keep away from the things devoted to destruction, so as not to covet and take any of the devoted things and make the camp of Israel an object for destruction, bringing trouble upon it. 19 But all silver and gold, and vessels of bronze and iron, are sacred to the LORD; they shall go into the treasury of the LORD." 20 So the people shouted, and the trumpets were blown. As soon as the people heard the sound of the trumpets, they raised a great shout, and the wall fell down flat; so the people charged straight ahead into the city and captured it.

| | | |
|---|---|---|
| *Monday, Nov. 15* | Joshua 5:10-15 | *The Passover Celebrated at Gilgal* |
| *Tuesday, Nov. 16* | Joshua 6:1-7 | *Israel Begins Conquest of Jericho* |
| *Wednesday, Nov. 17* | Joshua 6:8-14 | *Six-Day March around Jericho's Walls* |
| *Thursday, Nov. 18* | Joshua 6:15-20 | *Destruction of Jericho by Israel* |
| *Friday, Nov. 19* | Joshua 6:22-25, 27 | *Rehab and Her Family Are Spared* |
| *Saturday, Nov. 20* | Joshua 8:30-35 | *Joshua Renews the Covenant* |
| *Sunday, Nov. 21* | Psalm 44:1-8 | *A Sacred Song of Remembrance* |

## BACKGROUND

Joshua had gained a lot of experience as Moses' aide during the 40 years of Israel's wandering in the wilderness. Undoubtedly, this experience enabled Joshua to devise a shrewd military strategy for conquering the promised land. In fact, his methods are still being studied in modern times. For example, British General Allenby in World War I used the book of Joshua as a key resource in his campaign against the Ottoman forces in Palestine, and the Israeli forces copied many of Joshua's battle plans in their 1947–48 campaign for independence.

Speed and surprise were the main parts of Joshua's military policy. Jericho smugly thought that it was safe from any siege by the desert forces under Joshua, which had just crossed the flood waters of the Jordan. The great trading center was first settled in 7,500 B.C., according to carbon 14 dating, making it the oldest remaining city in the world. Its massive mud-brick walls seemed to provide security from any attack. Undoubtedly, Joshua's army appearing in front of those walls after fording the Jordan was unexpected.

German surveyors excavated Jericho before World War I, and famous archaeologists (including Pere Vincent and Kathleen Kenyon) have carefully studied the ruins of Jericho. Unfortunately, they cannot shed much light on the capture by Joshua, for many sun-dried bricks dissolved into mud after many rains, and there has been considerable dispute about how to interpret the date of the remaining evidence. The details really don't matter as much as they may interest us. The fall of the mighty city of Jericho was attributed not to Joshua's generalship but to God's leadership.

## NOTES ON THE PRINTED TEXT

Israel's entry into the promised land had not gone undetected. The people of Jericho, suspicious of Israel's intent, braced for the inevitable attack behind the walls and gates of the city's fortifications. Archaeological excavations have revealed a well defended city fortified by a double ring of walls, the outer one being 6 feet thick and the inner one being 12 feet thick. Timbers were laid across these to support houses on the walls.

Israel surrounded the city and laid siege to it. *Now Jericho was shut up inside and out because of the Israelites; no one came out and no one went in* (6:1). Often those sieging a city suffered as much as those within the city. It's uncertain what the situation at Jericho was like. But we do know that the Lord gave Joshua a supernatural plan for taking the city.

Assuring Joshua of victory, God ordered the Israelites to march around Jericho on six consecutive days, while the priests carried the ark of the covenant and the seven trumpets made from rams' horns. On the seventh day, Israel was to make the circuit seven times and the priests were to blow the trumpets. Following the final lap, a great blast of the trumpets was to be sounded and the soldiers were to shout. The Lord promised that the massive walls would collapse (6:2-5).

Whatever the reason the Israelites were called upon to keep circling around the city, the routine was God's master strategy for Joshua and the Israelites. They followed that plan by marching around Jericho with the ark of the covenant for six days (6:6-14).

On the seventh day, the Israelites executed the final portion of God's plan (6:15). *And at the seventh time, when the priests had blown the trumpets, Joshua said to the people, "Shout! For the LORD has given you the city"* (6:16). As the army shouted, the massive walls collapsed, leaving the city defenseless (6:17-20).

The phrase *devoted . . . for destruction* (6:17) indicated that Jericho, along with its inhabitants and everything in it, was completely consecrated as an offering to the Lord. God wanted the Israelites to keep themselves undefiled in order to reflect His holiness. That's why Jericho had to be sacked and burned to the ground. Everything was to be destroyed, except for items made from silver, gold, bronze, and iron. These were sacred to the Lord and were to be brought into His treasury. The inhabitants were to be massacred, except for Rahab and her family, for Rahab had previously hidden the spies that Joshua had infiltrated into the city.

## SUGGESTIONS TO TEACHERS

A Vietnam veteran had lost both legs and an arm. He also suffered severe internal injuries and disfigurement of his face from a land mine explosion. Others had written him off as a hopeless casualty. Despite a series of painful operations and a struggle with narcotic addiction, he overcame all obstacles. Plastic surgery and artificial limbs helped, but this man attributes his ability to lead a productive life to his Christian faith.

This week's lesson offers a powerful reminder of the way the Lord enables faithful members of His community to persevere in the face of obstacles. God stands with those who trust and obey Him!

**1. GOD GAVE A PLAN.** The invasion of Canaan and the capture of Jericho appeared to be impossible tasks, but God provided the guidance and the strength for the Israelite victory. Instead of focusing on the obstacles, Joshua and his army centered on the divine plan. God always offers possibilities when we listen and obey!

**2. JOSHUA GUIDED THE ATTACK.** Marching around Jericho's walls for six days with the ark of the covenant might have seemed silly and pointless to some. But Joshua faithfully followed God's orders. Joshua did not question the Lord's command, even when it might have been questioned by others. God often uses unorthodox ways to accomplish His purposes!

**3. ISRAELITES CAPTURED THE CITY.** Significant victories come when God's people cooperate, take courage, and act in obedience to the Lord.

**4. GOD GOT THE CREDIT.** Don't get bogged down in useless discussion in your class over the precise details of the fall of Jericho by trying to "explain" the collapse of the walls by an earthquake or pursuing other earthly causes. The credit for the miracle went to the Lord!

**5. VICTORS PROTECTED RAHAB.** The protection of Rahab won her and her family safety during the battle and an enduring place in the covenant community. Sometimes the most unlikely persons turn out to be the most faithful!

---

**FOR ADULTS**

■ TOPIC: Overcoming Obstacles

■ QUESTIONS: 1. What was unusual about God's plan to capture Jericho? 2. How did Joshua and the Israelites respond to God's plan? 3. What are some aspects of the Christian faith that might seem unusual to the lost? 4. What are the fundamental choices in life for each person? 5. What happens when we follow God's plan for living the Christian life?

■ ILLUSTRATIONS:

**Doing Your Best for God.** When Jimmy Carter as a young naval officer applied for an assignment in Admiral Hyman Rickover's nuclear submarine program, Rickover asked him, "How did you stand in your class at the Naval Academy?" "Sir, I stood 59th in my class of 820." Expecting to be congratulated, Carter was surprised to hear Rickover say, "Did you do your best?"

At first Carter was going to say yes, but then he remembered the times when he had not learned all that he could have in a class. So he answered, "No, sir, I didn't always do my best." Rickover then hit him with a stinger that touched a spot in the soul of a Christian striving to serve God: "Why not?"

We might learn something from the example of Jimmy Carter, who has lived by the conviction that all God expects of us is that by faith in Christ we do the best we can with what we have. Carter was always starting over again, learning from his failures and moving on, trying to do his best with the God-given means at hand. Serving the Lord has driven Carter's career through a series of defeats and victories. Carter accepted his weaknesses, and determinedly drew on the power of Christ at work within him.

Carter's greatest defeat as president came when his rescue mission failed to save the American hostages held in Tehran. But in the midst of a desperate campaign for re-election, which he also lost, Carter continued to negotiate for the safe return of the hostages. In his first act as a former president, Carter flew to Germany to welcome the released hostages.

Returning to Plains, Georgia, Carter found his farming business $1 million in debt. An even greater threat to his mental health was the realization that he was no longer president. Losing the presidency to Ronald Reagan might have led him into bitterness and recrimination. Instead, the former president launched the Carter Center in Atlanta, Georgia, as a base for his efforts to reconcile warring factions abroad, to eradicate diseases in developing countries, and to address domestic problems of housing and poverty. Carter relied on his well-honed ability to put setbacks behind him and focus only on the future. He received a letter from Rickover that said: "As long as a man is trying as hard as he can to do what he thinks to be right, he is a success regardless of the outcome."

Writing books and building houses for the poor have consumed the time of both Rosalynn and Jimmy Carter since that defeat, but the former president's greatest legacy is still unfolding—his work for world peace and toward eliminating poverty and eradicating disease. Carter's faith in Christ led him to strive for the same objectives by whatever means were at hand while he was in Georgia, during his tenure as president of the United States, and even after he left office.

**Impossible Obstacles?** Joseph Butler had gifts as a writer and thinker. He served as Dean at St. Paul's in London and later as Bishop of Durham, and he wrote "Analogies of Christian Religion." Yet when others asked Butler to serve as the Archbishop of Canterbury, he flatly refused, saying that it was too late for him to try to support a falling church. The obstacles appeared impossible because he seemed to overlook the Lord's involvement in the world.

**FOR YOUTH**  ■ TOPIC: Sticking to the Plan
■ QUESTIONS: 1. How do you think the Israelites felt as they anticipated the attack on Jericho? 2. How did the Israelites respond to Joshua's unusual battle plan? 3. What aspects of living for Christ might seem strange to you? 4. What is your spiritual life like when you obey the Lord? 5. How might you encourage other believers to follow the Lord?

■ ILLUSTRATIONS:
**Celebration.** Returning from their surprising win of the Pennsylvania Class AA state championship on November 26, 1997, the South Park Eagles football team arrived at the high school at almost midnight. As the buses carrying the team came up the driveway, hundreds of students, parents, community people, teachers, and administrators began a joyous welcome and a victory celebration. For an unranked team to beat several of the state's ranked favorites had been quite a feat!

Joy and pride exploded into a celebration.

This team was no different from any other team in that they were excited about the victory. Most people love to celebrate victories. Israel was no different. The celebration of God's victory must have been combined with equal joy and enthusiasm.

**Specific Directions.** A story is told of an old hand-operated pump in the badlands of the American West. A thirsty visitor to the pump found a note with these instructions and a bottle of water. The note read: DO NOT DRINK THE WATER IN THIS BOTTLE. POUR THE CONTENTS DOWN THE HOLE AT THE TOP OF THE PUMP. ALLOW THE WASHER AND THE PACKING A FEW MINUTES TO SOAK UP THE WATER. THEN PUMP AND DRINK YOUR FILL. BEFORE LEAVING, FILL UP THE BOTTLE, AND LEAVE IT FOR THE NEXT PERSON.

The instructions might have seemed absurd, particularly when an individual was thirsty. Why pour good water away when the precious liquid might be wasted? However, these were the instructions, and they worked.

Israel heard what must have seemed like equally absurd instructions about capturing Jericho. No general or military leader in their right mind would have thought of such a scheme. However, the idea was God's plan. In faith, Joshua and his army were to follow the plan, and it was their key to achieving success.

**Bold Plan.** On the evening of May 1, 1863, Generals Lee and Jackson conferred in the woods. The situation looked grim. Hooker and the Union Army were at Chancellorsville, Virginia. He had outflanked the Confederate forces and moved 130,000 men across the Rappahannock River. Lee's army had 60,000. It appeared that the butternut army was caught in a trap and would be crushed.

Jackson proposed taking his corps of 26,000 men and slipping around the Union flank. It would be a 10-mile end sweep through dense woods at night. The plan seemed crazy. However, the execution of the plan was perfect. The Union line cracked in panic as Jackson's soldiers swept in, boxing in the Union forces.

Thousands of years earlier, another army listened to a plan that seemed absolutely crazy. Yet the Israelites, too, followed the plan with similar victorious results.

# CHOOSING TO SERVE THE LORD

**BACKGROUND SCRIPTURE:** Joshua 24
**DEVOTIONAL READING:** Joshua 24:14-24

---

**KEY VERSE:** The people said to Joshua, "The LORD our God we will serve, and him we will obey." Joshua 24:24.

*KING JAMES VERSION*

JOSHUA 24:1 And Joshua gathered all the tribes of Israel to Shechem, and called for the elders of Israel, and for their heads, and for their judges, and for their officers; and they presented themselves before God.

2 And Joshua said unto all the people, . . . .

14 Now therefore fear the LORD, and serve him in sincerity and in truth: and put away the gods which your fathers served on the other side of the flood, and in Egypt; and serve ye the LORD.

15 And if it seem evil unto you to serve the LORD, choose you this day whom ye will serve; whether the gods which your fathers served that were on the other side of the flood, or the gods of the Amorites, in whose land ye dwell: but as for me and my house, we will serve the LORD.

16 And the people answered and said, God forbid that we should forsake the LORD, to serve other gods;

17 For the LORD our God, he it is that brought us up and our fathers out of the land of Egypt, from the house of bondage, and which did those great signs in our sight, and preserved us in all the way wherein we went, and among all the people through whom we passed:

18 And the LORD drave out from before us all the people, even the Amorites which dwelt in the land: therefore will we also serve the LORD; for he is our God.

19 And Joshua said unto the people, Ye cannot serve the LORD: for he is an holy God; he is a jealous God; he will not forgive your transgressions nor your sins.

20 If ye forsake the LORD, and serve strange gods, then he will turn and do you hurt, and consume you, after that he hath done you good.

21 And the people said unto Joshua, Nay; but we will serve the LORD.

22 And Joshua said unto the people, Ye are witnesses against yourselves that ye have chosen you the LORD, to serve him. And they said, We are witnesses. . . .

25 So Joshua made a covenant with the people that day, and set them a statute and an ordinance in Shechem.

*NEW REVISED STANDARD VERSION*

JOSHUA 24:1 Then Joshua gathered all the tribes of Israel to Shechem, and summoned the elders, the heads, the judges, and the officers of Israel; and they presented themselves before God. 2 And Joshua said to all the people, . . .

14 "Now therefore revere the LORD, and serve him in sincerity and in faithfulness; put away the gods that your ancestors served beyond the River and in Egypt, and serve the LORD. 15 Now if you are unwilling to serve the LORD, choose this day whom you will serve, whether the gods your ancestors served in the region beyond the River or the gods of the Amorites in whose land you are living; but as for me and my household, we will serve the LORD."

16 Then the people answered, "Far be it from us that we should forsake the LORD to serve other gods; 17 for it is the LORD our God who brought us and our ancestors up from the land of Egypt, out of the house of slavery, and who did those great signs in our sight. He protected us along all the way that we went, and among all the peoples through whom we passed; 18 and the LORD drove out before us all the peoples, the Amorites who lived in the land. Therefore we also will serve the LORD, for he is our God."

19 But Joshua said to the people, "You cannot serve the LORD, for he is a holy God. He is a jealous God; he will not forgive your transgressions or your sins. 20 If you forsake the LORD and serve foreign gods, then he will turn and do you harm, and consume you, after having done you good." 21 And the people said to Joshua, "No, we will serve the LORD!" 22 Then Joshua said to the people, "You are witnesses against yourselves that you have chosen the LORD, to serve him." And they said, "We are witnesses." . . . 25 So Joshua made a covenant with the people that day, and made statues and ordinances for them at Shechem.

| | | |
|---|---|---|
| *Monday, Nov. 22* | Joshua 23:1-5 | *Joshua Summons Israel to Remember God* |
| *Tuesday, Nov. 23* | Joshua 23:6-10 | *Israel Exhorted to Love and Obey God* |
| *Wednesday, Nov. 24* | Joshua 23:11-16 | *Joshua Warns against Unfaithfulness to God* |
| *Thursday, Nov. 25* | Joshua 24:1-7 | *Joshua Rehearses Israel's History* |
| *Friday, Nov. 26* | Joshua 24:14-18 | *Israel Promises to Be Faithful* |
| *Saturday, Nov. 27* | Joshua 24:19-24 | *Israel Renews the Covenant* |
| *Sunday, Nov. 28* | Joshua 24:25-33 | *Death of Joshua and Eleazar* |

# BACKGROUND

The Book of Joshua can be divided into four literary sections. The first part deals with the Israelites' entrance into the promised land (1:1—5:12), while the second part concerns the people's conquest of Canaan (5:13—12:24). In this section, we learn that the Israelites first conducted a central campaign, then a southern campaign, and finally a northern campaign. These military successes were not due to Joshua's skill or the Israelites' prowess, but rather to God's intervention. In fact, His providence enabled Joshua to distribute the land among Israel's tribes. The third section of the book discusses this in detail (13—21).

Joshua was not only a great military commander but also a capable civil and spiritual leader. He knew that simply occupying Canaan was only part of the job. The Israelites, as the people of Yahweh, also had to wage a holy war against the ungodly inhabitants of the land. The Canaanites had become so steeped in iniquity that God would use the Israelites to spew them out of Palestine. Of course, Israel's conquest of Canaan would be in fulfillment of the covenant that the Lord had pledged to Abraham and his descendants.

Once the land had been conquered and divided up among Israel's tribes, it was necessary for God's people to build a nation there for themselves. The key to their success was their obedience to the Mosaic covenant. Just as God had been faithful to the Israelites, so too they needed to remain faithful to Him. Ultimately, their continued possession and prosperity in Canaan was dependent on their observance of the law.

Chapters 22 through 24 are the epilogue—and fourth section—of the book. Here we find Joshua, the nation's preeminent soldier-statesman, exhorting the Israelites to accept the challenge of following the Lord. The glory days of conquest were gone. But perhaps more important would be the challenge to remain faithful to God in the ordinary activities of life.

This would not be easy. After all, God's people would be surrounded by paganism. There would be a tremendous temptation on the part of the Israelites to adopt the thinking and practices of their ungodly neighbors. That's why the renewal of the covenant at Shechem was so pivotal in the life of the faith community. The ceremony was Joshua's last opportunity, before his death, to underscore to the current generation of Israelites that following the Lord wholeheartedly was in their long-term best interests.

## NOTES ON THE PRINTED TEXT

Under Joshua's leadership, the Israelites took possession of Canaan. However, much of the land was still controlled by the original inhabitants (see 13:1). Because of Joshua's advanced age, he would have to rely upon others to lead the Israelites in their conquest of the Philistines and their neighbors to the south, the Phoenician coastland to the north, and the northern, mountainous territories of Lebanon.

In the meantime, Joshua summoned all the Israelites to Shechem, including *the elders, the heads, the judges, and the officers* (24:1). Shechem was a city in the tribal allotment of Manasseh in the vicinity of Mount Gerizim and Mount Ebal. The site had a long tradition of religious significance and covenant making in Israel, going back to Abraham's day. Shechem thus was a fitting place to observe a covenant renewal ceremony.

The solemnity of the occasion is evident by the fact that the people *presented themselves before God* (24:1). In verses 2-13, Joshua reviewed all the great things the Lord had done for the Israelites. For example, God had chosen the patriarchs to be the recipients of His blessings. And He commissioned Moses to lead the Israelites out of Egypt and safely across the Red Sea. God had been with His people during their time in the desert, during their crossing of the Jordan and conquest of Jericho, and during each phase of their military campaign in Palestine.

In light of all that God had done for His people, Joshua commanded them *to revere the LORD* (24:14). They could do this by honoring and serving Him wholeheartedly. In times past, the ancestors of the Israelites had worshiped idols. Now that God had redeemed and claimed the Israelites as His own, they were to put away these pagan deities and exclusively serve Him.

The people only had two choices. Either they would follow God or idols. When Joshua and his family vowed to serve the Lord, the Israelites wisely followed suit (24:15-16). Unlike the pagan deities of the ancient Near East, which were powerless and lifeless, the God of Israel was all-powerful, all-knowing, and always present. He had lavished His people with His mercy and deliverance. It thus was only fitting for them to serve Him exclusively (24:17-18).

Joshua warned the Israelites against having a nominal, superficial faith. If they became smug and overconfident, it would prove disastrous for them. God's holiness meant that the people needed to be completely devoted to Him (24:19). In accordance with the stipulations of the covenant, if the people forsook the Lord and served *foreign gods* (24:20), He would bring calamity on them.

The people responded by boldly claiming that they would never abandon their relationship with God (24:21). When Joshua reminded them that they were responsible for their decision to serve the Lord, they affirmed their accountability. Their own words would condemn them in the future should they abandon their pledge (24:22). This prompted Joshua to ratify the covenant with the people at Shechem. This committed them to a permanent and binding agreement with the Lord (24:25).

The people started out well that day. They understood that God was calling them to be a holy nation that would influence the rest of the world for the Lord. Sadly, the Israelites' pledge would not last indefinitely. Succeeding generations would become so preoccupied with the land that they would drift away from the Lord.

## SUGGESTIONS TO TEACHERS

Life demands making choices. Some are relatively insignificant. Whether you have orange juice or grapefruit juice for breakfast, or wear the blue suit or the gray one are not momentous decisions. But deciding whether to make a lifetime commitment in marriage to a person, or choosing a career path that will not be as financially rewarding as other jobs—these are the choices that are major.

Encourage the members of your class to relate some of the toughest decisions they have faced in their lives and to explain why these were so hard to make. In light of this week's lesson, help them to consider how God calls His people to make the big decisions in the context of the biggest choice of all, namely, to put the Lord first by trusting and obeying Him.

**1. CHART.** Joshua reminded the Israelites of what God had done for them in the past. A good point in making the right choices in life is to recall the Lord's mighty acts in the past, both those recorded in Scripture and those remembered in one's personal life.

**2. CHALLENGE.** Joshua challenged the people to make a conscious, public declaration of their loyalty to God. Regardless of what we, as believers, think, say, or do, everyday we are faced with the challenge of consciously deciding to serve the Lord exclusively. Discuss with your students what the most important challenges are that God has presented to them.

**3. CHANGE.** Choosing to worship and serve God means forsaking all the idols prevalent today in society. List the following items on a chalkboard, overhead, or sheet of newsprint: knowledge, success, popularity, money, pleasure, power, physical attractiveness, and consumerism. Then explain that these are just some of the many "idols" that people in our society typically worship. Discuss with the class how difficult it is to replace these things with exclusive devotion to the Lord.

**4. CHARGE.** Joshua called upon a new generation of Israelites to renew their pledge to worship and serve the Lord. As Christians, we do the same each time we gather together to observe the Lord's Supper. Remind your students about the New Covenant that we have through faith in Christ.

---

**FOR ADULTS**

■ TOPIC: Making the Right Choice

■ QUESTIONS: 1. What momentous decision did the Israelites have to make? 2. What would be the consequence of the choice the people made? 3. What are some tough decisions you have had to make? 4. How has your relationship with Christ made a difference? 5. What can you do to encourage other believers to serve the Lord exclusively?

■ ILLUSTRATIONS:

**From Klan to Christ.** Aaron Daniels came home from a conference of Promise Keepers in Birmingham, Alabama, in May 1997, determined to make some different choices. For starters, he burned his Ku Klux Klan robe. He announced that he would no longer use racial epithets in his home or anywhere else. Daniels also began to pray, asking the Lord to help him choose to live a new life.

The 34-year-old TV cable lineman had grown to hate African Americans in high school. Daniels also had started taking drugs. Eventually flunking out of school, he drifted to New Mexico to live with a sister and her husband. Daniels married in 1988, but divorced his wife two years later. In 1991, he was invited to the KKK, and found a focus for his simmering hatreds. By 1993, Daniels had risen to be the second-in-command in two counties for the Klan. He then was elevated to Grand Dragon. When his bosses found out about his Klan involvement, they demanded that he choose between the Klan or his job. Daniels reluctantly quit the Klan.

Daniels remarried, and then was introduced to Promise Keepers by his father, Dan Daniels. But Aaron wanted no part of Promise Keepers or the Christian faith. He was furious when he read an article in a Promise Keepers' magazine sent by his father that criticized the Klu Klux Klan. Finally, Aaron reluctantly accompanied his father to the Birmingham conference in May, 1997. But Aaron only went to please his father.

The message given that day hit Aaron hard. God changed the thinking of this former Grand Dragon when Dr. Raleigh Washington preached on racial reconciliation. Aaron, weeping, found himself hugging the African American man beside him. Since the conference, Daniels' new life in Christ has involved making serious choices, including regular church attendance and introducing other men to Promise Keepers.

**Why God Gives Us Choices.** "The problem of pain, of war, and the horror of war, of poverty, and disease is always confronting us. But a God who allows no pain, no grief, also allows no choice. There is little unfairness in a colony of ants, but also there is little freedom. This ability to make choices, to help write our own story, is what makes us human . . . even when we make the wrong choices, abusing our freedom and the freedom of others" (Madeleine L'Engle, *Walking on Water,* Harold Shaw, 1972).

Consider the the following. If God gave you 70 years of life, you would spend:

- 24 years sleeping
- 14 years working
- 8 years in amusement
- 6 years at the dinner table
- 5 years in transportation
- 4 years in conversation
- 3 years in education
- 3 years reading.

If you went to church every Sunday and prayed five minutes every morning and night, you would be giving God five months of your life. That's only five months out of 70 years!

---

**FOR YOUTH**

■ TOPIC: Making Life's Choices
■ QUESTIONS: 1. How were the Israelites to show their reverence for the Lord? 2. What would life be like for God's people if they chose to serve Him exclusively? 3. Why should you give God supreme control of your life? 4. Why is it often tough to live for the Lord? 5. What would your life be like without God?

■ ILLUSTRATIONS:
**Lure of Gold.** On a Philadelphia stage, the Master of Ceremonies leaned on a glittering gold bowl. Behind the pounding beat of rock music, Dick Clark, the guest host, stood beside Miss Pennsylvania on the blinking stage covered with neon strips and bright blue lights. The star-studded extravaganza was part of the Pennsylvania Lottery.

But not everyone was excited. Tony Milillo, President of the Council on Compulsive Gambling of Pennsylvania, was unhappy with the gold curtains, canned applause, and hype. He not only worried about the effects on the compulsive gamblers, but also on the youth who live in his state.

Milillo noted that teenagers are warned not to smoke, take drugs, or engage in premarital sex. But they are told that games of chance, which can feed on a person's greedy desire for money, are acceptable. He also pointed out that as daily drawings lose their appeal, the state has turned to other gimmicks, especially instant tickets, which appeal to teenagers and have pushed some to become addicted to gambling.

The love of money is just one kind of "idol" that can enslave teens, even those who are Christians. Adolescents within the community of faith should make the Lord the exclusive object of their devotion.

**Competing Loyalties.** Nine-year-old John Rosemond's bike broke. Because it could not be repaired, he asked his stepfather to buy him a new one. Several days later, at the bike shop, John looked over the rows of shiny new bikes and made his selection. When he showed it to his stepfather, he was told that he was in the wrong section and that he did not need a new bike. A used one would be fine.

When John protested, his stepfather took him outside and showed him the family car, which was purchased a few months earlier. "Do you know what year's model this is?" the stepfather asked. John learned that even though his parents could have bought a new car, they chose not to so that some of their income could be used in charitable ways. Their loyalty was in helping others, not in merely gratifying their own desires. John's stepfather was trying to teach him the same lesson about the choices he made.

Like John and his family, you need to decide where you want your loyalties to be. Will they reside with you, or will you offer your loyalty to God and His people? If you chose the first option, this will lead to an inflated sense of your own importance, intolerance of others, and a lack of charity.

**No Fear:** A Barna Survey indicated that half of the population becomes annoyed when a stranger tries to share his or her religious beliefs with the listener. However, when a family member, close friend, or trusted associate does the same, the listener is not annoyed and often expresses interest and gratitude.

Joshua had no fear about telling others that he trusted and served the Lord. He even challenged others to live exclusively for God. Does fear prevent you from sharing your faith with others?

.

DECEMBER 1999;
JANUARY, FEBRUARY 2000

# STUDIES IN MATTHEW

# KING'S HERALD AND BAPTISM

**BACKGROUND SCRIPTURE:** Matthew 3
**DEVOTIONAL READING:** Matthew 21:23-27

**KEY VERSE:** I baptize you with water for repentance, but one who is more powerful than I is coming after me; I am not worthy to carry his sandals. He will baptize you with the Holy Spirit and fire. Matthew 3:11.

*KING JAMES VERSION*

MATTHEW 3:1 In those days came John the Baptist, preaching in the wilderness of Judæa,

2 And saying, Repent ye: for the kingdom of heaven is at hand.

3 For this is he that was spoken of by the prophet Esaias, saying, The voice of one crying in the wilderness, Prepare ye the way of the Lord, make his paths straight.

4 And the same John had his raiment of camel's hair, and a leathern girdle about his loins; and his meat was locusts and wild honey.

5 Then went out to him Jerusalem, and all Judæa, and all the region round about Jordan,

6 And were baptized of him in Jordan, confessing their sins.

7 But when he saw many of the Pharisees and Sadducees come to his baptism, he said unto them, O generation of vipers, who hath warned you to flee from the wrath to come?

8 Bring forth therefore fruits meet for repentance: . . .

11 I indeed baptize you with water unto repentance: but he that cometh after me is mightier than I, whose shoes I am not worthy to bear: he shall baptize you with the Holy Ghost, and with fire:

12 Whose fan is in his hand, and he will throughly purge his floor, and gather his wheat into the garner; but he will burn up the chaff with unquenchable fire.

13 Then cometh Jesus from Galilee to Jordan unto John, to be baptized of him.

14 But John forbad him, saying, I have need to be baptized of thee, and comest thou to me?

15 And Jesus answering said unto him, Suffer it to be so now: for thus it becometh us to fulfil all righteousness. Then he suffered him.

16 And Jesus, when he was baptized, went up straightway out of the water: and, lo, the heavens were opened unto him, and he saw the Spirit of God descending like a dove, and lighting upon him:

17 And lo a voice from heaven, saying, This is my beloved Son, in whom I am well pleased.

*NEW REVISED STANDARD VERSION*

MATTHEW 3:1 In those days John the Baptist appeared in the wilderness of Judea, proclaiming,

2 "Repent, for the kingdom of heaven has come near."
3 This is one of whom the prophet Isaiah spoke when he said,
> "The voice of one crying out in the wilderness:
> 'Prepare the way of the Lord,
>    make his paths straight.' "

4 Now John wore clothing of camel's hair with a leather belt around his waist, and his food was locusts and wild honey. 5 Then the people of Jerusalem and all Judea were going out to him, and all the region along the Jordan, 6 and they were baptized by him in the river Jordan, confessing their sins.

7 But when he saw many Pharisees and Sadducees coming for baptism, he said to them, "You brood of vipers! Who warned you to flee from the wrath to come? 8 Bear fruit worthy of repentance. . . .

11 "I baptize you with water for repentance, but one who is more powerful than I is coming after me; I am not worthy to carry his sandals. He will baptize you with the Holy Spirit and fire. His winnowing fork is in his hand, and he will clear his threshing floor and will gather his wheat into the granary; but the chaff he will burn with unquenchable fire."

13 Then Jesus came from Galilee to John at the Jordan, to be baptized by him. 14 John would have prevented him, saying, "I need to be baptized by you, and do you come to me?" 15 But Jesus answered him, "Let it be so now; for it is proper for us in this way to fulfill all righteousness." Then he consented. 16 And when Jesus had been baptized, just as he came up from the water, suddenly the heavens were opened to him and he saw the Spirit of God descending like a dove and alighting on him. 17 And a voice from heaven said, "This is my Son, the Beloved, with whom I am well pleased."

## BACKGROUND

The Greek word translated as "gospel" means "good news." It is a fitting title for the first four books of the New Testament, which record the good news about the life, sacrificial death, and resurrection of Jesus of Nazareth. The gospels are not biographies in the modern sense of the word, for they do not present a complete written history of Jesus' life. In fact, apart from the birth narratives, they give little information about the first 30 years of Jesus' life. Each Gospel discusses various aspects of Christ's earthly ministry. But most of their attention is devoted to the last week of His life.

The primary purpose of the Gospels is theological and apologetic. They provide authoritative answers to questions about Jesus' life and ministry, and they strengthen the assurance of believers regarding the reality of their faith. All this having been said, it is nonetheless true that the Gospels are completely accurate historically, and present important biographical details of Jesus' life.

The author of each Gospel wrote from a unique perspective and for a different audience. For instance, Matthew wrote mainly to a Jewish audience. He presented Jesus as the long-awaited Messiah and rightful King of Israel. Matthew intended such things as the genealogy of Christ, the many Old Testament quotations, and the five large sections of teaching material to strengthen the faith of Jewish believers.

This week's lesson introduces us to John the Baptist. (According to Luke 1:36, Elizabeth and Mary, the mothers of John and Jesus, respectively, were members of the same family.) John was a forerunner of Jesus as well as a moral reformer and proclaimer of the messianic hope that would dawn in Christ. God used John's ministry to prepare the Jews for the first advent of their Redeemer.

## NOTES ON THE PRINTED TEXT

As the forerunner of Christ, *John the Baptist* (Matt. 3:1) preceded the Savior in birth, ministry, and death. John ministered *in the wilderness of Judea* (a barren region to the immediate west of the Dead Sea) and summoned his fellow Jews to repent. He did so because *the kingdom of heaven [had] come near* (3:2) in the person of Christ.

Isaiah 40:3 had long ago anticipated and described John's mission. The verse reflects the ancient practice in which a monarch traveling in wilderness regions would have a work crew go ahead to ensure that the road was clear of debris, obstructions, potholes, and other hazards that could make the journey difficult. In a spiritual sense, John was summoning the Jews to prepare their hearts for the arrival of the Messiah (Matt. 3:3).

Malachi 4:5 prophesied that God would send His people *the prophet Elijah before the great and terrible day of the LORD.* The New Testament identifies John the Baptist as this Elijah (Matt. 11:14). John's dress—*camel's hair with a leather belt around his waist* (3:4)—and his clothes evoked the image of Elijah (2 Kings 1:8). Though this outfit was practical, it was far from comfortable and fashionable.

John's message made a significant impact, for Jews from Jerusalem, from every section of Judea, and from all over the Jordan river valley went out to the wilderness to hear him preach (Matt. 3:5). In that day it would have been typical for Gentile proselytes converting to Judaism to be baptized. But, oddly enough, John was baptizing Jews *in the river Jordan* (3:6). What's more they were confessing, or acknowledging, their sins. It's clear that the people were sincere in spiritually preparing themselves for the arrival of the Messiah.

During the time of Christ, the *Pharisees and Sadducees* (3:7) were two prominent groups in Judaism. The Pharisees held not only to the law of Moses, but also to a whole body of oral tradition. Their activities were centered mainly in the synagogue, and despite their small number, they enjoyed the favor of the majority of Jews in Palestine. In contrast, the Sadducees were aristocratic Jews who were the recognized guardians of the temple policy and practices. Except for the Pentateuch (the first five books of Scripture), they rejected the Old Testament as well as any teaching that they believed was not found in the Torah.

In John's day, many of the Pharisees and Sadducees were characterized by hypocrisy and arrogance. Like the prophets of the Old Testament, John issued a stinging rebuke to the religious leaders and addressed them as deadly snakes. He said that like the rest of humankind, they had to repent if they wanted to escape *the wrath to come* (3:7). John urged them to prove by the way they lived that their repentance was genuine (3:8).

John clearly knew his place in God's order of things. As the humble forerunner of Christ, John's baptism was meant to symbolize the moral cleansing associated with repentance. But the Messiah, who was infinitely greater than John, would baptize believers with the Holy Spirit and unbelievers with the fire of judgment (3:11). At Jesus' second coming, He would judge the wicked (3:12).

One can only imagine how shocked John was when Jesus came to be baptized (3:13). When John balked at doing this (3:14), Jesus explained that it would *fulfill all righteousness* (3:15). Though sinless Himself, Jesus identified with sinners and satisfied all God's righteous requirements. Verses 16 and 17 point to the Son's voluntary humiliation, the Father's delight in Him, and the Spirit's desire to glorify Christ. (Notice the simultaneous presence of all three Persons of the Trinity.)

## SUGGESTIONS TO TEACHERS

You are already in the Advent season. During the Sunday morning worship service, someone may be lighting the second candle on the Advent wreath and reflecting on the significance of Christ's first coming. This week's lesson ties in with your congregation's observance of the second Sunday of Advent by stressing the need to prepare for the Jesus' birth.

**1. READINESS.** For weeks the malls have been screaming their messages about preparing for Christmas by urging everyone to buy. The Scripture text reminds us that God's people are to be more focused on the Savior, not the holiday. John the Baptist's words apply in this season of frantic spending. "Get ready!" John would say. Talk with the class about specific ways they could better ready themselves for the Christmas season.

**2. REPENTANCE.** John the Baptist warned his fellow Jews that having godly ancestors would not make things right with the Lord for ungodly descendants (see 3:9-10). That's why he called the people to repentance (3:2). This was no mere change of mind or just regret and remorse. Rather, it signified a turning away from sin. Discuss with you students what they think it means to repent. Also have them consider what it means to *bear fruit worthy of repentance* (3:8). Why is this often so hard to do consistently?

**3. RENUNCIATION.** John the Baptist refused to focus on himself, but rather insisted on pointing to Christ. John referred to the Messiah as the one and the only person worthy of emulating. Sadly, our age has glorified the loudmouthed, self-indulging, and self-promoting "superstars" in sports, entertainment, and government. Encourage the class members to notice the way John diminished himself so that Jesus could be held up as most important.

**4. RIGHTEOUSNESS.** Allow time in the lesson to comment on the meaning of Jesus' baptism. Explain that through this rite, the Messiah inaugurated His public ministry, identified with the repentant people of God, and showed support for what John was doing. Jesus also submitted to the will of His heavenly Father, and God in turn voiced His approval of His Son.

---

| FOR ADULTS | ■ TOPIC: Time for Preparing |
| | ■ QUESTIONS: 1. What kind of sins did John want his fellow Jews to abandon? 2. Why was it important for the people to repent? |

3. What are some sins in your life that you are seeking to forsake? 4. How can turning away from them better prepare you for the Christmas season? 5. Why is God pleased when you turn away from sin and pursue righteousness?

**Trumpet Call.** Every hour on the hour, in Krakow, Poland, a trumpeter blares out an oddly truncated call. The trumpet call begins sounding from the pinnacled tower of ancient Saint Mary's Church, but then abruptly stops after a few notes. Some strangers think that the trumpeter has forgotten the tune. Then the same brief fanfare blares again.

The reason behind the sudden stop to the call in mid-note lies in an historic event. In 1241, a watchman in the tower caught sight of a band of invading tartars and sounded the alarm on his bugle. He had gotten as far as the first few notes when an arrow struck him in the throat. But the warning allowed Krakow time to prepare itself.

Today, hourly, the same brief, sad call rings out over the city, and at midday it is broadcast to the nation. The trumpeter then and now reminds his people to be ready and to serve!

John the Baptist was the herald of God to call people to be ready and to serve the King whose coming was at hand. Today, John's summons to repentance and acceptance of God's rule is just as clear and compelling!

**What Are the Priorities?** It was a 99-degree September day in San Antonio, Texas, when a 10-month-old baby girl was accidentally locked inside a parked car by her aunt. Frantically the mother and aunt ran around the auto in near hysteria, while a neighbor attempted to unlock the car with a clothes hanger. Soon the infant was turning purple and had foam on her mouth.

It had become a life or death situation when Fred Arriola, a wrecker driver, arrived on the scene. He grabbed a hammer and smashed the back window of the car and set the baby free. Was he heralded as a hero? Fred said, "The lady was mad at me because I broke the window. I just thought, "What's more important, the baby or the window?"

Sometimes priorities get out of order, and we need to be reminded of what's most important. Perhaps this is more true of the weeks leading up to Christmas than of any other time of the year.

Every day our letter carrier provides us with a minimum of three catalogs from companies far and near encouraging us to do our Christmas shopping with them. "Consume, indulge, and gorge." "Spend yourself into debt." These seem to be the messages of the Christmas season. In order to acquire all the needed items for countless family members and friends, we might find ourselves running around in a frenzy like the women in the above story, or we might plan our shopping for months like a military strategist. Why do we do these things? Is it really to express our love and celebrate the birth of our Savior?

If one doesn't join in the spending frenzy, but rather seeks to provide more humble or homemade gifts, one is accused of being a Scrooge, cheap, or uncaring. In the flurry of shopping and family and social gatherings, it is easy for our priorities to be misplaced. We can even complain that we are too busy to take the time to worship the first coming of Christ! (Douglas Scalise, *The Beacon*, Brewster Baptist Church, December, 1997).

**The Congregation with the "$100 Holiday."** Bill McKibben, the author and environmentalist, teaches Sunday school and is active in his local church. A few years ago, he and fellow members of his congregation and others in the northern New York and Vermont conference of the United Methodist Church began a campaign for "$100 holidays." They and the church leaders voted to urge their parishioners not to spend more than $100 per family on gifts at Christmas, but to offer homemade presents or gifts of services.

McKibben made walking sticks the first year for his friends, and spicy chicken sausage the following. Others' gifts took the form of stacking a cord of firewood or regular backrubs or handmade calendars illustrated with photographs of family. McKibben and the others set the $100 figure as "an anchor against the constant seductions of advertisers" and as a way of explaining to children why they weren't getting everything on their holiday wish lists.

Christmas was the big season for merchants and suppliers, and they did about one-third of their business in the time before the holiday. Many were angry at McKibben and wrote letters to local papers complaining that their livelihoods were being threatened by the "$100 holidays." Even some news editors felt that the practice of the $100 limit would do too much damage to the economy.

McKibben and the many others now limiting themselves to the $100 Christmas point out that their campaign tries to address the problem of consumer addiction. And consumer addiction, they remind others, keeps people from building a fair society and preserving the environment. More important, this group of Christians insist that the focus of the Advent season is to celebrate the birth of Christ, not buy presents. Having felt cheated by the commercialized, big-spending holidays, these church people report that they can relax and enjoy the season.

The local ministers in that Methodists Conference now begin to talk about the $100 Christmas after Labor Day, but it's not too late for each of us to ponder whether the stacks of merchandise we feel compelled to buy truly reflect the meaning of the advent of Christ. The price of one silk necktie, McKibben reminds us, could feed a village for a day in many places!

**The Father He Was Ready to Meet**. Sir Alec Guinness, the great actor, never was able to find out who his father was or to meet him. Being an illegitimate child, his birth certificate in London in 1914 registered him as Alec Guinness de Cuffe, since his mother's name was Miss Agnes Cuffe.

When Guinness was five years old, his mother married a harsh man named David Stiven, and the boy carried the stepfather's name. At fourteen, he was told that his real name was Guinness and was instructed to call himself by that surname. Alec's mother would never reveal any information about who his father was, though there were several men who seemed to come and go in the home.

In his late teens, Alec Guinness determined to discover the man who was his natural father, but could find no clues. He went to the solicitor in charge of his family's flimsy and meager financial affairs when he was 21, and again learned nothing. Alec Guinness also privately held hopes that his father might have left him a gold watch, and asked the solicitor whether there was a watch left to him. The word again was, "No."

Guinness decided that someday when he had a bit of extra money, he would buy a gold watch. Many years later, with the first week's salary from playing in T. S. Eliot's *The Cocktail Party*, he bought himself the gold vest-pocket watch that had never materialized. Still hoping to know the father he had never met whose identity he wanted to learn, Alec Guinness had engraved on the inside of the watch, "The readiness is all." This inscription symbolized his dreams and readiness to meet the man who had fathered him and whom he longed to know.

Guinness's readiness to meet his earthly father should be matched by our readiness to meet the Father who has come to us in the person of Christ. Are we in a state of readiness always?

**FOR YOUTH**

■ TOPIC Fire and Water

■ QUESTIONS: 1. Why was it important for John's fellow Jews to get ready to meet their Savior? 2. Why did John's message have a note of urgency to it? 3. What changes do you need to make in the way you think and act? 4. How would making these changes affect your life? 5. How do you think your friends and peers would respond to such changes?

■ ILLUSTRATIONS:

**Holding Power.** As the Constitutional Convention met in Philadelphia in 1789, the participants debated how much to pay the newly elected president. Benjamin Franklin stood up and said that every human being had two terrible instincts. The first was the desire for wealth, and the second was the lust for power. Should the two be combined in the office of the president, he feared mischief would result. He urged that the president be paid nothing!

Franklin was correct in his belief that humans love power. That's why John the Baptist is so striking. Though a morally powerful man in his own right, John humbly acknowledged that someone who was far more powerful than himself was coming, and he willingly stepped aside to make way for the Messiah's advent.

**Found Direction.** Steve sat in his car rolling some marijuana in cigarette paper. The rock music was blasting. At 17, he was a drug addict and a dope dealer at his high school. While parked at a gas station, he became so preoccupied with preparing his joint to smoke that he failed to see the police officer walking up to his car window. The officer was suspicious that Steve was preparing to rob the gas station. Steve and his date were arrested and jailed.

After being freed that afternoon, Steve went out and got drunk. He then went to a fast food restaurant. There, the manager asked him to leave. When Steve took a swing at the manager, the police arrived again and arrested him a second time that day. At his court hearing, he was given a choice of either entering a chemical dependency treatment program or a correctional facility.

Robin was a girl at Steve's school who had originally been part of his drug taking group but who had gone clean and become a committed Christian. She knew Christ could change Steve. She provided Christian comic books to Steve and challenged him to come to a Bible study.

After his two arrests, Steve felt miserable. His life lacked direction. One day, he saw Robin sitting alone in the cafeteria. He sat down with her. Without even thinking he spilled out his story about believing that he was going to hell because there was no escape. Robin then shared with Steve the truth about Jesus. Steve trusted in Christ for salvation and asked the Lord to help him kick his drug habit and give him a new sense of direction.

Following Steve's drug treatment program, he began to preach against drug abuse. Later, at college, he volunteered in a youth ministry. None of this would have happened had it not been for Robin's efforts to point him to Christ. Now Steve is an ordained youth minister who tells other adolescents about Jesus. Both Steve and Robin are now acting as John had acted by pointing people to the Savior.

**Attracted to Celebrity.** Martin Koukal, a cross country skier for the Czech Republic, was excited. Martin had the opportunity to represent his tiny country at the Winter Olympic Games in Nagano, Japan, in February, 1998. As exciting as that was, it was nothing compared with the fact that he would get to meet one of the greatest hockey players in the world. A hockey player himself since age 11, Martin had heard that the NHL players would be staying in the Olympic Village. That meant that he would get to meet one of his heroes and fellow countrymen, Jaromir Jagr, the Pittsburgh Penguins forward, and possibly get his autograph for himself and his little brother.

Martin Koukal is no different from you. Youth tend to be attracted to unique persons, particularly celebrities. People were attracted to John, but he used his position to point to a far more unique individual—God's own Son!

# TEMPTATIONS AND MINISTRY

**BACKGROUND SCRIPTURE:** Matthew 4:1-17

**DEVOTIONAL READING:** Luke 4:14-21

**KEY VERSE:** Jesus said to him, "Away with you, Satan! for it is written, 'Worship the Lord your God, and serve only him." Matthew 4:10.

*KING JAMES VERSION*

MATTHEW 4:1 Then was Jesus led up of the Spirit into the wilderness to be tempted of the devil.

2 And when he had fasted forty days and forty nights, he was afterward an hungred.

3 And when the tempter came to him, he said, If thou be the Son of God, command that these stones be made bread.

4 But he answered and said, It is written, Man shall not live by bread alone, but by every word that proceedeth out of the mouth of God.

5 Then the devil taketh him up into the holy city, and setteth him on a pinnacle of the temple,

6 And saith unto him, If thou be the Son of God, cast thyself down: for it is written, He shall give his angels charge concerning thee: and in their hands they shall bear thee up, lest at any time thou dash thy foot against a stone.

7 Jesus said unto him, It is written again, Thou shalt not tempt the Lord thy God.

8 Again, the devil taketh him up into an exceeding high mountain, and sheweth him all the kingdoms of the world, and the glory of them;

9 And saith unto him, All these things will I give thee, if thou wilt fall down and worship me.

10 Then saith Jesus unto him, Get thee hence, Satan: for it is written, Thou shalt worship the Lord thy God, and him only shalt thou serve.

11 Then the devil leaveth him, and, behold, angels came and ministered unto him.

12 Now when Jesus had heard that John was cast into prison, he departed into Galilee;

13 And leaving Nazareth, he came and dwelt in Capernaum, which is upon the sea coast, in the borders of Zabulon and Nephthalim:

14 That it might be fulfilled which was spoken by Esaias the prophet.

*NEW REVISED STANDARD VERSION*

MATTHEW 4:1 Then Jesus was led by the Spirit into the wilderness to be tempted by the devil. 2 He fasted forty days and forty nights, and afterwards he was famished. 3 The tempter came and said to him, "If you are the Son of God, command these stones to become loaves of bread." 4 But he answered, "It is written,

'One does not live by bread alone,

but by every word that comes from the mouth of God.'"

5 Then the devil took him to the holy city and placed him on the pinnacle of the temple, 6 saying to him, "If you are the Son of God, throw yourself down; for it is written,

'He will command his angels concerning you,'

and 'On their hands they will bear you up,

so that you will not dash your foot against a stone.'"

7 Jesus said to him, "Again it is written, 'Do not put the Lord your God to the test.'"

8 Again, the devil took him to a very high mountain and showed him all the kingdoms of the world and their splendor; 9 and he said to him, "All these I will give you, if you will fall down and worship me."

10 Jesus said to him, "Away with you, Satan! for it is written,

'Worship the Lord your God,

and serve only him.'"

11 Then the devil left him, and suddenly angels came and waited on him.

12 Now when Jesus heard that John had been arrested, he withdrew to Galilee. 13 He left Nazareth and made his home in Capernaum by the sea, in the territory of Zebulun and Naphtali, 14 so that what had been spoken through the prophet Isaiah might be fulfilled.

| | | |
|---|---|---|
| Monday, Dec. 6 | Matthew 4:1-11 | *Jesus Is Tempted by the Devil* |
| Tuesday, Dec. 7 | Matthew 4:12-17 | *Jesus Begins His Ministry in Galilee* |
| Wednesday, Dec. 8 | Luke 4:14-19 | *Jesus in the Synagogue at Nazareth* |
| Thursday, Dec. 9 | Luke 4:20-30 | *Jesus Is Rejected in Nazareth* |
| Friday, Dec. 10 | Luke 4:31-37 | *Jesus Casts out a Demonic Spirit* |
| Saturday, Dec. 11 | Luke 4:38-44 | *Jesus Heals and Preaches* |
| Sunday, Dec. 12 | Luke 5:12-16 | *Jesus Heals a Man with Leprosy* |

## BACKGROUND

One of the burdens and blessings of being human is having to make choices. And connected with decision-making is the reality of temptations in which we must decide to either please ourself or God. What makes temptation so appealing is that it promises great payoffs. An enticement to sin always seems to make good sense! In fact, the tempter can convince a victim that succumbing to his way will be helpful to others!

At first we might think that God is the agent of temptation. But James 1:13 teaches otherwise. Because God is holy, He has no capacity for evil or vulnerability to it. It's true that the Lord permits trials to occur and in them He allows temptation to happen. But He has promised not to allow more than believers can endure and never without a way to escape (1 Cor. 10:13). They must choose whether to take the way of escape that God provides or to give in to the temptation.

The English reformer and theologian John Wycliffe (1330–1384) wrote the following: "Let no man think himself to be holy because he is not tempted, for the holiest and highest in life have the most temptation. How much higher the hill is, so much is the wind there greater; so, how much higher the life, so much stronger is the temptation of the enemy."

Jesus was not a robot who was preprogrammed to conform automatically and mindlessly to the divine will. Rather, He was both truly human and truly divine. This means He had the ability to choose from a range of ethical alternatives.

This week's Scripture text presents one situation in which Jesus had to choose to put the will of His heavenly Father above other goals and values. The Gospel writers make it clear that throughout Jesus' earthly career, He was confronted with many such temptations. Of course, dying on the cross was the greatest test of His devotion to God.

## NOTES ON THE PRINTED TEXT

After John baptized Jesus, the Spirit sent Him out into the desert *to be tempted by the devil* (4:1). The area northwest of the Dead Sea and west of Jericho is traditionally identified as the location where Jesus was tempted. During Jesus' sojourn in the wilderness, He *fasted forty days and forty nights* (4:2). When the devil launched his attacks, Jesus was at an outward disadvantage from a human perspective.

Satan said to Jesus that if He was truly the *Son of God* (Matt. 4:3), He would have no problem turning stones into loaves of bread. Rather than yield to the tempter's suggestion, Jesus quoted Deuteronomy 8:3. This verse teaches that people live not only by consuming food; they also need to take in God's Word for spiritual nourishment (Matt. 4:4).

The devil next escorted Jesus to Jerusalem and stood Him on the pinnacle of the temple (4:5). The tempter invited Jesus to prove in a spectacular way that He was God the Son. Satan also told Jesus to throw Himself down to prove that the Father would protect Him (4:6).

A common interpretation of Malachi 3:1 held that the Messiah would appear in the sky, descend to the temple, and proclaim deliverance. Satan wanted Jesus to combine such an appearance with a sensational descent, complete with angels, to win popular approval for His kingdom.

The tempter had cleverly misquoted Psalm 91:11-12 by leaving out the phrase *to guard you in all your ways*. Satan claimed that God would protect Jesus as He plummeted to the ground. Since the stunt was not within the will of God, the passage could not be legitimately claimed as a promise of divine protection.

Rather than yield to the devil's suggestion, Jesus quoted from Deuteronomy 6:16 (see Matt. 4:7). The passage commands believers not to see how far they can go in presuming on God's goodness or attempt to discover how much they can disobey God before He judges them.

In Satan's third temptation, he transported Jesus to a high mountain. In a moment of time, the devil paraded before Christ *all the kingdoms of the world and their splendor* (4:8). The devil would give the Son of God all that He saw if He would fall prostrate before the tempter and worship him as lord (4:9).

Through Jesus' death and resurrection, God intended to free the world from the control of Satan (see Heb. 2:14-15). If Jesus had paid homage to the devil, God's plan would have failed. And if Christ had yielded to the proposal of Satan, He would have been merely a false messiah and the devil's slave.

Rather than oblige His tempter, Jesus shouted, *"Away with you, Satan!"* (Matt. 4:10). There was good reason for this command. It was written in Deuteronomy 6:13 and 10:20 that worship and service were to be given only to God.

When the devil was finished, he departed from the Savior. When the time was opportune, Satan would return to tempt Jesus again (see Luke 4:13). Matthew 4:11 notes that angels came and attended to the needs of Christ.

Jesus learned that John the Baptist had been imprisoned (4:12). According to Mark 6:17-18, this occurred because John had rebuked the immoral Herod Antipas (the tetrarch of Galilee and Perea) for his illicit marriage to Herodias, the wife of his brother Philip.

Jesus decided it would be safer for Him to minister in Galilee. After arriving there, Jesus spent some time in Nazareth, but experienced rejection from the residents (Luke 4:16-30). He then traveled northeast to Capernaum, which was by the Sea of Galilee *in the territory of Zebulun and Naphtali* (Matt. 4:13).

Verse 14 says that Jesus' relocation to Capernaum fulfilled what was written in Isaiah 9:1-2. This passage alludes to the suffering that northern Israel experienced under Assyrian rule. God had promised to reverse His judgment by allowing the people to be the recipient of His blessing. He fulfilled that pledge by enlightening the people living near the Sea of Galilee with the glorious presence of the Messiah (Matt. 4:15-16).

## SUGGESTIONS TO TEACHERS

Jesus faced temptation, and so do you and every member of your class. Your particular temptations might seem trivial or silly to someone else, and what tempts another might surprise you. But no one is exempt from the lures of the devil. The issue is not whether you will be tempted but how you will respond to temptation when it occurs.

This week's lesson can help you to accomplish two goals. First, it will enable the members of your class to deepen their appreciation of Jesus' mission and ministry. Second, this study will heighten their awareness of the tricks of the tempter in their personal lives.

**1. MISAPPROPRIATION OF POSITION.** Consider how the tempter challenged Jesus to turn the stones into loaves of bread. What could be better than to meet the needs of the hungry? But examine Jesus' answer to the tempter. We humans have other needs besides the requirement for food, important though it is. Thankfully, Jesus realized that God had sent Him to earth to do more than hand out loaves. He rejected a lesser good to meet a greater good that only He could accomplish. Some temptations are to substitute a second-best way when God calls for obedience to a higher good. Jesus realized that obeying the will of His Father in heaven was of foremost priority.

**2. MISUSE OF POWER.** The sensational leap from the pinnacle of the temple would have instantly grabbed the attention of onlookers. And Jesus' supernatural powers would have been recognized by everyone. But this stunt would have been a shortcut to glory. The Messiah would have been misusing His remarkable abilities and gained undesirable admirers (for instance, fans concerned only with seeing spectacular performances). Rather than oblige the devil, Jesus chose to serve God in an honorable way. The Messiah made it clear that He would look to His Father to meet His need for significance in life.

**3. MISPLACEMENT OF PRIORITIES.** The third temptation before Jesus was to take the world as a political ruler right then, without having to carry out His mission to die on the cross for the sins of humankind. Satan was trying to distort Jesus' perspective by making Him focus on worldly power and not on God's priorities.

■ **TOPIC:** Time of Testing

■ **QUESTIONS:** 1. Why do you think Satan tempted Jesus when He was very hungry? 2. What did Jesus prove by resisting the attacks of the devil? 3. Why do some believers deny the reality of temptation in their lives? 4. What can you do to resist temptations? 5. Why is it important for you to say *no* to enticements to sin?

■ **ILLUSTRATIONS:**

**Fighting Temptation this Season at the Malls.** Several years back, news correspondent Patricia McLaughlin wrote: "Christmas seems to be more about shopping than worship. . . . No wonder so many adults dread it. It costs too much, and it's too much work. Even stout hearts quail at the prospect of all that schlepping through the stores and standing in lines and agonizing over whether Aunt Agnes would prefer the pink nightgown or the blue one and whether it'll break little Johnny's heart if you can't find that particular thuggish plastic action figure he's counting on" (*Cape Cod Times*, November 21, 1994).

Ms. McLaughlin is right! Present-day Western culture has, to a large extent, taken the Christ out of Christmas. This season has been turned into a frenzied shopping spree.

**Tested for the Storms.** In the days when ships were built out of wood, great care was taken in selecting the piece of timber for the bow. This timber had to be exceptionally strong, for the bow, as it crashed through the waves, had to absorb the pounding of the seas and withstand the constant pressure of the water. No ordinary tree would do. The shipwrights understood that only a hardwood that had been buffeted and bent by long exposure to harsh winds could be used. Tested and toughened, the gnarled tree was deemed suitable for the critically important part of the ship.

So it is with us. Only the believer who has learned to stand up to the tests of life is fit for the most important spiritual tasks in God's kingdom. We should learn to accept the trials in our lives as opportunities for God to make us stronger and more suitable to carry out His program. Scripture reveals that He wants to use believers who are particularly able to withstand the storms and pressures of life.

**Tested at the Bakery.** Did you ever hear the story about the overweight man who tried to shed some pounds during Lent? He announced to his friends that he was giving up the rich pastries that he picked up at the bakery each day on the way to work. Everything seemed to be going well for the first couple of weeks. His friends asked, "Harry, how do you stand up to the temptation not to stop at the bakery these days?" Harry would piously reply that the Lord helped him to resist his urges.

However, one morning during the third week of Lent, Harry arrived at work with a big sugary coffee cake. His buddies asked why he had given in to his desire. Harry explained, "Well, I was driving past the bakery this morning and saw that luscious array of coffee cakes in the window. I whispered to the Lord, 'God, if You say it's really all right for me to eat one of those coffee cakes, You'll let me find a parking space right in front of the bakery.' " Harry's friends looked at him with keen interest. Harry continued, "Sure enough, on the eighth time around the block, there was a place right there in front of the bakery!"

Temptation is clever and persistent. If we listen long enough to the lures of the devil, we can be duped to think that the Lord is a party to our choices, just as Harry did!

---

■ **FOR YOUTH**  ■ TOPIC: Temptation!
■ QUESTIONS: 1. What is significant about the three temptations Jesus experienced? 2. Why did Jesus refuse to give in to these temptations? 3. What are some temptations in your life? 4. How can God help you to resist these enticements? 5. How can you encourage other believers to say *no* to temptations?

■ ILLUSTRATIONS:

**Succumbed to Temptation.** Eddie Warner wanted a set of walkie-talkies, the top prize for selling the most candy and wrapping paper for his school's PTA. The 11-year-old sixth grader went door to door, and sales were good. He flashed a wad of bills with over 200 hundred dollars to his friends. However, Eddie was a victim of his success. The Toms River, New Jersey boy was found murdered. He had been strangled by a 15 year old who wanted his money. Sadly, this teenage murderer had succumbed to temptation. He simply took what he wanted, despite the fact that he knew it was wrong.

The Gospel of Matthew presents a Savior who resisted temptation. Jesus was tempted like any other human being, but He trusted God for the strength to say *no* to sin. You too can resist temptation with the Lord's help.

**Temptation Costs.** He wanted excitement, attention, respect, and fun. So a McKeesport, Pennsylvania, teenager put in an emergency call to Twin Rivers Emergency Dispatch Center at 10 A.M. on Wednesday, February 11, 1998. He claimed to be a hiker who had lost his footing, stumbled over a hillside, and had fallen into a sink hole. The caller alleged that he did not know where he was, but that he could see the Duquesne-McKeesport Bridge. The phone then went dead.

The call mobilized over 50 people from West Mifflin and Duquesne fire, police, and ambulance companies, as well as a Pennsylvania State Police helicopter. For hours they searched the hillsides.

Then at noon, a call was received at the dispatch center with the caller threatening to blow up McKeesport Area High School. The school complex was immediately evacuated, forcing students into the chilly winter air, including one swimming class that stood shivering in towels.

Police analyzed the dispatch tape and discovered that the voices were the same. The big break came when a teacher overheard the youth bragging to other students about making the calls. Police spoke with the adolescent, who admitted making the calls after a patrolman punched *redial* on the boy's cellular phone and discovered that the 911 center answered. As a result of succumbing to the temptation, the teenager faced two counts of false alarms, filing false reports, and other related charges.

**Madison Avenue Devils.** Researchers at the University of California at San Diego conducted interviews with 1,752 adolescents between the ages of 12 and 17 in 1993 through 1996. The study showed that tobacco advertising and promotions, not peer pressure, lured a significant proportion of the teenagers to start smoking. An author named John Pierce wrote in *The Journal of the American Medical Association* that more than half of the subjects were influenced by strong advertising that had been specifically targeted to entice adolescents. A whopping 83 percent were affected by the advertising behind two of the most popular brands of cigarettes! In short, three times as many people were tempted into smoking by advertising as were by peer pressure.

The devil specifically targets you with various temptations. You are not alone, for Jesus also experienced temptations. He understands what you are experiencing and is ready to help you overcome your sinful desires.

# BIRTH OF JESUS

**BACKGROUND SCRIPTURE:** Matthew 1
**DEVOTIONAL READING:** John 1:1-14

3

**KEY VERSE:** She will bear a son, and you are to name him Jesus, for he will save his people from their sins. Matthew 1:21.

*KING JAMES VERSION*

MATTHEW 1:1 The book of the generation of Jesus Christ, the son of David, the son of Abraham.

2 Abraham begat Isaac; and Isaac begat Jacob; and Jacob begat Judas and his brethren;

3 And Judas begat Phares and Zara of Thamar; and Phares begat Esrom; and Esrom begat Aram;

4 And Aram begat Aminadab; and Aminadab begat Naasson; and Naasson begat Salmon;

5 And Salmon begat Booz of Rachab; and Booz begat Obed of Ruth; and Obed begat Jesse;

6 And Jesse begat David the king; and David the king begat Solomon of her that had been the wife of Urias; . . .

18 Now the birth of Jesus Christ was on this wise: When as his mother Mary was espoused to Joseph, before they came together, she was found with child of the Holy Ghost.

19 Then Joseph her husband, being a just man, and not willing to make her a publick example, was minded to put her away privily.

20 But while he thought on these things, behold, the angel of the Lord appeared unto him in a dream, saying, Joseph, thou son of David, fear not to take unto thee Mary thy wife: for that which is conceived in her is of the Holy Ghost.

21 And she shall bring forth a son, and thou shalt call his name JESUS: for he shall save his people from their sins.

22 Now all this was done, that it might be fulfilled which was spoken of the Lord by the prophet, saying,

23 Behold, a virgin shall be with child, and shall bring forth a son, and they shall call his name Emmanuel, which being interpreted is, God with us.

24 Then Joseph being raised from sleep did as the angel of the Lord had bidden him, and took unto him his wife:

25 And knew her not till she had brought forth her firstborn son: and he called his name JESUS.

*NEW REVISED STANDARD VERSION*

MATTHEW 1:1 An account of the genealogy of Jesus the Messiah, the son of David, the son of Abraham.

2 Abraham was the father of Isaac, and Isaac the father of Jacob, and Jacob the father of Judah and his brothers, 3 and Judah the father of Perez and Zerah by Tamar, and Perez the father of Hezron, and Hezron the father of Aram, 4 and Aram the father of Aminadab, and Aminadab the father of Nahshon, and Nahshon the father of Salmon, 5 and Salmon the father of Boaz by Rahab, and Boaz the father of Obed by Ruth, and Obed the father of Jesse, 6 and Jesse the father of King David. . . .

18 Now the birth of Jesus the Messiah took place in this way. When his mother Mary had been engaged to Joseph, but before they lived together, she was found to be with child from the Holy Spirit. 19 Her husband Joseph, being a righteous man and unwilling to expose her to public disgrace, planned to dismiss her quietly. 20 But just when he had resolved to do this, an angel of the Lord appeared to him in a dream and said, "Joseph, son of David, do not be afraid to take Mary as your wife, for the child conceived in her is from the Holy Spirit. 21 She will bear a son, and you are to name him Jesus, for he will save his people from their sins." 22 All this took place to fulfill what had been spoken by the Lord through the prophet:

23 "Look, the virgin shall conceive and bear a son,
    and they shall name him Emmanuel,"

which means, "God is with us." 24 When Joseph awoke from sleep, he did as the angel of the Lord commanded him; he took her as his wife, 25 but had no marital relations with her until she had borne a son; and he named him Jesus.

## HOME BIBLE READINGS

## BACKGROUND

Matthew, like the other Gospel writers, was an author who carefully selected the material he included in his account of Jesus' life and ministry. The selections that Matthew made were intended to demonstrate that Jesus was the Jewish nation's long-awaited Messiah. Matthew also wrote to show that Jesus was the fulfillment of all for which Israel had hoped.

The Jewishness of Jesus is emphasized in Matthew's Gospel perhaps more than in any other. The writer began his account by presenting Jesus' genealogy. Matthew went back to Abraham, the progenitor of the faith. The writer then traced the line through David, the great king, to show that Jesus was the lawful heir to the throne. Matthew demonstrated that Jesus was the perfect King of Israel.

Matthew, of course, knew that there was more to say about Christ. For example, He is the Son of God. The account of Jesus' birth in the Gospel of Matthew contains the report of the supernatural or miraculous way Mary became pregnant, and how Joseph came to accept her as his wife and her child as coming from the hand of the Lord.

Thankfully, Matthew wrote about these matters with quiet restraint. Unlike crude pagan tales of miraculous appearances of gods and goddesses (such as in the Greek myths), Matthew avoided lurid details and sensational embellishments of Jesus' birth. The beauty of Matthew's report is in the simplicity of the words, *she had borne a son; and he named him Jesus* (1:25).

The Greek proper noun *Iesous* [ee-a-SOOS], which is rendered *Jesus* (1:21), is the equivalent of the Hebrew name *Yeshua* [YESH-you-uh], which means "the Lord will save." In ancient times, Jesus was a common name among the Jews (see Col. 4:11). But when used to refer to the Son of God, the name underscores Jesus' work on earth to save the lost (Mark 1:1; Luke 1:35). In fact, the early church proclaimed that Jesus is the Savior of humankind (Acts 5:31; 13:23).

## NOTES ON THE PRINTED TEXT

The ancient Israelites exercised great care in keeping records of family trees. Matthew traced Jesus' descent from Abraham through the direct royal line of David (1:1). Matthew organized his genealogy into three groups of names with 14 generations in each list. The significance of the number

14 is not clear. But Matthew's attention to numbers, which is a distinctly Hebrew characteristic, is evident throughout his Gospel. The systematic ordering may have been an aid for memorization.

Another possibility is that Matthew was drawing attention to the Davidic emphasis in the names of the genealogy. For example, in the first group, the Davidic throne is established. In the second group, the throne is cast down and deported to Babylon. And in the third group, the throne is confirmed in the coming of the Messiah. Furthermore, a basic covenant is set forth in each of these three periods: the Abrahamic covenant in the first (vss. 2-5), the Davidic covenant in the second (vss. 6-11), and the new covenant in the third (vss. 12-16).

Genealogies tended to be exclusively male. But Matthew's included women, both Jew and Gentile, saint and sinner. Tamar, a Jewess, played a prostitute but was called righteous. Rahab, a Canaanite prostitute, faithfully helped Israel. Ruth, a Moabitess, proved to be a loyal believer, while Bathsheba was not referred to by name, apparently because of her affair with David.

*Now the birth of Jesus the Messiah took place in this way* (1:18). Matthew knew that it was important to explain the nature of Jesus' birth. Joseph and Mary were engaged. The two had entered a legally binding obligation or covenant to marry. Part of the agreement was that the man and woman would be faithful to one another. Infidelity during that period was considered adultery and punishable by death. But prior to their marriage, before the two had lived together, Mary became pregnant. *When his mother Mary had been engaged to Joseph, but before they lived together, she was found to be with child from the Holy Spirit* (1:18).

Matthew revealed that Mary's conception was due to the supernatural work of the Spirit. At first Joseph did not know this. Because he was unwilling to publicly disgrace his fiancée, Joseph decided to quietly divorce Mary for supposedly violating their marriage agreement. *Her husband Joseph, being a righteous man and unwilling to expose her to public disgrace, planned to dismiss her quietly* (1:19).

God intervened to change Joseph's plans. Through a dream, an angel reassured Joseph that the child was from God. Joseph was to enter into marriage with Mary without any reservations. *"Joseph, son of David, do not be afraid to take Mary as your wife, for the child conceived in her is from the Holy Spirit"* (1:20).

The angel also gave Joseph a command. *"She will bear a son, and you are to name him Jesus, for he will save his people from their sins"* (1:21). When the male child was circumcised eight days after His birth, Joseph was to name the boy "Jesus," which is the Greek form of the Hebrew name "Joshua." The name indicated that Jesus came into the world to redeem the lost.

Matthew noted that the birth of Jesus was the fulfillment of the announcement made in Isaiah 7:14 (see Matt. 1:22). The prophet had declared that *the virgin shall conceive and bear a son* (1:23). Truly, God was with His people in Christ.

Joseph heeded the angel and took Mary as his wife (1:24). However, the two had no sexual relations until after the birth of Jesus (1:25).

# SUGGESTIONS TO TEACHERS

The conception and birth of Jesus Christ are supernatural events that defy human logic or reasoning. Use this week's lesson to get your class to shift their attention away from all the cute manger scene ideas about Christmas to the advent of Christ. Also encourage them to consider the significance of the Savior's genealogy and Virgin Birth. Doing this will help Christ's coming to have greater significance for them, perhaps even more so than ever before.

**1. DESCENDANT OF A MIXED GROUP OF ANCESTORS.** Matthew traced Jesus' family history to show His standing as the Messiah of God. We learn that Jesus is a descendant of Abraham, the ancestor of all Jews, and David, Israel's greatest king. Matthew wanted his Jewish readers to know that Jesus was the perfect King who fulfilled the Old Testament prophecies about the Messiah's line. Note that the roster of ancestors includes some interesting characters, such as Rahab, the Jericho prostitute, and Ruth, the Moabitess. From this we see that Jesus is not only the royal Deliverer, but also the Savior of all humankind. We also discover that God's work in history is not limited by human failures or sins, and that He works through ordinary people to accomplish His will.

**2. DREAM OF JOSEPH.** Take time to let the class ponder who Joseph was and what he did. Try to lift him from the obscurity to which he is often consigned by asking your students to describe the feelings this man might have experienced when he learned that his betrothed was pregnant. Don't try to explain away the miraculous aspect of the announcement in the dream, but rather let the details in Matthew's account speak for themselves.

**3. DETERMINATION OF THE NAME.** To Jews, the name of a child was (and still is in most families) extremely important. Jesus' name, which means "the Lord saves," carried immense significance. You could use this information to get the class to discuss what it means to be saved, how Jesus saves people from their sins, and what phony forms of salvation are being promoted today.

**4. DISCLOSURE OF THE DIVINE.** Let the students know that the name "Immanuel" means "God with us." Then comment on the mystery of Jesus' incarnation, namely, that God the Son became a human being and dwelt among us. In the midst of all the silliness of this season of Santas, Rudolphs, little drummer boys, and Frostys, your discussion about Emmanuel will prove to be refreshing!

---

**FOR ADULTS**

■ TOPIC: A Time of Rejoicing

■ QUESTIONS: 1. Why was it important for Matthew to begin his Gospel by noting that Jesus is the Messiah? 2. Why do you think Matthew wanted to stress the miraculous aspect of Jesus' conception and birth? 3. What are some details of Christ's genealogy that you find interesting? 4. How do you think you would have responded if you were in Joseph's situation? 5. In what sense is God with believers today?

**True Joy.** True joy comes from the awareness that this God is in our midst in the person of Jesus. We may not live in enjoyable circumstances. Furthermore, we do not need to be concerned about trying to feel happy. In fact, believers should not think about joy in terms of feeling happy. Joy is not feeling sparkling and chipper. Joy is not having fun. Joy is not getting more playthings or more playtime.

Ironically, our society has multiplied opportunities for pleasure as never before, but we seem to have more difficulty than ever in discovering a true sense of joy. We spent almost two billion dollars on Nintendo games in 1998 for our kids, but they are no more joyful than we were 50 years ago. One parent talked about skimping in order to save $260 for designer clothes for the Barbie doll that would make her daughter have a more joyful Christmas. But I'm certain that little girl will not be any more joyful than my sister was at her age back in the Depression, when my mother provided far simpler things for my sister.

**One Solitary Life.** Here is a man who was born of Jewish parents. He was the child of a peasant woman. He grew up in an obscure village. He worked in a carpenter's shop until He was 30, and then, for three years, He was an itinerant preacher.

This person never wrote a book, He never held a public or religious office, and He never owned a home. He never got married and had a family. He never went to college. He never traveled 500 miles from the place where He was born. He never did any of the things that the world usually associates with greatness. Ultimately, He had no credentials but Himself.

Though the world was made through Him, the world didn't recognize Him. Even in His own land and among His own people, He was not accepted. In fact, while He was still a relatively young man, the tide of popular opinion turned against Him. His closest friends ran away. One of them even denied Him. Another betrayed Him to His enemies.

This person then went through a bogus trial. He was nailed to a cross to die as a despised criminal. His executioners gambled for the one piece of property He had left on earth—His robe. After He died, two of His followers took Him down and laid Him in a borrowed tomb. Within three days, He rose from the dead.

Nineteen wide centuries have come and gone, and today He is the centerpiece of the human race, and the Redeemer of the world. It is fair to say that all the armies that ever marched, and all the navies that were ever built, and all the parliaments that ever sat, and all the kings that ever reigned, put together, have not affected humankind as powerfully as has the solitary life of Jesus of Nazareth.

**Mary's Dream.** Imagine Mary saying, "I had a dream, Joseph, and I don't understand it, but I think it was about a birthday celebration for our Son. The people had been preparing for it for about six weeks. They had decorated the house, and bought new clothes, and had gone shopping many times to buy elaborate gifts. It was peculiar, though, because the presents were for themselves, not for our Son.

"These people wrapped their gifts in beautiful paper, tied them with lovely bows, and stacked them under a tree. Yes, Joseph, the tree was right in their own house, and they decorated the tree with glowing balls and sparkling ornaments. There was a figure on top of the tree that looked like a tiny angel. It was so beautiful, and everyone was laughing and seemed happy. They were all excited about the gifts they were getting, too. But, you know, Joseph, no one had a gift to give to our Son. I don't think they even knew or cared about Him. Not one even mentioned His name. Doesn't it seem odd for people to go through all that trouble to celebrate someone's birthday, if they don't even remember Him?

"I had the strangest feeling, Joseph, that if our Son had gone to the celebration, He would have been intruding. Everything was so beautiful, and everyone was so full of cheer, but it made me want to cry. How sad for Jesus not to be wanted, not even to be recognized at His own birthday party. I'm glad that it was only a dream, Joseph. How terrible it would be if it had actually been real!"

---

**FOR YOUTH** ■ TOPIC: A King Is Born

■ QUESTIONS: 1. Who are some of the key ancestors in Jesus' family tree? 2. What is unusual about the Messiah's birth? 3. How would you describe the people in your "spiritual" family tree? 4. Why is Jesus' birth important to you? 5. Why is His coming important to the world?

■ ILLUSTRATIONS:

**Lived Up to His Name.** John was visiting his grandparents and went to their church. As he left, he shook hands with the minister. When the minister learned John's name, he remarked that one of Jesus' disciples—the one whom He especially loved—had the same first name. The minister also noted that this name had a long and noble tradition in such people as John Wycliffe, John Hus, John Calvin, John Knox, and John Wesley. The elderly pastor asked whether the youth knew what his name meant. When John responded that he did not, the clergyman told him that in Hebrew it meant "God is gracious." The minister gave John something to think about and talk about on his ride back to his grandparents' house.

The child born to Mary received a name to live up to and one that was also an announcement to the world. Let us use this holiday season to proclaim the wonderful truths about Jesus to unsaved family members, friends, neighbors, and work associates.

**What's in a Name?** There is a strange quasi-science called numerology. Numerologists claim that a name gives clues to one's traits and personality. A numerologist takes a person's name and birth date, assigns a numerical value to the letters in the name, adds these to the numbers in the date of birth, and establishes one's key numbers. The numerologist then "interprets" the meaning of these key numbers to describe the individual's personal characteristics. Some people take this nonsense seriously!

Joseph never consulted a numerologist. Instead, an angel of the Lord commanded him to give the unborn child in Mary's womb the name of "Jesus." That name perfectly described the child's purpose and character. As the Gospel of Matthew reveals, Jesus came to earth to redeem the lost from their sins.

**Child's Influence.** Over the winter of 1997–1998, El Niño touched the United States, dumping huge amounts of rain in California and spawning tornadoes in Florida. (El Niño is a Pacific warm water phenomenon that occurs about every seven years.) In California, the rain-saturated ground led to massive landslides. Within one three-week period, almost 300 million dollars of damage was caused in 22 counties. Over 40 deaths occurred in the U.S. during El Niño's February, 1998 rampage.

El Niño literally means "the child." The child promised to Mary and Joseph is truly the one who will change the climate of our lives, our relationships, our communities, and our world. This person is Jesus Christ, and He's the Savior for all people.

**Understood His Name.** Daniel F. Boone, 22, entered Army basic training. The fifth-generation descendant of the legendary frontiersman stated, "I consider it an honor to be named Daniel Boone. You can never live under another person's name without building up your own." Here is a wonderful understanding of names.

Your eternal name is "Christian." You live under another's name. All that you do must build up His name!

# COMING OF THE WISE MEN

**BACKGROUND SCRIPTURE:** Matthew 2
**DEVOTIONAL READING:** Psalm 98

**KEY VERSE:** "Where is the child who has been born king of the Jews? For we observed his star at its rising, and have come to pay him homage." Matthew 2:2.

**4**

### KING JAMES VERSION

MATTHEW 2:1 Now when Jesus was born in Bethlehem of Judæa in the days of Herod the king, behold, there came wise men from the east to Jerusalem,

2 Saying, Where is he that is born King of the Jews? for we have seen his star in the east, and are come to worship him.

3 When Herod the king had heard these things, he was troubled, and all Jerusalem with him.

4 And when he had gathered all the chief priests and scribes of the people together, he demanded of them where Christ should be born.

5 And they said unto him, In Bethlehem of Judæa: for thus it is written by the prophet,

6 And thou Bethlehem, in the land of Juda, art not the least among the princes of Juda: for out of thee shall come a Governor, that shall rule my people Israel.

7 Then Herod, when he had privily called the wise men, enquired of them diligently what time the star appeared.

8 And he sent them to Bethlehem, and said, Go and search diligently for the young child; and when ye have found him, bring me word again, that I may come and worship him also.

9 When they had heard the king, they departed; and, lo, the star, which they saw in the east, went before them, till it came and stood over where the young child was.

10 When they saw the star, they rejoiced with exceeding great joy.

11 And when they were come into the house, they saw the young child with Mary his mother, and fell down, and worshipped him: and when they had opened their treasures, they presented unto him gifts; gold, and frankincense, and myrrh.

12 And being warned of God in a dream that they should not return to Herod, they departed into their own country another way.

### NEW REVISED STANDARD VERSION

MATTHEW 2:1 In the time of King Herod, after Jesus was born in Bethlehem of Judea, wise men from the East came to Jerusalem, 2 asking, "Where is the child who has been born king of the Jews? For we observed his star at its rising, and have come to pay him homage." 3 When King Herod heard this, he was frightened, and all Jerusalem with him; 4 and calling together all the chief priests and scribes of the people, he inquired of them where the Messiah was to be born. 5 They told him, "In Bethlehem of Judea; for so it has been written by the prophet:

6 'And you, Bethlehem, in the land of Judah,
   are by no means least among the rulers of Judah;
   for from you shall come a ruler
   who is to shepherd my people Israel.' "

7 Then Herod secretly called for the wise men and learned from them the exact time when the star had appeared. 8 Then he sent them to Bethlehem, saying, "Go and search diligently for the child; and when you have found him, bring me word so that I may also go and pay him homage." 9 When they had heard the king, they set out; and there, ahead of them, went the star that they had seen at its rising, until it stopped over the place where the child was. 10 When they saw that the star had stopped, they were overwhelmed with joy. 11 On entering the house, they saw the child with Mary his mother; and they knelt down and paid him homage. Then, opening their treasure chests, they offered him gifts of gold, frankincense, and myrrh. 12 And having been warned in a dream not to return to Herod, they left for their own country by another road.

| | | |
|---|---|---|
| *Monday, Dec. 20* | Luke 2:1-7 | *The Birth of Jesus* |
| *Tuesday, Dec. 21* | Luke 2:8-20 | *Jesus' Birth Announced to Shepherds* |
| *Wednesday, Dec. 22* | Luke 2:21-27 | *Jesus Is Presented in the Temple* |
| *Thursday, Dec. 23* | Luke 2:28-38 | *Simeon and Anna Praise God* |
| *Friday, Dec. 24* | Matthew 2:1-6 | *Wise Men Inquire about Jesus' Birth* |
| *Saturday, Dec. 25* | Matthew 2:7-12 | *Wise Men Visit and Honor Jesus* |
| *Sunday, Dec. 26* | Matthew 2:13-18 | *Herod's Wrath Is Unleashed* |

## BACKGROUND

The familiar carol begins, "We three kings of Orient are." But there are at least two misconceptions in that line. First we don't know how many wise men came and worshiped the Christ child. Because three gifts—gold, frankincense, and myrrh—were presented, tradition has it that there were just three Magi [MAY-jeye] who traveled to Bethlehem from the East. Second, these visitors were not kings. While the magi were deeply respected in their homeland, they did not rule as monarchs.

So who were these gift-bearing *wise men from the East* (2:1)? They were members of an ancient priestly caste of scholars. In the ancient world, these learned men were respected as the research scientists of their day. They studied medicine, mathematics, and astronomy. Some magi examined nature and were proficient in what we know as the natural sciences. Other magi expanded their studies of the movement of the planets to include the practice of astrology.

Leaving their homeland, the Magi traveled at great expense and effort to Jerusalem to find out more about the promised King, whose unmistakable sign they had seen in the sky. They learned from ancient Jewish sources that the Messiah's birth would occur in Bethlehem, as recorded in Micah 5:2. They were undoubtedly glad for the opportunity to go to Bethlehem so that they could pay homage to the newborn King of the Jews.

Bethlehem was a village located on the edge of the Judean desert about five miles southwest of Jerusalem. Bethlehem was situated on a high ridge of Judean mountains about 2500 feet above sea level. The town was near the main road linking Hebron and Egypt. The climate of Bethlehem was somewhat Mediterranean; however, the town's higher elevation moderated the summer temperatures it experienced. This milder climate along with fertile surrounding fields made Bethlehem ideal for growing grapes and figs and grazing sheep and goats.

## NOTES ON THE PRINTED TEXT

*In the time of King Herod, after Jesus was born in Bethlehem of Judea, wise men from the East came to Jerusalem* (2:1). The birth of Jesus took place toward the end of the reign of Herod the king, who was also known as Herod the Great (37–4 B.C.). (Many Bible scholars think that the birth of Christ took place in the winter of 6–5 B.C.) Herod's reign was characterized by violence and bloodshed. Throughout his rule, he remained a loyal ally of Rome.

Sometime after the Messiah's birth, the wise men from the east arrived in Jerusalem. They may have been Gentiles from a priestly, royal background who served as official advisers to a ruling monarch. Their place of origin could have been Arabia, Mesopotamia, or Persia. They had been observing the skies and had witnessed a celestial phenomenon unlike anything they had seen before.

*"Where is the child who has been born king of the Jews? For we observed his star at its rising, and have come to pay him homage"* (2:2). There are differing views regarding the star referred to by the Magi. Some think the presence of the object was a natural phenomenon timed by God to attract notice, while others think it was a purely supernatural phenomenon (namely, one that God had miraculously produced). Some think the phrase *we observed his star at its rising* suggests that the Magi took note of the object as it appeared in the nighttime sky and were intrigued by it. Others render the phrase as "we saw his star in the east," and take this to mean that the Magi were still east of Palestine whey they had seen the object.

King Herod wanted no possible rivals to his throne. That is why he became distressed when the magi asked about the King of the Jews. Herod's uneasiness also caused the entire city of Jerusalem to be disturbed (2:3), for they knew how murderous Herod could be when he became paranoid.

Herod wanted to know what was going on. Thus, he assembled a team of religious experts to find out where the Messiah would be born (2:4). Bethlehem in Judea was the consensus of the Jewish scholars. Their answer was based on the prophecy of Micah 5:2, which had been given hundreds of years earlier (Matt. 2:5). Despite the village's small size and apparent insignificance, out of it would come a Ruler who would shepherd God's people (2:6).

Herod summoned the Magi to talk privately with them. The king may have held a secret meeting to avoid arousing the fears and suspicions of the people. Possibly after some questioning, he determined the time when the star had appeared (2:7). Herod then sent the Magi to Bethlehem with his permission to search for the Christ child. When they had located Him, they were to report their findings to Herod. He explained that he too wanted to visit Jesus and pay homage to Him (2:8). This excuse was bogus, however. The king's ultimate desire was to murder Jesus, whom he feared was a rival.

The Magi left Herod to find the Messiah. The prominent star they had previously seen went ahead of them until it *stopped over the place where the child was* (2:9). Perhaps the star had been low enough in the sky to indicate the approximate location of the house. The Magi were filled with joy over the sight of the unusual star that had appeared (2:10).

After the Magi had entered the house, they saw Jesus with Mary, His mother. Unlike Herod, who wanted to murder the Messiah, the Magi prostrated themselves in worship to the King of the Jews. After paying homage to Christ, they opened their belongings and gave Jesus their gifts of gold (a precious metal), frankincense (a fragrant gum resin), and myrrh (an aromatic gum resin; 2:11).

Herod had previously told the Magi to report their findings to him. But God warned them in a dream not to return to Herod. Perhaps they had learned that the king had sinister plans. They decided to return to *their own country by another road* (2:12).

## SUGGESTIONS TO TEACHERS

The visit of the Magi has become a great holiday throughout Latin America. For example, in the Spanish-speaking world, the Feast of the Three Kings comes after December 25th, and is the occasion of gift-giving and celebration. After the sentimental mish-mash of Santa Claus and the commercialized celebration of Jesus' birth, the members of your class might welcome the Latino touch of focusing on the Magi's visit to Bethlehem.

**1. SEARCH BY THE MAGI.** Relate to your students that we don't know much about the wise men. According to church tradition, they were individuals of high position from Parthia, near the site of ancient Babylon. Despite their official status and considerable learning, the Magi were humble enough to bow before Jesus! Wise men and women from the West must do no less!

**2. SUSPICIONS OF HEROD.** Herod felt threatened by the news of the arrival of the newborn King. Because Herod was an insecure ruler, he could tolerate no rivals. He thus tried to find and murder the Christ child. Have the class consider whether they are uneasy about Jesus being the Lord of their life. Explain that those who truly love Him submit to His will.

**3. SIGNIFICANCE OF BETHLEHEM.** Although Bethlehem now is world-renowned, at the time of Jesus' birth it was dismissed as an insignificant town. Jerusalem was the religious capital for the Jews, and Rome was the political capital of the mighty empire. Let the students know that God's ways often differ from our ways. He works through that which seems insignificant so that He might get all the glory for His marvelous work in our lives.

**4. SCENE OF JOY.** Finding Jesus was the fulfillment of the Magi's quest. With deep gratitude and joy, they worshiped Him and gave Him costly gifts. When we encounter the Savior-King, we too must humbly worship Him with an attitude of thanksgiving and joy.

**FOR ADULTS**

■ TOPIC: Time of Worshiping

■ QUESTIONS: 1. What was miraculous about the appearance of the star? 2. How was God's mighty power at work in the visit of the Magi? 3. What does it mean to worship the Savior? 4. Why is it important to be filled with joy and gratitude as you pay homage to Him? 5. How might you encourage others to worship Jesus as Lord?

## ■ ILLUSTRATIONS:

**Familiar Faces at the Manger.** An important early work by the Florentine painter Sandro Botticelli (1445–1510) was *Adoration of the Magi*. He painted it shortly after 1470, at the commission of a wealthy Italian merchant, who wanted to prominently display the work in the church of Santa Maria Novella. (Today the painting hangs in the Uffizi, a sixteenth-century Florentine palace.)

In the Botticelli painting, the Magi are given the faces of the Medici. (This was an Italian family that directed the affairs of Florence from the fifteenth to the seventeenth centuries.) Old Cosimo, the head of the family, kneels before the Christ child and holds Jesus' tiny foot in his hand. To the right of Cosimo, engaged in serious conversation, are his two sons, Giovanni, who died prematurely, and Piero, who succeeded his father as the head of state. The young man at the extreme left, somewhat arrogant in his bearing, is Lorenzo the Magnificent, while on the right is Giuliano de Medici (identifiable by his dark hair and downcast eyes), who would soon lose his life in the Pazzi Conspiracy. The young man at the extreme right, gazing unabashedly at us, is the painter himself, in his mid-twenties.

Above Giuliano and Botticelli is a remarkable succession of human faces watching the event. The child is illumined by the star of Bethlehem. The rude shed in which the birth has occurred is set amidst magnificent ancient ruins.

We may smile at the way Botticelli painted the faces of the famous Medici into the scene of the Magi at the manger. But we should remind ourselves that we too, despite our vast learning and technological superiority, must kneel in homage before the Messiah. Botticelli correctly understood that the advent of Christ was a pivotal event in redemptive history.


**Worshiping Celebrity over Substance.** Two people died within days of each other in September, 1997: They were Princess Diana and Mother Teresa. The way the news media covered these deaths reflects the value system of our time.

On the morning after the death of Mother Teresa, her photograph and the news of her passing occupied half the space and a less prominent position on the front page of *The Washington Post* than did a layout of two stories and a photo about Diana, Princess of Wales, who had perished six days earlier.

A day later, on the morning after Diana's burial ceremonies and the second day after the death of the Nobel Prize-winning nun, *The New York Times* gave the funeral of the former member of Britain's royal family two-thirds of its front page and three additional ad-free pages inside the main news section. The Times published six staff stories on the London rites, but barely found space on page 6—next to a large ad for the fall designer collection at Henri Bendel, a Fifth Avenue shop—for an Associated Press story from Calcutta. It reported that "crowds of weeping people gathered in the rain here today to pay homage to . . . the Roman Catholic nun who served as a tireless minister to the poorest of the world's poor."

Two French newspapers came closest to getting it right. *The Liberation* said, "Diana died as she had lived, through the baleful spells of the dream machine. . . . What an extraordinary modern tale. The demiurge of communication provoked the death of its own creation, and the public that it was trying to satisfy cries 'murder.' "

*Le Monde* said that Diana was the "incarnation of an epoch that practices, sometimes to the point of madness, the cult of the body, of hedonism, of physical beauty, an epoch in which the media are actors, models, grand couturiers. . . . The princess moved in the global media village in which celebrities are by turn victims, accomplices, and manipulators of the press."

There is a significant moral cost to western society when it worships people who are rich and famous. When glamour or charisma is valued over devotion and sacrifice, the real reason for living is obscured. Whom do you really worship? Celebrities? Princesses? Or Christ?

---

**FOR YOUTH**

■ TOPIC: Search Until You Find

■ QUESTIONS: 1. Why were the Magi looking for the Christ child? 2. How did the Magi respond to God's warning? 3. What makes Christ different from all other people? 4. What attitude should you have as you worship Christ? 5. When was the last time you joined others to pay homage to Jesus?

■ ILLUSTRATIONS:

**On the Downside?** In the winter of 1998, Fran Drescher, star of television's *The Nanny,* appeared on *The Tonight Show.* Host Jay Leno asked her what was new in her life. Drescher related a harrowing tale of slicing open her finger while cutting a muffin. She described all the gory details, including the treatment by the paramedics. The story, though sensational, was completely fabricated.

Sadly, Drescher's deceit is commonplace. *Time* magazine's Richard Schichel noted that this sort of fabrication has reached epidemic proportions. Truth seems to be on the downslide.

The jettisoning of truth is not something new. When the wise men visited Herod, he lied when he said that he wanted to worship the Christ child. Thankfully, God revealed to the Magi that Herod was lying and warned them not to return to the king.

**The Voice of God.** My father had a practice that was somewhat exasperating to me as a teenager. I would ask him whether I could do something, or go somewhere, or participate in some activity. Instead of making my decision for me, he would often answer, "Let your conscience be your guide." Though I was looking for an easy way out, my dad forced me to take responsibility for my actions.

My dad's response presupposed that I have a conscience. His answer also assumed that I had the training and background to know the difference between right and wrong. Moreover, his response presumed that I had the ability to apply different rules to specific situations. My dad was right, for he knew that my conscience was the voice of God in my soul (see Rom. 2:14-15).

God wants you to do what is right. When faced with a difficult or morally perplexing situation (such as the Magi experienced), turn to Scripture for guidance and let the Lord use it to speak to your soul about what you should do.

**Governmental Deceit.** On April 9, 1997, the U.S. government apologized to eight African American men in Tuskegee, Alabama, whose syphilis had gone untreated as part of a federal study. Four of the survivors had come forward with their account after the government apologized to victims of secret radiation experiments.

In the Tuskegee incident, the U.S. Public Health Service withheld treatment from 399 men between 1932 to 1972 to see how syphilis spread and how it killed. For 40 years the men were not told that they had the disease. They were also not given penicillin, which is the standard medical treatment.

The revelation in 1972 forced changes in the government's research practices. It also generated a mistrust of public health efforts among African Americans that lingers to this day. A class action lawsuit paid out $10 million to the victims and their heirs.

Governments and leaders can deceive. The U.S. government deceived hundreds of innocent people. Herod tried to deceive a group of wise men. Thankfully, most deceptions are eventually exposed, as the Tuskegee incident and the Magi account both illustrate.

# THE TWELVE DISCIPLES

**BACKGROUND SCRIPTURE:** Matthew 4:18-22; 9:9-12; 10:1-4
**DEVOTIONAL READING:** Matthew 10:5-15

**KEY VERSE:** Follow me, and I will make you fish for people. Matthew 4:19.

## KING JAMES VERSION

MATTHEW 4:18 And Jesus, walking by the sea of Galilee, saw two brethren, Simon called Peter, and Andrew his brother, casting a net into the sea: for they were fishers.

19 And he saith unto them, Follow me, and I will make you fishers of men.

20 And they straightway left their nets, and followed him.

21 And going on from thence, he saw other two brethren, James the son of Zebedee, and John his brother, in a ship with Zebedee their father, mending their nets; and he called them.

22 And they immediately left the ship and their father, and followed him. . . .

9:9 And as Jesus passed forth from thence, he saw a man, named Matthew, sitting at the receipt of custom: and he saith unto him, Follow me. And he arose, and followed him.

10 And it came to pass, as Jesus sat at meat in the house, behold, many publicans and sinners came and sat down with him and his disciples.

11 And when the Pharisees saw it, they said unto his disciples, Why eateth your Master with publicans and sinners?

12 But when Jesus heard that, he said unto them, They that be whole need not a physician, but they that are sick. . . .

10:1 And when he had called unto him his twelve disciples, he gave them power against unclean spirits, to cast them out, and to heal all manner of sickness and all manner of disease.

2 Now the names of the twelve apostles are these; The first, Simon, who is called Peter, and Andrew his brother; James the son of Zebedee, and John his brother;

3 Philip, and Bartholomew; Thomas, and Matthew the publican; James the son of Alphæus, and Lebbæus, whose surname was Thaddæus;

4 Simon the Canaanite, and Judas Iscariot, who also betrayed him.

## NEW REVISED STANDARD VERSION

MATTHEW 4:18 As he walked by the Sea of Galilee, he saw two brothers, Simon, who is called Peter, and Andrew his brother, casting a net into the sea—for they were fishermen. 19 And he said to them, "Follow me, and I will make you fish for people." 20 Immediately they left their nets and followed him. 21 As he went from there, he saw two other brothers, James son of Zebedee and his brother John, in the boat with their father Zebedee, mending their nets, and he called them. 22 Immediately they left the boat and their father, and followed him. . . .

9:9 As Jesus was walking along, he saw a man called Matthew sitting at the tax booth; and he said to him, "Follow me." And he got up and followed him.

10 And as he sat at dinner in the house, many tax collectors and sinners came and were sitting with him and his disciples. 11 When the Pharisees saw this, they said to his disciples, "Why does your teacher eat with tax collectors and sinners?" 12 But when he heard this, he said, "Those who are well have no need of a physician, but those who are sick." . . .

10:1 Then Jesus summoned his twelve disciples and gave them authority over unclean spirits, to cast them out, and to cure every disease and every sickness. 2 These are the names of the twelve apostles: first, Simon, also known as Peter, and his brother Andrew; James son of Zebedee, and his brother John; 3 Philip and Bartholomew; Thomas and Matthew the tax collector; James son of Alphaeus, and Thaddaeus; 4 Simon the Cananaean, and Judas Iscariot, the one who betrayed him.

| | | |
|---|---|---|
| *Monday, Dec. 27* | Matthew 4:18-22 | *Jesus Calls the First Disciples* |
| *Tuesday, Dec. 28* | Matthew 9:9-13 | *Jesus Calls Matthew* |
| *Wednesday, Dec. 29* | Matthew 10:1-4 | *Authority Conferred upon the Disciples* |
| *Thursday, Dec. 30* | Matthew 10:5-15 | *The Twelve Proclaim God's Kingdom* |
| *Friday, Dec. 31* | Matthew 10:16-25 | *Disciples Told of Coming Persecutions* |
| *Saturday, Jan. 1* | Matthew 10:26-33 | *The Disciples Told Not to Fear* |
| *Sunday, Jan. 2* | Matthew 10:34—11:1 | *Not Peace, But a Sword* |

## BACKGROUND

When Jesus had heard that the authorities had arrested and executed John the Baptist, He left Judea and returned to Galilee (4:12). He went to Capernaum, which was beside the Sea of Galilee, and used the town as His base of operations (4:13). As He went about preaching, He commanded people to repent, *for the kingdom of heaven has come near* (4:17).

Rabbis in the first century A.D. often had a circle of students who came to them for instruction. In this week's lesson, we learn that Jesus also had a group of followers. But unlike other disciples, these ones were anything but stellar material. From rough commercial fishermen to chiseling tax collectors, the 12 Jesus chose as His pupils seemed hardly qualified to carry on His work. But despite outward appearances, all but Judas eventually proved to be faithful to the Lord.

Being a true follower of Christ was demanding. Jesus' disciples not only agreed to obey the Savior but also to leave all things for His sake. They both believed in Him and served Him as a slave would his master. The followers of Jesus sought to be like Him in their thoughts and actions. Their desire was to abide in His words and heed His commands.

The disciples of Christ did not merely perpetuate His teachings, transmit His sayings, or imitate His life. They bore witness to the Savior. Jesus was not merely a teacher or philosopher to His followers. He was their Lord. Whatever He asked of them, they willingly did.

## NOTES ON THE PRINTED TEXT

Matthew related an incident in which Jesus had been walking along the shore of the Sea of Galilee. The Messiah noticed two brothers named Simon (also named Peter) and Andrew hard at work. They were fishermen, and they had been casting their nets into the Sea of Galilee (4:18).

Jesus summoned these two brothers to follow Him, or become His disciples. If they did so, they would be fishing *for people* (4:19). By this Christ meant that they would be winning other converts to Him. Without a moment's hesitation, Simon and Andrew abandoned their nets and accepted Christ's invitation to become His disciples (4:20).

As Jesus continued to walk farther down the shoreline of the Sea of Galilee, He saw two other brothers, *James son of Zebedee and his brother John* (4:21). These men evidently had been fishing in their boats and had returned to shore.

Zebedee and his two sons were in their boat getting their nets ready for the next time they would go out fishing. This advance preparation involved repairing any broken portions, washing the nets, and hanging them to dry.

Jesus invited James and John to follow Him. Perhaps He summoned them the way He had Simon and Andrew. Their response was similar. When they heard the Messiah's call, the sons of Zebedee immediately left their father in the boat with his hired servants (Mark 1:20) and became Christ's disciples (Matt. 4:22).

On another occasion, as Jesus was walking through the town of Capernaum, He saw a tax collector named Matthew sitting at the booth where he gathered tolls and customs (9:9). Matthew was surnamed Levi (Luke 5:27) and was the son Alphaeus (Mark 2:14).

In Jesus' day, the Romans used tax farmers to collect indirect levies (for example, tolls and customs) from the people. It was the job of tax farmers to obtain the largest amount of money possible for Rome. They would do so by employing residents from the local population (such as Matthew) as tax collectors. Those who wanted the job had to bid for the position. The person with the highest offer was allowed to collect tariffs and tolls in a designated area.

In order to make a profit, tax farmers and collectors would charge several times more than what the Roman government required. The desire for personal gain would invariably lead to the exorbitant inflation of tolls and customs. Each person involved in the tax collection process would greedily pocket some of the excess money being charged.

Undoubtedly, Matthew had a lucrative business. Nevertheless, when Jesus said, *"Follow me"* (Matt. 9:9), he immediately went with the Savior. Matthew demonstrated the sincerity of his decision by hosting a large banquet in his house (Luke 5:29). This would have given his associates an opportunity to meet Jesus (Matt. 9:10).

As Jesus dined with Matthew, He ate with *tax collectors and sinners* (9:11). The religious leaders considered sinners to be non-practicing Jews. They thus were unclean and unworthy of any association. The Pharisees, not understanding why Jesus would befriend these moral outcasts, began to complain (Luke 5:30) and asked the Savior's disciples for an explanation (Matt. 9:11). The religious leaders had failed to realize that they, like all people, were sinners in God's sight.

Jesus either overheard the Pharisees' question or was told it by His followers. Instead of becoming defensive, He explained, *"Those who are well have no need of a physician, but those who are sick"* (9:12). By this He meant it was not the upright who needed His healing touch, but rather those who were spiritually ill.

In 10:1-4, we read about Jesus' choosing of the 12 disciples. He *gave them authority over unclean spirits, to cast them out, and to cure every disease and every sickness* (10:1). Jesus delegated His power to the Twelve to show that He and His kingdom controlled the physical and spiritual realms, the effects of sin, and the efforts of Satan.

## SUGGESTIONS TO TEACHERS

We have tended to regard Jesus' disciples (except for Judas) either as a crew of super-Christians or as a collection of bearded look-alikes in medieval art. Probably few in your class can name more than a couple of the Twelve. Use this opportunity to reintroduce your students to them.

**1. CALLING THE COMMON TYPES.** Jesus neither selected the brainiest from the groves of Athens' academe nor the most pious from the precincts of the Jerusalem temple. Jesus bypassed the wealthy from Alexandria and the powerful from Rome. Instead, He chose a group of mostly ordinary people. Look at the backgrounds of these men. What an unlikely group to carry out the work that Jesus wanted them to perform! Remind the class that Jesus calls ordinary persons like us, just as He called fishermen and tax collectors, to do His work.

**2. CONFOUNDING THE CRITICS.** Have your students take a close look at Matthew, the tax collector whom Jesus chose to be one of the Twelve. Jesus' opponents criticized Him for associating with such dubious people as Matthew. The religious leaders were more concerned with their own appearance of holiness than with helping people. But God is concerned with all people, including those who are sinful and hurting. That's why Jesus insisted on reaching sinners. Discuss the implications of Jesus' calling Matthew and His reply to His critics.

**3. CONFERRING AUTHORITY.** Explain that Jesus conferred extraordinary authority on ordinary people to do His work. Then let your students know that we serve the same Messiah today. He can use anyone, no matter how insignificant he or she might appear to be.

**4. COUNTING THE CREW.** The Twelve weren't drafted or forced into service. Rather, Jesus chose each disciple to serve Him in a special way. Likewise, Jesus wants every member of your class to follow Him and be committed to doing His will. He doesn't twist their arms to get them to submit. Instead, He wants them to respond willingly to His summons.

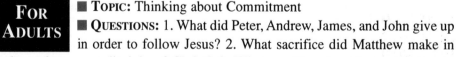

**FOR ADULTS**

■ **TOPIC:** Thinking about Commitment

■ **QUESTIONS:** 1. What did Peter, Andrew, James, and John give up in order to follow Jesus? 2. What sacrifice did Matthew make in order to become a disciple of Christ? 3. What sacrifice does Jesus call you to make to be His faithful follower? 4. What are some obstacles you have to overcome to heed the call of Jesus to be His disciple? 5. Who are some believers whom you would consider to be faithful followers of Christ?

■ **ILLUSTRATIONS:**

**Called to Commitment.** The Calvary Chapel association has caught the essence of Jesus' call to His original disciples by training lay persons to live out their Christian commitment. Founded in 1965 by Chuck Smith, Calvary Chapel now claims over 600 congregations in the United States and another hundred world-wide, including the former Soviet bloc. Chuck Smith and his fellow pastors stress strong lay leadership, and they plant new churches by sending these lay people as a small core from parent churches. The leadership often quote the following slogan: GOD DOES NOT CALL THE QUALIFIED; HE QUALIFIES THE CALLED. Are those in your class aware of the truth of this saying?

**What Kind of Commitment?** The Roper Center for Public Opinion Research at the University of Connecticut publishes a journal entitled *Public Perspective*. In it the Center shows the results of careful polls carried out by George Gallup. One survey a couple of years ago indicated what Gallup called "gaps" in the religious affairs by Americans. For instance, "the ethics gap" showed the disturbing difference between what people said and what they did.

Gallup also identified what he labeled "the knowledge gap." He pointed out the huge difference between what persons in this country claim to believe and their appalling lack of the most basic knowledge about that their faith.

The third was "the church gap." Gallup found that Americans tended to view their faith mostly as a matter between themselves and the Lord, and not tied to or affected by any congregation or religious institution. They were not influenced by the church or any form of organized religion, and saw no need to be committed to any faith community.

Gallup summed up his report by suggesting that Americans want the fruits of faith but few of its obligations. Of the list of 19 social values tested in the polls, "following God's will" ranked low on the list, coming after "happiness, satisfaction, and a sense of accomplishment."

**What Kind of Service?** "I'm in the Lord's service, too," the man announced loudly, trying to impress a saintly visiting missionary. The man's wife, who knew the big-mouth better than anyone else, chimed in, "Yeah, the secret service." Is your commitment to Christ evident to those closest to you?

---

■ **TOPIC:** Follow Me

■ **QUESTIONS:** 1. Why would the disciples whom Jesus called make such big sacrifices to follow Him? 2. What sorts of things were the Twelve called to do? 3. What aspect of following Christ scares you the most? 4. What aspect of being Jesus' disciple excites you the most? 5. What would prevent you from being a committed follower of Christ?

■ **ILLUSTRATIONS:**

**Committed.** Maura Donohue and Carla Sherred were juniors at Thomas Jefferson High School in Pleasant Hills, Pennsylvania. Both took a day off from school to board buses and ride to Washington, D.C., to participate in an important religious rally. They joined a group at 5:30 A.M. for worship and then rode to the nation's capital. The two said they had a strong passion for their organization's moral cause. Maura and Carla are two youth committed to making a difference in their community.

Jesus called people to become His disciples and commit themselves to His cause. You also have been called to discipleship. Support it as much as these two young people have chosen to support their religious group's cause.

**Showcased.** There are good paying jobs for high school and college graduates, especially those competent in math and English. Sadly, many young people do not meet potential employers in person. In January 1998, Century III Mall in Pittsburgh hosted an Employee Showcase in order to bring the two groups together. Students from six school districts participated in the event. Many of these students had already participated in individual Career Days programs at their respective high schools, which had enabled them to explore various vocational options.

Jesus made the effort to meet potential disciples in person. He then called several fishermen to follow Him. He also called others such as Matthew, who was a tax collector, to be His disciples. Each willingly accepted the challenge to learn from Jesus and tell others about Him.

**Taking a Stand.** On March 25, 1997, Amy Stolar, 18, and Jamie Huwar, 16, were preparing to attend the National Honor Society induction ceremony at Ambridge High School in Ambridge, Pennsylvania. A few hours before the ceremony, Principal Dave Perry approached the two girls and five others and ordered them to go home and change their clothes. He claimed that, according to "tradition," the young women had to wear dresses. All of the girls were in pants suits. Stolar and Huwar refused. The girls were sent to gym class and not allowed at the induction ceremony.

The young women went to the school board. They pointed out that all seven girls were honor students, and that this ceremony was to praise them for their leadership and their character. They also pointed out that no dress codes had been established. The letter that had been mailed stated only that students were to wear "dress clothes." The board agreed and ordered the ceremony to be repeated with everyone in attendance.

If these two young women could be so committed to a cause such as being treated fairly by their principal, how much more should you actively support and demonstrate your commitment to Jesus? He has called you to follow Him wholeheartedly. You should do so with equal enthusiasm and commitment.

**Everyone Has Seen It.** In 1998 the movie *Titanic* outperformed all the other movies at the box office. One reason is that teenagers went to the movie over and over again. Exit surveys showed that many of those in attendance were repeat customers. In the middle-school age group, a child who had not seen the movie was simply out of the loop, a situation that most students want to avoid. Erica Mignogna and Elene Tyler, both 14, had seen the movie five times. Asked why they would see it repeatedly, they responded simply because their friends were all seeing it.

Youth want to belong to something, whether it is a club or a group that has seen a movie. Jesus has called you to be one of His disciples. Accept His invitation and join His group. Also, get involved and make a difference!

# TEACHINGS ON PRAYER

**BACKGROUND SCRIPTURE:** Matthew 6:1-15
**DEVOTIONAL READING:** Luke 11:1-13

**KEY VERSE:** Whenever you pray, go into your room and shut the door and pray to your Father who is in secret; and your Father who sees in secret will reward you. Matthew 6:6.

*KING JAMES VERSION*

MATTHEW 6:1 Take heed that ye do not your alms before men, to be seen of them: otherwise ye have no reward of your Father which is in heaven.

2 Therefore when thou doest thine alms, do not sound a trumpet before thee, as the hypocrites do in the synagogues and in the streets, that they may have glory of men. Verily I say unto you, They have their reward.

3 But when thou doest alms, let not thy left hand know what thy right hand doeth:

4 That thine alms may be in secret: and thy Father which seeth in secret himself shall reward thee openly.

5 And when thou prayest, thou shalt not be as the hypocrites are: for they love to pray standing in the synagogues and in the corners of the streets, that they may be seen of men. Verily I say unto you, They have their reward.

6 But thou, when thou prayest, enter into thy closet, and when thou hast shut thy door, pray to thy Father which is in secret; and thy Father which seeth in secret shall reward thee openly.

7 But when ye pray, use not vain repetitions, as the heathen do: for they think that they shall be heard for their much speaking.

8 Be not ye therefore like unto them: for your Father knoweth what things ye have need of, before ye ask him.

9 After this manner therefore pray ye: Our Father which art in heaven, Hallowed be thy name.

10 Thy kingdom come. Thy will be done in earth, as it is in heaven.

11 Give us this day our daily bread.

12 And forgive us our debts, as we forgive our debtors.

13 And lead us not into temptation, but deliver us from evil: For thine is the kingdom, and the power, and the glory, for ever. Amen.

14 For if ye forgive men their trespasses, your heavenly Father will also forgive you:

15 But if ye forgive not men their trespasses, neither will your Father forgive your trespasses.

*NEW REVISED STANDARD VERSION*

MATTHEW 6:1 "Beware of practicing your piety before others in order to be seen by them; for then you have no reward from your Father in heaven.

2 "So whenever you give alms, do not sound a trumpet before you, as the hypocrites do in the synagogues and in the streets, so that they may be praised by others. Truly I tell you, they have received their reward. 3 But when you give alms, do not let your left hand know what your right hand is doing, 4 so that your alms may be done in secret; and your Father who sees in secret will reward you.

5 "And whenever you pray, do not be like the hypocrites; for they love to stand and pray in the synagogues and at the street corners, so that they may be seen by others. Truly I tell you, they have received their reward. 6 But whenever you pray, go into your room and shut the door and pray to your Father who is in secret; and your Father who sees in secret will reward you.

7 "When you are praying, do not heap up empty phrases as the Gentiles do; for they think that they will be heard because of their many words. 8 Do not be like them, for your Father knows what you need before you ask him.

9 "Pray then in this way:
Our Father in heaven,
hallowed be your name.
10 Your kingdom come.
Your will be done,
on earth as it is in heaven.
11 Give us this day our daily bread.
12 And forgive us our debts,
as we also have forgiven our debtors.
13 And do not bring us to the time of trial,
but rescue us from the evil one.
14 For if you forgive others their trespasses, your heavenly Father will also forgive you; 15 but if you do not forgive others, neither will your Father forgive your trespasses.

## HOME BIBLE READINGS

## BACKGROUND

One of the dangers of practicing a religious tradition is the desire to show off one's piety. Exhibitionists crop up in every faith community. As this week's lesson shows, the Judaism of Jesus' day had its share of people who paraded their holiness in public.

Many Jewish prayers were (and are) beautiful expressions of devotion. The problem was not always in the prayers but in the participants. In some cases, the required recitations of long prayers and short prayers three times a day became empty rote. Some who were praying these lovely petitions rattled them off without thinking. Their main desire was to be seen and heard by others. Some rabbis preached against such empty formality, but the practice continued.

Some on the Jerusalem streets also took pride in offering public prayers to God. They uttered long, windy addresses that were characterized by ornate language. One old Hebrew prayer actually began with 16 different adjectives to describe the Almighty's name. And some worshipers delighted in mumbling these words over and over, often before awed spectators.

Jesus insisted that His followers avoid any forms of ostentatious piety. Part of what we know as the Sermon on the Mount records the Messiah's warnings against hypocrisy in praying.

To aid His disciples in praying, Jesus offered a model prayer. Rabbis sometimes gave a prayer for their students, and this is apparently what Christ did too. But the so-called Lord's Prayer excelled by summarizing the kind of things a genuine worshiper of God would want to say while praying. This model prayer can be repeated in 15 seconds, but it takes a lifetime to understand fully!

## NOTES ON THE PRINTED TEXT

In Matthew 5:20, Jesus warned that unless a person's righteousness exceeded that of Israel's religious leaders, one could not enter the heavenly kingdom. Christ stressed that it was inadequate to obey God outwardly but not let Him transform one's attitude and actions. Internal conformity to the spirit of the law was just as vital as an external compliance to the letter of the law.

In 6:1-18, Jesus showed how the righteousness of the scribes and Pharisees was deficient in three areas: charitable deeds (vss. 1-4), prayer (vss. 5-15), and fasting (vss. 16-18). This week's lesson focuses on the first two categories.

When certain religious leaders performed their acts of *piety* (6:1), they sought to win the praise of the people. Jesus condemned such self-serving motives. He declared that good deeds should be done with no thought of being admired. When engaging in religious activities, the motives of Jesus' followers were to remain pure. Otherwise, they could expect to receive no reward from their heavenly Father. The acclaim they obtained from others would be their only reward.

When these religious leaders performed a charitable deed, a trumpet blast would announce it to the public *in the synagogues and in the streets* (6:2). In this way the leaders obtained praise from the people. Jesus condemned such pretense. The term rendered *hypocrites* had its origins in Greek theater, and described a character who wore a mask. In this verse, hypocrites were those who claimed to have a relationship with God but who were self-seeking and self-deceived.

Jesus encouraged His followers to give to those who were impoverished. He cautioned, however, *do not let your left hand know what your right hand is doing* (6:3). This means the disciples were not to draw attention to themselves. Rather, their motive was to honor God and give Him recognition.

The Savior told His disciples to do their charitable giving *in secret* (6:4), that is, in a private and inconspicuous manner. This implies that their acts of kindness and compassion did not need to be announced to the public. Their heavenly Father was well aware of what they had done and would eternally reward them.

Many leaders prayed in such conspicuous places as *in the synagogues and at the street corners* (6:5). They were frauds, for they wanted as many people as possible to see them praying. Undoubtedly, the people admired what appeared to be religious devotion. But God knew it was a sham.

Jesus did not specifically condemn praying in public, for even He did so (see John 11:41-42). Rather, He censured praying with impure, self-serving motives. His followers could avoid drawing attention to themselves by praying in a private, secluded spot (Matt. 6:6).

When the Gentiles prayed, they were known for their *empty phrases* (6:7). The disciples were not to mechanically resay their words in prayer, for the Father already knew what they needed even before they asked (6:8). Jesus was not condemning lengthy or repeated prayers, for at times He prayed all night (see Luke 6:12) and on occasion repeated His prayers (see Matt. 26:44). He sought to dispel the notion that prayers could force God to respond in a certain way.

The Lord's Prayer is recorded in 6:9-13. It teaches that when believers pray, they are to acknowledge God's holiness (6:9). They are also to long for the establishment of His future kingdom and for the completion of His will on earth even though it had been fully accomplished in heaven (6:10).

Jesus encouraged His followers to pray to God about their personal needs, for He ultimately provides their daily bread (6:11). This does not mean they will get all they want. Instead, God is promising to meet their needs, not satisfy their greedy desires.

Believers are to confess their sins, or moral and spiritual debts, to God. Jesus noted that God's forgiveness of them was to be reflected in their willingness to forgive those who had wronged them (6:12). The more aware and appreciative believers are of God's forgiveness, the more inclined they will be to forgive others.

Believers should pray to God about their spiritual well-being. For example, they can petition Him to steer them away from temptation. Only the Lord can deliver them from all evil influences, including the father of wickedness, the devil (6:13; see John 8:44).

Matthew 6:14-15 may be taken in two ways. Some say that the forgiveness God extends is conditional on how much His people forgive their offenders. Others say that believers enjoy the forgiveness of their sins to the same extent that they either forgive or withhold forgiveness from others who have wronged them. In either case, Jesus' point remains clear. God has freely pardoned believers from their transgressions. And He wants His people, in turn, to freely forgive others who have sinned against them (see Eph. 4:32).

## SUGGESTIONS TO TEACHERS

This week's lesson is so packed with material that you might have difficulty covering all of it. For example, Jesus' teachings on prayer cannot be easily squeezed into one class session. But don't fret. Touching on the subjects in the Sermon on the Mount relating to prayer will plant thoughts that the students can ponder during the upcoming week.

**1. PLAY-ACTING POSES.** Jesus warned His followers about trying to make a public spectacle of their piety. He taught that praying was not meant to impress others. That's why He admonished the disciples to find a quiet place where they could pray in private. Use this admonition to encourage your class to talk seriously about their need to set aside time each day for personal, private prayer.

**2. PRETENTIOUS PRATTLE.** Some have the mistaken notion that elaborate phrases and long-winded addresses to God are the key to a relationship with Him. In fact, some church leaders have given the impression that their "eloquent" prayers are the way everyone must pray. Jesus dismissed the idea that God wants us to approach Him with flowery speeches and lengthy orations. Honesty and simplicity, authenticity and humility are what counts to Him.

**3. PROTOTYPE PIETY.** Discuss each verse of the Lord's Prayer. An entire series of lessons could well be devoted to studying this model prayer. Nonetheless, allow ample time in this lesson to discuss the meaning of each verse.

**4. PURPOSEFUL PARDONING.** Highlight Matthew 6:14-15, in which Jesus emphasized the place of forgiveness. Appreciating God's mercy means being merciful to others. Invite your students to discuss the connection between receiving God's forgiveness and extending forgiveness to those who have wronged them in some way.

---

<table>
<tr><td>

**FOR ADULTS**

</td><td>

■ TOPIC: Thinking about Prayer

■ QUESTIONS: 1. In what ways were some of Israel's religious leaders hypocrites? 2. What is the connection between God's for-

</td></tr>
</table>

giveness of believers and their willingness to forgive those who have wronged them? 3. What do you like most about praying to God? 4. What are some of your recent prayers that God has answered? 5. Who is someone you could pray for today?

■ **ILLUSTRATIONS:**

**Strange Petition.** A mother, while listening to her little girl's bedside prayer, heard her say, "Dear God, please make Boston the capitol of Vermont!" Astonished by the strange petition, her mother asked, "Why did you pray for that?" "Because," answered the child, "that's the way I wrote it down on my examination paper today."

We often wonder whether God hears and answers our prayers. Some people, if posed with the question, would unhesitatingly answer, "I doubt it."

Perhaps we have difficulty acknowledging the efficacy of prayer because we find that we want to set the ground rules for it. In prayer, we often bombard God with petitions for this or that, and we neglect an important aspect of prayer, namely, letting God speak to our hearts. We expect God to hear our prayers but we don't wait around for His answer. It's like the person who prayed, "God give me patience, and I demand it now!"

If we approach prayer with an attitude of openness, seeking it to be an offering of ourselves and our needs, God will answer. His response might not be when we expect it. We might not always like the answer, for God gives His blessings according to His purposes, not ours. But He will answer, especially when we listen to Him.

**Eyes Open and Shut.** In Christian history, there are two traditions of prayer. One is praying with the eyes shut and is called "apophatic prayer." The other is praying with the eyes open and is known as "kataphatic prayer." Apophatic praying is centering on the divine in silence, knowing that all human expressions are inadequate. In contrast, kataphatic prayer attempts to experience in a limited way the majesty of God's grace that is present. Both approaches, at their deepest level, see prayer as listening for God's peace and presence.

We should pray remembering both kinds of methods—with eyes open as well as shut. We are open to the needs of the world around us and also shut in meditation and wonder before the mysteries of God, which cannot ever be completely understood. We are open to God's summons to live in response to His love by committing ourselves to share His mercy and work for justice. And we are shut in private, personal listening to the gentle leading of the Spirit.

**The Story behind the Song.** Albert Malotte's is the most popular version of the musical rendition of the Lord's Prayer. You have undoubtedly heard it sung many times, and with millions of others felt thrilled by the composition.

Malotte had once been a choirboy but then he ran away from home. He tried to support himself in small town theaters by playing the piano while standing on his head, but then he realized that he could not survive this way indefinitely. He also became aware that he had hurt his parents. Finally, one day, he went to a telegraph office and sent the message: "Dad, please forgive me. Wire me money to come home."

Al Malotte's father did forgive him, and welcomed him home. The boy never forgot the meaning of his father's love and acceptance. Years later, while relying on the power of prayer, Malotte began a series of jobs. He worked as a pilot and then as a church organist. There were ups and downs. But the Lord's Prayer, along with the memory of running away and being received home by his father, remained the constant form of praying for him. In his leisure, Malotte began writing music. He wrote the music for ballets in Hollywood, which were accepted, and then music for Walt Disney films. He was accorded recognition. But Malotte wanted to express his faith in a composition, saying, "I am so grateful to God."

The root of the melody of the piece, "The Lord's Prayer," began to grow. One night, he called to his parents and said, "Listen, Mom! Listen, Pop!" And he sang to them the prayer the Lord Jesus had given to us.

Subsequently, artists such as the great John Charles Thomas performed Malotte's "The Lord's Prayer." Though G. Schirmer had already published 19 other versions of the Lord's Prayer, not one reached the popularity of Malotte's. Malotte himself modestly insisted that his musical arrangement of Jesus' prayer was simply his way of wanting to bow in grateful, forgiving prayer.

**FOR YOUTH**

■ TOPIC: Private Conversation

■ QUESTIONS: 1. Why were the religious leaders so eager for others to see their acts of piety? 2. What are the key elements of the Lord's Prayer? 3. What time of the day is best for you to pray? 4. What do your friends think about praying to God? 5. How has praying helped you?

■ ILLUSTRATIONS:

**A Better Model.** Wayne Lee Jones is a student of religion and languages at Harvard University. While doing research, he discovered that most children's books on prayer were similar to ones in the fifteenth or sixteenth century. All were primers, but did not satisfy a child and lacked theological and spiritual content. He thus wrote *God, Good Morning: Prayers for Children from Around the World* to introduce youngsters to 100 prayers from various religious traditions. His view was that this varied collection would enhance the prayer life of children.

Jesus offered a model prayer. It has a simple form, which suggests that God is caring and compassionate. Why buy any book on praying when God's own Son gave us a model that is free of charge?

**The Shelter of Your Life.** Workers excavating for Berlin's Holocaust Memorial in the winter of 1997–1998 discovered the bunker of Joseph Goebbels, Hitler's minister of propaganda. The bunker was a series of dark, cramped concrete-lined tunnels. Even at best, living there would have been a miserable existence. It was built for protection from Allied bombers. As the Third Reich crumbled in the closing days of World War II, Goebbels urged his fellow citizens to fight to the last German, while he stayed in the protection and safety of his bombproof shelter. When the end came, Goebbels and his wife poisoned their six children and then committed suicide. Lost and forgotten in the no-man's land of the old Berlin Wall, the bunker is now a focal point of debate as to whether it should be destroyed or turned into a museum.

Jesus urged His followers to seek spiritual shelter with God. That protection came through a relationship with the Lord that was maintained through prayer. Christ urged His followers to find a place of solitude, and develop a prayer life that would enable them to experience God's enduring peace.

**Challenged.** In 1997, Ted Turner gave one billion dollars to the United Nations amidst great hoopla. He also challenged Bill Gates, the head of Microsoft, to do the same. Despite the media hype, isn't Turner's giving the kind that Jesus condemned? All that was lacking was the sound of trumpets! Jesus said that giving should be done in a private, quiet way, without fanfare or promotion.

# MIRACLES OF COMPASSION

**BACKGROUND SCRIPTURE:** Matthew 9:18-38
**DEVOTIONAL READING:** Matthew 11:2-6

**KEY VERSE:** When [Jesus] saw the crowds, he had compassion for them, because they were harassed and helpless, like sheep without a shepherd. Matthew 9:36.

*KING JAMES VERSION*

MATTHEW 9:18 While he spake these things unto them, behold, there came a certain ruler, and worshipped him, saying, My daughter is even now dead: but come and lay thy hand upon her, and she shall live.

19 And Jesus arose, and followed him, and so did his disciples.

20 And, behold, a woman, which was diseased with an issue of blood twelve years, came behind him, and touched the hem of his garment:

21 For she said within herself, If I may but touch his garment, I shall be whole.

22 But Jesus turned him about, and when he saw her, he said, Daughter, be of good comfort; thy faith hath made thee whole. And the woman was made whole from that hour.

23 And when Jesus came into the ruler's house, and saw the minstrels and the people making a noise,

24 He said unto them, Give place: for the maid is not dead, but sleepeth. And they laughed him to scorn.

25 But when the people were put forth, he went in, and took her by the hand, and the maid arose.

26 And the fame hereof went abroad into all that land.

27 And when Jesus departed thence, two blind men followed him, crying, and saying, Thou Son of David, have mercy on us.

28 And when he was come into the house, the blind men came to him: and Jesus saith unto them, Believe ye that I am able to do this? They said unto him, Yea, Lord.

29 Then touched he their eyes, saying, According to your faith be it unto you.

30 And their eyes were opened; and Jesus straitly charged them, saying, See that no man know it.

31 But they, when they were departed, spread abroad his fame in all that country. . . .

35 And Jesus went about all the cities and villages, teaching in their synagogues, and preaching the gospel of the kingdom, and healing every sickness and every disease among the people.

36 But when he saw the multitudes, he was moved with compassion on them, because they fainted, and were scattered abroad, as sheep having no shepherd.

*NEW REVISED STANDARD VERSION*

MATTHEW 9:18 While he was saying these things to them, suddenly a leader of the synagogue came in and knelt before him, saying, "My daughter has just died; but come and lay your hand on her, and she will live." 19 And Jesus got up and followed him, with his disciples. 20 Then suddenly a woman who had been suffering from hemorrhages for twelve years came up behind him and touched the fringe of his cloak, 21 for she said to herself, "If I only touch his cloak, I will be made well." 22 Jesus turned, and seeing her he said, "Take heart, daughter; your faith has made you well." And instantly the woman was made well. 23 When Jesus came to the leader's house and saw the flute players and the crowd making a commotion, 24 he said, "Go away; for the girl is not dead but sleeping." And they laughed at him. 25 But when the crowd had been put outside, he went in and took her by the hand, and the girl got up. 26 And the report of this spread throughout that district.

27 As Jesus went on from there, two blind men followed him, crying loudly, "Have mercy on us, Son of David!" 28 When he entered the house, the blind men came to him; and Jesus said to them, "Do you believe that I am able to do this?" They said to him, "Yes, Lord." 29 Then he touched their eyes and said, "According to your faith let it be done to you." 30 And their eyes were opened. Then Jesus sternly ordered them, "See that no one knows of this." 31 But they went away and spread the news about him throughout that district. . . .

35 Then Jesus went about all the cities and villages, teaching in their synagogues, and proclaiming the good news of the kingdom, and curing every disease and every sickness. 36 When he saw the crowds, he had compassion for them, because they were harassed and helpless, like sheep without a shepherd.

## BACKGROUND

During Jesus' earthly ministry, He was surrounded by people who clamored for His attention almost constantly, except perhaps when He withdrew for times of prayer before daybreak. Christ was subjected to pressures, was the target of critics, and experienced fatigue and stress. Yet the Savior never became irritable when people crowded around Him and pleaded for some kind of help.

No person in history was ever confronted with the number or size of human demands as was Jesus. Other public figures were known to lose their cool and snap at those around them, but not Christ. His patience and compassion toward the hurting and helpless knew no limits.

Matthew and the other Gospel writers gave examples of the patience and compassion that Jesus demonstrated through His healings. These miracles were never stunts. In fact, Jesus seemed to go out of His way to avoid being sensational or making a great spectacle out of the people whom He healed. The miracles were acts of kindness and revealed that the power of God was manifesting itself in the world through Jesus the Messiah.

This in-breaking of the Almighty through Jesus was done out of compassion for suffering persons and without fanfare. But eyewitnesses were astounded. Despite Jesus' instructions not to publicize His miraculous healings, people spread the reports.

Perhaps one of Jesus' harshest critics would have been the leaders of the local synagogues. Many possibly would have welcomed an opportunity to have Jesus silenced for good as a blasphemer. But on one occasion, when a synagogue leader's daughter became dangerously ill and the local physicians could not help, the father came to Jesus. Instead of turning him away, the Savior immediately responded with compassion.

On the way to the leader's house, Jesus was interrupted by a woman with a debilitating hemorrhage (perhaps some sort of menstrual disorder). Again, with sensitivity and compassion, Jesus restored the unfortunate sufferer to full health. When He arrived at the residence of the synagogue leader, Jesus encountered noisy crowds and funeral music. Despite the jeers of the people, Jesus restored the official's daughter to life.

While the Savior was ministering to a large crowd of people along the shore of the Sea of Galilee, a synagogue official named Jairus fell prostrate at His feet (Mark 5:21-22). This undoubtedly was a display of deep reverence and respect.

In the first century A.D., such an official would have supervised the synagogue worship services, maintained order, invited a visitor to address the congregation, and handed the Scripture scroll to a rabbi for reading. In this incident, the leader said to Jesus, *"My daughter has just died; but come and lay your hand on her, and she will live"* (Matt. 9:18).

Jesus evidently was moved by the man's faith, for He responded immediately. *And Jesus got up and followed him, with his disciples* (9:19). On the way, a woman who had suffered a hemorrhage for twelve years touched Christ (9:20). Perhaps out of superstition, she had convinced herself that if she touched the fringe of His robe, she would be healed (9:21).

In Jesus' day people wore cloaks, which were ankle-length robes. Over their head or shoulders they draped a tallith, which was a shawl with fringed corners. Four dangling ornaments called tassels were sewed to the four lower corners on the fringe of the tallith. These tassels were made from cords or threads of even length that had been fastened together at one end.

Jesus encouraged the woman's faith in His healing, saving power. Only He could take away her illness. *Jesus turned, and seeing her he said, "Take heart, daughter; your faith has made you well"* (9:22). Because of her trust in Christ, the woman was instantly healed.

The funeral ritual had already begun when Jesus and His disciples arrived at the official's home. The crowd at a funeral usually included professional mourners, whose task it was to wail while they recited the name of the departed loved one (9:23). Because Jesus knew that He could conquer death, He announced to all who were present that the child was only sleeping and not dead. *"Go away; for the girl is not dead but sleeping"* (9:24.) Jesus' statement, however, was met with ridicule and laughter.

Jesus had the crowd ushered out of the house. He then went to the girl and touched her. The girl was immediately restored to life! *But when the crowd had been put outside, he went in and took her by the hand, and the girl got up* (9:25). Inevitably, the news about this miracle spread throughout the countryside. *And the report of this spread throughout that district* (9:26).

After Jesus left the official's home, two blind men followed behind Him. They were shouting, *"Have mercy on us, Son of David!"* (9:27). Their use of this messianic title demonstrated their faith in Jesus' ability to heal them.

When He arrived at His destination, Jesus questioned the faith of the two in Him. *"Do you believe that I am able to do this?"* (9:28). They replied that they believed in His ability to heal them. Jesus then touched their eyes and gave them their sight (9:29). He also sternly warned them, *"See that no one knows of this"* (9:30). But instead they *spread the news about him throughout that district* (9:31).

Jesus continued to travel as an itinerant preacher throughout *all the cities and villages* (9:35) in the area. He taught in the synagogues and announced the good news that God's kingdom was about to draw near. The Savior's message was confirmed by the healing of every kind of disease and sickness among the people. The physicians of the day evidently would not or could not cure the infirm.

The large crowds of needy people placed tremendous demands on Jesus. When He saw them, He was moved with compassion. The term rendered *compassion* (9:36) means "to have pity on" or "to feel sympathy for." Christ was genuinely concerned for the well-being of the lost. He could see that they were tired and distressed, bewildered and destitute.

## SUGGESTIONS TO TEACHERS

Here is another bounteous helping of scriptural material that could serve up a dozen class sessions! This lesson should give you so much for the class members to feast on that you might find yourself quickly running out of time to discuss everything.

**1. CONCERN FOR A FRANTIC PARENT.** Any father or mother can empathize with the ruler of the synagogue whose daughter had died. Point out that Jesus willingly acceded to this parent's request. Though the Savior had many demands placed on His time, He was never too busy to glorify His heavenly Father through acts of compassion and kindness.

**2. SENSITIVITY TOWARD A FAITH-FILLED INVALID.** Explain to the class that the woman with the hemorrhage had endured this affliction for 12 years. Undoubtedly many would have considered her unclean. But Jesus changed that and restored her. In our times of desperation, we should look to God in faith, for we know that He will respond to our plight.

**3. LIFE FOR A DEAD GIRL.** Jesus had compassion on a little girl. The class should understand that in ancient times female children were seldom regarded as having any worth. In addition, no rabbi would touch a female or defile himself by touching a corpse. But Jesus' compassion was not limited by these considerations. He thus did not hesitate to restore the girl to life.

**4. SIGHT TO TRUSTING, BLIND VICTIMS.** Jesus healed two blind men, wanting them not only to have the gift of sight but also the ability to live productive lives in their community. He no longer wanted them to be reduced to the indignity of begging.

**5. DEEP COMPASSION.** Relate to the class members that Jesus, unlike the religious leaders of His day, felt great pity for the crowds. He could see that they had many problems and didn't know where to go for help. The situation has not changed much today. Remind your students that Jesus came to be the Shepherd. He is the One who can show people how to avoid the pitfalls of life.

■ TOPIC: Thinking about Wholeness

■ QUESTIONS: 1. How was Jesus' power evident in each of the miracles He performed? 2. How did the miracles confirm Jesus' claim to be the Messiah? 3. What are some difficulties in your life that Jesus wants to resolve? 4. When was the last time you reached out in faith to Jesus and asked Him to help you with a problem? 5. How might you encourage others to do the same thing?

■ **ILLUSTRATIONS:**

**Healing Is Wholeness.** A taxi driver was called to an address where a sad-faced and sick-looking woman lived. She got into the cab and directed the driver to stop at a florist shop. She came out with an expensive bouquet and then told the man to drive to a certain cemetery. After telling him to wait, she got out of the cab and was gone for several minutes. Her face was drawn and tear-stained when she returned.

When the driver dropped off the woman at her home, she paid him, and then told him to pick her up the following day at the same time. He returned the next day as requested. To his surprise, the same routine happened. He drove first to the florist shop and then took the woman to the cemetery, where she left the fresh flowers. Again, she requested the driver to return the next day. And, again, she repeated the pathetic routine, usually weeping quietly on the ride back to her home.

The driver finally grew curious after six or seven days of this in succession. One day, when the woman got out at the cemetery, he quietly followed at a discreet distance. He saw that she was placing the new flowers on a grave and carefully laying aside the previous day's floral spray. When the woman got back in the taxi, the driver asked her whether the flowers were for someone she loved. Sighing deeply, she replied, "My son. I just can't get over it. I can't sleep at night. I'm on so much medication I'm not supposed to drive. That's why I have to have you drive me." Then she turned her ashen face away, looking ill and haggard.

A week later, when the familiar cemetery ride had started and the woman came out of the florist shop bearing the usual bouquet, the cabbie finally worked up the nerve to say quietly, "Excuse me, Ma'am, but would you mind if I asked you if we might leave a few of them flowers at the hospital. Y'see, my little boy is there. He's in a special ward because he can't walk right. And well, if you don't mind too much, I think he'd like a couple of them pretty flowers. I won't charge you none if we'd drive past the hospital on the way back."

The woman grew even more pale, and said nothing. The cab driver silently helped her in the cab, closed her door, got in the driver's seat, started the engine, and turned toward the now-familiar route to the cemetery. "Driver," she whispered hoarsely. "Please take me to the hospital first so I can leave a couple of flowers for your boy."

That was the start of a remarkable healing for that woman. She never made it to the cemetery that afternoon or ever again with flowers. She began to make regular visits to the children in the pediatric orthopedic section of that hospital, and then became a volunteer chaplain's assistant. Her health improved. Once crippled with grief and self-pity, she received healing as she brought emotional restoration to others.

This woman discovered that the healing presence of Christ is encountered as we reach out in compassion toward others who are hurting. It's no wonder that the Hebrew word for "healthy" is *shalem*. It comes from the familiar term *shalom*, which means "harmony" and "connectedness." In the New Testament, the Greek word for "health" or "wholeness" is the same term that is rendered "salvation." It suggests that being connected to the Lord and with other persons in loving, healing relationships leads to spiritual wellness.

**Jesus' Compassion.** When Jesus went with Jairus to heal the official's daughter, He was doing something highly unusual for that time. Jesus showed concern for the health of a little girl. Tragically, caring about young females was almost unheard of in the first century A.D. One example of this callousness toward little girls can be seen in a letter written in A.D. 10 by a Greek businessman named Hilarion on a trip in Egypt. He sent the following message to his wife in Greece.

"Hilarion to Alis his wife, heartiest greetings, and to my dear Berous and to Apollonarion. I want you to know that we are still in Alexandria. Don't worry that when all the others come back, if I stay on in Alexandria. . . . If—good luck be with you—you bear a child, if it is a boy, let it live; if it is a girl, throw it out. You told Aphrodisias to say to me not to forget you. How can I forget you? So I beg you not to worry."

In the midst of the affection expressed toward his wife and to Berous and Apollonarion, this man also displayed a shockingly calloused attitude toward female babies. In contrast, Jesus cared about the welfare of a young girl whom He had never seen before.

**FOR YOUTH**

■ TOPIC: Healing Touch

■ QUESTIONS: 1. How vibrant was the faith of the synagogue official? 2. In what way did Jesus have mercy on the two blind men? 3. What are some seemingly impossible situations in your life that God wants to change? 4. How might you encourage your peers to turn to Christ for spiritual healing? 5. What might prevent them from reaching out to Him in faith?

■ ILLUSTRATIONS:

**Beliefs.** A June, 1996, TIME/CNN poll done by Yankelovich Partners indicated that 77 percent of Americans believe that God sometimes intervenes to cure people who have serious illnesses. The survey also discovered that 73 percent believe that praying for others can help cure their illnesses. However, only 28 percent believe that faith healers can make people well.

The crowd at the house of the synagogue official were skeptical of Jesus' ability to conquer death. However, Jesus touched the girl and told her to awake. The Lord had mercy on her and restored her to life.

**Showed Care and Compassion.** At the end of August, 1997, Princess Diana was killed in an automobile accident in Paris. People of all ages were stunned at her senseless death. Emotion surged and was evidenced by the thousands who brought flowers to Buckingham Palace. While Great Britain mourned, the royal family seemed aloof and uncaring. Public sentiment rose as the nation stingingly criticized Queen Elizabeth II for her seclusion and her lack of compassion. She was finally forced to speak to her nation's people.

Contrast this queen's response with that of King Jesus. Far from being indifferent and unconcerned, He got involved in the lives of people. Jesus showed genuine care and compassion.

**Troubles Are Over.** While still a child, Cleveland Amory read *Black Beauty*. It became his desire to build a ranch for animals where they could be free to end their days, like the fictional horse. Amory fulfilled his dream by starting *The Fund for Animals* and by building the *Black Beauty Ranch* in Murchison, Texas. This ranch has become a sanctuary for many animals who have been mistreated.

A cat, the ranch's first animal, literally dragged itself to the gate. Its foot had been seized by a hunter's leghold trap. The leg was so badly damaged that it had to be amputated. Now there are numerous three-legged animals, cats, foxes, coyotes, and a deer. The ranch also houses elephants, horses, wild burros, buffaloes, prairie dogs, and Nim (the talking chimp). All are animals that had been mistreated, experimented upon, or simply considered inconvenient to keep, and were subsequently abandoned or abused. Amory has proven to be compassionate to these creatures.

If an individual can be so compassionate to animals, how much more should people demonstrate compassion to their fellow human beings.

# OPPOSITION TO JESUS

**BACKGROUND SCRIPTURE:** Matthew 12:22-45
**DEVOTIONAL READING:** Matthew 12:1-14

**KEY VERSE:** Whoever is not with me is against me, and whoever does not gather with me scatters. Matthew 12:30.

*KING JAMES VERSION*

MATTHEW 12:22 Then was brought unto him one possessed with a devil, blind, and dumb: and he healed him, insomuch that the blind and dumb both spake and saw.

23 And all the people were amazed, and said, Is not this the son of David?

24 But when the Pharisees heard it, they said, This fellow doth not cast out devils, but by Beelzebub the prince of the devils.

25 And Jesus knew their thoughts, and said unto them, Every kingdom divided against itself is brought to desolation; and every city or house divided against itself shall not stand:

26 And if Satan cast out Satan, he is divided against himself; how shall then his kingdom stand?

27 And if I by Beelzebub cast out devils, by whom do your children cast them out? therefore they shall be your judges.

28 But if I cast out devils by the Spirit of God, then the kingdom of God is come unto you.

29 Or else how can one enter into a strong man's house, and spoil his goods, except he first bind the strong man? and then he will spoil his house.

30 He that is not with me is against me; and he that gathereth not with me scattereth abroad.

31 Wherefore I say unto you, All manner of sin and blasphemy shall be forgiven unto men: but the blasphemy against the Holy Ghost shall not be forgiven unto men.

32 And whosoever speaketh a word against the Son of man, it shall be forgiven him: but whosoever speaketh against the Holy Ghost, it shall not be forgiven him, neither in this world, neither in the world to come. . . .

38 Then certain of the scribes and of the Pharisees answered, saying, Master, we would see a sign from thee.

39 But he answered and said unto them, An evil and adulterous generation seeketh after a sign; and there shall no sign be given to it, but the sign of the prophet Jonas:

40 For as Jonas was three days and three nights in the whale's belly; so shall the Son of man be three days and three nights in the heart of the earth.

*NEW REVISED STANDARD VERSION*

MATTHEW 12:22 Then they brought to him a demoniac who was blind and mute; and he cured him, so that the one who had been mute could speak and see. 23 All the crowds were amazed and said, "Can this be the Son of David?" 24 But when the Pharisees heard it, they said, "It is only by Beelzebul, the ruler of the demons, that this fellow casts out the demons." 25 He knew what they were thinking and said to them, "Every kingdom divided against itself is laid waste, and no city or house divided against itself will stand. 26 If Satan casts out Satan, he is divided against himself; how then will his kingdom stand? 27 If I cast out demons by Beelzebul, by whom do your own exorcists cast them out? Therefore they will be your judges. 28 But if it is by the Spirit of God that I cast out demons, then the kingdom of God has come to you. 29 Or how can one enter a strong man's house and plunder his property, without first tying up the strong man? Then indeed the house can be plundered. 30 Whoever is not with me is against me, and whoever does not gather with me scatters. 31 Therefore I tell you, people will be forgiven for every sin and blasphemy, but blasphemy against the Spirit will not be forgiven. 32 Whoever speaks a word against the Son of Man will be forgiven, but whoever speaks against the Holy Spirit will not be forgiven, either in this age or in the age to come." . . .

38 Then some of the scribes and Pharisees said to him, "Teacher, we wish to see a sign from you." 39 But he answered them, "An evil and adulterous generation asks for a sign, but no sign will be given to it except the sign of the prophet Jonah. 40 For just as Jonah was three days and three nights in the belly of the sea monster, so for three days and three nights the Son of Man will be in the heart of the earth."

| | | |
|---|---|---|
| Monday, Jan. 17 | Matthew 12:1-8 | Plucking Grain on the Sabbath |
| Tuesday, Jan. 18 | Matthew 12:22-32 | Jesus Accused as Beelezebul's Man |
| Wednesday, Jan. 19 | Matthew 12:33-45 | Understand the Signs of the Times! |
| Thursday, Jan. 20 | Matthew 13:54-58 | Jesus Is Rejected at Nazareth |
| Friday, Jan. 21 | Matthew 15:1-9 | Confrontation between Jesus and the Pharisees |
| Saturday, Jan. 22 | Matthew 16:1-12 | Jesus' Enemies Demand a Sign |
| Sunday, Jan. 23 | Matthew 16:13-20 | Peter Declares That Jesus Is Messiah |

## BACKGROUND

Matthew wrote his Gospel to present Jesus of Nazareth as Israel's long-awaited Messiah and rightful King. Disciples such as Peter would eventually recognize Jesus' true identity (John 6:68-69). But the religious leaders not only rejected the Savior's messianic claims but also planned how they might eliminate Him (Mark 14:1).

Jesus' acts of kindness toward those who were suffering from afflictions often became the target of the religious leaders' attacks. This is sad, for disease was rampant in the ancient world. Medical knowledge was limited and physicians were often unable to cure people of their ailments. Consequently, magical charms and incantations were used along with folk remedies to heal the sick.

Many thought that demons were the cause of all sicknesses, and there were those who used a variety of occult means to cast out evil spirits. In general, the Gospels make a careful distinction between sickness and demon possession. While the writers affirmed that demons could possess people and physically afflict them, none of the Gospels perpetuated the superstition that all illnesses were somehow linked to demon possession. In fact, Jesus Himself made a careful distinction between casting out demons and performing cures (Luke 13:32).

The Gospels reveal that Jesus performed many miracles, such as healing the sick, expelling demons, and restoring the dead to life. The miracles were not mere displays of power. Rather, the Savior's intent was to validate His claim to be the Son of God (John 20:30-31). Beyond that, the miracles showed that God is Lord over life and death, and over temporal and eternal matters.

The miracles directly fulfilled God's purposes and were consistent with His majesty and holiness. Tragically, the religious leaders in Jesus' day failed to understand this. Instead, they accused Christ of being in league with Satan, a charge that He flatly denied.

## NOTES ON THE PRINTED TEXT

Jesus' popularity continued to grow as more and more people witnessed His teaching and healing ministry. On one occasion, some people brought a man who was demon-possessed, blind, and mute to the Savior. Perhaps others had tried unsuccessfully to help this person. And so the man's loved ones turned to Jesus in desperation.

With little fanfare Jesus *cured him* (12:22). In other words, the man no longer was demon-possessed, and he could see and speak normally. To say the least, the crowds were astounded. In fact, they questioned whether Jesus could be *the Son of David* (12:23). Their question could be translated, "This one can't be the Son of David, can He?" In other words, the question expected a negative answer.

Matthew wrote his Gospel to demonstrate that Jesus is the Son of David (1:1), or the Messiah of Israel. Though the Jewish leaders possessed the Scriptures, which testified to Messiah's person and coming, most still did not accept Jesus as the expected one (John 1:11). This is evident by what the Pharisees said about Jesus: *It is only by Beelzebul, the ruler of the demons, that this fellow casts out the demons* (Matt. 12:24).

Beelzebul was a Philistine deity associated with demonic rituals and idolatry (2 Kings 1:2). The name came to be used of Satan, the prince of demons. In effect, the Pharisees accused Jesus of being the devil's agent and using his power to cast out evil spirits.

The Savior could not allow this indictment to go unchallenged. He thus made a three-part defense. First, Jesus declared that a kingdom, city, or even a family cannot continue to exist if it is divided against itself (Matt. 12:25). For example, if Satan expelled his own demons from people, his kingdom was divided and could not endure (12:26).

Second, Jesus noted that when Jewish exorcists cast out evil spirits, they claimed to do so by the power of God. In this regard, their assertions were no different than the one made by Christ. Thus, they would stand in judgment over the Pharisees for having spoken slanderously against the Messiah (12:27).

Third, Jesus' expulsion of demons by means of the Spirit indicated that *the kingdom of God has come* (12:28). Jesus wanted the religious leaders to know that the King was in their presence. In fact, His ability to bind Satan and his demons proved what He said (12:29). Incidentally, Jesus' opponents thought they were serving God, but in reality they were the devil's slaves (John 8:44) and would be judged by Christ (Matt. 12:30).

Jesus wasted no time in confronting the Pharisees' deliberate rejection of Him as the Messiah. Because they attributed to Satan a work that was God's, they were guilty of *blasphemy against the Spirit* (12:31). Such an offense could never be forgiven, for they stubbornly refused to heed the Spirit's conviction and accept the pardon that Christ offered. Because those religious leaders rejected all proofs regarding the messiahship of Jesus, they stood eternally condemned (12:32).

The scribes and Pharisees had received a number of proofs concerning Jesus' messiahship, including the ministry of John, the testimony of the Father, the prophecies of the Old Testament, Christ's own testimony, and the work of the Spirit. Despite such overwhelming evidence, they still clamored, *Teacher, we wish to see a sign from you* (12:38).

Perhaps the religious leaders were demanding a sign of cosmic proportions (see Luke 11:16). Instead, Jesus would give them a "sign" from Scripture, namely, *of the prophet Jonah* (Matt. 12:39). At one point, Jonah had been as good as dead, and then God restored him back to life. The Son of Man's resurrection from the dead would be the greatest sign of all that the kingdom had come (12:40).

Christ's response was proper, for the religious leaders' demand for a sign was an indication of their unbelief and unfaithfulness to God. Jesus declared that His resurrection would be the ultimate sign, or proof, of His claim to be the Messiah (see Rom. 1:4).

## SUGGESTIONS TO TEACHERS

Was the source of Jesus' unique powers demonic or divine? His opponents tried to discredit Him by claiming that His powers were from Satan. But the miracles that Jesus performed, such as the one described in Matthew 12:22, should compel the members of your class to take what He did seriously. The bland response that church people often show toward Jesus indicates that they dismiss Him as being either harmless or unimportant. But His miracles and teaching reveal that He is eternally relevant.

**1. ANSWER TO ACCUSERS.** When some Pharisees accused Jesus of being in league with Satan, Jesus flatly denied their assertions. He made it clear that He was empowered by the Spirit of God, not evil, to restore sight, speech, and health to suffering persons. Invite your students to discuss how Jesus has spiritually healed them.

**2. THE UNPARDONABLE SIN.** The notion of the unpardonable sin has caused needless anxiety. Let your class know that anyone who has been convicted by the Spirit and now believes the truth cannot possibly have committed an unforgivable transgression. Only those who have hardened themselves to the Gospel and who have rejected Christ stand eternally condemned. The reason is that they have spurned God's only provision for their salvation.

**3. THE SIGN OF JONAH.** When Jesus' critics demanded that He perform a sign to prove that He came from God, He refused to oblige them. Instead, Jesus told the religious leaders that His resurrection would validate His messianic claims. Let your students know that there is sufficient evidence—namely, Christ's birth, life, death, resurrection, and ascension—to prove that He is the Son of God and Redeemer of the world.

**4. DANGERS OF A SPIRITUAL VACUUM.** When Jonah grudgingly went to Nineveh and preached God's message, the entire city repented. In contrast, when Jesus came to His people, they refused to repent. The spiritual vacuum in their lives could not have been greater. Likewise, the tragedy of rejecting Christ could not have been more eternal. Ask your students to consider the evidence they have regarding the messianic claims of Christ. After a few moments of quiet reflection, have them ponder how they have responded to the evidence. Stress that belief, not unbelief, is the only proper response.

| | |
|---|---|
| **FOR ADULTS** | ■ TOPIC: Thinking about Jesus' Power<br>■ QUESTIONS: Why were the crowds amazed at what Jesus had done? 2. What was preposterous about the accusation that the reli- |

gious leaders made against Jesus? 3. What would be your response if someone said to you that Christ was an agent of Satan? 4. Why is it impossible to be neutral in your opinion about Christ? 5. What new insights about our Lord did you obtain from this week's lesson?

■ **ILLUSTRATIONS:**

**False Accusation.** We were appalled when we learned that Susan Smith had pushed her two little sons into a lake to drown them, then blamed an African American carjacker for the monstrous deed, and thereby stirred up racial animosity. Smith finally confessed to the crime. But in her statement, she wrote, "I dropped to the lowest point when I allowed my children to go down that ramp into the water without me. I took off running and screaming, 'Oh God! Oh God, no! Why did *You* allow this to happen?' "

The Pharisees tried to accuse Jesus of being in league with demonic powers, and villains like Susan Smith continue to try to make the Lord responsible for their horrible acts. Because they refuse to believe that Jesus always acts out of compassion for others, they twist the truth to try to make themselves look good and God to appear hardhearted.

**Slandering Jesus.** A few years ago, the *Columbus Dispatch* reported on hearings in Columbus, Ohio, regarding a bill to ban certain types of semiautomatic weapons. Charles E. Mainous of High Street Baptist Church argued that bearing arms, even assault weapons, is a God-given right. He said, "If the AK-47 was around back then, Jesus would have ordered His disciples to get one." The bill passed. What a slanderous way to use the name of Jesus!

**Self Only?** Jean Rhys was the author of a series of popular novels during the 1920s and 1930s, but then fell into obscurity. She was rediscovered and showered with fame with the publication of her fifth and last novel, *Wise Sagasso Sea,* in 1966. She died in 1979. Her unfinished autobiography, which appeared in 1980, revealed an intensely self-centered woman. Critics and readers had suspected that Rhys was herself the subject of her fiction, but the depth of her egoism was disclosed in her candid remarks about herself. "People have always been shadows to me," she wrote. "I have never known other people. I have only ever written about myself."

Contrast this person to Jesus. He always regarded others, not as mere "shadows," but as beloved fellow members of the human race. Unlike people such as Rhys, Jesus would never arrogantly disregard others and focus on His own comfort and security. Though He is the Lord of heaven and earth, Jesus cared about the blind, the mute, and the distressed. He did not hesitate to help others in need so that they might come to a knowledge of the truth.

---

**FOR YOUTH**
■ TOPIC: Trouble!
■ QUESTIONS: 1. What prompted the crowds to wonder whether Jesus is the Son of David? 2. How did Jesus refute the charge of the religious leaders that He was in league with Satan? 3. How has Jesus demonstrated His healing power in your life? 4. What do your peers tend to think about Jesus? 5. What can you do to encourage them to have a proper view of Christ?

■ **ILLUSTRATIONS:**

**Unconvinced.** On February 17, 1998, President Clinton televised an explanation of the United States government's efforts to force Iraq to comply with resolutions made by the United Nations. He outlined Iraq's failure to abide by the agreements after Desert Storm, their failure to allow U.N. monitoring teams to check possible weapons sites, and evidence detailing the continued manufacture of weapons of mass destruction, particularly chemical and biological weapons.

The Clinton policy team then took to the road to test-market a military response. At St. John Arena at Ohio State University, which was their first stop, 5,000 people listened to Secretary of State Madeleine Albright, Defense Secretary William Cohen, and National Security Adviser Samuel Berger explain various military options, if Iraq did not yield to repeated diplomatic pressures.

To the amazement of these officials, not everyone agreed with their point of view. In fact, demonstrators—mostly young people—heckled the president's representatives and demanded more proof. They were skeptical of Saddam Hussein's nuclear and chemical potential. These students were like the religious authorities. They wanted visible proof before they would believe in someone or something.

**House Divided Speech.** The Kansas-Nebraska Act of 1854 was designed to open the new western territories to slavery. It was championed by Stephen A. Douglas. Standing in opposition was a new politician, Abraham Lincoln, who wanted to check the extension of slavery and to preserve the Union, which was rapidly dividing over the issue of slavery.

In 1858, Lincoln accepted the Republican nomination for the Senate. His acceptance reiterated his desire to preserve and defend the Union, amidst rumblings of secession from various southern states. His speech began, "A house divided against itself cannot stand. I believe the government cannot endure permanently half slave and half free."

Lincoln was right. The United States could not withstand division. His quote, which was based on the teachings of Jesus, proved to be tragically true. Division brought disaster.

**Consequence of Division.** In the 1997–1998 season, the Toronto Raptors of the National Basketball Association were a sorrowful team. They were locked in last place at the All-Star break and some 20 games behind Indiana in the Eastern Conference Central Division.

The front office was unstable. General Manager Isaiah Thomas left. The unhappy team, in its third season, was sold. Coach Darrell Walker resigned. In an effort to restore stability and unity, the new owners traded Damon Stoudamire (the Raptor's premier point guard and the 1996 Rookie of the Year) to the Portland Trail Blazers. The trade, however, brought only more division. Kenny Anderson refused to play! Within a week the disgruntled Anderson was traded to the Boston Celtics.

The consequences of division for the Raptors was a losing season. From this we see that no team can ever hope to win if its members cannot play together. Ultimately, disunity produces losers. Jesus pointed out a similar truth to the religious leaders. Division leads only to increased problems and defeat.

# LABORERS IN THE VINEYARD

**BACKGROUND SCRIPTURE:** Matthew 19:16—20:16
**DEVOTIONAL READING:** Matthew 20:20-28

**KEY VERSE:** The last will be first, and the first will be last. Matthew 20:16.

*KING JAMES VERSION*

MATTHEW 20:1 For the kingdom of heaven is like unto a man that is an householder, which went out early in the morning to hire labourers into his vineyard.

2 And when he had agreed with the labourers for a penny a day, he sent them into his vineyard.

3 And he went out about the third hour, and saw others standing idle in the marketplace,

4 And said unto them; Go ye also into the vineyard, and whatsoever is right I will give you. And they went their way.

5 Again he went out about the sixth and ninth hour, and did likewise.

6 And about the eleventh hour he went out, and found others standing idle, and saith unto them, Why stand ye here all the day idle?

7 They say unto him, Because no man hath hired us. He saith unto them, Go ye also into the vineyard; and whatsoever is right, that shall ye receive.

8 So when even was come, the lord of the vineyard saith unto his steward, Call the labourers, and give them their hire, beginning from the last unto the first.

9 And when they came that were hired about the eleventh hour, they received every man a penny.

10 But when the first came, they supposed that they should have received more; and they likewise received every man a penny.

11 And when they had received it, they murmured against the goodman of the house,

12 Saying, These last have wrought but one hour, and thou hast made them equal unto us, which have borne the burden and heat of the day.

13 But he answered one of them, and said, Friend, I do thee no wrong: didst not thou agree with me for a penny?

14 Take that thine is, and go thy way: I will give unto this last, even as unto thee.

15 Is it not lawful for me to do what I will with mine own? Is thine eye evil, because I am good?

16 So the last shall be first, and the first last: for many be called, but few chosen.

*NEW REVISED STANDARD VERSION*

MATTHEW 20:1 "For the kingdom of heaven is like a landowner who went out early in the morning to hire laborers for his vineyard. 2 After agreeing with the laborers for the usual daily wage, he sent them into his vineyard. 3 When he went out about nine o'clock, he saw others standing idle in the marketplace; 4 and he said to them, 'You also go into the vineyard, and I will pay you whatever is right.' So they went. 5 When he went out again about noon and about three o'clock, he did the same. 6 And about five o'clock he went out and found others standing around; and he said to them, 'Why are you standing here idle all day?' 7 They said to him, 'Because no one has hired us.' He said to them, 'You also go into the vineyard.' 8 When evening came, the owner of the vineyard said to his manager, 'Call the laborers and give them their pay, beginning with the last and then going to the first.' 9 When those hired about five o'clock came, each of them received the usual daily wage. 10 Now when the first came, they thought they would receive more; but each of them also received the usual daily wage. 11 And when they received it, they grumbled against the landowner, 12 saying, 'These last worked only one hour, and you have made them equal to us who have borne the burden of the day and the scorching heat.' 13 But he replied to one of them, 'Friend, I am doing you no wrong; did you not agree with me for the usual daily wage? 14 Take what belongs to you and go; I choose to give to this last the same as I give to you. 15 Am I not allowed to do what I choose with what belongs to me? Or are you envious because I am generous?' 16 So the last will be first, and the first will be last."

9

## HOME BIBLE READINGS

## BACKGROUND

The parable of the laborers in the vineyard might better be called "the story of the generous owner-boss." The stinger in the parable is the unexpected generosity of the owner-boss toward those hired near the close of the day. This underscores the meaning of grace. Keep in mind throughout your work in this week's lesson that God's grace is His undeserved goodness toward us.

It's helpful to understand the background of Jesus' parable. As with most parables, this one starts out by focusing on a slice from real life. Every hearer recognized the scene. The time for gathering grapes had come, and the owner wanted to collect the clusters of fruit before they began to rot and spoil, or before rains came to wreck the crop.

Typical of most villages, a labor pool gathered early in the morning. The owner promised the laborers he hired a fair day's wage, namely, the going rate for their work. As the day progressed, the owner took on additional help at various times. Perhaps the weather began to appear threatening, and he wanted to get the vineyard's produce in more quickly.

The workday typically was from sunup to sundown, or a 12-hour shift. The usual practice was to pay workers at the end of each day. The usual wage was enough to feed a person's family for a day. No pay meant lean times and undoubtedly a hungry household.

When the owner lined up the last-hired at the front of the procession to be paid, people were surprised. But when he gave these five o'clock laborers a full-day's wage, those who had been hired early in the morning complained that they should have been paid more. The owner reminded them that they were receiving what they had agreed upon. He then insisted on generously giving the last-hired what they had not earned. Such is God's mysterious grace!

## NOTES ON THE PRINTED TEXT

Perhaps you have noticed how many of Jesus' parables begin with this phrase, *"for the kingdom of heaven is like"* (20:1). The reason is that the parable was a form of teaching that compared the unknown with what was known, and often with something from everyday life. In fact, the Greek verb, which is the basis for "parable," literally means "to throw alongside." In this week's Scripture text, Jesus laid the grace mentality of God's kingdom alongside the contract mentality of the world to compare the two.

*"A landowner . . . went out early in the morning to hire laborers for his vineyard. After agreeing with the laborers for the usual daily wage, he sent them into his vineyard"* (20:1-2). Early in the morning at 6 A.M., the owner of a vineyard went to the marketplace. His fully ripe grapes needed to be picked immediately. He hired some laborers, who agreed to be paid the standard minimum daily wage of one denarius.

*"When he went out about nine o'clock, he saw others standing idle in the marketplace; and he said to them, 'You also go into the vineyard, and I will pay you whatever is right.' So they went"* (20:3-4). Perhaps the harvest was threatened by undesirable weather. Thus, time was a big factor; so the landowner hired additional help and promised to pay them a fair wage. The combination of time and the amount of grapes that remained to be picked led the owner to hire more workers at noon and at three o'clock. In each case, he agreed to pay them fairly (20:5).

At five o'clock, which was just an hour before the workday ended, the owner saw men standing around idle. Incredulous that they had not worked and since there was still harvesting left to do, he hired them. *And about five o'clock he went out and found others standing around; and he said to them, 'Why are you standing there idle all day? They said to him 'Because no one has hired us.' He said to them, 'You also go into the vineyard' "* (20:6-7).

At 6 P.M., which was the end of the workday, the owner instructed the supervisor to pay the workers, beginning with the last hired (20:8). As these laborers extended their hands, each received a denarius. *"When those hired about five o'clock came, each of them received the usual daily wage"* (20:9).

Naturally, those who had toiled the full 12 hours expected a nice bonus for their work. *"Now when the first came, they thought they would receive more; but each of them also received the usual daily wage"* (20:10). In other words, each 12-hour laborer was given a denarius.

The people hired first did not like the idea of being treated the same as those who were hired last (20:11-12). From the world's perspective the grumblers had a valid point. However, what may have been true in the world was not necessarily true in the kingdom of God.

The owner told one particular grumbler that he had treated him properly (20:13). The worker got exactly what he had contracted for, and thus it was a fair deal. The owner had every right to pay a worker hired last the same amount as a worker hired first, for the money originally belonged to him (20:14-15). The owner surmised that the real issue was envy and greed, not fairness. The grumbler resented the owner's generosity to the other workers (20:15)

Jesus noted that many believers who are first in rank and status in this life will be last in God's kingdom, for they approached their service for Christ with a greedy mentality (20:16). It is much better to trust God to be generous and gracious with us. Then we will be set free from all inclinations to be jealous and resentful of other believers.

## SUGGESTIONS TO TEACHERS

Jesus wanted His disciples to understand that when their service for Him was approached from a mercenary attitude (namely, on the basis of greed), they were misguided. Love and commitment, not pride and a desire for personal gain, were to be their motive for service.

**1. REFUSAL OF THE WEALTHY.** Wealth and power in Jesus' day were considered to be signs of God's favor. This is evident from Christ's encounter with the rich young man (see Matt. 19:16-22). This well-to-do person was interested in eternal life. However, his obsession with money prevented him from drawing close to God. This person refused to part with his possessions in order to become one of Christ's followers. We can see that Jesus correctly diagnosed the man's problem.

**2. RICHES AS A BARRIER.** The disciples found it hard to accept that riches could prevent someone from being saved. They were shocked when Jesus said that it was easier for a big lumbering camel to squeeze through a needle's eye than for someone who was wealthy to enter God's kingdom (19:23-24). In this era of flagrant greed, conspicuous consumption, and lavish lifestyles, Jesus' words hit us all where it hurts!

**3. RENUNCIATION FOR CHRIST.** The disciples, being astonished at what Christ had said, asked Him, *"Then who can be saved?"* (19:25). Jesus was candid in His response. Only by forgetting the greedy, materialistic values of society and renouncing self can people know God's acceptance (19:26). At this point in the conversation, Peter self-righteously said that he and the others had already given up everything for Jesus and therefore deserved to be given special places in God's kingdom (19:27). Be sure to underscore to the students that God's eternal blessings are given on the basis of His grace, not our good works (19:28-30).

**4. REWARDS OF THE GRACIOUS OWNER.** In Jesus' parable (recorded in 20:1-16), the owner of the vineyard showed graciousness and generosity toward those whom he had hired last. The key idea here is grace, which is God's undeserved mercy and acceptance. His grace is what saves us (Eph. 2:8-9).

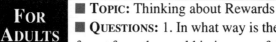

**FOR ADULTS**

■ TOPIC: Thinking about Rewards

■ QUESTIONS: 1. In what way is the kingdom of God radically different from the world in its way of thinking? 2. What was the point of Jesus' parable? 3. Why is it difficult for most believers to rejoice when God prospers their fellow Christians? 4. What causes believers to approach Christian service with a greedy mentality? 5. Why is it always better for believers to trust God to be generous and gracious with them?

**Refused Royalties and Rewards.** If you've ever grown vegetables or raised fruit or flowers, Professor Elwyn M. Meader's work has probably touched your life. Always a generalist, Meader introduced more than 60 varieties from beets to peaches, from kiwi fruit to chrysanthemums. His dedication and unselfishness in sharing germplasm ideas with colleagues throughout the world may have been an even greater contribution than his varieties.

At least half of Meader's introductions came after he "retired" from a distinguished 18-year career as a plant breeder at the University of New Hampshire. He could have gotten rich from royalties on all his releases, but instead he gave them away "as payment for his space on the planet." "I was working for the taxpayers," he would say in his broad Yankee accent, "and the results of my work belonged to them."

A deeply religious Quaker, Meader was always modest about his creations, but not shy about his opinions. He disdained plant patenting. "Plants shouldn't be patented if there has been one dollar of federal or state money used to fund development." At one point in the 1950s, he refused to serve on university committees (except one to abolish all committees). He maintained that he had been hired only to do breeding work. Meader offered inspiring advice to the wave of homesteaders who arrived in the sixties. He said, "Try all things. Hold on to that which is good." But he also added curtly, "If you can't make it without bringing along your TV, you'd better forget the whole thing."

While Meader served in Korea as a horticulturist for the U.S. army command from 1946–1948, he found much of his original material. Present strains of gynoecious (all female) hybrid pickling cucumbers, which have revolutionized the pickling industry, derive from germplasm that he collected in Korea. Meader recognized cold hardiness, photoperiod adaptation, and disease resistance in Korean plant material, and later introduced those traits into his squash, soybean, melon, and raspberry varieties. While traversing a Korean mountainside, he found seeds that became a nursery industry standard.

Meader credited his development of the Royalty Purple Pod bean to his wife's suggestion that it would be easier to pick beans if the pod color differed from the vine color. He also did considerable work reselecting Kohlrabi.

Meader became legendary for his acute powers of observation, his precision of detail, and his almost total recall of information that he had gleaned from decades of studying plant characteristics. His passing away in 1996 may have closed an era. Proud of his self-reliance, Meader asserted that "a committee of one works best." But he also believed that the most valuable thing he had ever done was to give away his findings. God is also pro-generosity.

**Two Types of C.E.O.'s.** In 1996, a large communications company announced that it was firing some 40,000 employees. Shortly afterward, the company then gave the CEO stock options that boosted his total compensation package to 16 million dollars. Earlier, he had been making a mere 6.7 million dollars!

Compare this corporate leader to Aaron Feuerstein. Feuerstein is the owner of Malden Mills. His plant manufactures synthetic fleece, and the company is located in Lawrence, Massachusetts. One night in 1996, the old factory caught fire. The smoking ruins the next morning seemed to spell the end of the Malden Mills manufacturing in the mill town of Lawrence. Everyone assumed that Feuerstein would do what experts advised, namely, to take the insurance money and relocate in another place where cheaper labor and lower taxes would be available.

But Feuerstein knew that his plant was the main source of employment for the town of Lawrence, and that thousands of people were dependent on Malden Mills for their income. Though he could have made vague promises to try to do what he could to help sometime in the distant future, Aaron Feuerstein announced the morning after the disastrous blaze that he would continue paying his workers' health benefits and some compensation, and he would even rebuild his factory right there in Malden!

Not one of Feuerstein's employees was fired. Everyone was taken back as soon as various parts of the manufacturing process were started up again and as the new mill was built and put into operation. The town of Lawrence was saved from becoming another dying New England industrial center. At great cost financially, Aaron Feurerstein put his employees and his town ahead of his own personal profit. Malden Mills now has been rebuilt and is busier than ever, with all the workers busy producing the synthetic fleece for which the company is renowned. Like the generous landowner of Jesus' parable, Feuerstein put people first.

**For Youth**

■ **Topic:** Turn It Around

■ **Questions:** 1. What's unusual about Jesus' parable? 2. In what way had the owner treated all the workers fairly? 3. What is your reason for serving the Lord? 4. In what ways might believers sometimes be like the workers whom the owner first hired? 5. How can believers cultivate the modest attitude of the workers whom the owner hired last?

■ **Illustrations:**

**Experienced a Turnaround.** Elizabeth Eckford and Minnijean Brown Trickey were students entering Central High School in Little Rock, Arkansas. What made their entrance different from many others is that they were two of the nine black students, who, in 1957, brought about the beginning of the end of organized resistance to school integration.

At the 40th anniversary of the event, the former students gathered to recall their experiences. They had seen discrimination in schooling, neighborhoods, restaurants, and travel facilities. They had observed the differences between the white and black communities. Segregation seemed unfair and unjust. Those concerned students chose to turn the situation around. Armed caravans of angry whites gathered at the school and sales of weapons increased. The Arkansas National Guard was brought into the school to turn the nine students away. Mobs followed them, all the while shouting at and threatening them. A famous photograph, which was made by Will Counts, shows a white woman sneering at Eckford.

At the anniversary, Eckford related that the woman contacted her in the late 1960's to apologize and to ask forgiveness. Her conscience had bothered her, and she wanted to make peace.

Like Elizabeth Eckford and Minnijean Trickey, you might experience unfair and unjust treatment. You also might face criticism and perhaps even opposition. However, you too should turn the situation around and allow the grace of God to show through your acts of kindness and compassion.

**Even Before God!** French playwright Jean Anouilh's rendition of the last judgment describes the good and virtuous people standing at heaven's gate. As the crowd waits for the celestial gates to open, a rumor circulates that God is also going to forgive others. The saved are furious, and they complain that they put in a lifetime of living moral lives only now to discover that sinners are going to be admitted to paradise. The redeemed moan that it did not seem fair. They wondered how God could welcome murderers, adulterers, thieves, and other sinners.

By human standards, God's actions do not seem fair. However, God's grace is given freely to all who will accept it by faith. Who are we to complain with that policy?

**Laborers on the Golf Course.** In February, 1998, Casey Martin won a court ruling, which allowed him to use a cart in his golf tournaments. The PGA rules stated that the players had to walk the course. But Martin, who had leg problems, wanted to ride in a cart.

The PGA and many big name players argued that riding was unfair. They contended that fatigue could be a factor in games, given that players must walk six miles during a round. Martin would only walk some 300 yards. It was argued that Martin might gain a competitive edge.

Casey's lawyers maintained that the only important factor was how many times a player struck the golf ball. The law was specific. Handicapped people had to have access to golf courses. Thus, the PGA could not discriminate against Martin.

If Martin had a withered hand and wanted to hit from a tee closer to the green, perhaps his opponents would have had a justifiable objection. However, the mode of transportation to the ball's location was not an integral part of the game. The "it's not fair" murmurs sounded a lot like the vineyard workers in Jesus' parable who complained!

# COMING TO JERUSALEM

**BACKGROUND SCRIPTURE:** Matthew 21:1-17
**DEVOTIONAL READING:** Luke 19:29-44

**KEY VERSE:** Tell the daughter of Zion, Look, your king is coming to you, humble, and mounted on a donkey, and on a colt, the foal of a donkey. Matthew 21:5.

*KING JAMES VERSION*

MATTHEW 21:1 And when they drew nigh unto Jerusalem, and were come to Bethphage, unto the mount of Olives, then sent Jesus two disciples,

2 Saying unto them, Go into the village over against you, and straightway ye shall find an ass tied, and a colt with her: loose them, and bring them unto me.

3 And if any man say ought unto you, ye shall say, The Lord hath need of them, and straightway he will send them.

4 All this was done, that it might be fulfilled which was spoken by the prophet, saying,

5 Tell ye the daughter of Sion, Behold, thy King cometh unto thee, meek, and sitting upon an ass, and a colt the foal of an ass.

6 And the disciples went, and did as Jesus commanded them,

7 And brought the ass, and the colt, and put on them their clothes, and they set him thereon.

8 And a very great multitude spread their garments in the way; others cut down branches from the trees, and strawed them in the way.

9 And the multitudes that went before, and that followed, cried, saying, Hosanna to the Son of David: Blessed is he that cometh in the name of the Lord; Hosanna in the highest.

10 And when he was come into Jerusalem, all the city was moved, saying, Who is this?

11 And the multitude said, This is Jesus the prophet of Nazareth of Galilee.

12 And Jesus went into the temple of God, and cast out all them that sold and bought in the temple, and overthrew the tables of the moneychangers, and the seats of them that sold doves,

13 And said unto them, It is written, My house shall be called the house of prayer; but ye have made it a den of thieves.

*NEW REVISED STANDARD VERSION*

MATTHEW 21:1 When they had come near Jerusalem and had reached Bethphage, at the Mount of Olives, Jesus sent two disciples, 2 saying to them, "Go into the village ahead of you, and immediately you will find a donkey tied, and a colt with her; untie them and bring them to me. 3 If anyone says anything to you, just say this, 'The Lord needs them.' And he will send them immediately." 4 This took place to fulfill what had been spoken through the prophet, saying,

5 "Tell the daughter of Zion,
Look, your king is coming to you,
    humble, and mounted on a donkey,
        and on a colt, the foal of a donkey."

6 The disciples went and did as Jesus had directed them; 7 they brought the donkey and the colt, and put their cloaks on them, and he sat on them. 8 A very large crowd spread their cloaks on the road, and others cut branches from the trees and spread them on the road. 9 The crowds that went ahead of him and that followed were shouting,

"Hosanna to the Son of David!
    Blessed is the one who comes in the name
        of the Lord!
Hosanna in the highest heaven!"

10 When he entered Jerusalem, the whole city was in turmoil, asking, "Who is this?" 11 The crowds were saying, "This is the prophet Jesus from Nazareth in Galilee."

12 Then Jesus entered the temple and drove out all who were selling and buying in the temple, and he overturned the tables of the money changers and the seats of those who sold doves. 13 He said to them, "It is written,

'My house shall be called a house of prayer';
    but you are making it a den of robbers."

| | | |
|---|---|---|
| *Monday, Jan. 31* | Luke 9:51-56 | *Jesus Sets His Face toward Jerusalem* |
| *Tuesday, Feb. 1* | Matthew 21:1-11 | *Jesus Enters Jerusalem amid Hosannas* |
| *Wednesday, Feb. 2* | Matthew 21:12-17 | *Jesus Cleanses the Temple* |
| *Thursday, Feb. 3* | Matthew 21:23-27 | *Chief Priests and Elders Resist Jesus* |
| *Friday, Feb. 4* | Matthew 21:33-46 | *Parable of the Wicked Tenants* |
| *Saturday, Feb. 5* | Matthew 22:23-33 | *A Question about the Resurrection* |
| *Sunday, Feb. 6* | Matthew 22:34-46 | *The Greatest Commandment of All* |

## BACKGROUND

The Gospel of Matthew reveals that Jesus is the King of the Jews and the promised Messiah of Israel. No event illustrated these claims better than the Savior's triumphal entry into Jerusalem. Matthew added details that Mark and Luke did not include in their accounts, such as the prophecy about the Messiah riding on a donkey (Zech. 9:9). Matthew wanted to show the unmistakable connection between the prophecies and promises of the Old Testament and Jesus' life and ministry.

Christ's triumphal entry into Jerusalem was a carefully staged event. He was deliberately showing that He was not coming to the Passover celebration as another pilgrim, but as the Messiah. Every detail in Matthew's record of Jesus' entrance underlined this fact.

The bystanders as well as the disciples clearly understood the symbolism of Christ's entrance. The messianic King was presenting Himself to the people of Israel, and the crowds realized this. Of course, so did the religious authorities. A showdown was inevitable, and it occurred when Jesus cleansed the temple.

The court of the Gentiles had been intended as a place where non-Jews could come to worship the Lord. However, the religious authorities had allowed this area to become a busy bazaar where sacrificial animals could be bought and Roman coins could be exchanged for Jewish currency. Jesus quoted from Isaiah 56:7 and Jeremiah 7:11 to make it clear that He controlled the Lord's house.

## NOTES ON THE PRINTED TEXT

Jesus and His disciples arrived at Jerusalem on the first day of the week preceding Passover. Before entering the holy city, they *reached Bethphage, at the Mount of Olives* (21:1). This was a village located east of Jerusalem on the lower slopes of the Mount of Olives. Bethphage [BETH-fah-jee] was also near the road leading from Jericho to Jerusalem. The Mount of Olives was a mile-long ridge east of Jerusalem and separated from the city by the Kidron Valley. Being approximately 2,700 feet in elevation and thus about 200 feet higher than Jerusalem, the Mount of Olives commanded a superb view of the city and its temple.

Jesus instructed two of His followers to go into Bethphage. As soon as they entered the village, they would *find a donkey tied, and a colt with her* (21:2). The colt, which had never been ridden (Mark 11:2), would be outside in the street and tethered beside a doorway (vs. 4). In ancient times religious ceremonies often called for the use of an animal that had never done any work (Num. 19:2; Deut. 21:3; 1 Sam. 6:7). The mother of the colt would need to be by the animal's side to keep it calm as it carried its rider.

In Scripture a donkey symbolized gentleness, peace, and regality (Judg. 10:4; 12:14; 2 Sam. 16:2; 1 Kings 1:33, 44). By riding into Jerusalem on a colt instead of a war stallion, Christ proclaimed Himself as Israel's humble Messiah (Zech. 9:9). As the son of David and heir to the throne, He came to offer God's people righteousness, peace, and redemption.

Jesus instructed His two disciples to untie the animals and bring them to Him (Matt. 21:2). If they were questioned by the owner, they were to explain that Jesus needed the donkey and its colt. Upon hearing this, the inquirers would permit the disciples to take the animals (21:3; see Mark 11:5-6). Some think the owner was a follower of Christ and thus eager to comply with His request.

Matthew 21:4 says that Christ's entry into Jerusalem on the back of a colt fulfilled Zechariah 9:9. Jerusalem and its inhabitants, here personified as the *daughter of Zion* (Matt. 21:5), were about to see their long-awaited King and Messiah humbly ride into the holy city and accomplish what had been promised in Scripture (Isa. 9:6-7; Mic. 5:2-4; Luke 1:32-33).

The two disciples successfully carried out Jesus' instructions (Matt. 21:6). Having obtained the donkey and its colt, they placed their cloaks (or outer garments) on the animals. As Jesus rode the colt (21:7; see Luke 19:35), a large crowd spread their cloaks on the road. In ancient times, such a gesture would have been considered a display of honor to royalty (2 Kings 9:13). Meanwhile, other people were cutting palm branches off the trees and spreading them on the road (Matt. 21:8; see John 12:13).

Christ had entered Jerusalem during the Feast of Passover, a time when many pilgrims from all over the Roman empire flocked to the holy city to observe this religious holiday (John 12:12). Perhaps it was numerous pilgrims along with residents from Jerusalem that were ahead and behind the Savior and shouting, *"Hosanna to the Son of David!"* (Matt. 21:9). "Hosanna" means "Save now" or "Save, we pray" (see Ps. 118:25).

*"Blessed is the one who comes in the name of the Lord!"* (Matt. 21:9) is a quote from Psalm 118:26. (Psalms 113—118 were usually sung at the Feast of Tabernacles and at Passover). The crowds acclaimed Jesus to be Israel's blessed and promised Messiah, who came in the authority and approval of the Lord. Shouts of *"Hosanna in the highest heaven!"* (Matt. 21:9) implied that the angels were to praise the King as He rode into Jerusalem (see Ps. 148:1-2).

Christ's triumphal entry stirred the entire city with excitement and prompted many to ask, *"Who is this?"* (Matt. 21:10). They were wondering what kind of person could generate such enthusiasm from the crowds. The multitudes explained that Jesus was a prophet from the town of Nazareth in Galilee (21:11).

Christ had ministered in Palestine for several years, teaching many and performing numerous miracles. Sadly, His true identity remained obscure to the people. They saw Him as a great man of God but not as the Son of God. In less than a week shouts of praise would be turned into vehement cries for His crucifixion (see 27:23).

Mark 11:11 indicates that after Jesus had entered Jerusalem, He went into the temple and looked around at everything. Because of the lateness of the hour, He went out to Bethany with the Twelve. It was not until the following day, Monday, that He returned to Jerusalem with His disciples (vs. 12).

Christ entered the large outer court of the Gentiles, the only spot at the temple where non-Jews were permitted to worship. The place was filled activity and noise as Jewish merchants and bankers did business with the people.

During the Passover celebration, many types of sacrifices were made by pilgrims who had traveled from distant locations. Vendors near the temple would sell ceremonially pure animals to the worshipers. Money changers would convert foreign coins into Jewish currency so that visitors could buy the animals they needed and also pay the required half-shekel temple tax.

Jesus would not permit the activity He saw to continue. He purged the court of the Gentiles of those who were *selling and buying* (Matt. 21:12). He also flipped over the tables of the money changers and the benches of the merchants who sold doves (the recognized offering of the impoverished; see Lev. 12:6; 14:22; 15:14, 29; Luke 2:24). Christ did not even permit vendors to carry their merchandise through the temple courts (Mark 11:16). Undoubtedly, many were dismayed and outraged by His actions (vs. 18).

Quoting from Isaiah 56:7, Jesus declared that God's house was to be a place where all people could come to pray and worship Him. And quoting from Jeremiah 7:11, the Savior announced that the money-hungry vendors and bankers had made the temple a *"den of robbers"* (Matt. 21:13).

Gentile worshipers were being defrauded in two ways. First, money changers charged them inflated exchange rates and merchants demanded exorbitant prices for their animals. Second, the non-Jewish pilgrims were prevented from worshiping Israel's God in His temple. Thankfully Jesus put a stop to all this.

## SUGGESTIONS TO TEACHERS

The account of Jesus entering Jerusalem on a donkey and cleansing the temple may be so familiar to your students that they might think they don't have to pay attention to the lesson. You thus will want to present this material in a way that seems fresh, interesting, and relevant.

**1. PROVIDING THE MASTER'S ASSIGNMENT.** Mention the compliance of the two disciples who obeyed Jesus. They readily went and obtained what He wanted for His grand entrance. How willing are we to carry out His commands?

**2. PRESENTING THE MESSIAH'S ANNOUNCEMENT.** Jesus' coming to Jerusalem on the back of a donkey amidst the shouts of the crowds was His public announcement of His identity as the promised Messiah. Explain to the class that Jesus did not accidentally stumble into being arrested and crucified. Also emphasize that He was not merely another worshiper. Rather, He was presenting Himself as the King-Deliverer of Israel.

**3. PRAISING THE MESSIAH'S ARRIVAL.** The people on the streets immediately recognized the symbolism of the entrance and responded accordingly. How do we show our awareness of Jesus' rule in our lives? Is our religion merely a Palm Sunday show, or is our recognition of Christ's lordship evident in our spending, our use of spare time, and our efforts to promote justice in society?

**4. PREVENTING THE TEMPLE'S ABUSE.** Jesus genuinely cared for all people—whether Jews or Gentiles—and that's why He cleansed the temple. The religious leaders had allowed the sacred space to be turned into a bustling market. Are there any programs or activities in our church that prevent those who come from being able to worship the Lord?

---

| | |
|---|---|
| **FOR ADULTS** | ■ TOPIC: The Guidance of the Word |
| | ■ QUESTIONS: 1. In what way was Jesus' entrance into Jerusalem |

grand? 2. How did Jesus demonstrate His humility? 3. In what ways do you recognize the messiahship of Jesus? 4. How can you guard against giving Jesus superficial acclaim? 5. What can you do to encourage others to freely worship the Lord?

■ **ILLUSTRATIONS:**

**Powerful Symbol.** Waving palm branches during Jesus' entry into Jerusalem had immense political meaning. Like a flag is to moderns, so palm branches were a symbol of nationalism to people in Judea. The Jews, while living under Roman occupation forces, regarded palm branches as a way of expressing their long-suppressed traditions of freedom.

Palm branches reminded the people of the great revolt by the Jewish hero, Simon Maccabeus, against the cruel Antioches Epiphanes IV, who had desecrated the temple and tried to stamp out Judaism. In 142 B.C., Simon Maccabeus drove out the occupation army. (The Jewish festival of Hanukkah celebrates this victory). When Maccabeus paraded down the Mount of Olives in his victory procession, the grateful people threw down palm branches to welcome the national liberator. From then on, palm branches stood as the symbol of liberation by a great national hero. The coins carried the likeness of the palm branches. Like firecrackers and red-white-and-blue bunting on July 4th for Americans, palm branches symbolized national pride and freedom for those in Jerusalem the day that Jesus rode into the city on a donkey.

When Jesus arrived, some people evidently mistook Him for the national liberator in the mold of Simon Maccabeus. They looked to Jesus to bark commands and rally troops. They thought He would be another powerful generalissimo who would bring victory to the nation.

**Missing the Real Event.** The story is told of the boy from the country who came to town many years ago to see the circus. He had never seen one before, and was excited at the prospect of watching the clowns, the elephants, the lions, and the tigers. The boy got up early and drove his horse and wagon to town in time for the big parade. Standing at the curb, he clapped enthusiastically as the steam calliope tooted and the stream of gaudily painted circus wagons rumbled by.

The boy shrieked with delight at the clowns and acrobats, and he grew wide-eyed with wonder at the sight of the wild animals in their cages. He laughed at the shuffling lines of elephants and watched the jugglers with wonder. When the parade reached its end, the boy rushed up to the last man in the procession and handed him his money, and then the boy went back home. The lad didn't discover until later that he hadn't seen the circus but had merely watched the parade. He missed the acts under the big top and merely caught sight of the procession leading to the performance.

Some church members are a bit like that boy. They watch the Palm Sunday procession, but they never go any farther. They enjoy a brief emotional experience but miss the real action of the cross and the empty tomb. They enjoy the pageantry and watch the parade briefly, but they never participate in the meaning of the resurrection. Sadly, they never get beyond Palm Sunday's events.

**FOR YOUTH** ■ TOPIC: Greatness through Humility
■ QUESTIONS: 1. What impresses you the most about Jesus' entry into Jerusalem? 2. Why did Jesus have the authority to cleanse the temple? 3. How do you think you would have responded if you had been in Jerusalem and saw Jesus riding on a donkey? 4. What can you do to let others know that you worship Jesus as the Messiah? 5. How might you encourage them also to worship Him?

■ ILLUSTRATIONS:
**Understand the Excitement.** On Sunday, January 25, 1998, the Denver Broncos defeated the highly favored Green Bay Packers 31-24 to win Super Bowl XXXII. The win gave the AFC its first victory over an NFC team in 13 long years. It also gave Quarterback John Elway and the Denver team their first Super Bowl win in four tries. The city of Denver celebrated wildly. Some fans, fueled by too much alcohol consumption, destroyed property in their exuberance.

While people in society expect and accept the wild joy and excitement of a football team winning the Superbowl, they have difficulty understanding how the entire city of Jerusalem could be thrown into turmoil over Jesus' arrival. They fail to understand that Jesus is no ordinary person. He is the King and Messiah!

**Unwanted Royalty.** On November 10, 1997, Australians voted for 76 elected delegates to a constitutional convention to be held in 1998. One surprise was that over 50 percent of all Australians supported key governmental figures in wanting the Queen of England to bow out as Australia's head of state, in removing her face from Australian currency, and in deleting any reference to Australia as part of the British crown. The governor-general would replace the queen and become the country's president.

In Jerusalem, key religious and governmental leaders wanted Jesus out of the picture. He was a King nobody wanted around. But without the finesse and political correctness demonstrated by the Australian politicians, these leaders pulled the strings and made backroom deals to have Jesus discredited and murdered.

**Fleeting Greatness.** In July 1997, 16-year-old Martina Hingis won her first Wimbleton Ladies Singles title. She was ranked No. 1 in the world and was the youngest champion in more than a century. Between the ages of 14 and 16, she won several Grand Slam titles, the Australian Open, and various other matches throughout the tennis world. She travels with her mother and her male hitting partner-coach. When asked whether she can get the ball back to him if he hits it really hard, she replied that she could because she is No. 1 in the world.

Evidently Hingis has not learned how fleeting greatness can be. Named for tennis star Martina Navratilova, Martina Hingis grew up hearing about Steffi Graf. However, some of you probably have not heard about either Graf or Navratilova. At some point Hingis also will slip out of people's memories.

Jesus reminded us that true greatness comes through humility, not dancing on a tennis court with a single finger in the air yelling, "I'm No. 1!" Model your humility and life on Him who is truly great.

# WATCHING FOR CHRIST'S RETURN

**BACKGROUND SCRIPTURE:** Matthew 24:1—25:13
**DEVOTIONAL READING:** Matthew 24:36-44

**KEY VERSE:** Keep awake therefore, for you know neither the day nor the hour. Matthew 25:13.

*KING JAMES VERSION*

MATTHEW 24:45 Who then is a faithful and wise servant, whom his lord hath made ruler over his household, to give them meat in due season?

46 Blessed is that servant, whom his lord when he cometh shall find so doing.

47 Verily I say unto you, That he shall make him ruler over all his goods.

48 But and if that evil servant shall say in his heart, My lord delayeth his coming;

49 And shall begin to smite his fellowservants, and to eat and drink with the drunken;

50 The lord of that servant shall come in a day when he looketh not for him, and in an hour that he is not aware of,

51 And shall cut him asunder, and appoint him his portion with the hypocrites: there shall be weeping and gnashing of teeth.

25:1 Then shall the kingdom of heaven be likened unto ten virgins, which took their lamps, and went forth to meet the bridegroom.

2 And five of them were wise, and five were foolish.

3 They that were foolish took their lamps, and took no oil with them:

4 But the wise took oil in their vessels with their lamps.

5 While the bridegroom tarried, they all slumbered and slept.

6 And at midnight there was a cry made, Behold, the bridegroom cometh; go ye out to meet him.

7 Then all those virgins arose, and trimmed their lamps.

8 And the foolish said unto the wise, Give us of your oil; for our lamps are gone out.

9 But the wise answered, saying, Not so; lest there be not enough for us and you: but go ye rather to them that sell, and buy for yourselves.

10 And while they went to buy, the bridegroom came; and they that were ready went in with him to the marriage: and the door was shut.

11 Afterward came also the other virgins, saying, Lord, Lord, open to us.

12 But he answered and said, Verily I say unto you, I know you not.

13 Watch therefore, for ye know neither the day nor the hour wherein the Son of man cometh.

*NEW REVISED STANDARD VERSION*

MATTHEW 24:45 "Who then is the faithful and wise slave, whom his master has put in charge of his household, to give the other slaves their allowance of food at the proper time? 46 Blessed is that slave whom his master will find at work when he arrives. 47 Truly I tell you, he will put that one in charge of all his possessions. 48 But if that wicked slave says to himself, 'My master is delayed,' 49 and he begins to beat his fellow slaves, and eats and drinks with drunkards, 50 the master of that slave will come on a day when he does not expect him and at an hour that he does not know. 51 He will cut him in pieces and put him with the hypocrites, where there will be weeping and gnashing of teeth.

25:1 "Then the kingdom of heaven will be like this. Ten bridesmaids took their lamps and went to meet the bridegroom. 2 Five of them were foolish, and five were wise. 3 When the foolish took their lamps, they took no oil with them; 4 but the wise took flasks of oil with their lamps. 5 As the bridegroom was delayed, all of them became drowsy and slept. 6 But at midnight there was a shout, 'Look! Here is the bridegroom! Come out to meet him.' 7 Then all those bridesmaids got up and trimmed their lamps. 8 The foolish said to the wise, 'Give us some of your oil, for our lamps are going out.' 9 But the wise replied, 'No! there will not be enough for you and for us; you had better go to the dealers and buy some for yourselves.' 10 And while they went to buy it, the bridegroom came, and those who were ready went with him into the wedding banquet; and the door was shut. 11 Later the other bridesmaids came also, saying, 'Lord, lord, open to us.' 12 But he replied, 'Truly I tell you, I do not know you.' 13 Keep awake therefore, for you know neither the day nor the hour."

| | | |
|---|---|---|
| Monday, Feb. 7 | Matthew 24:1-8 | *Signs of the End* |
| Tuesday, Feb. 8 | Matthew 24:9-14 | *Jesus' Followers Will Be Persecuted* |
| Wednesday, Feb. 9 | Matthew 24:15-28 | *Beware of False Messiahs* |
| Thursday, Feb. 10 | Matthew 24:29-35 | *Coming of the Son of Man* |
| Friday, Feb. 11 | Matthew 24:36-44 | *Be Watchful and Expectant* |
| Saturday, Feb. 12 | Matthew 24:45-51 | *Call to Be Faithful Servants* |
| Sunday, Feb. 13 | Matthew 25:1-13 | *Parable of the Ten Bridesmaids* |

## BACKGROUND

Even sophisticated world travelers were awed by the splendor of Herod's temple. When simple peasants from the dusty towns and villages of mud huts and basalt-block hovels gazed at the gleaming expanses of white marble and gold leaf, they were amazed. Jesus' disciples were so impressed by this architectural marvel that they called Him to admire it with them. Christ's reply startled them. The gorgeous edifice would be reduced to rubble (Matt. 24:1-2).

Jesus was aware of the seething unrest in the Jewish land, which threatened to erupt into armed revolt against the despised Roman conquerors. Jesus prophesied that the Romans would ruthlessly squash any uprising. Later, at the disciples' insistence, Jesus explained that terrible times were in store and that many false messiahs would arise. He warned the disciples to be wary of them and to watch and be ready for His return (24:3-44). Jesus' parables about the unfaithful slave and the ten bridesmaids, which are the subjects of this week's lesson, underscored the need for watchfulness.

Jesus' prophecy about the future of temple was literally fulfilled. Open rebellion broke out in A.D. 66. In A.D. 70, the Romans under Titus razed Jerusalem and burned the temple. Many Jews were executed and others were enslaved. The Tenth Legion was stationed in Jerusalem, and Titus held a triumphal procession in Rome (in which he displayed the golden candelabra from the temple).

## NOTES ON THE PRINTED TEXT

Christ did not want His disciples to waste their time trying to figure out the date of His return. If they could have predicted or calculated it, they might have discontinued serving Him and just waited for the momentous day to arrive. The key to spiritual preparedness was faithfully doing the Lord's work in anticipation of His eventual arrival.

Jesus related the story of a man who was away from his property for awhile. He chose a *"faithful and wise slave"* (24:45) to be in charge of the other workers in his household. The head servant had the important responsibility of providing food (and perhaps other necessities) for the rest of his master's laborers. If these servants did not have their needs met during their master's absence, his household would have fallen into disarray. Because so much was at stake, it behooved the head servant to obey his master while he was gone (24:46).

Jesus solemnly assured the Twelve that if the master, upon his return, had found his servant to be faithful, he would *"put that one in charge of all his possessions"* (24:47). Christ was urging His disciples to be His trustworthy and devoted servants. For example, they were to minister to one another in love and reach out to the lost with the gospel. In the heavenly kingdom, He would reward them with increased responsibilities for their faithful and consistent service.

Christ then had His disciples imagine the head servant being wicked and self-centered rather than good and faithful. Convinced that his master would be away a long time (24:48), this servant treated the other members of the household abusively by having them beaten. He also lived indulgently by eating and drinking *"with drunkards"* (24:49). His irresponsible behavior undoubtedly wreaked havoc in his master's household.

Jesus told the Twelve that the servant's master would return on a day when he would least expect it, *"at an hour that he does not know"* (24:50). Christ's words were stern and sobering. The master would *"cut him in pieces and put him with the hypocrites, where there will be weeping and gnashing of teeth"* (24:51). This means the master would swiftly judge and severely punish the servant for his evil, dishonest behavior. Jesus was teaching that those who rejected Him and refused to serve Him were foolish and faced eternal ruin.

Jesus grew more specific in His counsel by comparing Himself to a bridegroom at a typical village wedding. *"Then the kingdom of heaven will be like this"* (25:1). Jesus made it clear that readiness was necessary for His return and the inauguration of God's rule, just as the participants at a wedding feast had to be prepared for the celebration.

*"Ten bridesmaids took their lamps and went to meet the bridegroom. Five of them were foolish, and five were wise"* (25:1-2). Each of the young women had a small clay lamp to dimly light their way. Since the lamps held only a little olive oil, it was necessary to carry extra supplies in a small clay jug. Only five out of the ten bridesmaids had brought along their flasks. *"When the foolish took their lamps, they took no oil with them; but the wise took flasks of oil with their lamps"* (25:3-4).

The bridegroom was delayed and the bridesmaids fell asleep (25:5). Near midnight, the men of the wedding party arrived. They shouted that the bridegroom was there. *"But at midnight there was a shout, 'Look! Here is the bridegroom! Come out to meet him' "* (25:6).

The bridesmaids awoke. They found their tiny lamps either sputtering out or completely extinguished (25:7). The five who had brought extra oil poured it into their lamps. Sadly, the other five had run out of lamp fuel. *"The foolish said to the wise, 'Give us some of your oil, for our lamps are going out' "* (25:8).

Those with extra olive oil refused to share it. If they had shared, it was highly likely that all ten lamps would have gone out before the group arrived at the wedding. Thus, the five prepared bridesmaids urged the other five to hurry off and buy some oil. *"But the wise replied, 'No! There will not be enough for you and for us; you had better go to the dealers and buy some for yourselves' "* (25:9).

While the five bridesmaids were gone, the bridegroom arrived and everyone went into the wedding banquet. The door to the residence was then shut (25:10). By this time, those remaining outside would not be allowed to enter.

Having bought their refills, the five other bridesmaids finally arrived. Perhaps over the laughter and the music of the reception, they were able to get the attention of the bridegroom. They begged that the door be opened so that they could join the festivities (25:11). The bridegroom evidently thought that they were party crashers, for he told them to leave. *"But he replied, 'Truly I tell you, I do not know you' "* (25:12).

Jesus hammered home His main point once again to the disciples. They were to be ready at all times, for no one knew the time of His return. *"Keep awake therefore, for you know neither the day nor the hour"* (25:13).

## SUGGESTIONS TO TEACHERS

The coming of the year 2000 has stirred enormous talk about the new millennium. And with such talk has come speculation by some about the day of Christ's return. Undoubtedly a few of the members of your class are curious about when Jesus will come again.

**1. WARNINGS.** As you cover the Scripture text for this lesson, be sure to emphasize the following salient points. First, there is a summons for endurance. In other words, despite the presence of dire reports and desperate conditions, believers must persevere in the faith. Second, there will be sightings of false messiahs. Jesus warned that phony prophets and fake saviors would continually present themselves and threaten to mislead the unwary. Third, there is the silence of the Father. Only God knows the day of Christ's return. We thus must never presume to think that we can second-guess the Lord!

**2. WATCHFULNESS.** Jesus commanded His followers to be busy serving Him rather than speculating when He might return.

**3. PREPAREDNESS.** For the remainder of the class time, explain the way the parable of the ten bridesmaids applies to believers today. The key idea to stress is preparedness!

---

| FOR ADULTS | ■ TOPIC: The Joy of Being Prepared |
|---|---|

■ QUESTIONS: 1.Why did Jesus urge His followers to be ready at all times for His return? 2. In what ways did the two groups of bridesmaids differ from each other? 3. Why is it important to remember that Jesus will one day return? 4. What can you do to get yourself ready for Christ's return? 5. How can you avoid becoming preoccupied with the Savior's advent?

■ ILLUSTRATIONS:

**Daily Preparedness.** Annie Sherwood Hawkes was born in Hoosick, New York, which is a tiny upstate village. She was only 14 when she began writing poems for newspapers. She became a member of the Hanson Place Baptist Church in Brooklyn, New York, when she married and moved there in 1859. Dr. Robert Lowry, the pastor, was the person responsible for her career of hymn-writing, and he wrote music for several of her hymns, including "I Need Thee Every Hour." Her hymns were published in various popular hymn books.

Annie Hawkes wrote this hymn while doing her regular household tasks. It expressed her great joy in the constant companionship of the Master. She was surprised at how well received the hymn was in churches. It was only when Annie experienced the loss of her husband that she realized how comforting the hymn could be in times of sorrow. Like Annie Hawkes, it is imperative that we develop strong, spiritual lives during peaceful hours so that we might be victorious when difficulties come.

**Wacky Watching.** In Jerusalem, a bumper sticker that is popular among a certain faction of Orthodox Jews states, "PREPARE FOR THE COMING OF THE MESSIAH!" Some apparently feel compelled to get ready in strange ways in the ancient holy city. For example, in Jerusalem's Kfar Shaul Psychiatric Hospital, about fifty patients each year are received who are under delusions that they are the messiah or some other biblical figure. Dr. Moshe Kalian, a psychiatrist at Kfar Shaul, and his colleagues have labeled this disorder the "Jerusalem Syndrome."

Some tourists who visit the area become convinced that they have been divinely ordained to carry out a special mandate or message, usually in bizarre ways. Some claim to be Jesus Christ. Others insist that God has commanded them to undertake a strange mission in anticipation of the advent of the Messiah.

Cases are split about equally between Christians and Jews. About half are from North America, usually the United States, and the rest mostly from Western Europe. At times these cases are comical, such as the German who angrily telephoned police to complain that the hotel staff had prevented him from preparing the Last Supper, or the naked, sword-wielding man who raced through Jerusalem claiming that he was sent on a mission to heal the blind.

It's clear that these are not the ways to prepare for the Lord's return. Jesus calls us to please Him where we live each day. As we await His return, we are to live in a manner that is characterized by diligence, virtue, and integrity.

**Eyes on the Prize.** In a 1995 convocation address given at Harvard Divinity School, Dr. Cornel West (professor of the philosophy of religion at Harvard Divinity School and professor of Afro-American studies in Harvard's Faculty of Arts and Sciences) said the following. "It takes tremendous audacity and a deep sense of folly to be a Christian at the end of this dreadful and ghastly century. I hope you always hold on to the notion that however dark and difficult the moment may be, the world is still incomplete, history is still unfinished, and the future is still open-ended. What you think and what you do can make a difference. You can energize and galvanize even a cynical and world-weary people in the oldest surviving democracy.

"Maybe we can keep alive the tradition of struggle for decency and dignity. Maybe not. T. S. Eliot says in *The Four Quartets* that 'Ours is in the trying; the rest is not our business.' He is absolutely right. There are no guarantees. But, you see, I come from a black tradition of combative spirituality. It has always looked the absurd in the face and has seen the misery, but it has never allowed misery to have the last word, even if all we could do at the moment was sing a song, pray a prayer, shed a tear, crack a smile, try to preserve our sense of dignity and decency in the midst of brutality, no matter how subtle.

"I rest my all on that tradition. . . . I hope that all of you will keep your heads to the sky. . . . Keep your hands on the plow, . . . even when what you are doing takes the form of unadvertised service and nobody may see it but you. You are still making a difference. You are preserving your sense of personal and moral . . . integrity. Last but not least, keep your eyes not so much on each other and our own inadequacies and shortcomings, or on the evil that lurks in the hearts of each and every one of us. . . . Keep your eyes on the prize."

---

**FOR YOUTH**

■ TOPIC: Be Ready!

■ QUESTIONS: 1. What was the faithful and sensible servant doing when his master returned? 2. What is the main point of the parable of the 10 bridesmaids? 3. Do you look forward to Christ's return? 4. What can you do right now to get ready for Jesus' coming? 5. How can you encourage your friends to get ready?

■ ILLUSTRATIONS:

**Watch as Well!** John McMillan was a noteworthy Presbyterian missionary, evangelist, and educator to frontier western Pennsylvania. On his way to a meeting of the Presbytery of Pittsburgh, McMillan and Pastor Joseph Patterson, one of the Board of Trustees of Jefferson College, stopped at an inn. Two glasses of refreshment were placed on the table before them. Patterson closed his eyes and prayed. His prayer was extremely long. When he opened his eyes, there were two empty glasses on the table. McMillan is reputed to have said, "My brother, you must watch as well as pray!" Jesus also urged vigilance. Faithful disciples are to be watchful and prepared for His return.

**Two-Minute Drill.** Football teams develop and practice two-minute drills. These are important in the final minutes of a close or tie game. The hope is to develop a series of plays that can be run without the need of a huddle. Each athlete must be prepared to carry out his assignment as a blocker, receiver, or runner when seconds count. Obviously, preparation is extremely important.

Disciples are to have the same sort of spiritual readiness. We have designated assignments as God's people, and we should carry them out faithfully as our Lord has outlined.

**Happy in Serving.** Jillian Woodruff, a sophomore at Duke University, taught a freshman course entitled *An Introduction to American Sign Language and Deaf Culture*. Fluent in sign language, Spanish, Italian, and Chinese, the young woman has always used her skills to communicate with others.

As the daughter of former Pittsburgh Steeler cornerback Dwayne Woodruff, Jillian grew up watching her father do charity and volunteer work. In the eighth grade, she began to volunteer at the Regency Hall Nursing Home, playing games with the residents and creating a music program. She was also a candy-striper at Allegheny General Hospital's cardiology and oncology units.

However, Jillian's real passion became signing. In the sixth grade at Carson Middle School, she watched a deaf girl sign in her class with an interpreter. Jillian bought a book on signing so that she could converse with the student. Jillian got better and better through practice and lessons. By the tenth grade she was volunteering at Western Pennsylvania School for the Deaf. Even at college in North Carolina, she continues to serve at the Duke University Medical Center, signing in the center for deaf toddlers and using her Spanish as an interpreter.

Jillian is one who has learned the joy that comes from serving others. This is the joy and service that Jesus spoke about to the disciples and each of us.

# DEATH OF JESUS

**BACKGROUND SCRIPTURE:** Matthew 27:32-61
**DEVOTIONAL READING:** John 19:16-30

**KEY VERSE:** Truly this man was God's Son! Matthew 27:54b.

*KING JAMES VERSION*

MATTHEW 27:38 Then were there two thieves crucified with him, one on the right hand, and another on the left.

39 And they that passed by reviled him, wagging their heads,

40 And saying, Thou that destroyest the temple, and buildest it in three days, save thyself. If thou be the Son of God, come down from the cross.

41 Likewise also the chief priests mocking him, with the scribes and elders, said,

42 He saved others; himself he cannot save. If he be the King of Israel, let him now come down from the cross, and we will believe him.

43 He trusted in God; let him deliver him now, if he will have him: for he said, I am the Son of God.

44 The thieves also, which were crucified with him, cast the same in his teeth.

45 Now from the sixth hour there was darkness over all the land unto the ninth hour.

46 And about the ninth hour Jesus cried with a loud voice, saying, Eli, Eli, lama sabachthani? that is to say, My God, my God, why hast thou forsaken me?

47 Some of them that stood there, when they heard that, said, This man calleth for Elias.

48 And straightway one of them ran, and took a spunge, and filled it with vinegar, and put it on a reed, and gave him to drink.

49 The rest said, Let be, let us see whether Elias will come to save him.

50 Jesus, when he had cried again with a loud voice, yielded up the ghost.

51 And, behold, the veil of the temple was rent in twain from the top to the bottom; and the earth did quake, and the rocks rent;

52 And the graves were opened; and many bodies of the saints which slept arose,

53 And came out of the graves after his resurrection, and went into the holy city, and appeared unto many.

54 Now when the centurion, and they that were with him, watching Jesus, saw the earthquake, and those things that were done, they feared greatly, saying, Truly this was the Son of God.

*NEW REVISED STANDARD VERSION*

MATTHEW 27:38 Then two bandits were crucified with him, one on his right and one on his left. 39 Those who passed by derided him, shaking their heads 40 and saying, "You who would destroy the temple and build it in three days, save yourself! If you are the Son of God, come down from the cross." 41 In the same way the chief priests also, along with the scribes and elders, were mocking him, saying, 42 "He saved others; he cannot save himself. He is the King of Israel; let him come down from the cross now, and we will believe in him. 43 He trusts in God; let God deliver him now, if he wants to; for he said, 'I am God's Son.'" 44 The bandits who were crucified with him also taunted him in the same way.

45 From noon on, darkness came over the whole land until three in the afternoon. 46 And about three o'clock Jesus cried with a loud voice, "Eli, Eli, lema sabachthani?" that is, "My God, my God, why have you forsaken me?" 47 When some of the bystanders heard it, they said, "This man is calling for Elijah." 48 At once one of them ran and got a sponge, filled it with sour wine, put it on a stick, and gave it to him to drink. 49 But the others said, "Wait, let us see whether Elijah will come to save him." 50 Then Jesus cried again with a loud voice and breathed his last. 51 At that moment the curtain of the temple was torn in two, from top to bottom. The earth shook, and the rocks were split. 52 The tombs also were opened, and many bodies of the saints who had fallen asleep were raised. 53 After his resurrection they came out of the tombs and entered the holy city and appeared to many. 54 Now when the centurion and those with him, who were keeping watch over Jesus, saw the earthquake and what took place, they were terrified and said, "Truly this man was God's Son!"

## BACKGROUND

This week's lesson focuses on the death of Jesus on the cross. Crucifixion as a means of torture and execution was invented in the East and adopted by the Romans, who used it for slaves and lower-class persons. Victims of Roman crucifixion typically had to carry the crossbeam of their cross to the place of execution. They (or someone else) would also often carry a tablet citing the charge against them, which was then sometimes nailed to the top of the cross.

At the execution site, a longer beam or stake would be placed on the ground, and the crossbeam would be attached perpendicularly to it at or near the top. Then the victims' hands, and sometimes their feet, would be affixed to the cross by means of cords or nails. Finally, the cross would be lifted and dropped into a hole.

Victims sometimes lasted for two or three days, finally succumbing to death due to poor blood circulation and heart failure. If the crucifiers wanted to make the victims last longer, they would have first outfitted the cross with a block of wood as a seat or a footrest. This would give the victims support and improve their circulation. If the crucifiers wanted to shorten the victims' life, they would break their legs with a club to remove their ability to support themselves with their legs.

## NOTES ON THE PRINTED TEXT

After Jesus had celebrated the Lord's Supper with His disciples, they went out to the Mount of Olives. There Judas betrayed Jesus with a kiss, the authorities arrested Him, and His disciples abandoned Him. Caiaphas the high priest interrogated Jesus, the Sanhedrin condemned Him to death, and He was then treated abusively. Meanwhile, out in the courtyard, Peter denied his allegiance to Christ three times (Matt. 26:17-75).

Early the following morning, the religious leaders finalized their decision to execute Jesus and placed Him in Pilate's custody. After the governor questioned Jesus further, Pilate turned Him over to the soldiers for crucifixion. Meanwhile, Judas, who was now filled with remorse, tried in vain to return his thirty coins to the religious leaders. He then threw the money into the temple and went off and hanged himself (27:1-37).

Two robbers were crucified with Jesus. He was positioned in the center, with each of these criminals on either side of Him (27:38). By being executed with transgressors, Jesus identified Himself with the sin of humankind. He became the substitute for even the worst offenders (see Isa. 53:12).

A number of people walked by Jesus as He hung on the cross and derided him (Matt. 27:39). They taunted Him to rescue Himself from His dilemma (27:40). Certain religious leaders also hurled abusive remarks at Christ (27:41-43). Moreover, the thieves on either side of Jesus launched the same type of insulting remarks at Him (27:44). One of the criminals, however, later repented and asked Christ to include him in His kingdom (see Luke 23:39-43).

At the sixth hour, or noon, *darkness came over the whole land* (Matt. 27:45). Darkness in Scripture is often associated with God's judgment. The darkness during Jesus' crucifixion symbolized the fact that the Father had turned His back on the Son, for on the cross the Son had borne the sins of humanity.

At the ninth hour, or 3 P.M., Jesus cried out in a loud voice, *"Eli, Eli, lema sabachthani"* (Matt. 27:46). When translated, this statement meant, *"My God, my God, why have you forsaken me?"* This is a quote from Psalm 22:1, and indicates that Jesus was experiencing separation from His heavenly Father.

Because Jesus used the word *"Eli"* (Matt. 27:46), some bystanders imagined He was calling for Elijah to rescue Him from His deplorable situation (27:47). According to Jewish tradition, Elijah would one day return and deliver the upright from their suffering.

One of the bystanders ran, obtained a sponge, and soaked it with *sour wine* (27:48), which was a popular beverage among infantry soldiers and poorer people in Palestine. Placing the sponge on a reed (that is, the stalk of a hyssop plant), the bystander extended it to Jesus so that He might drink from it. But others standing around told the person with a sponge to leave Jesus alone (27:49). They superstitiously thought that Elijah might come to rescue Him.

After Jesus took a drink of the wine vinegar, the end finally came as He cried out once and died (27:50). From John 19:30, it would appear that what Jesus cried out was a declaration of victory. Suddenly, the curtain that covered the entrance to the most holy place in the temple was ripped from top to bottom, as if by the hand of God (Matt. 27:51). This symbolized that, because of Christ's death, access to God was no longer barred to believers.

Many people were resurrected when an earthquake occurred, splitting rocks and opening their tombs (27:52). These people went into Jerusalem and *appeared to many* (27:53). Little is known about who the resurrected people were or how the resurrection occurred. But clearly this was a foretaste of the future resurrection of the righteous, which is made possible by Christ's death.

The earthquake and the other strange phenomena frightened a centurion at the cross, as well as other soldiers standing there. They accurately connected these phenomena with Jesus' death and exclaimed, *"Truly this man was God's Son!"*

(27:54). These soldiers who had just mocked Jesus and treated Him with the utmost cruelty, now believed (at least on some level) His claim to divinity.

## SUGGESTIONS TO TEACHERS

There were a number of people involved in the drama of Jesus' crucifixion. Spend a few moments with the members of your class discussing each person. This will help the students to identify more readily with the events that occurred.

**1. SIMON OF CYRENE.** The soldiers forced a man named Simon, from the North African city of Cyrene, to carry Jesus' cross (27:32). Simon may have become a follower of Christ as a result of this unexpected meeting, for it appears that later his sons were known to the Christian community (see Mark 15:21).

**2. THE CROWD.** Onlookers jeered Christ because He had claimed He could destroy and rebuild the temple in three days (Matt. 27:40; see John 2:19). They evidently were taking their cues from Israel's religious leaders, who ridiculed Jesus by asserting that He could rescue others but was powerless to deliver Himself (Matt. 27:41-42). Remark to the class how easy it is for people to be manipulated. What evil forces and values attempt to control our thinking, and how can we keep from being manipulated by them?

**3. THE CENTURION AND THE SOLDIERS.** At first the squad thought that Jesus was just another criminal they were executing. But then all the strange phenomena that occurred during the time of Jesus' crucifixion changed their minds about Him (27:54). Though these Gentile soldiers might not have understood fully the phrase they used, they made an appropriate confession. In contrast, the Jewish leaders present continued to deride their Messiah.

**4. THE WOMEN.** A number of Jesus' female followers stood at a distance from Golgotha and watched His crucifixion as well as the events that followed. Earlier, as Jesus had journeyed from Galilee to Jerusalem, many of these women had accompanied Him and provided for His material needs (Matt. 27:55; see Luke 8:2-3). They were prepared to do so until the end.

**5. JOSEPH OF ARIMATHEA.** Once Jesus had died, the question became what to do with His body. The Roman officials no doubt would have preferred to let Jesus' body hang on the cross until it had decayed. But Jesus' friends wanted His body to be given a more dignified burial. Joseph of Arimathea, who was wealthy and a member of the Sanhedrin, asked Pilate for permission to take the body of Jesus and bury it (Matt. 27:57-58). After Joseph placed Jesus' body in a nearby rock tomb, he left the burial chamber and rolled a large disc-shaped stone along a sloped groove to close off the tomb's entrance (vss. 59-60).

**6. JESUS.** The main focus of this week's lesson is that Jesus, the Messiah, suffered for the sins of all people. His death on the cross is astonishing. Who could have imagined that God would choose to offer salvation to the world through a humble, suffering servant rather thank a glorious king? The idea is contrary to human pride and worldly thinking. But God often works in ways we don't expect. The Messiah's strength is shown by His humility, suffering, and mercy.

**FOR ADULTS**

■ TOPIC: Jesus' Death on Our Behalf
■ QUESTIONS: 1. In what ways did Jesus suffer on the cross? 2. How do you think Jesus' disciples felt as He was being crucified? 3. What stands out most to you about Jesus' execution at Golgotha? 4. Where would your salvation in Christ be without His crucifixion? 5. How might you give thanks to God for the atoning sacrifice of His Son?

■ **ILLUSTRATIONS:**

**Skip the Crucifixion?** I recall talking with a woman after a Palm Sunday service, and hearing her tell what a glorious worship experience it had been, and how she was looking forward to the music and celebration of the following Sunday at the Easter service. As she turned to walk away, I said something about looking forward to seeing her at the Holy Week services. She turned back and announced, "Oh, I won't be coming to any of them." Assuming that she had to work or might be traveling, I said, "If your job keeps you busy or if you're away, we'll miss you but understand."

"Oh, it's not that at all," the woman blurted. "I don't want to hear all that morbid stuff about a cross. I don't need any more tragedy and suffering, defeat, and death reports. Forget that dreary stuff about betrayals by Judas and agony in Gethsemane and dying on Calvary. Give me the positive upbeat message of Palm Sunday and Easter! I want the happy news of a triumphant Jesus, not the gloomy report of a helpless victim."

This woman is not the only person who would like to skip directly from the motorcade, confetti, and cheering crowds of Palm Sunday to the Hallelujah Chorus of Easter. Many people want to ignore the disappointment, hurt, loneliness, pain, and suffering that Jesus experienced at Calvary. Perhaps it's because we Americans prize victory and success.

But the events of Holy Week tell about some defeats and failures. Jesus' friends betrayed Him, and He experienced agony in the garden of Gethsemane. He endured the humiliation of being arrested, falsely accused, wrongfully condemned to death, and tortured by goons. But the agony of the cross was nothing compared to Jesus' experience of separation from the Father. That must have been the worst suffering of all, and it was necessary for Christ to experience in order to atone for our sins.

**Who Is Jesus to You?** People today have some of the most irreverent notions about Jesus. For instance, advertising and marketing expert Bruce Barton saw Jesus as a Madison Avenue salesperson who was promoting His "product." Norm

Evans, onetime lineman for the Miami Dolphins, portrayed Jesus as a 6-foot, 6-inch, 260-pound defensive tackle who always crashed through into the opponents' backfield. Former Yankee Fritz Peterson regarded Jesus as a baseball player, stating that if Jesus were sliding into second base, He'd knock the second baseman into left field to break up a double play. Andrew Lloyd Webber, the composer of musical hits, fancied Jesus Christ as a "Superstar."

For a reality check, consider the way the people around the cross saw Jesus. Ponder the words and the reactions of the centurion, the two bandits being crucified along with Jesus that day, the bystanders, and the disciples. Now consider who Jesus is to you. Is He the Savior who laid down His life on your behalf?

---

**FOR YOUTH**

■ TOPIC: Darkness before Dawn

■ QUESTIONS: 1. What are some of the unusual events that took place as Jesus hung on the cross? 2. How did the onlookers react to these events? 3. As you think about Jesus' sufferings on the cross, what do you want to say to Him in prayer? 4. Have you ever received the effect of Jesus' death for you by placing your faith in Him? If not, will you do it today? 5. What are some ways you can make the sacrifice of Christ known to others in your world?

■ ILLUSTRATIONS:

**Misplaced Confidence.** "Had we been on duty at the sepulcher, the holy body would ne'er have left it!" An officer of The Royal Scots, history's oldest extant regiment, uttered those words to a French general in 1633. While we may smile like those 17th century soldiers at the claim of the Royal Scots, their nickname, "Pontius Pilate's Bodyguard," still points to a fact.

The religious leaders, Pilate, and the guards all thought they had Jesus locked away in His tomb. All that supposedly remained were His body and the quiet shuffle of the guards' feet. However, at least one of the guards who had been at the cross suspected something greater. The centurion (a noncommissioned Roman officer) declared, *"Truly this man was God's Son!"* (Matt. 27:54).

**No More Sting.** Years ago, while I was walking in the field with my two young boys, a bee stung the older of the two just above his eye. He quickly brushed it away and threw himself in the grass, kicking and screaming. No sooner had the bee been brushed away when it went straight for the younger son and began buzzing around his head. He tried to hide in the tall grass and began screaming for help. I picked him up and told him not to worry, for the bee had lost its stinger.

This particular bee can sting only once. It leaves its stinger in the victim and becomes harmless. So I took my younger son over to his older brother and showed him the little black stinger in his brother's brow. I told him, "The bee can still buzz and scare you, but it is powerless to hurt you. Your brother took the sting away."

In 1 Corinthians 15:56, Paul said that the sting of death is sin. But Jesus took the sting for us by dying in our place on the cross. Thus, death is now powerless to hurt believers. Though death may try to hurt them, it can't anymore. They need not fear God's judgment. All death can do is open the door to glory (M. R. De Haan).

**Role Models or Rascals?** It is said that youth are searching for role models. What qualities do you look for in a role model? Would it be faith, speech, or a perfect lifestyle? Strangely, some entertainers are totally unconcerned about being role models. For example, Cheryl James, who is nicknamed "Salt" of Salt-N-Pepa, does not feel it is her job to teach teenagers. Her sentiments are echoed by Dennis Rodman of the Chicago Bulls basketball team.

Almost 2000 years ago, many at a state execution never saw Jesus as a model to be exemplified. However, a few there saw Him as far more than a role model. Some declared Him to be the Son of God!

# RESURRECTION AND COMMISSION

**BACKGROUND SCRIPTURE:** Matthew 27:62—28:20
**DEVOTIONAL READING:** John 20:19-31

**KEY VERSES:** Go therefore and make disciples of all nations, baptizing them in the name of the Father and of the Son and of the Holy Spirit, and teaching them to obey everything that I have commanded you. And remember, I am with you always, to the end of the age. Matthew 28:19-20.

*KING JAMES VERSION*

MATTHEW 28:1 In the end of the sabbath, as it began to dawn toward the first day of the week, came Mary Magdalene and the other Mary to see the sepulchre.

2 And, behold, there was a great earthquake: for the angel of the Lord descended from heaven, and came and rolled back the stone from the door, and sat upon it.

3 His countenance was like lightning, and his raiment white as snow:

4 And for fear of him the keepers did shake, and became as dead men.

5 And the angel answered and said unto the women, Fear not ye: for I know that ye seek Jesus, which was crucified.

6 He is not here: for he is risen, as he said. Come, see the place where the Lord lay.

7 And go quickly, and tell his disciples that he is risen from the dead; and, behold, he goeth before you into Galilee; there shall ye see him: lo, I have told you.

8 And they departed quickly from the sepulchre with fear and great joy; and did run to bring his disciples word.

9 And as they went to tell his disciples, behold, Jesus met them, saying, All hail. And they came and held him by the feet, and worshipped him.

10 Then said Jesus unto them, Be not afraid: go tell my brethren that they go into Galilee, and there shall they see me. . . .

16 Then the eleven disciples went away into Galilee, into a mountain where Jesus had appointed them.

17 And when they saw him, they worshipped him: but some doubted.

18 And Jesus came and spake unto them, saying, All power is given unto me in heaven and in earth.

19 Go ye therefore, and teach all nations, baptizing them in the name of the Father, and of the Son, and of the Holy Ghost:

20 Teaching them to observe all things whatsoever I have commanded you: and, lo, I am with you alway, even unto the end of the world. Amen.

*NEW REVISED STANDARD VERSION*

MATTHEW 28:1 After the sabbath, as the first day of the week was dawning, Mary Magdalene and the other Mary went to see the tomb. 2 And suddenly there was a great earthquake; for an angel of the Lord, descending from heaven, came and rolled back the stone and sat on it. 3 His appearance was like lightning, and his clothing white as snow. 4 For fear of him the guards shook and became like dead men. 5 But the angel said to the women, "Do not be afraid; I know that you are looking for Jesus who was crucified. 6 He is not here; for he has been raised, as he said. Come, see the place where he lay. 7 Then go quickly and tell his disciples, 'He has been raised from the dead, and indeed he is going ahead of you to Galilee; there you will see him.' This is the message for you." 8 So they left the tomb quickly with fear and great joy, and ran to tell his disciples. 9 Suddenly Jesus met them and said, "Greetings!" And they came to him, took hold of his feet, and worshiped him. 10 Then Jesus said to them, "Do not be afraid; go and tell my brothers to go to Galilee; there they will see me." . . .

16 Now the eleven disciples went to Galilee, to the mountain to which Jesus had directed them. 17 When they saw him, they worshiped him; but some doubted. 18 And Jesus came and said to them, "All authority in heaven and on earth has been given to me. 19 Go therefore and make disciples of all nations, baptizing them in the name of the Father and of the Son and of the Holy Spirit, 20 and teaching them to obey everything that I have commanded you. And remember, I am with you always, to the end of the age."

13

## HOME BIBLE READINGS

## BACKGROUND

Though Jesus had told His disciples that He would die on the cross and rise again from the dead, they did not seem to understand. Instead, they probably felt dejected at the execution of their Lord. We can only imagine how shocked they were when they heard the news that He was alive.

Had it not been for the resurrection of Christ, we would not be reading the Gospel of Matthew. We would also have no New Testament. We would not be gathering on Sundays for worship or at other times for Bible study. We would have no buildings called churches. Many scholars are convinced that the United States would not have its democratic form of government and the West would not have produced the present age of scientific inquiry. We would not have our finest music, literature, architecture, or art. Clearly, the resurrection of Christ is the most significant event in world history.

At first Jesus' disciples refused to believe the good news. And the Jewish religious establishment, upon hearing the reports of Jesus' resurrection, tried to discredit them as lies. But the disciples who saw the risen Lord could neither be silenced nor ignored. These devout followers of Christ were filled with joy and eager to live transformed lives. They wanted to show to others the kind of sacrificial love that Jesus had shown. The only explanation for this was that Jesus had risen from the dead!

## NOTES ON THE PRINTED TEXT

*After the sabbath, as the first day of the week was dawning, Mary Magdalene and the other Mary went to see the tomb* (28:1). In the predawn darkness of Sunday morning, Mary Magdalene and Mary (most likely the mother of James and Joses) returned to their lonely vigil at Jesus' tomb. Neither was expecting any miracle.

*And suddenly there was a great earthquake; for an angel of the Lord, descending from heaven, came and rolled back the stone and sat on it* (28:2). Seismic activity was, and still is, common in Palestine. In this case, however, it was a sign of God's activity. An angel of the Lord came down from heaven and rolled aside the huge circular stone from the entrance of the tomb and then sat on the stone

(28:3). The angel's appearance was so dazzling that the guards, whom the authorities had stationed at the tomb, were paralyzed with fright. *For fear of him the guards shook and became like dead men* (28:4).

The angel reassured the two women and delivered a startling announcement. *"Do not be afraid; I know that you are looking for Jesus who was crucified. He is not here; for he has been raised, as he said. Come, see the place where he lay"* (28:5-6). Jesus had been raised! His tomb was empty, a fact the two were invited to verify.

Then the angel commanded the women, *"Go quickly and tell his disciples, 'He has been raised from the dead, and indeed he is going ahead of you to Galilee; there you will see him'"* (28:7). The women were to share the resurrection announcement with Jesus' other disciples.

The two Marys believed the angel's announcement and ran quickly from the tomb. Though they were frightened, they were also filled with joy. As they rushed to find the disciples and tell them the good news, Jesus met the women (28:8-9). He said, *"Greetings!"* (28:9). The two Marys, perhaps feeling somewhat overwhelmed, ran to Jesus, held His feet, and worshiped Him.

Jesus personally encouraged the women and directed them to tell the disciples that He would meet them in Galilee. *Then Jesus said to them, "Do not be afraid; go and tell my brothers to go to Galilee; there they will see me"* (28:10).

God used the report of the two Marys to help convince the Eleven that Jesus had risen from the dead. *Now the eleven disciples went to Galilee, to the mountain to which Jesus had directed them* (28:16). When the disciples saw Jesus, they worshiped Him, though there were some doubts, hesitations, and questions. *When they saw him, they worshiped him; but some doubted* (28:17).

Jesus announced that the time of His humiliation had ended. The Father had given Him absolute authority *in heaven and on earth* (28:18). On the basis of Christ's authority, His followers were to *make disciples of all nations* (28:19). Those who trusted in Him were to be baptized into the fellowship of believers. Jesus' followers were also to teach the new disciples to obey all the commands He had given them.

At times the disciples would encounter disappointment and grief. The risen Lord gave them encouragement and hope when He declared, *"And remember, I am with you always, to the end of the age"* (28:20).

## SUGGESTIONS TO TEACHERS

Skeptics still ask, "How can we take seriously the report that Jesus rose from the dead?" The religious authorities tried to spread the story that Jesus' body had been stolen and that His followers concocted the lie about His resurrection. To this day, critics try to "explain" the resurrection on the grounds that Jesus was still alive when He was removed from the cross. In other words, the resurrection is just a giant hoax. But Matthew's Gospel says otherwise.

**1. SECURING THE TOMB.** The religious authorities did everything they could to ensure that no one would enter or leave the tomb where Jesus' body had been placed. This made it impossible for the disciples to steal His body.

**2. SURPRISING THE WOMEN.** All of Jesus' followers were convinced that He was dead. Otherwise, why would the two Marys go to the tomb before dawn to put burial spices on Jesus' body? Neither they nor anyone else anticipated finding Him alive. The women were astonished when they first met the angel and then the risen Lord.

**3. STATING THE NEWS.** The response of the women and every other disciple who met the living Christ was to share the good news of His resurrection with others. How has the resurrection of Christ affected your class members?

**4. SUPPRESSING THE TRUTH.** The religious leaders attempted to squelch the news of Jesus' resurrection. In our day, there are still doubters. Have the students consider how believers might inadvertently negate the glorious news of Christ's resurrection. For example, believers sometimes undermine the Gospel by their greedy, petty-minded ways, and cruel talk.

**5. SENDING THE DISCIPLES.** Have the class members think about Jesus' words in Matthew 28:18-20, which is sometimes called the Great Commission. Ask them to consider how they are carrying out that command.

**6. STRENGTHENING THE FOLLOWERS.** Have your students focus on the claim that the risen Lord has *"all authority in heaven and on earth"* (28:18) and on His promise, *"I am with you always"* (28:20). Draw out the implications of these great assertions for believers today.

---

**FOR ADULTS**

■ TOPIC: The Basis for Our Authority

■ QUESTIONS: 1. What proof did the angel offer the women concerning Jesus' resurrection? 2. What did Jesus commission His disciples to do? 3. What difference has Christ's resurrection made in your life? 4. How does the news of Jesus' resurrection affect your view of death? 5. Whom might God want you to tell about the Savior's resurrection?

■ ILLUSTRATIONS:

**Life on Earth?** The costly and complicated piece of gadgetry successfully reached Mars in 1997 after an intricately programmed journey through outer space. After landing, it began to relay a series of pictures back to earth. The big question was whether life ever existed on Mars. Hundreds of millions of dollars had been spent and the best brains of the scientific world had been employed to investigate that question. A scoop of Martian soil was gathered and studied intensely. Many scientists now think there is no evidence of any life on Mars.

Perhaps for countless people the more pertinent question is whether any life exists here on earth. Many wonder whether there is any hope or meaning to human existence. After all, death and decay seem to be everywhere. But the resurrection of Christ emphatically declares, "Yes, there is life on earth!" Because Jesus has conquered sin and death, those who trust in Him can share in His victory.

**The Big News.** Sometimes people fail to grasp what really matters. For example, on November 7, 1917, the Bolsheviks stormed the Winter Palace in Moscow, Russia, setting off the Russian Revolution, which is now accepted as one of the top history-making events of our century. That same day, however, the lead story in the *New York Times* dealt with Tamany Hall's victory in local elections. Similarly, when Tacitus wrote his authoritative chronicle of Rome around A.D. 100, he made only a passing reference to Christians. He dismissed everything about the Messiah and His followers with a brief reference to them as minor troublemakers during the reign of Nero. Today, of course, Nero gets only a passing reference, and the Roman Empire has long ago disappeared. But Jesus' resurrection continues to be big news. Nothing can eclipse that event!

**Guns into a Bell.** Bridgeport, Connecticut has had a homicide rate twice as high as New York city during the past years. In 1991, 63 murders were reported in Bridgeport, a city of 137,000. Christian leaders in the community determined to change the death rate caused by violence. Pastor Paul F. Merry picked up an idea from churches in the South, and introduced it to churchgoers in Bridgeport. The program, which is called "Guns for Bells," offers people gift certificates to grocery, toy, and department stores in exchange for weapons. Those who drop off their guns at the police station receive certificates of $25 to $100, depending on the type of gun and whether it is in working order.

The guns collected will be melted down to make a bell. And the bell, which will be almost a yard in diameter and 700 pounds in weight, will ride on wheels and be put on display at churches and parks throughout Bridgeport to remind people that good can be done despite the presence of violence. People are turning in their guns, and the bell will soon be a reality. "We are thinking about the future of the youth of Bridgeport," said Elena de Murias, a lay person active in the drive. "This is really a program of hope." The good news of Jesus' resurrection motivates believers to work to bring new life in the midst of death!

---

**FOR YOUTH**

■ TOPIC: Being a Winner

■ QUESTIONS: 1. Why were the two Marys frightened when they saw the angel? 2. Where did the disciples go to meet the risen Lord? 3. What is most significant to you about Jesus' resurrection? 4. How can the Savior's resurrection help you to handle life's problems? 5. How has Jesus' resurrection given you hope?

## ■ ILLUSTRATIONS:

**A Certainty.** At Arlington National Cemetery's Tomb of the Unknowns, the remains of X-26 were interred on Memorial Day, 1984, by then-President Ronald Reagan. The remains from an unidentified serviceman who was killed in Vietnam were added to those from the First and Second World Wars and the Korean War. The problem is that some military officials knew the identity of the remains of the Vietnam soldier but sought to conceal it.

The remains were believed to be those of Michael Joseph Blassie, a highly decorated 24-year-old Air Force Pilot who was shot down in May, 1972, near An Loc, on the Cambodian border, so said a CBS investigative report. In October, a ground patrol found Blassie's identity card, money, shreds of a flight suit, and skeletal remains. Over the next eight years, the remains believed to be those of Blassie were kept by the Army. Strangely, the identity card and money disappeared. Then, the documents referring to Blassie disappeared.

In 1980, an Army review board for unknown reasons declared that the bones were not those of Blassie and reidentified the remains as X-26. At the same time, the Army was under heavy pressure to add the body of an unidentified serviceperson from the Vietnam War for the memorial. Within nine days, X-26 was designated for inclusion in the memorial, even though Army scientists had the ability to identify the remains. In January, 1998, investigators called for the remains to be exhumed for DNA testing. Only recently has the identity of the soldier been confirmed.

Almost 2,000 years ago, Mary Magdalene and another woman named Mary had witnessed the crucifixion of Jesus and saw the tomb where Joseph had placed the Savior's body. Early Sunday morning the women went to the tomb to put burial spices on Jesus' body. But they soon discovered that the stone had been rolled away from the tomb's entrance and that the body was gone.

The two Marys learned from an angel that Jesus was alive. They then met the risen Lord and recognized His identity. They did not hesitate to report what they had seen to the other disciples.

**Does Heaven Exist?** A young man asked the pastor of his church that question after a funeral service had been given for the young man's mother. It is also a question that Americans were asked in a telephone survey by *TIME*/CNN on March 11-12, 1997. Eighty-one percent of Americans said that they believed in heaven, while 66 percent claimed that they believed a person has both a body and soul in heaven.

Perhaps the more important question concerns the reality of the resurrection. Matthew's Gospel leaves no doubt. Jesus rose from the dead, and His resurrection is the basis for the believer's hope of eternal life. Because the Son has conquered sin and death, His followers can also have victory over them. And Jesus has given them the wonderful privilege of sharing this good news with the entire world!

**Salute the Old Man.** On Wednesday, April 8, 1981, General Omar N. Bradley died. He had led American soldiers through some of the bloodiest fighting of World War II (for example, the defeat of the Afrika Korps, the landing at Normandy, and the Battle of the Bulge). Bradley had commanded the 1.3 million troops of the Twelfth Army Group, the largest American force under one man's command.

A creaking black caisson pulled by six matched gray horses carried Bradley's flag-draped casket to Arlington National Cemetery. It was followed by a riderless black quarterhorse symbolizing a fallen warrior. Air Force F-15 fighters passed overhead in tribute.

Prior to the trip, mourners passed by the deceased general's casket at Washington's Cathedral. An elderly veteran stopped at the coffin, stood at attention, saluted smartly, and then marched off. S. M. Smith, a 69-year-old retired truck driver who had driven a jeep as a private first class during World War II, waited with other veterans and dignitaries in the cold morning drizzle for the opportunity to enter a chapel door under the inscription, "The Man of Peace," and pay their respects. All that remained for Smith and others was to pay one final tribute to Bradley by giving him a salute.

Almost 2,000 years ago, two women went to a tomb to offer their final tribute to another man of peace. All that remained for them to do was anoint His body with burial spices and then walk back to their homes. Both the women were surprised by what they saw and heard that Easter morning. They saw an empty tomb and learned that Christ had risen from the dead.

Matthew's Gospel tells us that Easter is no final tribute to a fallen hero. Rather, it is the commemoration of Jesus' resurrection. Easter is not a time to offer a final salute. Instead, it is an opportunity to worship the risen Lord.

# CONTINUING JESUS' WORK

# HELPING A CHURCH CONFRONT CRISIS

**BACKGROUND SCRIPTURE:** 1 Corinthians 1:1-17
**DEVOTIONAL READING:** 1 Corinthians 1:18-25

**Key Verse:** Now I appeal to you, brothers and sisters, by the name of our Lord Jesus Christ, that all of you be in agreement and that there be no divisions among you, but that you be united in the same mind and the same purpose. 1 Corinthians 1:10.

*KING JAMES VERSION*

1 CORINTHIANS 1:2 Unto the church of God which is at Corinth, to them that are sanctified in Christ Jesus, called to be saints, with all that in every place call upon the name of Jesus Christ our Lord, both their's and our's:

3 Grace be unto you, and peace, from God our Father, and from the Lord Jesus Christ.

4 I thank my God always on your behalf, for the grace of God which is given you by Jesus Christ;

5 That in every thing ye are enriched by him, in all utterance, and in all knowledge;

6 Even as the testimony of Christ was confirmed in you:

7 So that ye come behind in no gift; waiting for the coming of our Lord Jesus Christ:

8 Who shall also confirm you unto the end, that ye may be blameless in the day of our Lord Jesus Christ.

9 God is faithful, by whom ye were called unto the fellowship of his Son Jesus Christ our Lord.

10 Now I beseech you, brethren, by the name of our Lord Jesus Christ, that ye all speak the same thing, and that there be no divisions among you; but that ye be perfectly joined together in the same mind and in the same judgment.

11 For it hath been declared unto me of you, my brethren, by them which are of the house of Chloe, that there are contentions among you.

12 Now this I say, that every one of you saith, I am of Paul; and I of Apollos; and I of Cephas; and I of Christ.

13 Is Christ divided? was Paul crucified for you? or were ye baptized in the name of Paul?

14 I thank God that I baptized none of you, but Crispus and Gaius;

15 Lest any should say that I had baptized in mine own name.

16 And I baptized also the household of Stephanas: besides, I know not whether I baptized any other.

17 For Christ sent me not to baptize, but to preach the gospel: not with wisdom of words, lest the cross of Christ should be made of none effect.

*NEW REVISED STANDARD VERSION*

1 CORINTHIANS 1:2 To the church of God that is in Corinth, to those who are sanctified in Christ Jesus, called to be saints, together with all those who in every place call on the name of our Lord Jesus Christ, both their Lord and ours:

3 Grace to you and peace from God our Father and the Lord Jesus Christ.

4 I give thanks to my God always for you because of the grace of God that has been given you in Christ Jesus, 5 for in every way you have been enriched in him, in speech and knowledge of every kind— 6 just as the testimony of Christ has been strengthened among you— 7 so that you are not lacking in any spiritual gift as you wait for the revealing of our Lord Jesus Christ. 8 He will also strengthen you to the end, so that you may be blameless on the day of our Lord Jesus Christ. 9 God is faithful; by him you were called into the fellowship of his Son, Jesus Christ our Lord.

10 Now I appeal to you, brothers and sisters, by the name of our Lord Jesus Christ, that all of you be in agreement and that there be no divisions among you, but that you be united in the same mind and the same purpose. 11 For it has been reported to me by Chloe's people that there are quarrels among you, my brothers and sisters. 12 What I mean is that each of you says, "I belong to Paul," or "I belong to Apollos," or "I belong to Cephas," or "I belong to Christ." 13 Has Christ been divided? Was Paul crucified for you? Or were you baptized in the name of Paul? 14 I thank God that I baptized none of you except Crispus and Gaius, 15 so that no one can say that you were baptized in my name. 16 (I did baptize also the household of Stephanas; beyond that, I do not know whether I baptized anyone else.) 17 For Christ did not send me to baptize but to proclaim the gospel, and not with eloquent wisdom, so that the cross of Christ might not be emptied of its power.

## HOME BIBLE READINGS

## BACKGROUND

Paul, the great missionary and founder of congregations throughout what we now know as Turkey and Greece, kept in touch with his fledgling congregations through letters. Many of these have been preserved, and are now part of the New Testament. He wrote two of his letters to the church that he established in the city of Corinth.

Paul apparently had not intended to found a church in that rip-roaring sinkhole of depravity. The apostle was weary from having been beaten and hounded from city to city in northern Greece. After a time in Athens, Paul traveled farther south to the great port of Corinth. There he preached the Gospel and witnessed the birth of a small colony of Christians.

But what unpromising material! The Greeks and Romans were never known for their morals, but even they were startled at the vices of the Corinthians. The immorality of the city was so well known that Aristophanes [air-iss-TAH-fuh-neez] coined the Greek verb *korinthiazomai,* which means "to act like a Corinthian," as a synonym for lewd behavior. The new converts to the Gospel came out of this depraved, pagan environment. Many in that struggling church found it difficult to leave behind their former, sinful lifestyle.

Paul ministered in Corinth for 18 months, and then left for Jerusalem and Syrian Antioch. Only in Ephesus did Paul ever remain for a longer period. He kept in close touch with the believers in Corinth, especially when disquieting reports about factions and conflict reached him. The letters of First and Second Corinthians give us valuable insights into the problems in this early Christian fellowship, and, more important, the epistles offer us godly advice on how to handle thorny problems in our congregations today.

## NOTES ON THE PRINTED TEXT

*To the church of God that is in Corinth* (1:2). Corinth was a thriving commercial and trading center. As such, it drew Greeks, Romans, Syrians, Asiatics, Egyptians, and Jews to its precincts. Business persons from many lands were represented as were the poor, who came looking for jobs. The Corinthian church was also a racial and social mix. Some believers were Jews, but most were Gentiles. While there were some people of wealth and social class, most members came from the lower classes. Despite their pagan backgrounds, they had trusted in Christ for salvation.

The Corinthian believers were *those who are sanctified in Christ Jesus, called to be saints, together with all those who in every place call on the name of our Lord Jesus Christ, both their Lord and ours* (1:2). The converts had been cleansed from sin and set apart to the Lord through the work of Christ. In spiritual union with Him they were holy! These saints were not paragons of moral perfection, but rather those dedicated to God. Paul pronounced a blessing on these people. *Grace to you and peace from God our Father and the Lord Jesus Christ* (1:3).

Paul followed traditional letter writing form by offering a thanksgiving, the foundation of which was God's grace in Christ. *I give thanks to my God always for you because of the grace of God that has been given you in Christ Jesus, for in every way you have been enriched in him, in speech and knowledge of every kind—just as the testimony of Christ has been strengthened among you—so that you are not lacking in any spiritual gift as you wait for the revealing of our Lord Jesus Christ* (1:4-7).

When we think about all the problems that existed in the church at Corinth, it's surprising that Paul would offer thanksgiving to God for the believers in the congregation. Perhaps the apostle realized that it was good to begin his letter to them on a positive note. Though he could not praise them for their noble deeds, he could praise God for the grace that He had given them in Christ. God's grace was seen in the abundance of spiritual gifts found in the Corinthian church, especially the ability to speak in tongues and prophesy.

The Messiah's work on the cross prompted Paul to remind the Corinthians that they should find strength in God's faithfulness. Christ's sacrifice on the cross had fully atoned for their sins. *He will also strengthen you to the end, so that you may be blameless on the day of our Lord Jesus Christ. God is faithful; by him you were called into the fellowship of his Son, Jesus Christ our Lord* (1:8-9).

Paul next underscored the purpose of his letter to the Corinthians. He appealed for unity, especially in light of what Christ had done for them at Calvary. *Now I appeal to you, brothers and sisters, by the name of our Lord Jesus Christ, that all of you be in agreement and that there be no divisions among you, but that you be united in the same mind and the same purpose* (1:10). Church members shared a relationship as brothers and sisters in God's spiritual family. While there would be differing viewpoints, they were to remember their common loyalty to Christ. They were to abandon their cliques, which created divisions in the church.

In a suburb of Corinth called Anaploga, archaeologists have excavated a first-century A.D. villa of a wealthy family. It was lavishly decorated and had mosaic floors picturing cats and panthers. The first Christian congregations in Corinth might have met in private homes such as this villa. Since it would have accommodated a group of only 30 to 40 people, the church might have been organized into sub-groups that assembled in various homes. This situation could have contributed to the divisions and quarrels in the church that had been reported to Paul. *For it has been reported to me by Chloe's people that there are quarrels among you, my brothers and sisters* (1:11).

Part of the division centered around loyalty to various church leaders such as Paul, Apollos (an eloquent Alexandrian Jew who had been tutored by Aquila [ACK-wih-luh] and Priscilla), Cephas (Peter), and Christ. (Little is known about the faction claiming allegiance to Him.) Though the church community at Corinth was divided, Christ was not divided. *Has Christ been divided?* (1:13). The believers' actions implied that the congregation was plagued by schisms.

Paul underscored the nature of his ministry in Corinth. *Was Paul crucified for you? Or were you baptized in the name of Paul?* (1:13). The apostle pointed out that he had not baptized the believers in Corinth (1:14). Paul further wrote that he baptized only Crispus (a prominent Jewish convert), Gaius, and the members of Stephanus's household (1:15-16). (Stephanus was one of the first believers in Corinth.) Paul stated that Christ sent him not to baptize but to preach the simple message of God's love through Christ. *For Christ did not send me to baptize but to proclaim the gospel, and not with eloquent wisdom, so that the cross of Christ might not be emptied of its power* (1:17).

## SUGGESTIONS TO TEACHERS

People rarely completely agree with all others in a group. Whether a nation, a congregation, or even a family, differences of opinion exist. With the streak of self-interest and self-righteousness (which Christians call "sin") in each person, those disagreements sadly are sometimes allowed to escalate into conflict.

If you serve on a church board or committee, or are an astute observer of congregational politics, you know some of the differences and tensions that are present in your church. Sadly, you may have experienced conflict in your congregation. You no doubt are also aware of the issues causing disagreement within your denomination. As you can see, you are touching on timely lesson material this week!

Familiarize yourself with the situation that existed in the Corinthian church. In the Scripture text for this week's lesson, note what Paul urged his readers to do in the face of church conflict.

**1. UNION WITH CHRIST.** Paul avoided the kind of "conflict resolution" double talk we often hear today. He reminded everyone about Christ and what it means to be committed to Him as Savior and Lord. Several important points emerge in Paul's letter, forming the basis for this week's lesson:

A. **Cleansed.** The act of baptism symbolizes the washing away of the self-interest and self-righteousness that cause separation from the Lord and others. Talk with the class members about the implications of their faith in Christ.

B. **Called.** The summons to salvation and Christian service is directed to each person, not only to clergy. The call to trust in Christ and follow Him should be made to every student in your class.

C. **Connected.** Christians, Paul wrote, should regard themselves as *called into the fellowship of [God's] Son, Jesus Christ our Lord* (1:9). As a result of being united by faith with the crucified, living Lord, believers are strengthened to endure anything—even quarrels and hurts within a congregation!

**2. UNITY WITHIN THE CHRISTIAN COMMUNITY.** Discuss frankly with the students how Paul's comments might help you and your church handle the issues that crop up in every congregation from time to time and that can become disruptive and even destructive.

A. **Conflict.** Christians can hold different opinions while holding fast to Christ and loving each other.

B. **Contentiousness.** Paul correctly warned against the quarrelsomeness that easily creeps into the life of a Christian community.

C. **Competition.** No believer should presume to place himself or herself ahead of others. Discuss with the class members what it means to *be united in the same mind and the same purpose* (1:10).

---

■ TOPIC: Appeal for Unity

■ QUESTIONS: 1. What did Paul thank God for with respect to the believers in Corinth? 2. What sort of divisions existed in the Corinthian congregation? 3. How has God's grace and peace made a difference in your life? 4. How can you encourage unity, rather than disunity, in your church? 5. Who among your acquaintances needs to hear the Gospel?

■ ILLUSTRATIONS:

**What Makes Them Tick.** I wish I knew what makes them tick. They are a strange breed, these folk. They are the backbone of every congregation in the world. I am talking about people who would be surprised to discover that their name was on my mind. Not only do they refrain from thinking more highly of themselves than they ought to think, but, in fact, seldom talk about themselves at all. They neither put themselves down, nor do they envision themselves as the object of the admiration of others. They make their contribution to the church with such consistency that they seldom appear to be doing anything special. Whatever their role happens to be, they quietly and without fanfare go about it. They never "sleep in" on Sundays. When strangers appear, they greet them with genuine warmth (Martin Pike, *Presbyterian Outlook,* Nov., 1997).

**Lessons from Jazz Musicians.** Wynton Marsalis, the virtuoso trumpet player, readily shares the secret of a good jazz group. His points could apply also to the way a church should and can coalesce into a harmonious community. In an interview in the October, 1995, *American Heritage,* Marsalis stated that first a musician must master the theme and catch its spirit. Second is the desire to play music with other people. He said that's learning to make room for others so that everyone can play. Third, each person must learn to respect the individuality of others. Jazz playing, Marsalis claimed, means reconciling differences, even when they're opposites. He insisted that "jazz teaches you how to have a dialogue, with integrity. Jazz is by nature social, and good manners are important." What better way to describe how members of a church can work together in unity!

**The Humans in the Church.** Kenneth C. Roscoe observed the following:
> I think that I shall never see
> A church that's all it ought to be,
> A church whose members never stray
> Beyond the straight and narrow way!
> A church that has no empty pews,
> Whose pastor never has the blues.
> A church where gossips never peddle lies,
> Or make complaints or criticize;
> Where all are always sweet and kind,
> And to all others' faults are blind.
> Such perfect churches there may be,
> But none of them are known to me.
> But still we'll work and pray and plan,
> To make our own the best we can!

■ **TOPIC:** What Unites?

■ **QUESTIONS:** 1. What does it mean to *call on the name of our Lord* (1:2)? 2. What appeal did Paul make to the believers in Corinth? 3. What spiritual gifts has God given to you? 4. How might you encourage your fellow believers to be *united in the same mind and the same purpose* (1:10)? 5. What difference has the cross of Christ made in your life?

■ **ILLUSTRATIONS:**

**Wrong Direction.** The San Francisco 49'er–Minnesota Vikings football game at San Francisco on October 25, 1964, featured one of the greatest goof-ups in NFL history. San Francisco's Bill Kilmer fumbled. The Vikings' Jim Marshall then grabbed the loose ball and raced 60 yards into the end zone. The only problem was that Marshall had run in the wrong direction! He scored a two point safety for San Francisco! The players that congratulated him after the score were 49ers!

The Corinthian church was like Jim Marshall. They were going in the wrong direction. They had divided into cliques, believing that their favorite church leader would make the difference. Pride in the ability of that particular leader had led to quarreling. All attention had been focused on this individual's ideas at the expense of unity and cooperation.

**Passing Down Passover.** At Pittsburgh's Jewish Education Institute, Rabbi Yale Butler teaches young people the symbolism of food in their faith. "Food," says Butler, "has many significances. Passover, for instance, begins with what is eaten; but what remains is the moral lesson that is absorbed." His 17 students learn about their faith through his hands-on food course. Dena Stern, a senior at Allderdice Hill School, learns to make *cholent*, a slow cooking Sabbath stew of beans and potatoes. She also learns to keep a kosher kitchen with two sets of dishes (one for meat and one for dairy products). Butler's school class stresses learning through food to create a stick-to-the-heart belief. The traditions of food, he preaches, brings each person closer to their faith.

Perhaps you, like these students, have found meaning through various significant acts or rituals. This was the message that Paul was sharing with the Corinthians. Spiritual union with Christ by faith was symbolized by the act of baptism, not by an allegiance to any particular church leader.

**Family Tradition.** Donna Meshanks and her family take a sampling of all her Easter food to Saint Maurice Church in Forest Hills, Pennsylvania. It is part of an old Orthodox celebration with an ethnic tradition mixed in. Easter food and baskets are token reminders of spiritual sustenance. Donna and her husband learned this tradition as youngsters and have continued it with their children.

The Corinthian church had associated water baptism with one person, failing to see that they were spiritually joined to Christ by faith. Sadly, the ceremony of baptism had become merely an empty ritual, a tradition that was passed down, but was devoid of any broader significance.

# THE HOLY SPIRIT AS TEACHER

**BACKGROUND SCRIPTURE:** 1 Corinthians 2—3
**DEVOTIONAL READING:** 1 Corinthians 3:1-9

**KEY VERSE:** Now we have received not the spirit of the world, but the Spirit that is from God, so that we may understand the gifts bestowed on us by God. 1 Corinthians 2:12.

---

*KING JAMES VERSION*

1 CORINTHIANS 2:1 And I, brethren, when I came to you, came not with excellency of speech or of wisdom, declaring unto you the testimony of God.

2 For I determined not to know any thing among you, save Jesus Christ, and him crucified. . . .

4 And my speech and my preaching was not with enticing words of man's wisdom, but in demonstration of the Spirit and of power:

5 That your faith should not stand in the wisdom of men, but in the power of God.

6 Howbeit we speak wisdom among them that are perfect: yet not the wisdom of this world, nor of the princes of this world, that come to nought:

7 But we speak the wisdom of God in a mystery, even the hidden wisdom, which God ordained before the world unto our glory:

8 Which none of the princes of this world knew: for had they known it, they would not have crucified the Lord of glory.

9 But as it is written, Eye hath not seen, nor ear heard, neither have entered into the heart of man, the things which God hath prepared for them that love him.

10 But God hath revealed them unto us by his Spirit: for the Spirit searcheth all things, yea, the deep things of God.

11 For what man knoweth the things of a man, save the spirit of man which is in him? even so the things of God knoweth no man, but the Spirit of God.

12 Now we have received, not the spirit of the world, but the spirit which is of God; that we might know the things that are freely given to us of God.

13 Which things also we speak, not in the words which man's wisdom teacheth, but which the Holy Ghost teacheth; comparing spiritual things with spiritual. . . .

15 But he that is spiritual judgeth all things, yet he himself is judged of no man.

16 For who hath known the mind of the Lord, that he may instruct him? But we have the mind of Christ.

*NEW REVISED STANDARD VERSION*

1 CORINTHIANS 2:1 When I came to you, brothers and sisters, I did not come proclaiming the mystery of God to you in lofty words or wisdom. 2 For I decided to know nothing among you except Jesus Christ, and him crucified. . . . 4 My speech and my proclamation were not with plausible words of wisdom, but with a demonstration of the Spirit and of power, 5 so that your faith might rest not on human wisdom but on the power of God.

6 Yet among the mature we do speak wisdom, though it is not a wisdom of this age or of the rulers of this age, who are doomed to perish. 7 But we speak God's wisdom, secret and hidden, which God decreed before the ages for our glory. 8 None of the rulers of this age understood this; for if they had, they would not have crucified the Lord of glory. 9 But, as it is written,

"What no eye has seen, nor ear heard,
     nor the human heart conceived,
what God has prepared for those who love him"—

10 these things God has revealed to us through the Spirit; for the Spirit searches everything, even the depths of God. 11 For what human being knows what is truly human except the human spirit that is within? So also no one comprehends what is truly God's except the Spirit of God. 12 Now we have received not the spirit of the world, but the Spirit that is from God, so that we may understand the gifts bestowed on us by God. 13 And we speak of these things in words not taught by human wisdom but taught by the Spirit, interpreting spiritual things to those who are spiritual. . . .

15 Those who are spiritual discern all things, and they are themselves subject to no one else's scrutiny.

16 "For who has known the mind of the Lord
     so as to instruct him?"

But we have the mind of Christ.

| | | |
|---|---|---|
| *Monday, Mar. 6* | 1 Corinthians 2:1-5 | *Proclaiming Christ Crucified* |
| *Tuesday, Mar. 7* | 1 Corinthians 2:6-16 | *The True Wisdom of God* |
| *Wednesday, Mar. 8* | 1 Corinthians 3:1-9 | *Put Away Quarrels and Jealousies* |
| *Thursday, Mar. 9* | 1 Corinthians 3:10-15 | *Build on the Foundation of Jesus Christ* |
| *Friday, Mar. 10* | 1 Corinthians 3:16-23 | *We Belong to God through Jesus Christ* |
| *Saturday, Mar. 11* | Romans 8:1-8 | *Life in the Spirit* |
| *Sunday, Mar. 12* | Romans 8:9-17 | *We Are Children of God* |

## BACKGROUND

The Greeks prided themselves on their love of wisdom. They delighted in abstract arguments and indulged in philosophical speculation. After all, Greece had been the home of Plato, Aristotle [AIR-iss-tott-uhl], and Heraclitis [herr-uh-KLEYE-tuss]. Greeks admired the orators with their rhetorical tricks and clever logic. Demosthenes [dih-MAHS-thuh-neez] was remembered as one of their greatest heroes. Wandering professionals paraded their wisdom, attracting followers and holding seminars while promulgating their lofty ideas. Corinth, like every Greek city, saw many golden-tongued speakers and self-styled philosophers come and go. In the little congregation in Corinth, many undoubtedly fancied themselves as heavy-duty intellectuals and eloquent thinkers.

Paul apparently was not an imposing speaker. Though he may have been schooled in the ways of the Greek academy, he deliberately avoided the forms of learned discourse in his preaching. Perhaps one time he showed his knowledge of Greek oratory style was in his address in Athens (see Acts 17:22-31).

Paul arrived in Corinth after his visit to Athens, an experience that had impressed him with the foolishness of worldly wisdom. Evidently the apostle's encounter with the philosophers at Athens also made him more determined than ever to preach the simple message of the cross.

With the support of an influential Christian couple named Aquila [ACK-wih-luh] and Priscilla (1 Cor. 16:19), Paul preached in the synagogue until Jewish opposition forced him to focus his ministry on the Gentiles. As a result of the apostle leading a number of people to faith in Christ, a church was established (consisting of both Jews and Gentiles) and soon began to grow (Acts 18:8-10). Paul's ministry in Corinth lasted a fairly long time (more than 18 months; vss. 11, 18), and he accomplished much while in the city.

Paul did not place his confidence in his keen intellect or speaking ability. Rather, he relied completely on the Spirit to help and guide him in his proclamation of the Gospel. At first this might have shocked the Corinthians, for they gloried in their strength, wealth, and abilities. By anchoring his confidence in the Lord, Paul was teaching his new converts to depend completely on God to do His will.

# NOTES ON THE PRINTED TEXT

Many Corinthians prided themselves on their intellectual prowess. Paul, concerned that their judgmental attitude reflected worldly wisdom and teaching, reminded his readers that the Holy Spirit was their ultimate Teacher. Their cleverness and knowledge was a far cry from God's wisdom. Paul used himself as an example of one who lived according to divine truth.

*When I came to you, brothers and sisters, I did not come proclaiming the mystery of God to you in lofty words or wisdom* (2:1). When Paul arrived in Corinth, he did not preach in a fancy or impressive style. He was not going to repeat in Corinth his eloquent and adroit presentation of the Gospel in Athens. He had arrived in Corinth determined to preach nothing but the cross and the resurrection. *For I decided to know nothing among you except Jesus Christ, and him crucified* (2:2). Given that crucifixion was abhorred by the Gentiles, Paul's mess. that God's Son had been executed on the cross must have sounded absurd.

Paul's speech was simple and direct, not flashy and flowery. The apostle reminded his listeners that his preaching had not moved them to faith. Instead, their commitment had been the result of the Spirit's miraculous power. The Spirit had enabled them to believe. *My speech and my proclamation were not with plausible words of wisdom, but with a demonstration of the Spirit and of power, so that your faith might rest not on human wisdom but on the power of God* (2:4-5).

Paul reminded the Corinthians that their faith did not rest on human wisdom. Worldly ways of thinking were human-centered and thus doomed to fail. Perhaps Paul had in mind those rulers and people of power who had condemned and murdered Jesus but whose actions produced exactly the opposite result of what they anticipated. Clearly, the cross of Christ was a demonstration of God's wisdom and power. *Yet among the mature we do speak wisdom, though it is not a wisdom of this age or of the rulers of this age, who are doomed to perish* (2:6).

Paul and his fellow Christians spoke about God's saving purpose and His plan to redeem human beings through the atoning sacrifice of His Son. *But we speak God's wisdom, secret and hidden, which God decreed before the ages for our glory* (2:7). Paul specifically spoke about those who crucified the Savior and their inability to discern God's purpose in the cross. *None of the rulers of this age understood this; for if they had, they would not have crucified the Lord of glory* (2:8). To reinforce his point that God's wisdom was often hidden and differed from worldly wisdom, Paul quoted Isaiah 64:4 (1 Cor. 2:9).

The apostle then reminded the Corinthian church that God's wisdom was made known through the Spirit. He is the Teacher and the Revealer who helped them to understand the significance of Jesus' death on the cross. *These things God has revealed to us through the Spirit; for the Spirit searches everything, even the depths of God* (2:10).

Paul used an analogy. Only a human being could understand people. Likewise, only the Holy Spirit can fathom God. *For what human being knows what is truly human except the human spirit that is within? So also no one comprehends what is truly God's except the Spirit of God* (2:11).

The apostle reminded the Corinthian church that all of them had received the Spirit. He enabled them to receive and believe God's saving message. *Now we have received not the spirit of the world, but the Spirit that is from God, so that we may understand the gifts bestowed on us by God. And we speak of these things in words not taught by human wisdom but taught by the Spirit, interpreting spiritual things to those who are spiritual* (2:12-13).

Paul noted that believers are distinguished by the Spirit's presence within them. He instructs, enlightens, and guides them. Because they operate from this perspective, they are able to evaluate the worth of all sorts of things (2:15-16). And the Spirit helps them to remain sensitive the Lord's will and leading (see Isa. 40:13). Unbelievers, of course, have no insight into the things of the Spirit, and that is why they are not qualified to judge Christians regarding spiritual matters (1 Cor. 2:14).

## SUGGESTIONS TO TEACHERS

In the popular movie *Titanic*, everyone thought that the great liner was a symbol of human achievement. One character, perhaps echoing the sentiments of an age proud of its wisdom, confidently bellowed, "Even God can't sink this ship!"

The worldly-wise people in every generation often prove to be the greatest fools. This week's lesson offers your students instruction in the wisdom given by the Holy Spirit and the way in which it holds a Christian group together.

**1. LIMITS OF LEARNING.** Some in our era erroneously think that human wisdom can solve every problem and meet every challenge. That mindset, which proved faulty in the case of the Titanic, was condemned by Paul in his letter to the Corinthians. He declared that only God is all-knowing and all-wise!

**2. LEADING OF THE SPIRIT.** Misplaced reliance on human wisdom inevitably causes difficulties. Only the guidance of the Spirit, not oratorical tricks or fancy arguments based on logic, can lead a congregation to live in unity.

**3. LOYALTY TO GOD.** Corinthian church members tried to build fan clubs around various leaders. Thankfully, Paul, Apollos, and others refused to let such personality cults continue. Only Christ was to be adored! Remind the students that human teachers and preachers are never to be put on a pedestal, only the Lord.

**4. LOGIC OF UNITY.** Paul insisted that allegiance to Christ meant allegiance to each believer in a congregation. Unity with the Lord cannot be separated from unity with fellow believers! Let the students know that unless such unity is present, the church cannot survive.

**5. LESSON IN WISDOM.** Finally, reflect on the true nature of godly wisdom. The wisdom that emanates from oneness with the Spirit of Christ draws a church together, and is the enduring source of true unity.

■ **TOPIC:** True Wisdom: A Basis for Unity

■ **QUESTIONS:** 1. What was the heart of Paul's preaching in Corinth? 2. How did Paul's preaching reflect the wisdom of God? 3. How might the Spirit of God enable you to share the Gospel with your unsaved acquaintances? 4. How can the wisdom of God help your church remain united? 5. How can wisdom from the Spirit help your church avoid becoming divided?

■ **ILLUSTRATIONS:**

**Dead in the Himalayas.** Mount Everest rises 29,029 feet above sea level, and it is the highest point on earth. Since 1924, when Englishman George Mallory lost his life trying to scale this mountain, 140 persons have died attempting to climb it. In 1953, New Zealander Edmund Hillary and Sherpa guide Tenzing Norgay led the first team of climbers to its summit. Scores have traveled to Nepal since then with the conceited ambition to stand "on the top of the world." Many of these have limited climbing experience. But all have deep pockets, paying professional guides $65,000 each to make the climb, not counting the cost of airfare to Nepal or the price of personal equipment.

On May 10, 1996, climbers from three expeditions attempting to reach the highest point in the world found themselves in a traffic jam as they approached the final ascent. An unexpected storm suddenly came up, claiming the lives of eight, including Rob Hall and Scott Fisher, two of the best high-mountain climbing guides in the world. The disaster was described in a best-seller, *Into Thin Air,* by Jon Krakauer (Villard Books, 1997), and in a television special. The story is not so much a tale about a mountain as it is the account of human pride and the naive notion that with enough money, determination, and skills, anything is possible.

One survivor, Sandy Hill, illustrates what went wrong. Hill, a 45-year-old New Yorker, wanted to be the first woman to climb the seven major peaks of the world. Krakauer describes how she caused delays by having to be pulled up on ropes by Sherpas for a period of five hours and insisting on having Sherpa porters carry her personal computer for the entire climb. The "money-can-buy-me-anything" approach, the drive for personal achievement, and the desire to conquer everything—including everything in God's creation—violated all relationships between persons and between humans and nature.

Those same attitudes can bring destruction within the church. A congregation maintains unity when it has godly wisdom to recognize the danger of human pride and the need to depend on the guidance of the Holy Spirit.

**Bringing Beauty and Harmony.** Fred Rogers, the beloved creator of the outstanding "Mr. Rogers' Neighborhood," and his great pianist, Johnny Costa, were asked to visit a Christmas party at Children's Hospital in Pittsburgh. The children were ecstatic. One little boy suffering from cerebral palsy wanted to sing a carol to honor the guests. The child's disease made his speech halting and uncertain.

When the little fellow began to sing "Silent Night," the sound was wavering. He not only had difficulty in framing the words for the carol but shifted key frequently. The first bar of the familiar carol was rendered so poorly that nearly everyone present involuntarily shuddered, everyone that is except Fred Rogers and Johnny Costa.

Costa was at the portable organ when he began quietly to provide background music for the cerebral palsy victim's attempted solo. As the youngster struggled on slowly and changed key frequently, Johnny wove lovely chords with each change in each line. The effect was such that the youngster's rendition took on a quality of rare beauty and harmony. Then others began to join the child. Costa seemed to anticipate where the next croak on the scale would be in the boy's singing, and worked each note into a performance of "Silent Night" in which everyone participated and enjoyed themselves.

In the same way, the Holy Spirit gives Christians wisdom and helps them build unity within the church. When the Spirit is allowed to lead, our faltering efforts are woven into a harmonious masterpiece of beauty for the Lord.

**FOR YOUTH**

■ TOPIC: In the Know

■ QUESTIONS: 1. Why did Paul emphasize in his preaching the cross of Christ? 2. In what way are spiritual persons able to discern all sorts of things? 3. How might the wisdom of God help you to grow in spiritual maturity? 4. How can the Spirit help you to better understand the things of God? 5. Why is it important to have the mind of Christ when making daily decisions?

■ ILLUSTRATIONS:

**Old to Young.** "I'm glad you're going to college, boy," the old man blurted to his grandson. "I went to the school of hard knocks and I learned to lay concrete block and put up dry wall!"

The grandfather's comment indicates that there are different ways of learning and different kinds of knowledge. Obviously some learn by experience and others by studying books. Some learn practical knowledge, while others learn more theoretical knowledge. Each type of knowledge and each kind of teaching technique is important. Both enrich the learner. One does not have greater importance than the other. This is one lesson that Paul was trying to explain to the Corinthians.

**Not Out of Touch.** How often is the wisdom of God viewed as foolishness on earth? For example, Christ urged His followers to be concerned about others. Jimmy Carter is one individual who faithfully tries to do that. The former president has worked for Habitat for Humanity, volunteering his time and efforts in the ghettos at home and abroad by doing manual labor and helping the underprivileged. Obviously it is not what former presidents usually do! It is a case of Carter's being a true example of practicing what he preaches. Here is one leader not out of touch with the world that youth know.

**Power of Knowledge.** As March madness erupts in the college basketball world, fans remember John Wooden, who led the UCLA Bruins to a record setting ten NCAA titles, including seven in a row during the 1960s and 1970s. NBA greats, such as Kareem Abdul-Jabbar, remember Wooden's coaching prowess and especially his priorities: education, basketball, and finally socializing. His message was that knowledge is power. Knowledge is what people use to get ahead throughout their life. Wooden is proud that his players have gone on to be doctors, lawyers, ministers, dentists, and teachers (to name a few occupations).

Paul reminded his readers that as important as knowledge and education are, knowing the power of God is of greater eternal importance.

# THE CHURCH AND ITS LEADERS

**BACKGROUND SCRIPTURE:** 1 Corinthians 4:1-13
**DEVOTIONAL READING:** 1 Peter 5:1-11

**KEY VERSE:** Think of us in this way, as servants of Christ and stewards of God's mysteries. 1 Corinthians 4:1.

*KING JAMES VERSION*

1 CORINTHIANS 4:1 Let a man so account of us, as of the ministers of Christ, and stewards of the mysteries of God.

2 Moreover it is required in stewards, that a man be found faithful.

3 But with me it is a very small thing that I should be judged of you, or of man's judgment: yea, I judge not mine own self.

4 For I know nothing by myself; yet am I not hereby justified: but he that judgeth me is the Lord.

5 Therefore judge nothing before the time, until the Lord come, who both will bring to light the hidden things of darkness, and will make manifest the counsels of the hearts: and then shall every man have praise of God.

6 And these things, brethren, I have in a figure transferred to myself and to Apollos for your sakes; that ye might learn in us not to think of men above that which is written, that no one of you be puffed up for one against another.

7 For who maketh thee to differ from another? and what hast thou that thou didst not receive? now if thou didst receive it, why dost thou glory, as if thou hadst not received it?

8 Now ye are full, now ye are rich, ye have reigned as kings without us: and I would to God ye did reign, that we also might reign with you.

9 For I think that God hath set forth us the apostles last, as it were appointed to death: for we are made a spectacle unto the world, and to angels, and to men.

10 We are fools for Christ's sake, but ye are wise in Christ; we are weak, but ye are strong; ye are honourable, but we are despised.

11 Even unto this present hour we both hunger, and thirst, and are naked, and are buffeted, and have no certain dwellingplace;

12 And labour, working with our own hands: being reviled, we bless; being persecuted, we suffer it:

13 Being defamed, we intreat: we are made as the filth of the world, and are the offscouring of all things unto this day.

*NEW REVISED STANDARD VERSION*

1 CORINTHIANS 4:1 Think of us in this way, as servants of Christ and stewards of God's mysteries. 2 Moreover, it is required of stewards that they be found trustworthy. 3 But with me it is a very small thing that I should be judged by you or by any human court. I do not even judge myself. 4 I am not aware of anything against myself, but I am not thereby acquitted. It is the Lord who judges me. 5 Therefore do not pronounce judgment before the time, before the Lord comes, who will bring to light the things now hidden in darkness and will disclose the purposes of the heart. Then each one will receive commendation from God.

6 I have applied all this to Apollos and myself for your benefit, brothers and sisters, so that you may learn through us the meaning of the saying, "Nothing beyond what is written," so that none of you will be puffed up in favor of one against another. 7 For who sees anything different in you? What do you have that you did not receive? And if you received it, why do you boast as if it were not a gift?

8 Already you have all you want! Already you have become rich! Quite apart from us you have become kings! Indeed, I wish that you had become kings, so that we might be kings with you! 9 For I think that God has exhibited us apostles as last of all, as though sentenced to death, because we have become a spectacle to the world, to angels and to mortals. 10 We are fools for the sake of Christ, but you are wise in Christ. We are weak, but you are strong. You are held in honor, but we in disrepute. 11 To the present hour we are hungry and thirsty, we are poorly clothed and beaten and homeless, 12 and we grow weary from the work of our own hands. When reviled, we bless; when persecuted, we endure; 13 when slandered, we speak kindly. We have become like the rubbish of the world, the dregs of all things, to this very day.

## BACKGROUND

The Greeks fancied themselves as intellectually superior. They enjoyed dabbling in philosophical discourse. They were delighted by impressive oratory and learned argumentation. Wandering speakers with a good line and smooth logic won audiences and approval. The people of Corinth were typical of this Greek mind-set. Leaders were expected to be eloquent and impressive. Those in the congregation apparently adopted their notions of leaders from the culture in which they lived.

Paul did not meet the expectations of the Corinthian Christians with respect to what a leader should be. For example, he was not a silver-tongued preacher with dramatic flourishes and winsome ways. His message centered not on clever methods of getting ahead or pleasing an audience but on the Good News that the Son of God died on the cross and rose from the dead. Between Paul's lack of dynamic presence and his unconventional message of God's sacrificial love in Christ, the apostle must have seemed like a lackluster leader to many in the congregation.

Shortly after Paul left Corinth, a group in the newly-organized congregation began complaining that he lacked the powerful stature and persuasive rhetoric that supposedly characterized "successful" leaders in Greek society. As time went on, the criticisms leveled against Paul grew sharper and more personal.

As you can imagine, there were some deep and recurring problems behind the great diversity of issues in 1 Corinthians. Challenges to Paul's authority, pride in personal spirituality, and especially a lack of love were fundamental issues that the apostle needed to address. In the course of responding to different problems in the church, Paul set forth his teaching on such key doctrines as God's sovereignty, the nature of the church, sanctification, and the bodily resurrection.

We learned in the first lesson that the Corinthians favored different ministers. Some followed Paul, while others were fans of either Apollos or Peter (1:12). Along with this party spirit was an undertow of opposition to Paul. In chapter 4 of his letter, the apostle explained why the church in Corinth should not turn against its founder and spiritual parent. Paul began by explaining that he and Apollos were mere servants of Christ. Paul also stressed that Christian ministry is characterized by humble service to the Lord.

Paul sensed the need to address the matter of divisions within the Corinthian church. These were caused in part by cliques gravitating around various leaders, such as Paul, Apollos, and Peter. Comparisons between them had produced a split.

Paul stated that the church and its leaders were God's slaves. *Think of us in this way, as servants of Christ and stewards of God's mysteries* (4:1). The function of leaders was to serve. God's representatives had no significance of their own but were to do their Master's work. The only requirement was absolute faithfulness to the Lord. *Moreover, it is required of stewards that they be found trustworthy* (4:2).

Because loyalty to the Master was the criterion of evaluation, Paul was not concerned whether the believers in Corinth judged him. For the apostle, God had the last word on the quality of his ministry, for only the Lord truly knew Paul's work. The apostle was not aware of anything wrong he had done as a servant of the Lord. *But with me it is a very small thing that I should be judged by you or by any human court. I do not even judge myself. I am not aware of anything against myself, but I am not thereby acquitted. It is the Lord who judges me* (4:3-4).

The Corinthians had no right to judge others such as Paul. That responsibility rested with Lord Jesus, which He would exercise at His return. Then, nothing would be concealed. *Therefore do not pronounce judgment before the time, before the Lord comes, who will bring to light the things now hidden in darkness and will disclose the purposes of the heart. Then each one will receive commendation from God* (4:5).

Paul had used himself and Apollos as illustrations of humble Christian service so that the Corinthians might learn from their example. Based on this, the apostle urged his readers not to go beyond the teaching of Scripture in their treatment of their spiritual leaders. While the believers at Corinth had the responsibility of confronting those who were sinning, they were not permitted to judge who was a better servant of Christ. *I have applied all this to Apollos and myself for your benefit, brothers and sisters, so that you may learn through us the meaning of the saying, "Nothing beyond what is written"* (4:6).

In a series of rhetorical questions, Paul pointed out that everything that the Corinthians believers had was a gift from God. Therefore, who were they to brag about one of their leaders at the expense of another? *For who sees anything different in you? What do you have that you did not receive? And if you received it, why do you boast as if it were not a gift?* (4:7).

Paul observed that the Corinthians Christians were acting as if God's kingdom had already been inaugurated. And they were behaving as rich and powerful rulers. *Already you have all you want! Already you have become rich! Quite apart from us you have become kings! Indeed, I wish that you had become kings, so that we might be kings with you!* (4:8).

Paul contrasted the Corinthians' pride with the humility and suffering of him and his co-workers. They were humble, living like those condemned to die in the spectacle of a gladiatorial game. *For I think that God has exhibited us apostles as last of all, as though sentenced to death, because we have become a spectacle to the world, to angels and to mortals* (4:9).

In the world's way of thinking, Christ's servants appeared foolish for proclaiming the Gospel. Instead of being honored, they were insulted and harassed. *We are fools for the sake of Christ, but you are wise in Christ. We are weak, but you are strong. You are held in honor, but we in disrepute* (4:10). Life for Christ's servants was grim. *To the present hour we are hungry and thirsty, we are poorly clothed and beaten and homeless, and we grow weary from the work of our own hands* (4:11-12).

Despite all that Paul and his colleagues had endured, they followed the teaching and example of their Lord. *When reviled, we bless; when persecuted, we endure; when slandered, we speak kindly* (4:12-13). Their gentle ways had done nothing to change the rough treatment they were receiving. In fact, the apostle said that they continued to be treated like the world's garbage. They humbly endured all this for the cause of Christ.

## SUGGESTIONS TO TEACHERS

A recent survey showed that church leaders do not enjoy the trust and respect they once had. Clergy were fairly low on the list, just ahead of government officials and used car dealers. The publicity surrounding immoral priests and philandering pastors has lowered the public's regard for them. The media reports of the failings of deacons, elders, and others in leadership positions has shown the need for mature ministers in the church.

This week's lesson offers helpful insights into what God requires of all church leaders. You should encourage the students to consider what qualities their congregation should look for when electing its officers and choosing its leaders.

**1. CONTENTMENT AS SERVANTS AND STEWARDS.** The haughty Corinthians had concluded that Paul was an insignificant church leader. Rather than try to defend himself, the apostle humbly told them that he and his associates were *servants of Christ and stewards of God's mysteries* (4:1). Be sure to discuss the meaning of these phrases with the members of your class.

**2. COMMENDATION LEFT UP TO CHRIST.** It's the egotistical leader who wants recognition and appreciation. True church leaders quietly continue serving the Lord without regard for acclaim, for they know that God's commendation is sufficient.

**3. CONTRAST TO THE PROUD CORINTHIANS.** Some in the Corinthian church were puffed up with notions of superior rank or wisdom. Paul reminded them that he and his associates regarded themselves as nobodies in the eyes of the world. Take time to discuss this with your students.

**4. CONCERN FOR UNITY.** Church leaders who are self-focused put themselves ahead of the faith community of Christ's people, and thereby undermine the unity of the church.

**5. COMMITMENT TO HUMILITY.** Be sure to underscore the importance of humility in Christian service. Explain that such an attitude derives from an awareness of being Christ's servant and a steward of God's truth, especially as it is revealed in Jesus' crucifixion and resurrection!

---

■ **FOR ADULTS**

■ **TOPIC:** Mature Leaders Bring Unity

■ **QUESTIONS:** 1. What does it mean to be a servant of Christ? 2. Why is it wrong to prejudge believers? 3. In what ways have you demonstrated your trustworthiness to God as His servant? 4. What are some ways that you have suffered for the cause of Christ? 5. How might you encourage other believers to remain faithful to the Lord?

■ **ILLUSTRATIONS:**

**Hostage Hero.** On December 17, 1996, fourteen guerrillas belonging to the Tupac Amaru Revolutionary Movement suddenly burst into a diplomatic reception at the Japanese ambassador's residence in Lima, Peru. They seized more than 500 guests as hostages, and held off the police and the military until the following April 22, 1997.

One of those captured by the invaders was the Reverend Juan Julio Wicht Rossel, a Jesuit priest. Wicht first drew public attention when he was chosen by the guerrillas to be one of the 225 hostages to be released just before Christmas, 1996. The priest stood up and asked to stay with the remaining hostages. His act of serving won the applause of the hostages and later even the admiration of the armed revolutionaries.

During the following terrifying four months of the ordeal, Wicht prayed regularly with the hostages and held services. On April 18th, a few days before the sudden rescue operation, Wicht celebrated his 65th birthday. To his surprise, he was summoned downstairs, and encountered the leader of the hostage takers, Nestor Cerpa Cartolini, who was surrounded by his armed henchmen. "Despite our differences, we want to greet you for your birthday and to tell you that we respect your decision to remain," Cerpa said.

After the commando force stormed the ambassadorial residence, killing the guerrillas and rescuing the hostages, Wicht was asked about his decision to stay with all the people who were seized four months earlier. "Like all priests, we are prepared to help others," he stated. "I said to myself, they need me, so I am staying. I am glad I stayed, for many of the hostages drew closer to God. My faith has grown beyond what I could possibly express." Mature leaders create and build this kind of community!

**Changed Baseball and Changed America.** On April 15, 1947, a 28-year-old rookie named Jackie Robinson started a professional baseball ball game as the first baseman for the Brooklyn Dodgers at Ebbets Field against the Boston Braves. He was the first African American to appear in a major league baseball game since well before the turn of the century.

The game and the nation would never be the same. The young athlete suffered horrid abuse from other players, many coaches, and fans. But Robinson, son of a sharecropper and grandson of a slave, was not only a skilled player but a mature leader. Accepting and enduring the slurs and curses day after day, he lead the nation through its national pastime, the game of baseball, in a sociological revolution. His sacrifice helped to integrate sports everywhere.

Today, a steady stream of visitors comes daily to the Cypress Hills Cemetery in New York near the Brooklyn-Queens border to visit the grave of Jackie Robinson. A stone bearing his family's name identifies the plot. Underneath, carved into the granite, are the words of one of Jackie Robinson's favorite sayings: "A life is not important except in the impact it has on other lives." There is no better description of true leadership!

**Godly Preaching.** One great pulpit figure of the earlier part of this century was J. H. Jowett. This humble man of Christ was once asked to state the goal of a sermon. His answer applies not only to preaching but to all phases of church leadership: "What you are after is not that folks will say at the end of it all, 'What an excellent sermon!' That is a measured failure. You are there to have them say, when it is over, 'What a great God!' It is something for people not to have been in your presence but in His."

**FOR YOUTH**

■ TOPIC: Lead and Serve

■ QUESTIONS: 1. What type of Christian service does God commend? 2. What hardships did Paul experience for the cause of Christ? 3. How might you avoid prejudging other Christians? 4. What spiritual blessings have you received from the Lord? 5. In what ways have you demonstrated humble Christian service to others?

■ ILLUSTRATIONS:

**Recommendations?** Imagine that you have been asked to serve on your church's Pulpit Nominating Committee, which has the responsibility of selecting your church's next pastor. You begin to look over resumés and interview possible candidates. One candidate has straight A's from one of the finest universities in America and has received a Phi Beta Kappa key. He has earned a Ph.D. in the minimum amount of time. On paper he has considerable experience, though you notice that his tenure at various churches tends to be from two to four years. Each time he changes congregations, he seems to go for a bigger and better paying position. His questions to your committee revolve around his salary, benefits, and perks. He wants to know about the country club and the golf course.

A second candidate has faithfully served his congregation for 15 years. He lacks any flashy academic credentials but asks about congregational commitment to the Lord, the attendance at worship, and the church's vision of its ministry. In light of Paul's statements on the role of servant leadership, whom would you recommend to the congregation to call?

**Cost of Judgment.** Pittsburgh Common Pleas Court Judge John W. O'Brien heard the case of Saint Mary's Ukranian Orthodox Church of McKees Rocks, Pennsylvania, against Mary Hoysan. Mary, who had been baptized in the church 59 years earlier, had been charged with defiant trespass by the pastor, the Reverend James Norton, and the congregation's president, J. Terry Winslow. Mary wanted to be allowed back in the church, even though she had been ejected for loud responses, off-key singing, and improper behavior. For instance, Mary would stand up and castigate the pastor and various members of the congregation, often laced with improper or profane language. Mary lost her appeal and the judge urged her to find another church.

Mary was too judgmental of others. She showed a problem that was similar to the one that plagued some in the Corinthian church. They were upset at others and the leadership.

**Teens' Terrible Secret.** What is the secret that teens hate to divulge? A May 1997 Roper Youth Report indicates that adolescents still think that their parents count. Youth—even rebellious young people—are concerned about their parents' opinion, and their influence is still felt, especially among 13 to 17 year olds. Only in areas of music and clothing do friends or peers exert a stronger influence to sway the opinion of the young.

While judgment belongs to the Lord, people are still called to make critical evaluations in life. Paul, however, noted that the most important decision in life was to remain faithful to the Lord. No other virtue would have more positive impact in the lives of others.

# THE NEED FOR DISCIPLINE IN THE CHURCH

**BACKGROUND SCRIPTURE:** 1 Corinthians 5:1—6:11
**DEVOTIONAL READING:** James 3:13-18

**Key Verse:** Let us celebrate the festival, not with the old yeast, the yeast of malice and evil, but with the unleavened bread of sincerity and truth. 1 Corinthians 5:8.

*KING JAMES VERSION*

1 CORINTHIANS 5:1 It is reported commonly that there is fornication among you, and such fornication as is not so much as named among the Gentiles, that one should have his father's wife.

2 And ye are puffed up, and have not rather mourned, that he that hath done this deed might be taken away from among you.

3 For I verily, as absent in body, but present in spirit, have judged already, as though I were present, concerning him that hath so done this deed,

4 In the name of our Lord Jesus Christ, when ye are gathered together, and my spirit, with the power of our Lord Jesus Christ,

5 To deliver such an one unto Satan for the destruction of the flesh, that the spirit may be saved in the day of the Lord Jesus.

6 Your glorying is not good. Know ye not that a little leaven leaveneth the whole lump?

7 Purge out therefore the old leaven, that ye may be a new lump, as ye are unleavened. For even Christ our passover is sacrificed for us:

8 Therefore let us keep the feast, not with old leaven, neither with the leaven of malice and wickedness; but with the unleavened bread of sincerity and truth.

9 I wrote unto you in an epistle not to company with fornicators:

10 Yet not altogether with the fornicators of this world, or with the covetous, or extortioners, or with idolaters; for then must ye needs go out of the world.

11 But now I have written unto you not to keep company, if any man that is called a brother be a fornicator, or covetous, or an idolater, or a railer, or a drunkard, or an extortioner; with such an one no not to eat.

12 For what have I to do to judge them also that are without? do not ye judge them that are within?

13 But them that are without God judgeth. Therefore put away from among yourselves that wicked person.

*NEW REVISED STANDARD VERSION*

1 CORINTHIANS 5:1 It is actually reported that there is sexual immorality among you, and of a kind that is not found even among pagans; for a man is living with his father's wife. 2 And you are arrogant! Should you not rather have mourned, so that he who has done this would have been removed from among you?

3 For though absent in body, I am present in spirit; and as if present I have already pronounced judgment 4 in the name of the Lord Jesus on the man who has done such a thing. When you are assembled, and my spirit is present with the power of our Lord Jesus, 5 you are to hand this man over to Satan for the destruction of the flesh, so that his spirit may be saved in the day of the Lord.

6 Your boasting is not a good thing. Do you not know that a little yeast leavens the whole batch of dough? 7 Clean out the old yeast so that you may be a new batch, as you really are unleavened. For our paschal lamb, Christ, has been sacrificed. 8 Therefore, let us celebrate the festival, not with the old yeast, the yeast of malice and evil, but with the unleavened bread of sincerity and truth.

9 I wrote to you in my letter not to associate with sexually immoral persons— 10 not at all meaning the immoral of this world, or the greedy and robbers, or idolaters, since you would then need to go out of the world. 11 But now I am writing to you not to associate with anyone who bears the name of brother or sister who is sexually immoral or greedy, or is an idolater, reviler, drunkard, or robber. Do not even eat with such a one. 12 For what have I to do with judging those outside? Is it not those who are inside that you are to judge? 13 God will judge those outside. "Drive out the wicked person from among you."

## BACKGROUND

Every form of sexual perversion could be found in Corinth. Male and female prostitutes openly plied their trade. The great temple of Aphrodite with its hundreds of courtesans flaunted sexual indulgence. Some of the practices of some of the cults were so disgusting that even the blasé Roman government refused to license these groups.

In this notoriously easy-going society, new converts to Christ often found it hard to leave behind their old, sinful ways. A situation in the Corinthian church arose that showed how these early believers sometimes retained their pagan practices. One prominent member of the congregation was living openly with his stepmother. This combination of adultery and incest was shocking even to some respectable non-Christians in Corinth. The small, struggling congregations were getting a bad name and bringing reproach to the cause of Christ.

More startling was the fact that the believers at Corinth seemed smug and indifferent to the man's offense. They apparently thought that having this person in their congregation was evidence of their grace and openness. They believed that by accepting him, they were "witnessing" to their community about the liberty they had in Christ to do whatever they wanted.

Paul was appalled at such indifference. He was not only indignant that this man would so flagrantly disregard basic morality, but also irate that the church was ignoring the matter. The apostle commanded that the faithful Christians not only break fellowship with the disobedient and unrepentant person, but also put him out of the church.

## NOTES ON THE PRINTED TEXT

Part of the disturbing news about the Corinthian church was a report of a case of incest. The church seemed to be condoning a sin that even shocked the licentious Corinthian unbelievers. Paul was infuriated at the church's toleration of the sin. *It is actually reported that there is sexual immorality among you, and of a kind that is not found even among pagans; for a man is living with his father's wife* (5:1).

A man was living together with his stepmother. Paul reprimanded the Corinthians believers for failing to act. Instead of being filled with grief and indignation for the man's sin and failure to repent, they seemed proud (perhaps based on a faulty understanding of Christian freedom). Paul declared that the man was to be excommunicated, that is, removed from the Christian community. *And you are arrogant! Should you not rather have mourned, so that he who has done this would have been removed from among you?* (5:2).

Paul's directive was a command, not a suggestion. Though not present with the Corinthians Christians, he reminded them that his authority as an apostle came from Jesus. *For though absent in body, I am present in spirit; and as if present I have already pronounced judgment in the name of the Lord Jesus on the man who has done such a thing* (5:3-4). So adamant was Paul on this matter that he told the church to hand over the man *to Satan for the destruction of the flesh, so that his spirit may be saved in the day of the Lord* (5:5).

There are several interpretations of what Paul meant. One view says the man would become so spiritually miserable under the torment of Satan that he would beg for forgiveness and repent of his sin. Another interpretation says that the devil would afflict the man's body with physical illness. His condition would become so intolerable that he would repent of his sin. And if he remained unrepentant, he might even die. Still another view says that the man would be forced to forfeit the power of the Spirit in his life. This would open the way for him to be directed and dominated by worldly desires and impulses. Regardless of which view is taken, the man's spiritual preservation was the ultimate goal.

Having commented on what to do with the unrepentant sinner, Paul next commented on the morally lax attitude of the church. It was not good that the congregation had tolerated such sin. The apostle said, *Your boasting is not a good thing. Do you not know that a little yeast leavens the whole batch of dough?* (5:6). Yeast was often used in Scripture to depict the corrupting power of evil. The violation of one moral standard would slowly affect the whole congregation. Paul then referred to the Jewish Passover practice of ridding the house of yeast. *Clean out the old yeast so that you may be a new batch, as you really are unleavened* (5:7). In other words, believers were not to accept or tolerate any form of immorality.

Paul explained that Christ, who had been sacrificed for the sins of the world, was the Corinthians' Passover lamb. Paul then alluded to the Feast of Unleavened Bread, which followed Passover. The apostle said that his readers should celebrate Jesus' sacrifice by living a pure and holy life dedicated completely to God. They were to put behind them the wickedness of their earlier life and, instead, live sincerely and truthfully. *Therefore, let us celebrate the festival, not with the old yeast, the yeast of malice and evil, but with the unleavened bread of sincerity and truth* (5:8).

Many scholars think that Paul had written the Corinthians a previous letter, which is now lost to us. In it the apostle told his readers not to associate with people who were *sexually immoral* (5:9). Paul did not mean by this that they should completely disassociate themselves from unbelievers, even when they behaved wickedly. Rather, Paul had urged the Corinthians to disassociate themselves from those who claimed to be Christians but whose behavior indicated otherwise. The Corinthians were not even to eat with so-called believers who habitually indulged in any form of immorality. This included such vices as sexual promiscuity, greed, idolatry, damaging others' reputations, drunkenness, and cheating (5:10-11).

Paul made a careful and important distinction in 5:12. He noted that it was not the responsibility of the church to pass judgment on the non-Christian society, for God reserved the right to do this. Instead, it was the church's responsibility to evaluate the behavior of people who were part of its fellowship. Those who flagrantly and persistently lived in sin were to be disciplined.

Consider the man involved in an incestuous affair. Paul told the Corinthians to exclude him from the church. The apostle based his directive on Deuteronomy 22:24. Paul wanted his readers to gently and yet firmly direct the offender toward repentance so that he could be restored to fellowship (1 Cor. 5:13).

## SUGGESTIONS TO TEACHERS

You need no statistics to document the widespread immorality in today's culture. Everyone in your class already knows the way traditional values of fidelity in marriage have declined in the past decades. The warped thinking of society has invaded the modern church in the same way it threatened the congregation in Corinth. This week's lesson should be studied by every member of the class who wants to be called a follower of Christ!

**1. RENOUNCING ALL DEPRAVITY.** Explain to the students that every person who claims to be a Christian has pledged to submit to the authority of Jesus. This calls for a higher morality than that of the community around us. We must discipline ourselves to resist the appeal of the pagan culture. Discuss the forms of disciplined living that individuals and families in the church may consider, such as choosing not to watch certain videos or TV programs or movies, or working to keep pornography out of the community, or holding courses on Christian marriage. Emphasize that believers abide by a higher ethical standard than the unsaved, especially in matters of sexual morality.

**2. REMOVING THE DESTROYER.** Paul bluntly told the Corinthians to discipline the unrepentant church member who was living in sin. The apostle also chastised the Corinthians for their casual acceptance of the offender's ungodly behavior. Immoral living within Christ's family wrecks the unity the church.

**3. RESOLVING THE DIFFERENCES.** Paul was appalled that the believers in Corinth would be so tolerant of such a notorious case of immorality. Of course, this was not the only problem in the church. There was factionalism, immaturity, and judgmentalism. These problems had become so acute that the unity of Christ's family was threatened. Paul called for differences to be handled by mature and trusted leaders within the church. Invite the members of the class to discuss how their church might best resolve its differences.

**4. REMEMBERING YOUR DEDICATION.** Finally, discuss with the class members the need to preserve the moral and spiritual integrity of the congregation and encourage offenders within it to abandon their evil ways. What approach should the leaders of the church take when disciplining an unrepentant member?

---

<table>
<tr>
<td>

**FOR ADULTS**

</td>
<td>

■ TOPIC: Discipline Brings Unity

■ QUESTIONS: 1. What was the nature of the sexual offense with-in the church at Corinth? 2. Why did Paul urge such stern discipli-

</td>
</tr>
</table>

nary measures be taken against the unrepentant, sinning church member? 3. What should be the attitude of Christians when they learn that a fellow believer is living in sexual sin? 4. How might the leaders of the church encourage God's people to live morally pure lives? 5. Why is it often so difficult for a church to discipline members of the congregation who are living in flagrant sin?

■ **ILLUSTRATIONS:**

**Call for Public and Private Morality.** In contrast to the immoral lives of many of our modern leaders, John Adams stands as a person who was convinced that public and private morality are interconnected. He speaks to self-indulgent baby boomers who prefer to use pundits and polls as their moral guides and divorce their actions from the traditional biblical moral codes. Adams was convinced that a corrupt people could not long remain free. An immoral person, he insisted, could not be free, but was instead a slave to unreasoning passion.

This great leader, who was a force behind the American Revolution and the establishment of our nation, demanded strict discipline, excellence, and integrity as the characteristics required in all persons, and especially in leaders. To attract and keep virtuous, disciplined people, Adams stated that society as a whole must foster virtue and discipline in its citizens.

"The best republics," Adams wrote, "will be virtuous and have been so." He noted that to remain virtuous, one must adhere to the rule of law and keep private passions in check. "A passion continually indulged feeds upon itself, eventually warping the owner's inherent capacity to judge right from wrong. People entrusted with unlimited power thrive upon their passions. The passion that is long indulged and continually gratified becomes mad; it is a species of delirium; it should not be called guilt, but insanity."

**Origin of the Word.** True leaders and genuine Christians know that they must live disciplined lives. The English word "true" has an interesting origin. It derives from the old English word "try." This term meant "firm and dependable, like a tree." What a significant way to define the type of individual who practices personal discipline! He or she is firm and dependable like a tree, standing strong and steady, useful and fruitful.

**How to Build a Cathedral.** The philosopher Heinrich Heine [HI-nuh] and a companion were visiting Avignon [aah-veh-YOHN], France, and gazed at the magnificent cathedral. Awed by the ancient edifice, the friend asked, "Why is it that we can't seem to build cathedrals anymore? Heine replied, "Ah, my friend, in those days people had convictions. We moderns merely have opinions. It takes more than opinions to build a cathedral."

Convictions arise from a life of discipline before the living Lord. And such disciplined living produces convictions that bind God's people together to a great common effort such a erecting a cathedral.

---

**FOR YOUTH**
■ TOPIC: Who Enforces God's Moral Standard?
■ QUESTIONS: 1. Why do you think the believers in Corinth were so indifferent about the presence of sexual sin within their congregation? 2. What was wrong about the boastful attitude of the Corinthian Christians? 3. What can believers do to encourage one another to abandon all forms of sexual immorality? 4. What can Christians do to encourage their fellow believers to pursue holiness? 5. What affect does the presence of unchecked sin have on a church?

■ **ILLUSTRATIONS:**

**Still Condemned.** The Department of Justice states that every year our judicial system deals with roughly 500,000 cases of incest. If that statistic does not sadden you, then read on. Researchers believe that between 5 and 15 percent of the American population is or has been involved in incest. Other studies claim that 1 in 7 boys and 1 in 4 girls will be sexually abused before they reach the age of 18. Ninety-seven percent of the molesters are male and 75 percent of them are family members. All segments of society are susceptible, for this type of crime is no respecter of either income level or professional and educational level.

Paul was specific. Incest was heinous and could not be tolerated. This immorality was condemned, and he called for the perpetrator, not to be tolerated, but to be punished swiftly

**Sex Sells.** While some suggestive ads are pulled due to a protest from viewers, the truth is that sexuality is used to promote items as varied as cologne, toiletries, traveler's checks, underwear, chicken, clothing, vegetables, and automobiles. It's no wonder that youth are uncertain about immorality. Advertisers know that they can make money off of the human desire for physical intimacy.

Paul urged his fellow believers not to tolerate any form of immorality. He was concerned that even a little toleration was like yeast, and would spread throughout the entire congregation. You are wise to listen to Paul and resist the temptations around you to be immoral.

**Missing Ingredient.** Realizing that 13 million people each year contract a sexually transmitted disease (STD), Stanford University introduced an interdisciplinary undergraduate course in STDs. The course covers such topics as Acquired Immune Deficiency Syndrome, genital herpes, syphilis, hepatitis, and pelvic inflammatory disease. The course features leaders from the Federal Center for Disease Control and experts in biology, law, public policy, sociology, and history. Noticeably absent is the religion department and any discussion on abstinence or celibacy. Paul certainly would have condemned this as condoning immorality.

# COUNSEL CONCERNING MARRIAGE

**BACKGROUND SCRIPTURE:** 1 Corinthians 6:12—7:16
**DEVOTIONAL READING:** 1 Corinthians 7:25-35

**KEY VERSE:** Do you not know that your body is a temple of the Holy Spirit within you, which you have from God, and that you are not your own? 1 Corinthians 6:19.

## KING JAMES VERSION

1 CORINTHIANS 7:1 Now concerning the things whereof ye wrote unto me: It is good for a man not to touch a woman.

2 Nevertheless, to avoid fornication, let every man have his own wife, and let every woman have her own husband.

3 Let the husband render unto the wife due benevolence: and likewise also the wife unto the husband.

4 The wife hath not power of her own body, but the husband: and likewise also the husband hath not power of his own body, but the wife.

5 Defraud ye not one the other, except it be with consent for a time, that ye may give yourselves to fasting and prayer; and come together again, that Satan tempt you not for your incontinency. . . .

8 I say therefore to the unmarried and widows, It is good for them if they abide even as I.

9 But if they cannot contain, let them marry: for it is better to marry than to burn.

10 And unto the married I command, yet not I, but the Lord, Let not the wife depart from her husband:

11 But and if she depart, let her remain unmarried, or be reconciled to her husband: and let not the husband put away his wife.

12 But to the rest speak I, not the Lord: If any brother hath a wife that believeth not, and she be pleased to dwell with him, let him not put her away.

13 And the woman which hath an husband that believeth not, and if he be pleased to dwell with her, let her not leave him.

14 For the unbelieving husband is sanctified by the wife, and the unbelieving wife is sanctified by the husband: else were your children unclean; but now are they holy.

15 But if the unbelieving depart, let him depart. A brother or a sister is not under bondage in such cases: but God hath called us to peace.

16 For what knowest thou, O wife, whether thou shalt save thy husband? or how knowest thou, O man, whether thou shalt save thy wife?

## NEW REVISED STANDARD VERSION

1 CORINTHIANS 7:1 Now concerning the matters about which you wrote: "It is well for a man not to touch a woman." 2 But because of cases of sexual immorality, each man should have his own wife and each woman her own husband. 3 The husband should give to his wife her conjugal rights, and likewise the wife to her husband. 4 For the wife does not have authority over her own body, but the husband does; likewise the husband does not have authority over his own body, but the wife does. 5 Do not deprive one another except perhaps by agreement for a set time, to devote yourselves to prayer, and then come together again, so that Satan may not tempt you because of your lack of self-control. . . .

8 To the unmarried and the widows I say that it is well for them to remain unmarried as I am. 9 But if they are not practicing self-control, they should marry. For it is better to marry than to be aflame with passion.

10 To the married I give this command—not I but the Lord—that the wife should not separate from her husband 11 (but if she does separate, let her remain unmarried or else be reconciled to her husband), and that the husband should not divorce his wife.

12 To the rest I say—I and not the Lord—that if any believer has a wife who is an unbeliever, and she consents to live with him, he should not divorce her.
13 And if any woman has a husband who is an unbeliever, and he consents to live with her, she should not divorce him. 14 For the unbelieving husband is made holy through his wife, and the unbelieving wife is made holy through her husband. Otherwise, your children would be unclean, but as it is, they are holy. 15 But if the unbelieving partner separates, let it be so; in such a case the brother or sister is not bound. It is to peace that God has called you. 16 Wife, for all you know, you might save your husband. Husband, for all you know, you might save your wife.

5

**219**

## HOME BIBLE READINGS

## BACKGROUND

Apparently there were some in the congregation at Corinth who believed that, as Christians, they had the freedom to do whatever they desired. In fact, Bible scholars think that Paul may have been quoting some in the church who had asserted that *all things are lawful for me* (6:12). If this is true, the apostle affirmed that everything is permissible for the Christian; however, Paul said that not everything works for the believer's benefit.

Some of the members in the Corinthian church claimed that just as eating and digesting food was a natural, physical activity that had no bearing on their spiritual life, so promiscuous sexual activity had no effect on their moral and spiritual life (6:13). Paul admitted that food and the human body are transitory, but he denied that what believers do with their bodies is unimportant. Sexual promiscuity affects the personality and spiritual life of a human being in a far greater way than food does.

Undoubtedly the Corinthians were more prone to sexual sin than were Christians in some other cities because of the climate of immorality for which their city had become infamous. Corinth's temple of Aphrodite employed perhaps as many as a thousand temple priestess-prostitutes. In such an environment, some of the Corinthian Christians may have had trouble getting used to biblical standards for morality.

The apostle implied that a sexual act is more than physical; it is not completely divorced from the spiritual (6:16). To Paul, the sexual act is an expression of two people's whole personalities. It is a way they reveal and commit themselves to each other. We can see why Paul told the Corinthians to shun all forms of sexual immorality (6:18). They were to run away from temptations to express their sexuality in morally illicit ways. Because the Corinthians belonged to God, Paul urged them to glorify the Lord with their bodies by fleeing immorality and being sexually responsible (6:20).

The apostle's teaching on these matters set the stage for the counsel he gave in chapter 7 of his letter. He directed his attention to answering questions the Corinthians had about various issues. The first group of topics related to marriage.

# NOTES ON THE PRINTED TEXT

The Roman empire was going through a sexual revolution. Marriage, in the Roman view, was for the purpose of producing heirs. However, for sexual pleasure, the Romans sought satisfaction outside of marriage. Many Romans chose to forego marriage altogether.

In a previous letter, the Corinthians had asked Paul questions about relationships between men and women, about marriage, and about the single life. Paul began his response with these words, *Now concerning the matters about which you wrote* (7:1). The apostle then offered frank counsel concerning marriage. Far from being a prude who was hostile to women, Paul advocated marriage and saw women as an equal partner in the relationship. He wrote, *"It is well for a man not to touch a woman"* (7:1). Outside of marriage, a man and a woman should not be sexually intimate. Paul indicated that any illicit sexual relationship was forbidden.

For some a single life was the correct choice. But for others such a lifestyle would lead to temptation and sexual immorality. *But because of cases of sexual immorality, each man should have his own wife and each woman her own husband* (7:2). Paul's point was that sexual relations were an acceptable part of marriage. *The husband should give to his wife her conjugal rights, and likewise the wife to her husband* (7:3). Mutual concern and consideration of the other was important. Sex was to be equal and reciprocal, and each partner had a responsibility to the other. *For the wife does not have authority over her own body, but the husband does; likewise the husband does not have authority over his own body, but the wife does* (7:4).

Sex was not to be withheld except by mutual agreement for a limited time of prayer. Following that period physical relations were to be resumed, lest sexual temptation result. *Do not deprive one another except perhaps by agreement for a set time, to devote yourselves to prayer, and then come together again, so that Satan may not tempt you because of your lack of self-control* (7:5).

Another issue raised by the Corinthians was whether single people should marry. Paul advocated remaining single if a believer could practice celibacy. But if the individual was unable to exercise self-control over his or her own passions, marriage was preferable. *To the unmarried and the widows I say that it is well for them to remain unmarried as I am. But if they are not practicing self-control, they should marry. For it is better to marry than to be aflame with passion* (7:8-9).

Paul then addressed the issue of divorce. He stressed the importance of preserving the marriage relationship. *To the married I give this command—not I but the Lord—that the wife should not separate from her husband* (7:10). Neither Christian husband nor wife should initiate divorce, but if divorce occurred, the two should remain unmarried or be reconciled to each other. *(But if she does separate, let her remain unmarried or else be reconciled to her husband), and that the husband should not divorce his wife* (7:11).

Paul wrote that if a Christian was married to a non-Christian, the continuance of the marriage depended on the will of the non-Christian. *To the rest I say—I and not the Lord—that if any believer has a wife who is an unbeliever, and she consents to live with him, he should not divorce her* (7:12). Paul reassured the Corinthians that they would not be defiled through physical contact with the unbeliever. In fact, the unbelieving spouse was sanctified, or set apart to God, through the converted partner. *For the unbelieving husband is made holy through his wife, and the unbelieving wife is made holy through her husband* (7:14). And children in such relationships were holy. *Otherwise, your children would be unclean, but as it is, they are holy.*

Paul said that if the unbeliever desired a divorce, then the Christian partner should permit it. In such a situation, the Christian partner *is not bound* (7:15). Some say this means the Christian was under no obligation to try to preserve the marriage compact. Others interpret this to mean that the believer was free to remarry. In either case, Paul discouraged divorce, for God could use the believing partner to bring his or her unbelieving mate to Christ. *Wife, for all you know, you might save your husband. Husband, for all you know, you might save your wife* (7:16).

## SUGGESTIONS TO TEACHERS

Paul's teachings on sex and marriage recorded in this week's Scripture text has so much valuable counsel that you could easily develop a series of Sunday school lessons for your class. Be sure to accentuate the positives in this section as well as the "must nots" for Christians.

**1. REFUTATIONS.** The Corinthians spouted the same lines that we hear today to excuse their lack of responsibility in sexual relations. You and your class members can quickly state most of these. ("Everybody's doing it." "It's my private business." "Anything goes as long as nobody gets hurt.") Call attention to the way Paul answered these excuses.

To those claiming they weren't breaking any law or that God accepts everyone, regardless of their behavior, the Scripture states that Christians are called to be responsible. That means living always in ways that are beneficial and never dominated by anything other than Christ. Those who equate indulging their sexual urges with satisfying hunger pangs are warned that Christ totally rejects immoral acts.

The Corinthian letter tells us that our bodies belong to Christ, not to ourselves. Prostitution, therefore, is degrading what is Christ's and sinning against one's own body as well. Likewise, the extra-marital affair or casual sex is ruled out. We have given ourselves to Christ!

**2. RELATIONSHIPS.** God's gift of sex has been granted for one man and one woman who have mutually pledged to the Lord to live in a caring, faithful, and permanent marriage relationship with each other. True intimacy between those partners can grow only in the covenant bond of matrimony. Paul's sound counsel emphasized that the caring and sharing must be mutual. There doesn't exist any macho notion of male superiority or assertions of the husband only having conjugal rights! Christians always have understood that the husband and the wife stand as equals before the Lord, and each seeks to please the other in marital intimacy.

God's Word teaches that the marital bond between the husband and the wife is permanent. This means that sexual immorality and divorce are to be avoided. Throughout this week's lesson, stress that believers adhere to a higher form of morality than unbelievers because the former belong to Christ!

| **FOR ADULTS** | ■ TOPIC: Responsibility in Marriage and Singleness<br>■ QUESTIONS: 1. What conjugal rights do the husband and wife have in their married relationship? 2. What is God's attitude toward |

divorce? 3. In what ways is your inclination to remain single or to be married a gift from God? 4. What can you do to strengthen the integrity of marriage? 5. What can you do to ensure that your family lives in peace?

■ **ILLUSTRATIONS:**

**Hedgehog Morality.** The Isle of South Ulst lies far off the west coast of Scotland in the Outer Hebrides. Two rare species of birds are found on this remote place—corncrakes and waders. These birds nest in the fine grass near the shore. For years the waders and corncrakes laid their eggs and hatched their young in safety on the ground of South Ulst. A few years ago, however, someone decided to bring a few hedgehogs as pets to South Ulst. He knew that hedgehogs love to feast on birds' eggs, but he told others that the animals would simply be harmless pets and that a couple of cute little hedgehogs couldn't cause any trouble.

By 1998, there were 10,000 hedgehogs on South Ulst. The few brought as "harmless" pets that wouldn't cause any problems had escaped and multiplied. Even worse, they devoured the birds' eggs so that the number of corncrakes, waders, and other shore birds and sea birds were rapidly diminishing.

The same type of reasoning that the man used to justify the bringing in of hedgehogs on the island also pervades the minds of many when it comes to casual sex. They like to tell themselves, "What harm can it do? It can't make any difference, especially since it's my personal life!" But inevitably such "hedgehog morality" proves destructive by taking over one's life and harming others.

**Mother's Advice.** William Willimon, the Dean of the Chapel and Professor at Duke University, relates that when he was young and single and leaving to go out on a date, his mother would tell him, "Remember who you are!" Willimon knew that she was not referring to his name or his address. This wise mother was reminding her son to be aware always that he belonged to the Lord. What better advice could anyone offer in regard to dating, sex, and marriage!

**Quickie Weddings or Committed Marriages?** In May 1997, 100 Chicago-area couples were married in a quick mass ceremony aboard the *Giant Drop* at Six Flags Great America. And in Las Vegas, *The Little White Chapel Drive-up Wedding Window* advertises that couples can be married in 15 minutes. No car is required. "Roller skates are fine, too!" exclaims the chapel's manager, Joanie Richards.

To counter such hasty and casual marriages (as well as the high divorce rate in the United States) some legislators want potential newlyweds to take more time before saying "I do!" Bills are being introduced in some states requiring a 90-day waiting period prior to a wedding. Other legislators are considering bills encouraging a driver's-education-style course for couples planning marriage. Such laws may be helpful, but the counsel of Paul in 1 Corinthians 7 expresses best how Christians should approach marriage.

**For Youth**

■ **Topic:** Sex and Marriage

■ **Questions:** 1. What authority in sexual matters do the husband and wife have over each other's body? 2. Why does God stress the importance of preserving the marriage relationship? 3. What can you do to remain morally pure regardless of whether you are single or married? 4. How can you encourage your friends to stay away from sexual immorality? 5. Why do you think that God strongly discourages divorce?

■ **Illustrations:**

**Pure Love.** A situation that once was viewed by most people as unacceptable has become commonplace. According to the *National and International Religion Report*, the marjority of men and women who plan to get married are living together before the wedding ceremony. The report goes on to point out that this practice has devastating effects. "Marriages that are preceded by living together have 50 percent higher disruption (divorce or separation) rates than marriages without premarital cohabitation."

The temptations were no different in the first century. Paul had to make it clear to the believers at Corinth that they were not to be involved in anything that even expressed a hint of sexual immorality. He said that if they found their passions becoming so strong that they wanted to express their desires, there was an answer. It was not found in an immoral relationship; rather, it was found in marriage.

In a day when immorality continues to consume people's lives, Christians should do all we can to promote the joys and privileges of love that is honoring to God, namely, the love that is shared in marriage.

**Two Are Better than One.** In an age where 48 percent of students live in a one-parent family by the age of 18, new thoughts have emerged. The old belief was that children really did not need both parents at home to grow up well adjusted. The theory was that children were resilient and could endure a separation or a divorce without emotional problems.

A new study suggests that children do experience the painful effects of divorce. The National Association of Elementary School Principals surveyed 8556 students at 15 elementary and high schools around the country. The one-parent children showed substantially more absenteeism, truancy, discipline problems, suspensions, expulsions, and dropouts.

Clearly, the family is important! The study amply demonstrates the catastrophic effects of divorce on children. While Paul reaffirmed the sanctity of marriage and counseled strongly against divorce, he also stressed that children should not have to bear the effects of the divorce, for they are precious in God's eyes.

**Recipe for Success.** What makes for a good marriage? What qualities should be present in a couple? Two Brigham Young University researchers believe that communication is the mainstay of marriage. Drs. Thomas Holman and Wesley Burr of the family sciences department have concluded after surveying 15,000 couples in 12 cooperating colleges and universities that communication is more important than having something in common, the quality of their parents' marriage, agreement on values and role expectations, demographic similarities, and good emotional health. Good communication enabled couples to talk out problems without defensiveness or emotional outbursts, and produced a willingness to listen to the other's point of view.

Paul talked about maintaining mutuality and respect in the marriage relationship. The consistent presence of these virtues can enable a marriage to grow and remain strong.

# Concerning Love and Knowledge

**Background Scripture:** 1 Corinthians 8

**Devotional Reading:** 1 Corinthians 10:23—11:1

**Key Verse:** Anyone who claims to know something does not yet have the necessary knowledge; but anyone who loves God is known by him. 1 Corinthians 8:2-3.

*KING JAMES VERSION*

1 CORINTHIANS 8:1 Now as touching things offered unto idols, we know that we all have knowledge. Knowledge puffeth up, but charity edifieth.

2 And if any man think that he knoweth any thing, he knoweth nothing yet as he ought to know.

3 But if any man love God, the same is known of him.

4 As concerning therefore the eating of those things that are offered in sacrifice unto idols, we know that an idol is nothing in the world, and that there is none other God but one.

5 For though there be that are called gods, whether in heaven or in earth, (as there be gods many, and lords many,)

6 But to us there is but one God, the Father, of whom are all things, and we in him; and one Lord Jesus Christ, by whom are all things, and we by him.

7 Howbeit there is not in every man that knowledge: for some with conscience of the idol unto this hour eat it as a thing offered unto an idol; and their conscience being weak is defiled.

8 But meat commendeth us not to God: for neither, if we eat, are we the better; neither, if we eat not, are we the worse.

9 But take heed lest by any means this liberty of your's become a stumblingblock to them that are weak.

10 For if any man see thee which hast knowledge sit at meat in the idol's temple, shall not the conscience of him which is weak be emboldened to eat those things which are offered to idols;

11 And through thy knowledge shall the weak brother perish, for whom Christ died?

12 But when ye sin so against the brethren, and wound their weak conscience, ye sin against Christ.

13 Wherefore, if meat make my brother to offend, I will eat no flesh while the world standeth, lest I make my brother to offend.

*NEW REVISED STANDARD VERSION*

1 CORINTHIANS 8:1 Now concerning food sacrificed to idols: we know that "all of us possess knowledge." Knowledge puffs up, but love builds up.

2 Anyone who claims to know something does not yet have the necessary knowledge; 3 but anyone who loves God is known by him.

4 Hence, as to the eating of food offered to idols, we know that "no idol in the world really exists," and that "there is no God but one." 5 Indeed, even though there may be so-called gods in heaven or on earth—as in fact there are many gods and many lords— 6 yet for us there is one God, the Father, from whom are all things and for whom we exist, and one Lord, Jesus Christ, through whom are all things and through whom we exist.

7 It is not everyone, however, who has this knowledge. Since some have become so accustomed to idols until now, they still think of the food they eat as food offered to an idol; and their conscience, being weak, is defiled. 8 "Food will not bring us close to God." We are no worse off if we do not eat, and no better off if we do. 9 But take care that this liberty of yours does not somehow become a stumbling block to the weak. 10 For if others see you, who possess knowledge, eating in the temple of an idol, might they not, since their conscience is weak, be encouraged to the point of eating food sacrificed to idols? 11 So by your knowledge those weak believers for whom Christ died are destroyed. 12 But when you thus sin against members of your family, and wound their conscience when it is weak, you sin against Christ. 13 Therefore, if food is a cause of their falling, I will never eat meat, so that I may not cause one of them to fall.

| | | |
|---|---|---|
| *Monday, Apr. 3* | 1 Corinthians 8:1-6 | *Knowledge Puffs Up; Love Builds Up* |
| *Tuesday, Apr. 4* | 1 Corinthians 8:7-13 | *Don't Cause Another to Stumble* |
| *Wednesday, Apr. 5* | 1 Corinthians 9:1-12 | *Love Has Priority over "Rights"* |
| *Thursday, Apr. 6* | 1 Corinthians 9:13-18 | *Preaching the Gospel Is Reward Enough* |
| *Friday, Apr. 7* | 1 Corinthians 9:19-27 | *Being All Things to All People* |
| *Saturday, Apr. 8* | 1 Corinthians 10:1-13 | *Learn from Lessons of the Past* |
| *Sunday, Apr. 9* | 1 Corinthians 10:14-22 | *Flee from the Worship of Idols* |

## BACKGROUND

In ancient times pagan temples were a main source of meat in Corinth as well as in other cities. Animals were slaughtered and a token piece of the carcass was burned as a sacrifice to the pagan deities. The rest of the meat was then offered for sale. Anyone in Corinth wanting a steak for dinner simply bought it from the butcher shop affiliated with one of the sites of pagan worship.

Some in the church in Corinth were proud of knowing that such a steak was merely meat and not defiled by idolatrous associations. They announced that they were free to eat whatever they pleased and that they were not bound by any of the dietary regulations existing in Judaism. Sadly, the awareness that these believers had concerning their spiritual freedom in Christ led them to feel intellectually superior to other believers who thought that it was wrong to patronize meat markets affiliated with pagan temples.

There were others in the Corinthian church whose consciences bothered them about buying or eating such meat. They were newly converted from the rampant paganism of the Corinthian culture. Thus they were fighting a desperate battle to keep themselves from slipping back into their old idolatrous ways. We can understand why it bothered them deeply that their fellow believers would flaunt their freedom in Christ to enjoy meat that had been sacrificed to idols.

The believers in Corinth asked Paul to give godly instruction concerning this matter. The apostle noted that while knowledge might make us feel important, it is love that really builds up the church. Spiritually strengthening the community of believers by being sensitive to the needs and concerns of one another took priority over gratifying one's personal desires.

## NOTES ON THE PRINTED TEXT

In addition to answering questions about marriage, Paul gave instruction about whether believers could eat food that had been sacrificed to idols in pagan temples. It is helpful to note that meat was not abundant in the ancient world. Most individuals ate porridges, barley bread, olives, wine, and some fish as a relish. Because meat was extremely expensive, it was mostly eaten by the affluent.

The general public could only afford to buy discounted meat that had previously been sacrificed to a pagan deity in a temple.

*Now concerning food sacrificed to idols: we know that "all of us possess knowledge." Knowledge puffs up, but love builds up* (8:1). Paul affirmed that believers were spiritually free in Christ to eat meat that had been sacrificed to an idol. Sadly, some with this knowledge became arrogant and contemptuous of others who were not as spiritually "enlightened." In reality, the group that felt superior to others were missing the point about their spiritual freedom in Christ. They should have been using their knowledge to help other believers in the church, not tear them down. *Anyone who claims to know something does not yet have the necessary knowledge; but anyone who loves God is known by him* (8:2-3).

After underscoring the importance of Christian love, Paul wrote, *Hence, as to the eating of food offered to idols, we know that "no idol in the world really exists," and that "there is no God but one"* (8:4). This means that an idol is not really a god. In fact, there is only one God, the Lord of Israel (and over the universe). Paul acknowledged that the unsaved in Corinth worshiped *many gods and many lords* (8:5). This was evident by the presence of pagan temples. In fact, in Paul's day, statues of Athena and Apollo were prominent in the city's square and public buildings. Several temples have been unearthed at the west terrace of the forum, one of which commemorated the whole Greek pantheon and another of which was dedicated to Tyche (the goddess of good fortune and the protector of cities.)

Paul declared that there is only one God—the Father—who created everything. And there is only one Lord—Jesus Christ—through whom God made everything (8:6). But not all believers clearly understood these truths. Some had serious concerns about the consequences of eating food that had been offered to idols. *It is not everyone, however, who has this knowledge. Since some have become so accustomed to idols until now, they still think of the food they eat as food offered to an idol; and their conscience, being weak, is defiled* (8:7).

Paul noted that the issue lay with the individual believer, for the consumption of certain foods did not affect his or her spiritual relationship with God. *"Food will not bring us close to God." We are no worse off if we do not eat, and no better off if we do* (8:8). The apostle explained that while believers had the freedom to eat food sacrificed to idols, their concern for the sensitivity of other Christians overrode their exercise of their legitimate liberties. *But take care that this liberty of yours does not somehow become a stumbling block to the weak* (8:9).

Paul discussed a situation in which knowledgeable Christians, who were well grounded in their faith, ate in the temple of an idol. (Both Roman and Greek sources indicate that the temple precincts were the public restaurants of the day.) Such would encourage weaker Christians to violate their conscience by eating food that had been dedicated to an idol (8:10).

Paul censured such an exercise of Christian liberty, for it undermined the faith of the weaker believers. The apostle declared that this was a sin against Christ. *So by your knowledge those weak believers for whom Christ died are destroyed. But when you thus sin against members of your family, and wound their conscience when it is weak, you sin against Christ* (8:11-12).

Paul exhorted the stronger believers to show love to the weaker ones by refraining from offending them by their actions. The apostle said that he would not eat meat that had been sacrificed to an idol if his action would encourage other Christians to sin against their conscience. *Therefore, if food is a cause of their falling, I will never eat meat, so that I may not cause one of them to fall* (8:13).

## SUGGESTIONS TO TEACHERS

At first glance, you might think that you can skip over this section of 1 Corinthians, which concerns eating meat that has been sacrificed to idols in pagan temples. But don't be so hasty. Instead, dig into this week's Scripture text. You will quickly discover that important issues surface about how Christians should behave around one another.

**1. SUPERIORITY OF LOVE OVER "KNOWLEDGE."** Paul's argument on eating meat sacrificed to idols went like this: "Okay, we know that meat is really just meat. It's not changed by the fact the butcher got it from a pagan temple. But let's not get swelled heads because we think that we are so mature in our thinking. We should ask whether we're helping or hurting other Christians by our actions!" You could also try this line of thinking in more culturally relevant areas. You might ask, "What harm is there in doing thus and so? How might this questionable activity affect other believers?" Remind your students, *Knowledge puffs up, but love builds up* (8:1). How easy it is for us to grow conceited over how much we think we know! Be sure to stress that caring for the needs of others comes first!

**2. SENSITIVITY TOWARD OTHERS.** As Christians we are bound to one another as a spiritual family, a family in which the Lord is the head. Even as He has the best interests of each of us at heart, so too we are called to keep the best interests of others at heart. We reflect Jesus' sensitivity by showing the same concern toward one another. This may sometimes mean giving up certain practices that may seem harmless to us, but that could offend or lead others astray.

**3. SERIOUSNESS OF ABUSING FREEDOM.** This week's lesson opens up the subject of exercising our spiritual freedom in Christ. In this era of rampant individualism, our culture has come to think that everyone should do as they please. They excuse their selfishness by saying, "I wanna be free to be me!" Tell the members of your class that believers are free to care for others, not to gratify their sinful desires.

**4. SOURCE OF ENCOURAGEMENT FOR THE WEAK.** You will want to get the discussion down to specifics. Ask which personal practices hinder others and which ones help others. Which activities that we enjoy doing might undermine the faith of our fellow believers?

| FOR ADULTS | ■ TOPIC: Let Love Lead. ■ QUESTIONS: 1. Why do you think the Corinthian believers were so enamored with knowledge? 2. Why was showing Christlike |
| --- | --- |

love of supreme importance? 3. What are some of the ways that believers can show the Lord how much they love Him? 4. Which of your present attitudes and actions could weaken the faith of another believer? 5. Which of your present attitudes and actions could strengthen the faith of another believer?

■ ILLUSTRATIONS:

**Free to Care.** Gus runs a small convenience store. He sells candy, soft drinks, newspapers, magazines, greeting cards, bread, milk, and a few sundries. The profit margin is low, and Gus doesn't make much from his long hours behind the counter. One afternoon, the news agent who distributes the magazines and daily papers that Gus puts on his shelves presented a tempting offer for Gus to boost his earnings. The offer was to stock a selection of mildly pornographic magazines. "Look," the agent told him, "this stuff sells. And you'll get some new customers."

At first Gus thought that the magazines were fairly harmless, especially when compared to the hard-core pornography on videos and cable television, and in other magazines. He reasoned that he wouldn't be bothered to read that literature himself. So why not take a trial shipment for a month or two? Then Gus remembered how many kids hung around his store, and bought snacks and school supplies. This shopkeeper knew that it was lawful for him to sell the questionable magazines. But as a Christian, he was also called to care for others. Gus therefore decided to turn down the offer from the news agent.

**Aunt Millie's Testimony.** At 87, "Aunt" Millie (as everyone calls her) is a bit unsteady on her feet, even with her cane. Her eyesight isn't too good, either. The weather in her part of the country makes walking nasty during the winter months. But Aunt Millie has not missed walking the four blocks to worship on a Sunday morning at her church for over 12 years. Her family and friends sometimes tell her that she doesn't have to go to church every Sunday, especially on bad days. Her daughter and family often prefer to sleep in on Sunday mornings.

A few weeks ago, Aunt Millie's son-in-law teased her, "Aw, c'mon, you don't have to get up and go to church in this kind of weather. You're free to stay home and keep warm if you want!" Aunt Millie answered, "I just got to show what side I'm on." The following Sunday, with boots, cane, umbrella, and her offering envelope tucked inside a worn handbag, she trudged the four blocks to be present by 10:30 in her usual place. Though as an elderly person she might have felt free to lounge around at home, she also felt responsible to her fellow believers.

**Led to Heal.** Dr. Ronald Seaton is a surgeon with the finest training and skills imaginable. For over 35 years, he served as a missionary doctor in small hospitals run by the Church of North India. He was asked to move many times to bring his surgical expertise to various hospitals, often at great inconvenience to his family and himself, but always without complaint. Had Dr. Seaton maintained a medical practice in the United States, he could have made a high income and a great name for himself. But because he is a devout Christian, he gave up his freedom to earn money and prestige in this country. Dr. Seaton also knew about the need for villagers in rural areas of Maharashtra State in India to receive the love of Christ through the hands of a skilled, experienced, Johns Hopkins-trained surgeon.

Dr. Seaton and his wife, Edith, retired in 1996. But instead of settling down comfortably somewhere near a golf course for leisurely living, they carefully investigated where there was an area badly in need of the services of a medical doctor. They finally selected a pocket of mountainous West Virginia that lacked a resident physician-surgeon. Dr. Seaton opened up a medical practice in Hinton, West Virginia, and he has deliberately chosen to serve the people in this remote area. He knew that he and Edith are free to enjoy themselves as retirees, but he also senses his responsibility to continue a ministry of healing!

## FOR YOUTH

■ TOPIC: You Can, But Don't

■ QUESTIONS: 1. What do you think was objectionable about the attitudes and actions of the Corinthians believers? 2. In what way were some in the Corinthian church undermining the faith of their fellow believers? 3. How might you demonstrate your Christian love to your family members and friends? 4. What are some things you can do to encourage other Christians to be faithful to Christ? 5. What are some of the ways that your behavior is modeled after the behavior of Christ?

■ ILLUSTRATIONS:

**Senseless Acts.** Nowhere in the Bible are you forbidden to smoke, though some Christians will tell you that it is a sin. However, the Surgeon General of the United States, the medical profession, and now even the tobacco industry have warned that smoking (as well as chewing tobacco) is hazardous to your health. Or consider how harmful the over-consumption of alcoholic beverages can be to you. The Bible speaks about moderation and the potential harm that can be experienced by overindulging in alcoholic beverages (see Prov. 23:29-35).

While smoking and drinking are not specified directly as sins in the Bible's pages, they are dangerous practices. As a Christian adult, you are permitted by law to smoke and drink. But you should also consider how your actions in these areas affect yourself and others.

**Setting an Example.** Larry Washington returned from his business trip to Cleveland, Ohio, nearly exhausted. However, he did not have time for a nap.

Washington, 25, remembered that he had promised to take 13-year-old James to the Pittsburgh-Syracuse basketball game. Washington is a mentor with the Big Brothers/Big Sisters program in his area. He is convinced that being a role model is important. Washington should know, for he grew up in a single parent family. His Sunday school teacher, a neighbor, and a first grade teacher that eventually became known to him as Aunt Bernice committed themselves to him. They guided him through a variety of pressures and problems that he encountered on the streets, at home, and in school.

Washington believes that it is his responsibility to set a godly example for others, as was done for him. This mature and caring attitude was also voiced by Paul to the Corinthians believers over the issue of eating meat sacrificed to idols. Have you considered how your attitudes and actions might affect others?

**Do as I Say, Not as I Do.** David Cline taught driver education at Northern High School near Durham, North Carolina. On September 19, 1997, Cline was teaching two students to drive when the car that he was riding in was cut off by Jon David Macklin. Cline, who preached careful and considerate driving, was infuriated and ordered the female driver to chase down Macklin. When they caught up with Macklin, Cline got out of the car and punched the offender in the nose.

Macklin sped off and Cline ordered the student to chase him again. The police pulled them over for speeding. Macklin returned and told the officer what had happened. Cline was arrested. The teacher who preached against road rage felt that he had gotten even. But Cline proved to be a poor role model. The horrible example he set was costly. He was forced to resign, after being suspended by the Durham School District.

Paul understood the importance of setting a godly example. Even if it meant sacrificing his own freedom to eat meat, he was willing to do so to build up, rather than undermine, the faith of his fellow believers.

# SPIRITUAL GIFTS

**BACKGROUND SCRIPTURE:** 1 Corinthians 12:1-30
**DEVOTIONAL READING:** Romans 12:1-8

**KEY VERSE:** Now there are varieties of gifts, but the same Spirit; . . . and there are varieties of activities, but it is the same God who activates all of them in everyone. 1 Corinthians 12:4, 6.

## KING JAMES VERSION

1 CORINTHIANS 12:4 Now there are diversities of gifts, but the same Spirit.

5 And there are differences of administrations, but the same Lord.

6 And there are diversities of operations, but it is the same God which worketh all in all.

7 But the manifestation of the Spirit is given to every man to profit withal.

8 For to one is given by the Spirit the word of wisdom; to another the word of knowledge by the same Spirit;

9 To another faith by the same Spirit; to another the gifts of healing by the same Spirit;

10 To another the working of miracles; to another prophecy; to another discerning of spirits; to another divers kinds of tongues; to another the interpretation of tongues:

11 But all these worketh that one and the selfsame Spirit, dividing to every man severally as he will.

12 For as the body is one, and hath many members, and all the members of that one body, being many, are one body: so also is Christ.

13 For by one Spirit are we all baptized into one body, whether we be Jews or Gentiles, whether we be bond or free; and have been all made to drink into one Spirit.

14 For the body is not one member, but many.

15 If the foot shall say, Because I am not the hand, I am not of the body; is it therefore not of the body?

16 And if the ear shall say, Because I am not the eye, I am not of the body; is it therefore not of the body?

17 If the whole body were an eye, where were the hearing? If the whole were hearing, where were the smelling?

18 But now hath God set the members every one of them in the body, as it hath pleased him.

19 And if they were all one member, where were the body?

20 But now are they many members, yet but one body. . . .

26 And whether one member suffer, all the members suffer with it; or one member be honoured, all the members rejoice with it.

## NEW REVISED STANDARD VERSION

1 CORINTHIANS 12:4 Now there are varieties of gifts, but the same Spirit; 5 and there are varieties of services, but the same Lord; 6 and there are varieties of activities, but it is the same God who activates all of them in everyone. 7 To each is given the manifestation of the Spirit for the common good. 8 To one is given through the Spirit the utterance of wisdom, and to another the utterance of knowledge according to the same Spirit, 9 to another faith by the same Spirit, to another gifts of healing by the one Spirit, 10 to another the working of miracles, to another prophecy, to another the discernment of spirits, to another various kinds of tongues, to another the interpretation of tongues. 11 All these are activated by one and the same Spirit, who allots to each one individually just as the Spirit chooses.

12 For just as the body is one and has many members, and all the members of the body, though many, are one body, so it is with Christ. 13 For in the one Spirit we were all baptized into one body—Jews or Greeks, slaves or free—and we were all made to drink of one Spirit.

14 Indeed, the body does not consist of one member but of many. 15 If the foot would say, "Because I am not a hand, I do not belong to the body," that would not make it any less a part of the body. 16 And if the ear would say, "Because I am not an eye, I do not belong to the body," that would not make it any less a part of the body. 17 If the whole body were an eye, where would the hearing be? If the whole body were hearing, where would the sense of smell be? 18 But as it is, God arranged the members in the body, each one of them, as he chose. 19 If all were a single member, where would the body be? 20 As it is, there are many members, yet one body. . . . 26 If one member suffers, all suffer together with it; if one member is honored, all rejoice together with it.

## HOME BIBLE READINGS

| | | |
|---|---|---|
| *Monday, Apr. 10* | 1 Corinthians 12:1-6 | *Understand the Source of Spiritual Gifts* |
| *Tuesday, Apr. 11* | 1 Corinthians 12:7-11 | *Many Spiritual Gifts, But One Spirit* |
| *Wednesday, Apr. 12* | 1 Corinthians 12:12-19 | *One Body, Many Members* |
| *Thursday, Apr. 13* | 1 Corinthians 12:20-31 | *We Need One Another* |
| *Friday, Apr. 14* | Romans 12:1-8 | *Transformed by New Life in Christ* |
| *Saturday, Apr. 15* | Romans 12:9-15 | *Marks of a Faithful Christian* |
| *Sunday, Apr. 16* | Romans 12:16-21 | *Guidance for Living the Christian Life* |

## BACKGROUND

Have you ever thought, "I wish my congregation could be more like the church of the first century"? Perhaps you have in mind a small, closely knit fellowship of Christians who are deeply committed to each other. Or maybe you're thinking about a congregation that, despite its modest financial means, is turning the community inside out with the Gospel.

As noble as this sentiment might be, it doesn't match what existed in most of the churches in the first century A.D. For example, consider the church at Corinth. It had several admirable preachers and teachers; yet it groaned under the weight of burdensome problems, many of which plague the church today. In reality, the Corinthian congregation was made up of sinners saved by the grace of God.

This week we will examine a portion of Paul's letter focusing mainly on spiritual gifts (chaps. 12—14). From what's said in chapter 14, it seems that the Corinthian Christians were emphasizing the gift of speaking in tongues almost to the exclusion of all other gifts. Perhaps they thought that this gift confirmed their mistaken view about their "spiritual" nature. Paul, after hearing abut the overemphasis on tongues, taught that a diversity of gifts was needed in the church.

It's helpful to note that the Greek word translated "gifts" in 1 Corinthians is usually *charismata*. The singular form of the word is *charisma*, which means "gift." Both terms are related to the word *charis*, which means "grace" or "favor." Thus *charismata* are gifts of grace. The Spirit gives these extraordinary abilities to believers to build up the church. Though such attributes as faith, teaching, and giving are considered gifts, all Christians are encouraged to use these traits.

## NOTES ON THE PRINTED TEXT

Spiritual gifts were another matter that had caused division in the Corinthian church and thus required Paul's attention. Some believers in Corinth had some spectacular spiritual gifts, chief of which was speaking in tongues. Paul both affirmed the power of these special abilities and addressed how Christians were to use them properly.

*Now there are varieties of gifts, but the same Spirit; and there are varieties of services, but the same Lord; and there are varieties of activities, but it is the same God who activates all of them in everyone* (12:4-6). Within the Corinthian church there existed various ministries, activities, and ways of serving. The Lord initiated each of them and oversaw them. The gifts differed by God's design. It thus was silly to expect uniformity within the body of Christ.

It is interesting to note that Paul linked each of three synonyms for spiritual gifts and ministries—*gifts, services,* and *activities* (12:4-6)—with different names for God—the Holy *Spirit,* the *Lord* Jesus, and *God* the Father. The idea is that the diversity of spiritual gifts within the unity of the church mirrors the diversity of the persons within the divine Trinity.

*To each is given the manifestation of the Spirit for the common good* (12:7). The various gifts bestowed by the Spirit were to be used for everyone's advantage and the good of the Christian community, not for personal gain.

Paul listed some of the gifts within the Corinthian church. Some believers had *the utterance of wisdom* (12:8), which refers to the ability to deliver profound truths consistent with biblical teaching. Others had *the utterance of knowledge,* which can either denote information received through supernatural means or the effective application of Bible teaching to people's lives.

Some Christians possessed the gift of *faith* (12:9), which refers to the ability to display amazing trust in God regardless of circumstances. (Of course, all Christians have saving faith.) Other believers had the gift of *healing,* namely, the ability to restore someone else to health through supernatural means. Still other believers could work *miracles* (12:10), which means they could do signs and wonders.

Within the church at Corinth there were believers who had the special ability of *prophecy* (12:10), that is, to proclaim revelations from God, including predictions about future events. Other Christians could discern between *spirits,* which refers to distinguishing which messages and acts come from the Spirit of God and which come from evil spirits. Finally, some members had the gift of *tongues,* while others had the ability to interpret what was spoken.

Paul noted that all the individual gifts came from *one and the same Spirit* (12:11). The apostle then explained, *For just as the body is one and has many members, and all the members of the body, though many, are one body, so it is with Christ* (12:12). Paul said that because the members of the Corinthian church belonged to the body of Christ, they were to act in harmony with one another. After all, the Spirit had united them in one community of faith. *For in the one Spirit we were all baptized into one body—Jews and Greeks, slaves or free—and we were all made to drink of one spirit* (12:13).

Paul used the analogy of a human body to drive home his point that all believers in Christ's body were united by faith. The unity and diversity of the church was comparable to the unity and diversity of a human body. All individuals were to work together harmoniously with their fellow believers for the good of the church and the glory of Christ. The idea in 12:14-20 is that God had wisely distributed spiritual gifts among the Corinthian believers so that the church could have a complete and well-rounded ministry. Thus it was wrong for them to emphasize just one spiritual gift to the exclusion of the others.

The parts of the human body illustrated how one spiritual gift was to work in relationship to others. The implication was clear. The entire congregation was to do what it could to help its suffering members through tough times, and to rejoice in the honor that an individual believer might receive. *If one member suffers, all suffer together with it; if one member is honored, all rejoice together with it* (12:26).

## SUGGESTIONS TO TEACHERS

Palm Sunday honors Jesus a, King. But He should not be thought of as a monarch who is surrounded by a retinue whose proximity to His royal presence is defined by the rank of each member. Dukes and duchesses, then lords and ladies, and so on down to the least significant footperson (all arranged in a pecking order) may be the way the world thinks. But it is not the way the Christian community is organized!

This week's lesson encourages the members of your class to ponder the importance of the gifts of the Spirit to everyone in the congregation. The lesson should also remind them that every ability given by the Spirit is equally valued and important to the proper functioning of the church.

**1. VALIDITY OF THE SPIRIT'S GUIDANCE.** Paul taught that we can determine whether a person's commitment to Christ is genuine by noting whether he or she is willing to affirm (by the power of the Spirit) that Jesus is Lord. The Spirit always focuses the attention of the church on Jesus. Thus, if people are promoting themselves or bullying Christians, they are truly misguided!

**2. VARIETIES OF THE SPIRIT'S GIFTS.** Examine with your class the different kinds of gifts bestowed by the Spirit to a congregation. Work to understand what each of these may mean for your church today. Consider who in your church seems to be blessed with what gifts. Are these persons encouraged to minister their gifts to others? How can the congregation give equal emphasis to all the gifts of the Spirit present within the church?

**3. VALUE OF INDIVIDUAL GIFTS.** Invite the members of your class to share how they might be a blessing to others through the exercise of their spiritual gifts. To get the discussion started, you might consider sharing a few personal thoughts about how the Spirit has equipped you to serve the church.

**4. VITALITY OF THE BODY.** End the class session by discussing the ways in which the church is similar to a human body. Be sure to stress that every member of the congregation—even the believers who seem the least significant—are needed to help the church remain healthy, growing, and productive.

<table>
<tr><td>

**FOR ADULTS**

</td><td>

■ TOPIC: Work Together

■ QUESTIONS: 1. What was the thinking of some in the Corinthian

</td></tr>
</table>

church regarding spiritual gifts? 2. What would the church look like if every person had the same spiritual gift? 3. How might you use your spiritual gifts for the common good of the church? 4. How might you help other believers to discover and use their spiritual gifts? 5. How might you help your church recognize the value of all the spiritual gifts present within it?

■ **ILLUSTRATIONS:**

**A Lesson in Importance.** When I was a child, I had a clear notion of who was most important in my home church. At the top of the pecking order was the minister. Then came the head usher. Next stood the superintendent of the Sunday school, who could offer the kind of elaborate prayers that are usually voiced only by the clergy. Following these people was the lead soprano in the choir, who commanded immense respect and whose word was law in the music department. At the foot of this flow chart was a moon-faced widow who sang off-key, could barely read or write, dressed poorly, and never held any church offices. I dismissed her as someone without any spiritual gifts and therefore of minimal importance.

Years later I remember (in retrospect) the countless acts of kindness that this woman performed with her mason jars of homemade soup and sincere prayers while visiting the sick and elderly. Her gift was more important to the life of my home congregation than I realized. This elderly, nearly illiterate widow taught me that the spiritual gifts of every church member are important, and that God has blessed every believer with some special ability that is indispensable for the ministry of the church!

**Mitten Theology.** Charlotte Burkholder tells us that fingers in a mitten are in contact with one another, and that each contributes body heat. Therefore, these fingers keep warmer than those in a glove where each finger is wrapped separately. It's a reminder that we must keep together and allow each other to contribute to the common good of the church. We are most useful to the Lord and to one another as the body of Christ when we are practicing a "mitten" faith together instead of "glove" living ("Mittens or Gloves" in *The Secret Place,* January 4, 1998).

**Lesson from the Hive.** Tommy decided that he would capture a honeybee, care for it, and eventually collect some honey. He carefully lowered a large jar over a flower on which a bee had settled to gather nectar. He snipped off the stem, capped the jar, and jubilantly carried the trapped bee to the little one-bee hive that he had painstakingly prepared. The new home for Tommy's lone bee had plenty of water, plenty of clover for food, plenty of warmth, and plenty of fresh air. Tommy was certain that he had provided all the necessary ingredients to care for his bee. But to his dismay, the bee was dead three days later. Only when he talked to an experienced beekeeper did Tommy learn that a bee cannot survive in isolation. Individual bees are kept alive by living in community with one another.

The same lesson might be applied to us as a community of faith. We need each other to survive as Christians. In isolation, we would find it impossible to remain faithful. But as we work together, we can encourage one another. Clearly, our unity as fellow believers is a great source of spiritual strength!

**FOR YOUTH**

■ TOPIC: Many Parts, One Body

■ QUESTIONS: 1. Where do the gifts of the Spirit come from? 2. What are some of the different spiritual gifts Paul discussed? 3. How might you discover and use the spiritual gifts that God has given to you? 4. Why is it important for every member of your church to serve in the ways that the Spirit has gifted them? 5. What would happen in your church if one spiritual gift was valued more than the others?

■ **ILLUSTRATIONS:**

**The Need for Diversity.** Imagine that the main hospital in your community is staffed only by heart specialists. They are all world famous experts who can deal with the unique needs of heart patients. In fact, these physicians can utilize the best and latest medical technology in their field. But how effective is the hospital in meeting the diverse medical needs of your community? In this situation there is no one to suture lacerations and set broken bones. There's also no one to care for the trauma victims and cancer patients. Furthermore, no one has any desire to treat patients who have problems of the stomach, liver, gall bladder, intestines, brain, or urinary tract.

A hospital cannot survive long with just heart specialists. Similarly, a church is ineffective if it only has believers with one spiritual gift. The congregation needs a whole spectrum of believers with a wide variety of special abilities to meet the needs of their fellow Christians.

**A Magical Johnson.** Senior Carrie Hoy, a guard on Pennsylvania defending Class A Champion Williamsburg, was attempting to prevent junior Erin Johnson of Claysburg-Kimmel High School from scoring in their February 1998 game. Johnson crossed the ball from left to right at the top of the key and swished in a three pointer. Hoy looked at her bench and said that she never would have believed it was possible.

The reason was that 5 foot 5 inch Erin Johnson has only one hand. Born with a left arm that extends only to her elbow, she must dribble, pass, and shoot with her right hand. In her third season as the starting shooting guard for the Bulldogs, Erin's game is one of lightning-quick flicks, while using her left arm as a guide. Erin also plays softball, halfback on her powder-puff football team, and is first chair in the trumpet section of the band. Lacking a second hand, Erin makes use of every other ability that she has, though she wishes she had a second hand in order to play the drums! Erin has developed all her abilities and talents. She is a superlative example of how all believers should discover and use of their spiritual gifts.

**Speaker of Tongues.** In early February 1998, Carl Gorman died. The 90 year old was a Navajo artist who taught at the University of California. He was also the father of celebrated artist R. C. Gorman.

Carl, though, gained fame as the original and oldest of 400 Navajo code talkers. During World War II, the Japanese broke the U.S. Army, Navy, and Air Corps codes. However, the Marines used the native Navajo tongue and turned the language into a secret weapon. Navajo is a language without an alphabet and has an irregular syntax. In 1942, only about 50,000 Navajos actually spoke the language, having resisted all the efforts by the U.S. government to Americanize them. (Gorman's teachers at a mission school had chained him one whole week to an iron pipe in an effort to force him not to use his native tongue!)

Gorman and his colleagues worked out words for military terms and used a two-tier code where English terms were represented by Navajo words. (For instance, a hummingbird was a fighter, and a swallow became a torpedo plane.) The code was so secure that it was never broken by the Japanese. And the code was so valuable that it remained top secret until it was finally declassified in 1969, when secure high-speed electronic coding was developed.

Gorman's gift was simple and plain. However without his gift and those few others that also had this special ability, the war effort in the Pacific might have gone differently. From this we can see that every believer's spiritual gifts, no matter how seemingly insignificant, are important to the body of Christ.

# CHRIST'S RESURRECTION AND OURS

**BACKGROUND SCRIPTURE:** 1 Corinthians 15
**DEVOTIONAL READING:** 1 Corinthians 15:12-19, 50-57

**KEY VERSE:** Christ has been raised from the dead, the first fruits of those who have died. . . . For as all die in Adam, so all will be made alive in Christ. 1 Corinthians 15:20, 22.

*KING JAMES VERSION*

1 CORINTHIANS 15:20 But now is Christ risen from the dead, and become the firstfruits of them that slept.

21 For since by man came death, by man came also the resurrection of the dead.

22 For as in Adam all die, even so in Christ shall all be made alive.

23 But every man in his own order: Christ the first-fruits; afterward they that are Christ's at his coming.

24 Then cometh the end, when he shall have delivered up the kingdom to God, even the Father; when he shall have put down all rule and all authority and power.

25 For he must reign, till he hath put all enemies under his feet.

26 The last enemy that shall be destroyed is death.

27 For he hath put all things under his feet. But when he saith all things are put under him, it is manifest that he is excepted, which did put all things under him. . . .

35 But some man will say, How are the dead raised up? and with what body do they come?

36 Thou fool, that which thou sowest is not quickened, except it die:

37 And that which thou sowest, thou sowest not that body that shall be, but bare grain, it may chance of wheat, or of some other grain:

38 But God giveth it a body as it hath pleased him, and to every seed his own body.

39 All flesh is not the same flesh: but there is one kind of flesh of men, another flesh of beasts, another of fishes, and another of birds.

40 There are also celestial bodies, and bodies terrestrial: but the glory of the celestial is one, and the glory of the terrestrial is another.

41 There is one glory of the sun, and another glory of the moon, and another glory of the stars: for one star differeth from another star in glory.

42 So also is the resurrection of the dead. It is sown in corruption; it is raised in incorruption:

43 It is sown in dishonour; it is raised in glory: it is sown in weakness; it is raised in power:

44 It is sown a natural body; it is raised a spiritual body. There is a natural body, and there is a spiritual body.

*NEW REVISED STANDARD VERSION*

1 CORINTHIANS 15:20 But in fact Christ has been raised from the dead, the first fruits of those who have died. 21 For since death came through a human being, the resurrection of the dead has also come through a human being; 22 for as all die in Adam, so all will be made alive in Christ. 23 But each in his own order: Christ the first fruits, then at his coming those who belong to Christ. 24 Then comes the end, when he hands over the kingdom to God the Father, after he has destroyed every ruler and every authority and power. 25 For he must reign until he has put all his enemies under his feet. 26 The last enemy to be destroyed is death. 27 For "God has put all things in subjection under his feet." But when it says, "All things are put in subjection," it is plain that this does not include the one who put all things in subjection under him. . . .

35 But someone will ask, "How are the dead raised? With what kind of body do they come?" 36 Fool! What you sow does not come to life unless it dies. 37 And as for what you sow, you do not sow the body that is to be, but a bare seed, perhaps of wheat or of some other grain. 38 But God gives it a body as he has chosen, and to each kind of seed its own body. 39 Not all flesh is alike, but there is one flesh for human beings, another for animals, another for birds, and another for fish. 40 There are both heavenly bodies and earthly bodies, but the glory of the heavenly is one thing, and that of the earthly is another. 41 There is one glory of the sun, and another glory of the moon, and another glory of the stars; indeed, star differs from star in glory.

42 So it is with the resurrection of the dead. What is sown is perishable, what is raised is imperishable. 43 It is sown in dishonor, it is raised in glory. It is sown in weakness, it is raised in power. 44 It is sown a physical body, it is raised a spiritual body. If there is a physical body, there is also a spiritual body.

| | | |
|---|---|---|
| *Monday, Apr. 17* | 1 Corinthians 15:1-11 | *The Resurrection of Christ the Lord* |
| *Tuesday, Apr. 18* | 1 Corinthians 15:12-19 | *How Can You Deny the Resurrection?* |
| *Wednesday, Apr. 19* | 1 Corinthians 15:20-28 | *The Resurrected Christ Destroys Death* |
| *Thursday, Apr. 20* | 1 Corinthians 15:29-34 | *The Dead Are Raised: Believe It!* |
| *Friday, Apr. 21* | 1 Corinthians 15:35-41 | *God Will Give the Glory* |
| *Saturday, Apr. 22* | 1 Corinthians 15:42-49 | *Raised a Spiritual Body* |
| *Sunday, Apr. 23* | 1 Corinthians 15:50-58 | *We Have Victory through Jesus Christ!* |

# BACKGROUND

The cornerstone of Paul's faith was the resurrection of Jesus Christ. The apostle had built his ministry on knowing that the Father had raised the Son from the dead after His crucifixion. In fact, Paul had endured all sorts of hardship because of his commitment to the risen, living Lord. Therefore, the apostle was dismayed that some in the fledgling church at Corinth were denying the bodily resurrection of the dead.

Greek philosophy offered little hope to humans after death. The wispy idea of immortal souls provided no comfort in the face of the finality and tragedy of death. Most in that society resigned themselves to the notion that they would cease to exist after they died. Life must have seemed short and cheap for the bulk of the population.

Most in the Corinthian church believed that Christians, after death, live on forever in heaven as spirits. But to some of them the idea of one's soul being rejoined with one's body was distasteful. It's clear that this distorted thinking reflected the mindset of the culture in which the members of the Corinthian church lived. Imagine the feelings of despair and hopelessness that overwhelmed some in the congregation when they heard others deny the reality of the resurrection.

Paul sensed the need to correct this erroneous thinking. He began his argument by establishing common ground with his readers. They all believed that God had raised Jesus from the dead. In fact, Christ's resurrection signified that He had conquered death and sin.

Paul called the Corinthian believers back to the central truths of their faith. He reminded them that apart from the good news of Christ's resurrection their hope was in vain, that they were still mired in guilt, and that life was futile. Of course, if Jesus was still dead, then Paul's preaching and the Corinthians' faith were both useless. Without the Resurrection, the Gospel was not worth spreading or believing. Thankfully, Paul firmly asserted that Christ was raised. In fact, He serves as a pledge that more resurrections will one day follow.

# NOTES ON THE PRINTED TEXT

Paul's first letter to the Corinthians next addressed a question over the reality and significance of the resurrection of the dead. Down through the centuries, the reality of eternal life has remained a message of great importance and a foundation of the Christian faith.

*But in fact Christ has been raised from the dead, the first fruits of those who have died* (15:20). Paul had presented the apostolic teaching about Jesus' resurrection. Paul also explained to the Corinthians how dismal it would be if Christ had not risen from the dead. Paul then boldly asserted that Jesus is the *first fruits of those who have died.* In ancient times, God's people were required to bring an offering from the first part of the crop (Lev. 23:10). This offering was a token of the whole harvest, namely, that all of it belonged to God. Similarly, Jesus not only was the first to rise from the dead, but also He serves as a pledge that more resurrections will one day follow.

Paul then explained, *For since death came through a human being, the resurrection of the dead has also come through a human being; for as all die in Adam, so all will be made alive in Christ* (1 Cor. 15:21-22). In other words, because Adam sinned, all people die. And because Jesus was raised from the dead, all Christians will be raised from the dead. Adam is responsible for death, and Jesus is responsible for eternal life.

Paul noted that the resurrection follows a specific order: first Christ, then His followers. Jesus has already been raised from the dead. At His return, He will resurrect the redeemed. *But each in his own order: Christ the first fruits, then at his coming those who belong to Christ* (15:23).

Jesus then will establish His lordship finally over His enemies. After that, the end will come in which Christ turns the kingdom over to God the Father (15:24). Paul explained that Jesus has to reign until He absolutely subdues and humbles His enemies (15:25). Death is the last enemy for Christ to conquer (15:26). Paul quoted from Psalm 8:6 to underscore that it was the Father's will to give the Son authority over all things (1 Cor. 15:27).

In 15:35 Paul wrote, *But someone will ask, "How are the dead raised? With what kind of body do they come?* Apparently some of the Corinthian believers wanted to know what form the resurrection body would take. The apostle thought this was a foolish question. After all, the natural world showed how entities of different types go through transformation.

Paul referred to plant life as an example. A seed is a sort of body, and it undergoes a sort of death when it is sown. But then the seed grows into a plant, which is another sort of body. There is continuity between the seed and the plant, and yet they are different (15:37-38).

Paul noted that just as there are different kinds of seeds and plants, so also there are different kinds of flesh—whether of humans, animals, birds, or fish (15:39). Heavenly bodies are glorious in a different way than are earthly bodies. Among the heavenly bodies (such as the sun, moon, and stars) there are differing kinds of glory. And even among a particular kind of heavenly body—namely, the stars—glory (or radiance) differs (15:40-41).

The apostle explained that like a seed, a human body is *sown* (15:42) in one form and *raised* in another. A person's earthly body is perishable, dishonored, weak, and natural. But that same body, when resurrected, is imperishable, glorious, powerful, and spiritual. The two bodies are different, just as entities in the natural world are different from one another. Though the idea of the resurrection body being spiritual may have seemed strange to the Corinthian believers, Paul nevertheless insisted on it (15:42-44).

## SUGGESTIONS TO TEACHERS

Start the teaching time with a quick quiz. Ask, "What is the most important fact in the Christian faith, and what is the most basic teaching to believers?" The possible answer, of course, is the resurrection of Jesus Christ. Your responsibility in this week's lesson is to stress to your students how central the good news of the risen Lord is for them.

**1. LIST OF WITNESSES.** Paul presented a catalog of reasons why the resurrection is of prime importance, and included a list of persons who saw the risen Christ. Paul added his own name to that list. Emphasize that the report of Jesus' resurrection was not fabricated. Rather, it was an historical event that many reliable people witnessed (15:1-11).

**2. LESSON IN FAITH.** Paul asked his readers to consider the significance of the resurrection. Take a few moments to discuss this with your students, especially the hope of our resurrection from the dead.

**3. LORD OVER DEATH.** Jesus' resurrection proved that He is sovereign over death and sin. Be sure to underscore to the members of your class that they worship and serve an all-powerful Lord. He cares for them immensely and will never abandon them.

| FOR ADULTS | ■TOPIC: What about the Resurrection? |
|---|---|

■ **Questions:** 1. Why is Christ's resurrection so important to affirm? 2. How does the resurrection of Christ affect believers? 3. How might you draw strength from the truth of Jesus' resurrection? 4. How might you encourage your family members and friends with the good news of Jesus' resurrection? 5. In what ways can you thank God for what He has done in raising Christ from the dead?

■ **ILLUSTRATIONS:**

**The Evidence.** A father was explaining to his five-year-old son how Jesus died and then revisited His followers after rising from the dead. "That's what we believe," the father said. "That's how we know Jesus is the Son of God, because He came back from the dead just as He said He would." "Do you mean like Elvis?" the boy observed.

We have no evidence that Elvis ever came back from the dead, but there is a great deal of evidence for Jesus' resurrection. Perhaps some of the greatest evidence is the fact that Christ lives in the hearts of believers today. For Christians, the resurrection of Jesus is at the core of their faith.

Without the resurrection, every word of Jesus is transformed into a lie, every belief we hold is undermined, and everything the church has accomplished for almost 2,000 years is pointless. But of course Christ did rise from the dead. Our preaching, believing, and hoping have not been in vain. That's why on Easter, throngs of people crowd the church. They know that Easter is the most glorious day of the year, and they know why that is true. It's Resurrection Day!

**Triumph of the Risen Lord.** For over 75 years, the Soviet Union had repressed the church by closing congregations, shooting or imprisoning religious leaders, seizing Bibles and other religious literature, and forbidding any public proclamation of the good news of Jesus' resurrection. The powerful government promoted atheism. In fact, religion was said to be "the opium of the people" (a statement originally made by Karl Marx).

In a prominent location in Moscow, a poster had printed on it, "Glory to the Communist Party!" A couple of years ago, a visitor was walking through that city with a Russian acquaintance when they came to the place where the poster had hung. "Look at that!" the Russian said, pointing to a large banner fluttering in the chill breeze of a Russian spring. "KHRISTOS VOSKRESE!" the banner proclaimed in swooping old Cyrillic letters. In other words, CHRIST IS RISEN!

The wonderful news of the Resurrection has outlasted all revolutions, all ideologies, and all empires. The risen, living Christ triumphs over all forever!

**Our Experience as Well.** D. T. Niles once said, "The resurrection that awaits us beyond physical death will be but the glorious consummation of the risen life that we have in Christ." I like the way F. B. Meyer said it in a sermon title: "Death— A Parenthesis in Life." He knew that Jesus' resurrection means that believers can conquer death through faith in Him. The resurrection of Christ means that believers don't have to fear death. We also don't have to be entombed in doubt, anxiety, loneliness, or guilt. By defeating death, Christ also broke death's power to hold us captive to sin. By being identified with His resurrection, we are freed to obey God and love others unconditionally and wholeheartedly.

**FOR YOUTH**

■ TOPIC: What's the Last Word?

■ QUESTIONS: 1. In what sense has Jesus become the first in a great harvest? 2. What specific order does the resurrection follow?

3. What danger is there in denying the biblical doctrine of the resurrection?
4. How can you help skeptical friends and peers to reconsider the truth of Jesus' resurrection? 5. How does your belief in Jesus' resurrection affect your day-to-day existence?

■ ILLUSTRATIONS:

**Failed Experiment.** It was billed as *Elvis—The Concert!* Advertisements promised to bring Elvis (live through the "magic" of video) along with his original band of James Burton, Glen D. Hardin, Jerry Scheff, Ron Tutt, and J. D. Sumner. The original back-up female and male touring group for Elvis was also to be present.

However, on March 18, 1998, fewer than 4,000 fans paid $25 to see Elvis. The music roared and Elvis stepped onto the stage's main screen. The response? Mostly everyone yawned. Those who attended agreed that Elvis was still dead. What was billed as the "beyond death experiment" had failed. Fans agreed and said that it was like watching television or a haunting music video complete with musicians who seemed like ghosts. One girl named Hilda said, "You almost think he's here, but then it's sad to look down at the stage and see that he's not." Despite all the hype, Elvis was still dead.

Paul assured the Corinthian Christians that there was life after physical death for them. God would one day give believers a resurrection body. Because of Jesus' rising from the dead, they had proof that the hope of eternal life is an absolute certainty.

**Death, Where Is Your Sting?** A small boy was allergic to bee stings. The allergy was so severe that doctors warned the family that a single bee sting could produce anaphylactic shock. This is a severe medical emergency that could kill the child by preventing him from breathing.

One day, a bee landed on the boy's cheek. The child was almost paralyzed with fright. Calmly the father allowed the bee to walk onto his own finger. The father agitated the bee and then allowed it to sting him. The bee flew back to the boy, but this time the child was unafraid. Death had been robbed of its power!

This story illustrates Paul's point to the Corinthian believers. They did not need to fear death, for Christ had removed its sting through His resurrection. And through faith in Christ, they could conquer death.

**Looking for Hope.** On the early morning of March 22, 1998, fire raced through a mountain cabin. Eight students from Line Mountain High School and three college students from Lititz, all from Herndon, Pennsylvania, were killed as they slept inside. They had come to camp to enjoy spring break.

As news of the tragedy spread, the high school opened to provide counseling and support to students looking for hope. It remained open through the night and the following day. Classes were canceled Monday as students came to the school, talked, cried, and hugged. Flags flew at half staff in the tight-knit community in Miles Township. Throughout the day, students wrote notes in which they spoke about their love, pledged to support the survivors of the fire, and promised to organize a reunion sometime later. That night, a prayer service led by local clergy was held in the gym, and a candlelight vigil followed in the school's stadium. The efforts were to soothe the souls of those in the community.

Paul understood such grief and loss. However, the apostle also knew about God's promise of the resurrection. Paul declared that for those who have trusted in Christ, eternal life awaited them in heaven with God!

# THE WAY OF LOVE

**BACKGROUND SCRIPTURE:** 1 Corinthians 12:31—13:13
**DEVOTIONAL READING:** 1 John 4:7-21

**KEY VERSE:** Now faith, hope, and love abide, these three; and the greatest of these is love.
1 Corinthians 13:13.

---

*KING JAMES VERSION*

1 CORINTHIANS 12:31 But covet earnestly the best gifts: and yet shew I unto you a more excellent way.

13:1 Though I speak with the tongues of men and of angels, and have not charity, I am become as sounding brass, or a tinkling cymbal.

2 And though I have the gift of prophecy, and understand all mysteries, and all knowledge; and though I have all faith, so that I could remove mountains, and have not charity, I am nothing.

3 And though I bestow all my goods to feed the poor, and though I give my body to be burned, and have not charity, it profiteth me nothing.

4 Charity suffereth long, and is kind; charity envieth not; charity vaunteth not itself, is not puffed up,

5 Doth not behave itself unseemly, seeketh not her own, is not easily provoked, thinketh no evil;

6 Rejoiceth not in iniquity, but rejoiceth in the truth;

7 Beareth all things, believeth all things, hopeth all things, endureth all things.

8 Charity never faileth: but whether there be prophecies, they shall fail; whether there be tongues, they shall cease; whether there be knowledge, it shall vanish away.

9 For we know in part, and we prophesy in part.

10 But when that which is perfect is come, then that which is in part shall be done away.

11 When I was a child, I spake as a child, I understood as a child, I thought as a child: but when I became a man, I put away childish things.

12 For now we see through a glass, darkly; but then face to face: now I know in part; but then shall I know even as also I am known.

13 And now abideth faith, hope, charity, these three; but the greatest of these is charity.

*NEW REVISED STANDARD VERSION*

1 CORINTHIANS 12:31 But strive for the greater gifts. And I will show you a still more excellent way.

13:1 If I speak in the tongues of mortals and of angels, but do not have love, I am a noisy gong or a clanging cymbal. 2 And if I have prophetic powers, and understand all mysteries and all knowledge, and if I have all faith, so as to remove mountains, but do not have love, I am nothing. 3 If I give away all my possessions, and if I hand over my body so that I may boast, but do not have love, I gain nothing.

4 Love is patient; love is kind; love is not envious or boastful or arrogant 5 or rude. It does not insist on its own way; it is not irritable or resentful; 6 it does not rejoice in wrongdoing, but rejoices in the truth. 7 It bears all things, believes all things, hopes all things, endures all things.

8 Love never ends. But as for prophecies, they will come to an end; as for tongues, they will cease; as for knowledge, it will come to an end. 9 For we know only in part, and we prophesy only in part; 10 but when the complete comes, the partial will come to an end. 11 When I was a child, I spoke like a child, I thought like a child, I reasoned like a child; when I became an adult, I put an end to childish ways. 12 For now we see in a mirror, dimly, but then we will see face to face. Now I know only in part; then I will know fully, even as I have been fully known. 13 And now faith, hope, and love abide, these three; and the greatest of these is love.

9

| | | |
|---|---|---|
| *Monday, Apr. 24* | 1 Corinthians 13:1-7 | *The Gift of Love* |
| *Tuesday, Apr. 25* | 1 Corinthians 13:8-13 | *Love Is the Greatest Gift* |
| *Wednesday, Apr. 26* | 1 John 2:7-17 | *Love: An Enduring Commandment* |
| *Thursday, Apr. 27* | 1 John 3:11-17 | *Show Your Love for One Another* |
| *Friday, Apr. 28* | 1 John 3:18-24 | *Believe in Jesus, and Love One Another* |
| *Saturday, Apr. 29* | 1 John 4:7-12 | *Let Us Love as God Loves* |
| *Sunday, Apr. 30* | 1 John 4:13-21 | *We Abide in God if We Love* |

## BACKGROUND

In 1 Corinthians 12:29-30, Paul asked some rhetorical questions. In those questions, the apostle wanted to know whether all Christians had the same spiritual gift. Each time the appropriate answer was "No!" The apostle knew that the Corinthian believers had so emphasized the special ability to speak in tongues that they forgot about the diversity of gifts within the body of Christ. Paul wanted his readers to see that each believer had his or her own unique gifts. All of these special abilities were important to the continued vitality and growth of the church.

After discussing the purpose and use of spiritual gifts, Paul in chapter 13 digressed from his argument to talk about the importance of Christlike love. Love, of course, is not a spiritual gift; rather, it is the way in which all special abilities should be used. By "love" Paul did not mean the mushy sentiment that our English word often conveys. Love is not simply the infatuation teenagers feel toward their first heartthrob. In fact, the Greek word has nothing to do with sensual experience or even with sentimental feelings.

By love, Paul was talking about the sacrificial concern that God has shown to us in Christ. The apostle's purpose was to set the issue of spiritual gifts within an ethical framework. Perhaps he thought the Corinthians were too fascinated with the spiritual gifts and had lost sight of a more basic concern: living out Christlike love.

First Corinthians 13 has been called a hymn of love. It is renowned for being sublime in tone and powerful in content. Some readers have found it helpful to substitute the word "Christ" whenever the word "love" appears in this chapter. This helps to clarify the meaning of what Paul intended in the use of "love."

## NOTES ON THE PRINTED TEXT

As Paul concluded his discussion about spiritual gifts, he wrote that they had no value unless they were exercised in love. Love had to be the motivating force behind the believers' use of their gifts. *But strive for the greater gifts. And I will show you a still more excellent way* (12:31).

In his discussion on love, Paul started off by naming certain representative gifts and actions, and then stating how they are worthless unless done in love. Imagine being able to speak in any language, whether in heaven or on earth. In the absence of love, however, such utterances would be meaningless noises, such as those made from a *noisy gong or a clanging cymbal* (13:1).

Paul next referred to three other spiritual gifts—prophecy, knowledge, and faith (13:2). Imagine having these gifts in abundance. One might be able to deliver eloquent messages from God, or display insight into all sorts of spiritual mysteries and truths, or have such a strong belief that mountains would be dislodged from their foundations. Yet in the absence of love, such impressive displays were robbed of any value.

What about giving all our possessions to the poor, or sacrificing our bodies in Christian service and martyrdom so that God might be glorified? Paul declared that in the absence of love, nothing would be gained by these actions (13:3). The apostle emphasized that love is the ingredient that makes whatever we do for the Savior worthwhile.

Using positive and negative terms, Paul described what he meant by love. *Love is patient; love is kind; love is not envious or boastful or arrogant or rude* (13:4-5). In other words, love accepts insults, hardships, and injuries without complaint. Christlike compassion does not demand its own way, is not irritable, and keeps no record of when it has been wronged. Love is never glad about injustice but rejoices whenever the truth wins out. (13:6). The love of Christ in the believer's heart never gives up, never loses faith, and is always hopeful. Even when tragedy strikes, it never collapses or quits. It remains strong to the end of the ordeal (13:7).

Such love never become obsolete, but rather will last forever (13:8). Its permanency contrasts with the gifts of the Spirit, which will one day come to an end. For example, *prophecies* will cease, *tongues* will be stilled, and *knowledge* will pass away. Paul admitted that the knowledge of the most informed Christians was partial. This was also true of the understanding that came from prophesying (13:9). The apostle then noted that *when the complete comes, the partial will come to an end* (13:10). The gifts of knowledge and prophecy (for example) put believers in touch with God only imperfectly. But in the later period, Christians will be in full and perfect contact with the Lord.

Paul was contrasting two periods—an earlier one in which the spiritual gifts are needed and a later one when they are not needed. Yet Bible interpreters differ over the time scheme that Paul had in mind. Some think that the first period extended between Pentecost and the completion of the New Testament, with the second period coming after. Others think that the first period is the time between Christ's first and second comings, with the second period following that.

Regardless of which view is taken, it's clear that there is a distinct difference between the two periods. Paul illustrated this difference by drawing an analogy involving childhood and adulthood (13:11). The apostle noted that when he was a child, he talked, thought, and reasoned as a child. But now that Paul had become a grown man, he had *put an end to childish ways.*

Paul was saying that the first period is like childhood, and that childish ways are like spiritual gifts. Just as childish ways are appropriate for a child, so spiritual gifts are suitable for people in the first period. The apostle's analogy implies that adulthood is like the second period. In that period, believers will put away their spiritual gifts, for they won't be appropriate any longer.

Paul noted that the glimpse of God reflected in the use of spiritual gifts is like looking in a mirror (13:12). It's not clear whether the reference to *dimly* implies a *blurry* sense of who God is or an *indirect* sense. Either way, in the first period our spiritual gifts give only a reflection of God's presence and power, whereas in the second period, we'll see the Lord face-to-face. In the first period, we know God only partially, but in the second period we will know Him fully.

In 13:13, Paul summarized his teaching about love. He said that love is for now and forever: *And now faith, hope, and love abide, these three; and the greatest of these is love.*

## SUGGESTIONS TO TEACHERS

Ask the class to tally some uses of the word "love" that they've heard recently. Use these examples to underscore how overworked is our English word "love." Next mention that "love" in 1 Corinthians 13 translates *agape* [ah-GAH-pay], which refers to unselfish, unconditional compassion, not sentimental feelings or erotic stirrings. Then note the following points.

**1. SUPREMACY OF LOVE.** Paul mentioned several gifts of the Spirit, such as speaking in tongues, profound thinking, and acts of philanthropy. Yet love surpasses them all!

**2. SHAPE OF LOVE.** Note the various qualities of Christian love. Then have the class members discuss times when either they or some other believers they know demonstrated the love of Christ. Remind the students that Jesus is the best example of love. Point out how consistently He exhibited a patient, unselfish compassion for others.

**3. STAMINA OF LOVE.** In any era of road rage and "in your face" confrontations, we may be persuaded that Christlike love is wimpish and futile. But love outlasts everything. In fact, love triumphs! The Cross and Resurrection pronounce God's verdict on violence and retaliation. Love proves to be more powerful than anything!

**4. SUPERIORITY OF LOVE.** Paul listed the top three virtues: faith, hope, and love. Each is great, and each is needed. But love is the greatest!

**FOR ADULTS**

■ **TOPIC:** What's Real Love?

■ **QUESTIONS:** 1. Why are any of the spiritual gifts valueless apart from love? 2. What are some ways that the love of Christ is different from the world's concept of love? 3. What are some ways that you can show the love of Christ as you use your spiritual gifts? 4. How does your life compare with Paul's description of love? 5. What can you do to become more Christlike in your love?

■ ILLUSTRATIONS:

**How Christ's Love Conquers.** Five missionaries—Nate Saint, Jim Elliot, T. Edward McCully, Peter Fleming, and Roger Youderian—were brutally slain while trying to share the Gospel to members of a wild tribe, the Huaorani people, in a remote part of Ecuador. Later, the Huaorani realized that the five men they had murdered were armed and could have defended themselves. To the amazement of the people in the tribe, the Christian missionaries had not tried to fight back, despite having rifles, ammunition, and time to prepare to open fire against their attackers. This realization ultimately opened the way for the Huaorani to listen to the truth about Jesus' love.

The martyrdom of these five young men in 1956 moved many, including Rachel Saint, Nate's sister, and Elizabeth Elliot, Jim's widow, who went to Ecuador to minister to the people who had murdered their loved ones. Young Steve Saint, Nate Saint's small son, moved to Ecuador with his Aunt Rachel, and was raised among the Huaorani people, and continues to witness as a Christian with them. Most of the Huaorani tribe are now faithful followers of Christ. The love of Christ, as exhibited through the sacrifice and witness of Jesus' valiant servants, has brought love to a once wild tribe in the remote vastness of South America.

**Reconciliation in South Africa.** Nelson Mandela was imprisoned for 27 years by the repressive apartheid government in South Africa. When he was released and soon elected to head the state, many feared that a race war would erupt. White supremacists assumed that Mandela would be a harsh, black dictator seeking reprisals against whites after the years of injustice and barbarities he had suffered. Instead, Mandela used his power to bring reconciliation.

For example, shortly after Mandela's election in 1995, he showed his greatness in a dramatic way in Johannesburg, South Africa. For many years rugby has been the sport of choice among whites, especially Afrikaners. In 1995, the World Cup rugby match was being played in Johannesburg. Against all odds, the South African Springboks had made it into the final playoff. Since rugby was predominantly a white person's game, people of color had scorned the Springboks and ignored rugby.

On the afternoon of the World Cup final, the stadium was jammed with South Africans, especially white Afrikaners, as the Springboks prepared to play New Zealand. To the surprise of the Springboks, Nelson Mandela walked into their locker room before the start of the match wearing the Number 6 green jersey of the Springboks' captain, greeted each team member, and wished them success. In a great upset, the Springboks won 15 to 12.

President Nelson Mandela, the nation's black head of state, walked onto the field at the close of the exciting game to present the trophy. At the time, he was still wearing the bright green Springbok jersey. The Afrikaner crowd broke into a chant, shouting "NEL-SON! NEL-SON! NEL-SON!" It was not only a great emotional moment, but also had a devastating effect on the white extremists. They had refused to vote in the 1994 elections and to recognize the new constitution of the nation. They had also threatened an armed uprising by saying, "It's not our country!"

The predicted white backlash simply evaporated because of Mandela's gesture of love! Through this act and many others to bring reconciliation, Mandela has become the symbol of a new, united South Africa.

**The Way of Love.** A converted drunkard of South India named Abraham had settled down to do honest work. But during the harvest season, some bullies attacked him, cut off his fingers with an ax, and stole his crops. The public conscience of the village was so roused that they gathered subscriptions to help the victim prosecute his attackers in court. The Indian Y.M.C.A. Secretary, whom God used to convert Abraham, urged him to go to court, for he could identify the bullies.

After Abraham spent several minutes considering the possibility, he said, "Sir, just two things would I say to you. You are an educated man; I am an illiterate man. You have been a Christian all your life, and I trusted in Jesus not long ago. But when I became believer, I promised to follow in His footsteps. You told me how He was crucified. The nails were driven through His hands and feet. The crown of thorns was placed on His head; but He never said: 'O God, punish My enemies.' Rather, His last words were, 'Father, forgive them, for they know not what they do.' So, just as my Master forgave His enemies and prayed for them, so must I pray for mine and forgive them, for they have done this in the ignorance of their hearts. They did not know anything better."

---

**FOR YOUTH**

■ TOPIC: What's Real Love?

■ QUESTIONS: 1. Why is it important for Christlike love to be present when believers exercise their spiritual gifts? 2. In what way is the love of Christ enduring? 3. How might you show the love of Christ to your family and friends? 4. How might you encourage your fellow believers to let the love of Christ permeate their attitudes and actions? 5. Do you long for the day when you'll see the Savior face-to-face?

■ ILLUSTRATIONS:

**Never Obsolete.** Thirteen years ago I bought my first computer, monitor, and printer. Though certain minor problems arose with the equipment, these were repairable. And I chose to ignore such inconveniences as an aging ribbon. But a few years later when the computer broke down again, the technician said that he could not repair the equipment, for it had become obsolete. In fact, I learned that it was cheaper simply to scrap the computer and buy a new one than to continue having the old one repaired.

Unlike aging computer equipment, Christlike love never grows obsolete. While even the most spectacular spiritual gifts will outlive their usefulness, this will never be true of love.

**What Is Love?** "I want to know what love is. I want you to show it to me," a certain rock group chants repeatedly in a refrain. The request is apt, for we tend to think and speak about love in many contradictory ways. For example, we say that we love God, our parents, baseball, hot dogs, apple pie, and a host of other things. Such a concept couldn't be more confusing!

The Greeks had several words for love. *Eros* [ERR-ahs] refers to passionate love of a sensual nature. *Philia* [fih-LEE-ah] primarily indicates the fondness, affection, or affinity that exists between family members or close friends. Finally, *agape* refers to the unselfish, unconditional love of God. It is this type of compassion that Paul urged us, as Christians, to cultivate and practice.

**Put Away Childish Things.** A radical German kindergarten program bans children from playing with toys for a three-month stretch. Originally begun in a nursery school in Penzberg (30 miles south of Munich), the program was designed to prevent children from becoming addicted to possessions. They learn to amuse themselves, develop new skills, and increase their greater creativity.

Paul urged his readers to put aside childish things. This means not spending all our time and energies seeking the attention and approval of others. It also means not buying the fanciest clothes or seeking to become the most popular person among our peers. Mature, loving Christians are not obsessed with the toys and trinkets of the world. Instead, they strive to serve the Lord.

**What Needs Love.** Nobel Peace Prize winner Mother Teresa died in the fall of 1997, but her example, words, and works continue to have a lasting influence. The woman who headed a religious community that cared for the victims of disease and starvation and demonstrated unconditional and enduring love for all declared that the greatest illness in the world was not cancer or leprosy, but a lack of love. She further said that the greatest evil was indifference and intolerance.

Paul declared that the love of Christ is the greatest gift that a believer can pass on to others. In light of Mother Teresa's words and Paul's teaching, how are you going to act?

# THE CHRISTIAN MARCH OF TRIUMPH

**BACKGROUND SCRIPTURE:** 2 Corinthians 1—2
**DEVOTIONAL READING:** 2 Corinthians 1:3-11

**KEY VERSE:** Thanks be to God, who in Christ always leads us in triumphal procession, and through us spreads in every place the fragrance that comes from knowing him. 2 Corinthians 2:14.

*KING JAMES VERSION*

2 CORINTHIANS 2:4 For out of much affliction and anguish of heart I wrote unto you with many tears; not that ye should be grieved, but that ye might know the love which I have more abundantly unto you.

5 But if any have caused grief, he hath not grieved me, but in part: that I may not overcharge you all.

6 Sufficient to such a man is this punishment, which was inflicted of many.

7 So that contrariwise ye ought rather to forgive him, and comfort him, lest perhaps such a one should be swallowed up with overmuch sorrow.

8 Wherefore I beseech you that ye would confirm your love toward him.

9 For to this end also did I write, that I might know the proof of you, whether ye be obedient in all things.

10 To whom ye forgive any thing, I forgive also: for if I forgave any thing, to whom I forgave it, for your sakes forgave I it in the person of Christ;

11 Lest Satan should get an advantage of us: for we are not ignorant of his devices.

12 Furthermore, when I came to Troas to preach Christ's gospel, and a door was opened unto me of the Lord,

13 I had no rest in my spirit, because I found not Titus my brother: but taking my leave of them, I went from thence into Macedonia.

14 Now thanks be unto God, which always causeth us to triumph in Christ, and maketh manifest the savour of his knowledge by us in every place.

15 For we are unto God a sweet savour of Christ, in them that are saved, and in them that perish:

16 To the one we are the savour of death unto death; and to the other the savour of life unto life. And who is sufficient for these things?

17 For we are not as many, which corrupt the word of God: but as of sincerity, but as of God, in the sight of God speak we in Christ.

*NEW REVISED STANDARD VERSION*

2 CORINTHIANS 2:4 For I wrote you out of much distress and anguish of heart and with many tears, not to cause you pain, but to let you know the abundant love that I have for you.

5 But if anyone has caused pain, he has caused it not to me, but to some extent—not to exaggerate it—to all of you. 6 This punishment by the majority is enough for such a person; 7 so now instead you should forgive and console him, so that he may not be overwhelmed by excessive sorrow. 8 So I urge you to reaffirm your love for him. 9 I wrote for this reason: to test you and to know whether you are obedient in everything.

10 Anyone whom you forgive, I also forgive. What I have forgiven, if I have forgiven anything, has been for your sake in the presence of Christ. 11 And we do this so that we may not be outwitted by Satan; for we are not ignorant of his designs.

12 When I came to Troas to proclaim the good news of Christ, a door was opened for me in the Lord; 13 but my mind could not rest because I did not find my brother Titus there. So I said farewell to them and went on to Macedonia.

14 But thanks be to God, who in Christ always leads us in triumphal procession, and through us spreads in every place the fragrance that comes from knowing him. 15 For we are the aroma of Christ to God among those who are being saved and among those who are perishing; 16 to the one a fragrance from death to death, to the other a fragrance from life to life. Who is sufficient for these things? 17 For we are not peddlers of God's word like so many; but in Christ we speak as persons of sincerity, as persons sent from God and standing in his presence.

## HOME BIBLE READINGS

| | | |
|---|---|---|
| *Monday, May 1* | 2 Corinthians 1:1-11 | *God Consoles Us in Our Afflictions* |
| *Tuesday, May 2* | 2 Corinthians 1:12-22 | *Sealed by God's Spirit* |
| *Wednesday, May 3* | 2 Corinthians 1:23—2:4 | *Love Prevails over Pain and Conflict* |
| *Thursday, May 4* | 2 Corinthians 2:5-11 | *Christian Forgiveness for the Offender* |
| *Friday, May 5* | 2 Corinthians 2:12-17 | *The Gospel: the Fragrance of Life* |
| *Saturday, May 6* | 2 Corinthians 3:1-11 | *Good News Written on Human Hearts* |
| *Sunday, May 7* | 2 Corinthians 3:12-18 | *Freed and Transformed by the Spirit* |

## BACKGROUND

In this week's lesson, we begin a selective study from 2 Corinthians. Paul wrote this letter to refute the accusations that false teachers were making against him. They asserted that Paul was untrustworthy and double-minded, and that he ministered solely for the purpose of self-elevation.

Unlike the false teachers, Paul's motivation for defending himself in this letter did not come from self-interest or pride. Rather, he had a desire to protect the church at Corinth. Because the apostle's integrity was so closely linked to the message of the Gospel, a successful effort to discredit him would have inevitably led to an undermining of the faith preached in the city by Paul and the members of his missionary team.

In the spring of A.D. 55 or 56, Paul learned about misunderstandings and other problems in the church at Corinth, and thus wrote 1 Corinthians in response (1 Cor. 1:11). This evidently did not resolve the problems, and so the apostle left Ephesus to make a *painful visit* to Corinth (2 Cor. 2:1). After he returned to Ephesus, Paul wrote a sorrowful letter to the Corinthians—a document that has since been lost (vss. 3-9). Then perhaps in May of A.D. 56, the apostle left Ephesus for Troas and Macedonia, and met with Titus in Macedonia (2:12-13; 7:5-16). Probably in September or October of that same year, Paul wrote 2 Corinthians.

In this letter, the apostle called on his readers to distinguish between true and false teaching, to separate themselves from all idolatrous associations, and to pray for him and his ministry. Paul urged the Corinthian believers to depend on God rather than themselves. The apostle testified that God's comfort and strength were more than adequate to meet the afflictions and challenges associated with being a Christian in that troubled city.

In this week's lesson, we pick up Paul's discussion concerning why he had changed his travel plans. He chose not to go to Corinth directly from Macedonia because he sensed that his discipline of the Corinthian believers might have caused them more pain than they could bear. He evidently thought that if he waited awhile before returning to the city, he would not have to discipline the wrongdoers when he came.

## NOTES ON THE PRINTED TEXT

Despite the thinking of Paul's critics, his decision to write the Corinthian believers (in lieu of visiting them) was not an easy way out for the apostle. He admitted that penning the document had caused him *much distress and anguish of heart* (2:4). Paul was willing to undergo such sadness in order to prevent his readers from experiencing similar heartache.

Second Corinthians 2:5-11 refers to a man at Corinth who had been the cause of some serious offense in the church. This incident might have been the cause of the painful visit. The believers in the church evidently took the apostle's advice in disciplining the offender, and he decided to repent of his misdeed. Because of the positive report Paul had received from Titus, the apostle was willing to forget the trouble caused by the incident. In fact, the apostle wrote that the offender had caused more sorrow for the church than for him (2:5).

Paul said that the congregation had sufficiently disciplined the wrongdoer (2:6). The apostle indicated that it was now time to forgive the repentant believer and console him (2:7). In the absence of such displays of *love* (2:8), the individual might be *overwhelmed by excessive sorrow* (2:7).

Paul had written his instructions about disciplining the man to test the obedience of the Corinthian believers (2:9). The apostle undoubtedly was pleased to see them pass the test. Paul was ready to offer his own forgiveness of the repentant man to that of the church. In fact, the apostle called on Christ as his witness of his willingness to forgive the man for the sake of the church (2:10). Paul realized that to needlessly prolong the painful matter would give Satan an opportunity to gain an advantage over the congregation (2:11).

While in Ephesus, Paul longed for news from the Corinthian church. When he did not hear anything about their response to his sharp letter, he departed for Troas and prepared to cross the Aegean Sea to Macedonia. Titus, whom Paul had sent to Corinth to straighten out the problems there, had not yet rejoined the apostle. *When I came to Troas to proclaim the good news of Christ, a door was opened for me in the Lord; but my mind could not rest because I did not find my brother Titus there. So I said farewell to them and went on to Macedonia* (2:12-13).

Paul eventually was reunited with Titus, who carried encouraging news about Corinth. The way God was working at Corinth led the apostle to thank God for all He had done in the midst of a difficult situation. Paul compared the steady advance of the Gospel to a Roman triumphal procession in which the victorious general and his soldiers celebrated their victory over a foreign enemy (2:14). The positive report of Titus renewed Paul's hope and brought to his mind this victorious image of the church.

Paul's references to *fragrance* (2:14) and *aroma* (2:15) were also connected to Roman triumphal parades. During these celebrations, priests used censers filled with burning incense to add fragrance to the air before the procession passed. Paul compared the aroma of the occasion to *the fragrance that comes from knowing Christ* (2:14), which was being spread by preachers of the Gospel. The Good News was an odor of death to unbelievers, but a life-giving aroma to believers.

Such an overwhelming responsibility caused Paul to question his own adequacy for preaching the Gospel (2:16). (Of course, we know that in Christ such adequacy can be found.) It was this consideration of sufficiency that set the apostle apart from false teachers, who expected to make a profit from *God's word* (2:17). Because the apostle recognized the awesomeness of his responsibility, he did not seek personal gain, especially when the eternal destiny of others was at stake.

## SUGGESTIONS TO TEACHERS

Nearly everyone in your class has experienced the pain of conflict and broken relationships. In the case of some, this week's lesson may touch on some hurtful memories and sensitive issues. Keep in mind that the overall theme is triumph through the work and power of Christ.

**1. CONSOLED AND CONSOLING.** The idea of consolation resonates throughout this week's Scripture text. We learn that there is consolation in union with Christ and in fellowship with other believers. Throughout all our afflictions, we are promised the encouraging presence of Jesus. Regardless of the hardship we face, we can go through it, for we know that our Savior is always there to lead and strengthen us.

**2. CRUSHED BUT COMFORTED.** We don't know exactly what had happened in the Corinthian church to cause Paul so much distress. But it is clear that the apostle experienced anguish. He noted that his hope was renewed by the comforting report that Titus brought. Paul could see from this that God was able to bring victory into the worst of circumstances.

**3. CONCERNED AND CORRECTING.** One of Paul's purposes in writing was to help the Corinthian believers to discipline a troublemaker in the church. The apostle's remedy may seem harsh, but it was meant to bring about the spiritual restoration of the offender.

**4. CONNECTED AND CARING.** Paul, the troublemaker, and the Corinthian church had experienced pain over the distressing situation. From this we see that there is a mutuality of suffering among all the members of a church! When the troublemaker repented, Paul then urged forgiveness. Remind your students that God wants all persons to be reconciled to Him and with one another.

**5. CONFIDENT AND COMMITTED.** End the class time by focusing on 2 Corinthians 2:14-17. Be sure to explain Paul's comparison of the steady advance of the Gospel to a Roman triumphal procession. That was the picture the apostle had of the church at it victoriously progressed across the world.

■ TOPIC: From Sorrow to Joy

■ QUESTIONS: 1. Why was it important for the Corinthian believers to reaffirm their love for the repentant offender? 2. Why was it important for the members of the church at Corinth to forgive this man? 3. How has your faith in Christ helped you to overcome difficult circumstances? 4. Why is it good for you to be part of a Christian congregation as you endure trying situations? 5. How might you comfort your fellow believers in the midst of their hardships?

■ ILLUSTRATIONS:

**Scorned and Ignored.** Some people in the church at Corinth had scorned and ignored Paul because they did not think that he had the credentials and commanding presence of an outstanding leader. There are times when we may be scorned and ignored by others, and thus can identify with how Paul may have felt.

A young man named Francis Harry Hinsley went through a painful experience early in World War II. Hinsley was a young undergraduate of Saint John's College in Cambridge, England, when the war broke out. He was studying history. Recruiters for the British code-breaking unit urged him to sign up. After briefly studying at the Government Code and Cypher School at Bletchley Park, he was assigned to analyze the radio transmissions of German warships in the Baltic.

In April, 1940, young Hinsley reported a massive movement of vessels toward Norway. But the British Admiralty refused to believe so young and untried a man. Scorning and ignoring Hinsley's intelligence reports, the British Navy discovered too late that what he said was correct, and lost the aircraft carrier *Glorious* to German warships.

From then on, however, the Royal Navy gave 21-year-old Hinsley its trust. His work with the codebreakers during the rest of the war enabled the Allies to win the Battle of the Atlantic. Eventually he was presented with a knighthood in gratitude for his labors. Like Sir Harry Hinsley, we must persevere even when treated with scorn and ignored by those claiming to have superior knowledge.

**From Ridiculed Runt to All-star Athlete.** Brett Butler, the Los Angeles Dodger star, is one of the smallest big-league players on record. He stands only 5 feet 9 inches and weights 156 pounds. His size 7 shoes are the smallest in baseball. As a boy, he was teased, picked on, and often laughed at because of his size. However, he was determined to succeed as an athlete.

While playing football in high school, Butler had to wear pads from the junior high because the equipment for the senior high boys was too large. But baseball was his first love. Brett wanted to go to Arizona State, one of the best colleges for baseball. His high school coach ridiculed him for this idea. Nevertheless Brett went off to Arizona State, even though he did not get the scholarship help he wanted.

After transferring to Southeastern Oklahoma State, Butler finally began to get some recognition, becoming All-American two times. Upon graduation from college, Brett pursued his dream of playing baseball professionally, but ended in the twenty-third round of the draft choices. Gradually, his ability was able to win him a position with the L.A. Dodgers. In fact, he became the best bunter in the sport. Each season he stole over 40 bases and scored over 100 runs. In 1991, Butler was named to the all-star team, and in 1992 was one of the top hitters.

**No Need to Bash Believers.** John B. Barker has noted that making fun of Christians is in vogue these days. Television is especially fond of producing comic caricatures of the faithful and their moral values. For every decent show, there are several comedies that bash believers.

What about the 350,000 churches across America, where people's spiritual needs are quietly being met? And what about the thousands of missionaries to the poor or the armies of Christian volunteers working in hospitals, food pantries, prisons, homeless shelters, half-way houses, and various counseling programs? It's not fair to stereotype and ridicule all believers as many sitcoms do.

**FOR YOUTH**

■ Topic: Discipline from Love

■ Questions: 1. What was the source of Paul's spiritual strength? 2. For what did Paul say he gave thanks to God? 3. Why is it important for you to be motivated by love in your dealings with others? 4. In what ways can people see the life of Jesus in you? 5. What, in your opinion, is God able to accomplish through His church in this world?

■ **Illustrations:**

**Poor Example.** Chuck Truitt was an administrator for the Red Bank Valley School District in Punxsutawney, Pennsylvania, where E. David Farley was the superintendent. Truitt was charged with criminal conspiracy in connection with the theft of two computers. He contends that Farley ordered him to take the computers and store them in his garage, where state police found them. Farley later threatened to kill Truitt.

Needless to say, everyone was surprised. Both administrators seemed sincere and good. But the incident left residents and students wondering whether both men were simply putting up a good front as leaders to mask much darker sides of their lives.

The Corinthian believers were faced with evaluating a Christian leader's integrity. Was Paul sincere, or were his critics accurate in their accusations against Paul? Like Red Bank Valley School District, the congregation at Corinth experienced pain. Nevertheless, the members of the church accepted Paul's leadership, took his advice, and resolved a thorny problem.

**Discipline Shows Care.** Noelle Bowman was at an off-campus party and went to the bathroom. When the 21-year-old junior at Indiana University of Pennsylvania came out of the door, she was met by a policeman. His gun was drawn and pointed at her. The officer ordered the frightened student to sit with others along a wall.

The raid was part of a concerted effort by local police and the university to avoid underage drinking. The university was and is serious that its zero tolerance of underage drinking be enforced, especially after a freshman girl was killed after a binge-drinking episode on New Year's Eve, 1998. Noelle, though upset, understood and accepted the school's policy.

Many youth struggle with the idea that firm discipline is an expression of care and love. The temporary infringement on their freedom is far outweighed by the possibility that no young people are lost due to underage drinking.

**Still No Forgiveness.** On October 8, 1997, the International Committee of the Red Cross handed over 60,000 pages of World War II documents at a modest ceremony at Yad Vashem, Israel's Holocaust Memorial Institute. The Red Cross acknowledged that the documents proved a "moral failure" in keeping silent as the Nazis murdered 6 million Jews. Included in the pages were reports from field workers about mass deportations and killings of Jews. The Red Cross, however, kept silent. They feared that they might compromise the neutrality of Switzerland, where the organization was based. The Red Cross also dreaded the possibility that the Nazis would retaliate by stopping the organization from helping Allied prisoners of war.

While officials at the memorial were pleased to receive the documents, the general populace of Israel was still unhappy. The Red Cross acknowledgment of moral failure was not an apology, such as the Roman Catholic Church of France had issued only one week earlier. From this we see that forgiveness is more difficult to extend as a group than it is for individuals. Knowing this about human beings, Paul wrote to the entire Corinthian church to urge them to forgive a repentant offender.

# TRIALS AND TRIUMPHS OF CHRISTIAN MINISTRY

**BACKGROUND SCRIPTURE:** 2 Corinthians 4
**DEVOTIONAL READING:** 2 Corinthians 6:1-10

---

**KEY VERSE:** We are afflicted in every way, but not crushed; perplexed, but not driven to despair; persecuted, but not forsaken; struck down, but not destroyed. 2 Corinthians 4:8-9.

---

*KING JAMES VERSION*

2 CORINTHIANS 4:5 For we preach not ourselves, but Christ Jesus the Lord; and ourselves your servants for Jesus' sake.

6 For God, who commanded the light to shine out of darkness, hath shined in our hearts, to give the light of the knowledge of the glory of God in the face of Jesus Christ.

7 But we have this treasure in earthen vessels, that the excellency of the power may be of God, and not of us.

8 We are troubled on every side, yet not distressed; we are perplexed, but not in despair;

9 Persecuted, but not forsaken; cast down, but not destroyed;

10 Always bearing about in the body the dying of the Lord Jesus, that the life also of Jesus might be made manifest in our body.

11 For we which live are alway delivered unto death for Jesus' sake, that the life also of Jesus might be made manifest in our mortal flesh.

12 So then death worketh in us, but life in you.

13 We having the same spirit of faith, according as it is written, I believed, and therefore have I spoken; we also believe, and therefore speak;

14 Knowing that he which raised up the Lord Jesus shall raise up us also by Jesus, and shall present us with you.

15 For all things are for your sakes, that the abundant grace might through the thanksgiving of many redound to the glory of God.

16 For which cause we faint not; but though our outward man perish, yet the inward man is renewed day by day.

17 For our light affliction, which is but for a moment, worketh for us a far more exceeding and eternal weight of glory;

18 While we look not at the things which are seen, but at the things which are not seen: for the things which are seen are temporal; but the things which are not seen are eternal.

*NEW REVISED STANDARD VERSION*

2 CORINTHIANS 4:5 For we do not proclaim ourselves; we proclaim Jesus Christ as Lord and ourselves as your slaves for Jesus' sake. 6 For it is the God who said, "Let light shine out of darkness," who has shone in our hearts to give the light of the knowledge of the glory of God in the face of Jesus Christ.

7 But we have this treasure in clay jars, so that it may be made clear that this extraordinary power belongs to God and does not come from us. 8 We are afflicted in every way, but not crushed; perplexed, but not driven to despair; 9 persecuted, but not forsaken; struck down, but not destroyed; 10 always carrying in the body the death of Jesus, so that the life of Jesus may also be made visible in our bodies. 11 For while we live, we are always being given up to death for Jesus' sake, so that the life of Jesus may be made visible in our mortal flesh. 12 So death is at work in us, but life in you. 13 But just as we have the same spirit of faith that is in accordance with scripture—"I believed, and so I spoke"—we also believe, and so we speak, 14 because we know that the one who raised the Lord Jesus will raise us also with Jesus, and will bring us with you into his presence. 15 Yes, everything is for your sake, so that grace, as it extends to more and more people, may increase thanksgiving, to the glory of God.

16 So we do not lose heart. Even though our outer nature is wasting away, our inner nature is being renewed day by day. 17 For this slight momentary affliction is preparing us for an eternal weight of glory beyond all measure, 18 because we look not at what can be seen but at what cannot be seen; for what can be seen is temporary, but what cannot be seen is eternal.

| | | |
|---|---|---|
| *Monday, May 8* | 2 Corinthians 4:1-7 | *God's Light Shines in Our Hearts* |
| *Tuesday, May 9* | 2 Corinthians 4:8-15 | *God Raised Jesus and Will Raise Us* |
| *Wednesday, May 10* | 2 Corinthians 4:16—5:10 | *We Walk and Live by Faith* |
| *Thursday, May 11* | 2 Corinthians 5:11-21 | *Reconciled to Be Reconcilers* |
| *Friday, May 12* | 2 Corinthians 6:1-11 | *Open Wide Your Hearts* |
| *Saturday, May 13* | 2 Corinthians 6:14—7:1 | *We Are Temples of the Living God* |
| *Sunday, May 14* | 2 Corinthians 7:2-13 | *Paul's Joy at the Corinthians' Repentance* |

## BACKGROUND

In 2 Corinthians, Paul wrote about some of his own triumphs and joys as well as some of his disappointments and despairs. Because he did so, probably no other letter gives us a clearer glimpse into the apostle himself. Paul certainly had good reason for feeling downhearted on occasion. The anguish he endured would have defeated most of us.

In 11:24-28, Paul disclosed some of the trials he had experienced. Five different times antagonistic fellow Jews flogged him. Three times the apostle was beaten with rods, and once he was stoned. Three times Paul was shipwrecked, and once he spent a whole night and a day adrift at sea. He had to face danger from flooded rivers and robbers, as well as in the cities, in the deserts, and on the stormy seas. The apostle had lived with weariness, pain, and sleepless nights. Often he had been hungry, thirsty, and cold. Perhaps worse than the physical sufferings was the emotional anguish. Enormous was the daily burden of how the churches that Paul had established were getting along.

By allowing his readers to identify with his struggles, Paul revealed that the same comfort and strength he had received from the Lord was available to them, too. Backed by the knowledge and strength of God's mercy, the apostle wrote *we do not lose heart* (4:1). The Lord had enabled him and other ministers to persevere in the midst of problems and setbacks. In fact, Paul's role as a minister of the Gospel more than compensated for all the afflictions and malicious charges he had endured for the sake of the Christians at Corinth.

## NOTES ON THE PRINTED TEXT

Paul and his fellow missionaries had been called to proclaim the Gospel. In light of such a glorious opportunity, it would have been foolish for them to have proclaimed themselves. While the apostle was forced at times to defend himself against the attack of his adversaries, he never focused his message on himself. *For we do not proclaim ourselves; we proclaim Jesus Christ as Lord and ourselves as your slaves for Jesus' sake* (4:5).

God, who brought light into existence, was shining the light of the Gospel of

Christ in the hearts of such people as Paul. Like all believers, the apostle had once had a heart darkened with sin. But then the Lord enabled him to understand the Good News and accept it, which led to his salvation. *For it is the God who said, "Let light shine out of darkness," who has shone in our hearts to give the light of the knowledge of the glory of God in the face of Jesus Christ* (4:6).

No amount of human effort could take away the darkness of the human heart. God alone could shine His light into the hearts of sinners and dispel the darkness of sin. Paul made it clear that the power of the Gospel was not diminished by the human frailties of those who proclaimed it. He said that this *treasure* (namely, the Gospel; 4:7) was being kept in jars of clay, which was a reference to himself and his co-workers. The apostle was pointing out how unworthy they were to serve as representatives of God's truth. Paul's frailty made it *clear that this extraordinary power belongs to God and does not come from us* (4:7).

Paul used four illustrations of how the Lord had delivered him out of desperate situations. *We are afflicted in every way, but not crushed; perplexed, but not driven to despair; persecuted, but not forsaken; struck down, but not destroyed* (4:8-9). Paul related his experiences to constantly carrying in his body the death of Jesus (4:10). The apostle's own experience reflected the suffering that Jesus endured on the cross. For Paul, living for Christ meant enduring mental and physical hardship, as well as facing hatred, violence, and even death.

Despite the suffering Paul endured, he said the life of Christ was manifested in his own life. Just as he felt Christ's sufferings to be a part of his own, the apostle also felt the power of Christ's resurrection in his many escapes from death. And the life of Christ that manifested itself in the midst of His dying was also a source of life for Paul's readers. *For while we live, we are always being given up to death for Jesus' sake, so that the life of Jesus may be made visible in our mortal flesh. So death is at work in us, but life in you* (4:11-12).

In 4:13, Paul quoted Psalm 116:10. The writer of this psalm thanked God for delivering him from a close call with death. Paul could identify with the writer's afflictions as well as with his faith in God's deliverance. Because of Paul's travails, he actually felt more compelled to speak about his belief in the resurrected Lord. Of course, Paul's hope went beyond deliverance from temporal dangers. He knew that after he had finally faced death, the Lord would raise him (and all other believers) from the dead (2 Cor. 4:14).

Paul contended that everything he had done and endured had been for the benefit of the Corinthians. His motive, though, was greater than spiritually building up his readers. Ultimately the apostle wanted to bring praise and glory to the Lord. *Yes, everything is for your sake, so that grace, as it extends to more and more people, may increase thanksgiving, to the glory of God* (4:15).

Paul was not discouraged. No matter what life presented he always had confidence in a better life after death. Earthly life was temporary. Life with Christ in heaven was eternal. *So we do not lose heart. Even though our outer nature is wasting away, our inner nature is being renewed day by day. For this slight momentary affliction is preparing us for an eternal weight of glory beyond all measure, because we look not at what can be seen but at what cannot be seen; for what can be seen is temporary, but what cannot be seen is eternal* (4:16-18).

## SUGGESTIONS TO TEACHERS

Saint Theresa of Avila, who experienced hardship as a servant of Christ, once remarked in exasperation in a prayer, "Lord, if this is how You treat your friends, no wonder You have so few of them!" Even highly committed people have their moments of feeling dejected.

**1. TRIALS IN MINISTRY.** Let the members of your class know that being a Christian isn't always easy. Shallow preaching sometimes leads people to think that becoming a Christian is always going to be fun, pleasant, and rewarding. But following Jesus means experiencing hardships. Invite your students to discuss what trials they encounter as servants of the Lord.

**2. TRUTH IN CHRIST, NOT ONE SELF.** Our spiritual power and guidance come from Christ. The world, in contrast, advocates self-reliance and advertises ways to enhance one's ego. The popular notion is that with enough know-how and drive, people can accomplish whatever they want to accomplish. Point out to the students the folly of such arrogance. It is only with the Lord's help that we can rise above the trials that sometimes overtake us.

**3. TREASURE IN CLAY JARS.** Have your students seriously consider Paul's analogy of the clay jars (4:7). The most important thing is the treasure, not the frail containers.

**4. TRUST IN RESURRECTING POWER.** God, who raised up Jesus from the dead, gives new life to all believers. The Lord is greater than we ever can begin to understand! Our worst situations are never beyond His ability to overcome. In Him there is true hope.

**5. TRIUMPH THROUGH CHRIST.** Yes, Christians suffer. And, yes, Christians often are subjected to trials. But God has the final word. Through the risen, living Lord, we can look beyond the present moment of hardship and heartache and live in confidence of ultimate victory! Ask the members of your class to consider the ramifications of 4:17-18 for their daily lives.

---

**FOR ADULTS**

■ TOPIC: From Suffering to Triumph

■ QUESTIONS: 1. What was the focus of Paul's Gospel proclamation? 2. How was Paul able to triumph in the midst of his sufferings? 3. Why is it important to rely on the Lord when seeking to lead others to faith in Christ? 4. When do you most depend on God's power—when everything is going well, or when you face difficult times? 5. Why is it helpful to see the crises that come into your life as opportunities to further the cause of Christ?

## ■ ILLUSTRATIONS:

**The Zero-Moment Point.** Seafaring people have an expression to describe the position from which a ship in distress cannot recover. It's called the "Zero-moment point." This results when the wind and waves become so severe that the vessel is unable to right itself and begins to founder.

Undoubtedly there were times when Paul almost came to a "zero-moment point" in his life as he faced the spectre of death (see 2 Cor. 1:8-10). While we don't know all the details, we can assume that it probably was related to some terrible beating and imprisonment, or acute disappointment over the attacks and rejection by others in the church, or a life-threatening bout of sickness, or a combination of any of these, or some other unnamed severe setback. Despite the hardship that would have devastated many other believers, Paul did not flounder. Why? It's because of Jesus Christ. Paul would attribute his recovery from his "zero-moment points" to the intervention of the Lord.

When such times arise in our lives and we see no hope for ourselves, we can depend on Jesus to always remain with us. With Him at our side, we can be confident of eventual triumph!

**Triumph of Hymn Writer.** The most prolific American hymn writer was a blind woman named Fanny Crosby. Many hymn books contain some of the 8,000 pieces that this remarkable woman wrote during her long (95 years) life. What is more remarkable is the way that Fanny Crosby overcame handicaps. As a baby, she developed a severe eye infection. Painful treatments by a quack doctor produced scars over both eyes, causing total blindness for her for the rest of her life. Shortly afterward, her father died, forcing her young mother to take work as a maid and leave the baby Fanny in the care of Grandmother Crosby.

Though the little girl felt depressed, the grandmother instilled in her a deep faith. Young Fanny was taught the importance of prayer. The grandmother also helped Fanny to develop her memory so that she could learn by heart long portions of Scripture.

Fanny Crosby eventually realized that God wanted her to serve Him even though she was blind. Never whimpering in self-pity, she entered the New York Institute for the Blind, where she stayed on as a teacher for 23 years. She became an accomplished pianist, harpist, and singer. She married Alexander van Alstine, a former pupil at the Institute, and at his encouragement began to compose hymns. Despite her prodigious outpouring of hymns over the next decades, she received little money for her efforts.

The evangelistic team of Dwight L. Moody and Ira D. Sankey introduced Fanny Crosby's hymns to a wider audience through their campaigns. Favorites such as *Jesus, Keep Me Near the Cross, Blessed Assurance, I Am Thine, O Lord, Tell Me the Story of Jesus, Jesus Is Tenderly Calling You Home,* and countless other well-known compositions from the pen of Fanny Crosby have inspired millions and enriched Christian worship. Fanny Crosby triumphed over hardships and handicaps because of her trust in Christ and gratitude as a believer.

**Persecution of Christians Continues.** In July 1997, the U.S. State Department issued a report on religious persecution around the world. It noted these atrocities being committed by the following countries:

• *Burma:* Government troops are reported to have attacked members of the largely Christian Karen ethnic minority, raping women and forcing men to act as porters.

• *China:* Only government-authorized religious organizations are allowed to function without official harassment. Repression has increased against Christians, Tibetan Buddhists, and Muslims in the western province of Xinjiang.

• *Iran:* Muslims who convert to another faith are considered apostates and face the death penalty. Dozens of members of the Bahai sect have been executed since the 1979 Islamic revolution.

• *Iraq:* The government has brutally repressed Kurds and Assyrian Christians in the north and Shiite Muslims in the south.

• *North Korea:* All but officially sanctioned religious activity is prohibited.

• *Saudi Arabia:* Islam is the official religion and no other can be practiced openly. Non-Muslim worshipers risk arrest, lashing, and deportation.

• *Sudan:* The Islamic government, which is engaged in a civil war with non-Muslims, tries to force conversions through rape, starvation, and abduction of children. Christians have also been forced into slavery.

---

**FOR YOUTH**

■ TOPIC: Power from Weakness

■ QUESTIONS: 1. How did Paul respond to the many hardships that he endured for the cause of Christ? 2. What was Paul's ultimate goal in proclaiming the Gospel? 3. How might you demonstrate to others the hope that you possess for an eternity with the Lord? 4. Why is it best to set your affections on the things of eternity rather than the things of earth? 5. What are some ways that you can praise God for helping you to endure your hardships?

■ **ILLUSTRATIONS:**

**School Spirit.** Alumni associations of American colleges and universities are jumping on the marketing bandwagon and generating millions of dollars of revenue through a variety of creative means. For instance, Carnegie Mellon University has four styles of Seiko watches with the school's logo on the face. West Virginia University offers lamps and furniture, while Ohio State alumni can have caskets with the buckeye leaf stitched into the lining. The University of Pittsburgh and dozens of other schools have deals with various credit cards, while Penn State even has a mortgage company. Alumni are proud and committed to their schools. They are happy to have the symbols of their affiliation, which generate money for their alma mater. If young people and alumni are this eager to serve their alma mater, how much more should you be willing to identify with and serve your Lord.

**Devoted to the Gold.** When 15-year-old Tara Lipinski of Sugar Land, Texas, won the gold medal in ladies figure skating at the 1998 Winter Olympic Games at Nagano, Japan, it was the culmination of an effort that began when she was two years old. She literally devoted almost all the waking hours of her young life in pursuit of the Olympic gold. That had been her goal and the cause to which she was committed. Americans watched and celebrated with her when she achieved that goal.

Perhaps you also have known persons whose lives reflect a cause to which they are devoted. Hopefully that cause or goal is a good and constructive one. God has called you to serve Him. May you do it with the enthusiasm and zeal that Tara has displayed for figure skating!

**Persecuted for His Sake.** In Cairo, Egypt, a teenage Coptic Christian girl was kidnapped by Muslim extremists. During her nine month captivity, she was forced to fast, pray, and memorize the Koran. She was physically and sexually abused. Sulfuric acid was poured on her wrist to obliterate a tattoo of the cross, and her captors threatened to pour it on her face if she dared to remove the Islamic veil that they had forced her to wear. Terrorized, she signed papers of conversion to Islam in order to escape. She is now being sheltered and treated by the Servants of the Cross.

This poor girl is only one of an estimated 200 to 250 million Christians whose lives are at risk. Nina Shea, director of the Puebla Program on Religious Freedom, notes that persecution, torture, enslavement, imprisonment, and the forcible separation of children from parents are only some of the trials that believers face in Islamic countries and in China.

Being a follower of Christ is not easy. Paul wrote that believers could expect to be persecuted (see 2 Tim. 3:12). If you have not suffered for your faith, then give God thanks. If you have endured affliction, then look to God for strength to remain faithful to Christ.

# THE COLLECTION FOR JERUSALEM CHRISTIANS

**BACKGROUND SCRIPTURE:** 2 Corinthians 9
**DEVOTIONAL READING:** 2 Corinthians 8:1-15

**KEY VERSE:** Each of you must give as you have made up your mind, not reluctantly or under compulsion, for God loves a cheerful giver. 2 Corinthians 9:7.

*KING JAMES VERSION*

2 CORINTHIANS 9:1 For as touching the ministering to the saints, it is superfluous for me to write to you:

2 For I know the forwardness of your mind, for which I boast of you to them of Macedonia, that Achaia was ready a year ago; and your zeal hath provoked very many.

3 Yet have I sent the brethren, lest our boasting of you should be in vain in this behalf; that, as I said, ye may be ready:

4 Lest haply if they of Macedonia come with me, and find you unprepared, we (that we say not, ye) should be ashamed in this same confident boasting.

5 Therefore I thought it necessary to exhort the brethren, that they would go before unto you, and make up beforehand your bounty, whereof ye had notice before, that the same might be ready, as a matter of bounty, and not as of covetousness.

6 But this I say, He which soweth sparingly shall reap also sparingly; and he which soweth bountifully shall reap also bountifully.

7 Every man according as he purposeth in his heart, so let him give; not grudgingly, or of necessity: for God loveth a cheerful giver.

8 And God is able to make all grace abound toward you; that ye, always having all sufficiency in all things, may abound to every good work:

9 (As it is written, He hath dispersed abroad; he hath given to the poor: his righteousness remaineth for ever.

10 Now he that ministereth seed to the sower both minister bread for your food, and multiply your seed sown, and increase the fruits of your righteousness;)

11 Being enriched in every thing to all bountifulness, which causeth through us thanksgiving to God.

12 For the administration of this service not only supplieth the want of the saints, but is abundant also by many thanksgivings unto God;

13 Whiles by the experiment of this ministration they glorify God for your professed subjection.

*NEW REVISED STANDARD VERSION*

2 CORINTHIANS 9:1 Now it is not necessary for me to write you about the ministry to the saints, 2 for I know your eagerness, which is the subject of my boasting about you to the people of Macedonia, saying that Achaia has been ready since last year; and your zeal has stirred up most of them. 3 But I am sending the brothers in order that our boasting about you may not prove to have been empty in this case, so that you may be ready, as I said you would be; 4 otherwise, if some Macedonians come with me and find that you are not ready, we would be humiliated—to say nothing of you—in this undertaking. 5 So I thought it necessary to urge the brothers to go on ahead to you, and arrange in advance for this bountiful gift that you have promised, so that it may be ready as a voluntary gift and not as an extortion.

6 The point is this: the one who sows sparingly will also reap sparingly, and the one who sows bountifully will also reap bountifully. 7 Each of you must give as you have made up your mind, not reluctantly or under compulsion, for God loves a cheerful giver. 8 And God is able to provide you with every blessing in abundance, so that by always having enough of everything, you may share abundantly in every good work. 9 As it is written,

"He scatters abroad, he gives to the poor;
    his righteousness endures forever."

10 He who supplies seed to the sower and bread for food will supply and multiply your seed for sowing and increase the harvest of your righteousness. 11 You will be enriched in every way for your great generosity, which will produce thanksgiving to God through us; 12 for the rendering of this ministry not only supplies the needs of the saints but also overflows with many thanksgivings to God. 13 Through the testing of this ministry you glorify God by your obedience.

| | | |
|---|---|---|
| *Monday, May 15* | 2 Corinthians 8:1-7 | *Exceeding Generosity* |
| *Tuesday, May 16* | 2 Corinthians 8:8-15 | *Show Your Love by Your Giving* |
| *Wednesday, May 17* | 2 Corinthians 8:16-24 | *A Generous Gift Glorifies God* |
| *Thursday, May 18* | 2 Corinthians 9:1-9 | *God Loves and Blesses Cheerful Givers* |
| *Friday, May 19* | 2 Corinthians 9:10-15 | *Generous Giving Brings Joy to All* |
| *Saturday, May 20* | 2 Corinthians 16:1-9 | *A Collection for Jerusalem Christians* |
| *Sunday, May 21* | Romans 15:22-29 | *Paul Intends to Visit Roman Christians* |

## BACKGROUND

The believers in Jerusalem were poor, and many had suffered hardship from it. Though we may never know all the reasons for their poverty, signs of their need existed from the earliest days of the church. Paul resolved to organize a special relief fund for the congregation in Jerusalem. He wrote to the churches he had established throughout Asia Minor and Greece, and called on them to collect money for the destitute in Jerusalem.

The collection of money for the impoverished believers in Jerusalem occupied a major place in Paul's thinking during the last year or two of his third missionary journey. The apostle was eager for the Gentile churches to remember the spiritual debt they owned to the Jewish Christians, who were represented by the church in Jerusalem (Rom. 15:27). This special offering would accomplish several things. It would meet basic human needs and relieve suffering in Jerusalem. But at the same time, this collection would demonstrate the unity of the church and show that Christ's followers truly loved one another.

When Paul had written an earlier letter to the Corinthians, he had instructed them to put aside some money every week for the needy believers in Jerusalem (see 1 Cor. 16:1-4). With this systematic manner of giving, the church members could gather a sizable sum without placing an undue burden on themselves. Paul had placed great importance on this collection throughout his missionary journey and had been promoting it for several years.

However, it is possible that the recent accusations against the apostle, the painful visit, and the resulting letter had distracted the Corinthians, taking their attention away from the project they had once embraced with enthusiasm (see 2 Cor. 9:2). But now that Paul sensed that the believers in Corinth had experienced a change of heart, he felt confident enough to bring up this matter once again.

Paul sent Titus and two other believers to Corinth as his representatives to receive the money the Christians in the church had collected. Paul did not assume anything when it came to collecting money for the poor. He involved others in the arrangements and carefully established their credentials (8:16-24).

## NOTES ON THE PRINTED TEXT

Paul was so confident in his expectations of how the Corinthians would receive Titus and the two others that the apostle did not feel it was necessary for him to spell out what their response should be to the visitors (9:1). Paul trusted that his readers knew what to do in such situations, and he was sure that they would follow through in displaying Christian love to his representatives.

Paul knew about the Corinthians' eagerness to help other believers. This zeal had been demonstrated in their initial response toward contributing money to meet the needs of the poor saints in Jerusalem (9:2). In fact, it was the Corinthians' original enthusiasm for the offering that had stirred the Macedonians to action.

While there was no need to go on commending the Corinthians for their Christian love, Paul did sense a need to urge them to finish the task they had earlier embraced. That was his reason behind sending Titus and the other workers (9:3). They would complete all the arrangements for the collection so that the apostle could deal with other matters when he arrived. Paul was eager to make sure that his boasting about the Corinthians did not turn out to be in vain.

Because Paul would be bringing representatives from the Macedonian churches with him on his upcoming trip to Corinth, he was especially eager for the Corinthians to finish their collection before the group arrived. That is why the apostle urged his readers to do all that was possible to keep from embarrassing him or themselves (9:4). To prevent such a mishap, Paul explained again that he was sending Titus and two other representatives to help the Corinthians finish their offering before he arrived with the Macedonian believers (9:5). The apostle wanted their gift to arise from a willing spirit and not be given grudgingly.

Paul compared the individual giver to a farmer sowing seed. The farmer who plants only a few seeds cannot expect to reap a large harvest. Rather, the way to receive a bountiful crop is to sow a lot of seeds (9:6). In other words, just as a sown seed is not lost, so the money given to the believers in Judea would likewise not be lost, but would bring a rich spiritual return for the Corinthians. Of course, Paul did not want his readers to feel obligated to contribute to the fund for the church in Jerusalem. He insisted that they were free to make their own decision. Godly giving is done by believers who are thankful that they can serve the Lord and help others in this way (9:7).

The apostle related that if the Corinthians responded to the need in Jerusalem in a generous and sacrificial manner, they would discover God's grace in abundance. His grace would more than compensate for any spiritual or material lack in their lives, and would also enable them to perform even more godly deeds for others (9:8). In fact, Paul said they would be like the person described in Psalm 112:9, whose generous gifts to the poor were as *righteousness [that] endures forever* (2 Cor. 9:9). From this we see that God's spiritual rewards for sacrificial giving will far exceed anything we can imagine.

To underscore God's ability to bless His people, the apostle pointed out that it is the Lord who gives seed to the sower in the first place (9:10). Only God can enable the believer to perform works of righteousness, such as sacrificial giving. To the Christians who generously give, the Lord will make a way for them to actually give even more (9:11). In each incidence of sacrificial giving, even the recipients of such gifts would be drawn closer to God as they expressed their thanks to Him.

Paul emphasized that the giving of the Corinthians would serve another purpose in addition to providing for needy believers in Jerusalem. The generosity of the Corinthians would also glorify God by encouraging others to worship Him (9:12). For the apostle, that aspect of the giving was just as important as helping the needy. Paul explained that not only would the recipients thank the Lord for the gift, but they would also praise Him for what the offering signified, namely, the proof of God's work in the lives of the Corinthians (12:13).

## SUGGESTIONS TO TEACHERS

Our giving to the financial needs of the church indicates how committed we really are to the cause of Christ. Though we may shy away from discussing money matters in church, the Bible has no such reticence. This week's lesson, in fact, could be preached as a sermon on Christian giving in most congregations! Have the members of your class take note of the following important points.

**1. BIDDING.** Paul reminded his readers of their responsibility to share their financial wealth with other needy believers. It doesn't matter what one's economic status might be. The main point is that God calls us, as His spiritual children, to be generous and sacrificial in our giving.

**2. BENEFITS.** Paul minced no words about stingy givers. Those who shared little showed the depth of their spiritual impoverishment. Those giving generously knew firsthand the abundance of God's grace, which overflowed in their life. Paul compared Christian giving and receiving to sowing and reaping. The farmer who sowed sparingly would gather a small harvest. And believers who were stingy in their giving would reap little from an eternal perspective.

**3. BOUNTY.** Paul assured his readers that God would provide for their needs. In a world where there is hunger in some quarters, the problem lies usually in the adequate distribution of wealth. If those who have more than enough share their abundance with others, everyone will have their needs met. Invite the students to discuss ways your church can do more to alleviate world hunger. Think together also about those who might be malnourished in the United States.

**4. BLESSINGS.** Giving is a way of testifying to our faith in Christ. Paul enumerated the spiritual blessings that come to believers who witness to their faith by their generous giving. Discuss how real stewardship of one's dollars can enhance the proclamation of the Gospel among the unsaved.

**5. BOND.** Paul told his readers how sacrificial sharing among Christians builds a deep bond between them. When a church is truly mission-minded and financially committed, a marvelous sense of community between believers develops. Both the givers and the recipients are enriched in their faith.

<table>
<tr><td rowspan="2">**FOR ADULTS**</td><td>■ TOPIC: From Reluctant to Joyful Giving</td></tr>
<tr><td>■ QUESTIONS: 1. In what way had the Corinthian believers shown</td></tr>
</table>

■ **TOPIC:** From Reluctant to Joyful Giving

■ **QUESTIONS:** 1. In what way had the Corinthian believers shown an eagerness to help the impoverished Christians in the Jerusalem church? 2. Why did Paul want the Corinthians to give willingly, not grudgingly? 3. What situations or needs might you know about to which you could make a generous financial contribution? 4. Do you respond to requests for contributions out of guilt or out of an eagerness to do what you can to serve the Lord with your money? 5. Why is it important to investigate carefully charities that ask you to contribute to their cause?

■ **ILLUSTRATIONS:**

**Pass the French Fries.** One day a mother and daughter walked into a fast food restaurant for lunch. The mother ordered a salad and her daughter got a cheeseburger and French fries. When the mother asked her daughter if she could have a few fries, her daughter whined, "No, they're mine!" The mother reflected on this incident and wrote that it made her sad for three reasons.

First, the child didn't understand where the fries came from in the first place. They had been provided by her mother. Second, if the mother wanted to, she could have taken every French fry from her child or bought enough fries to completely bury her daughter in greasy potatoes. Third, the mother really didn't need her child's fries, for she could have bought her own. But it would have been so much nicer if her child had shared willingly.

Do we believe that God is the source of our life and the one who provides for all of our needs? Do we enjoy being in God's presence and happily share with others a portion of what God has given us? If God gave us ten French fries, would we be willing to give one or two back to Him? Or would we whine, "These are mine!" Would we give God the best and biggest French fry in gratitude for giving us ten? Or would we take one or two small fries, break them into even smaller pieces and give God barely a nibble?

Our financial giving to the church is about gratitude and proportion. We express gratitude for what God has done for us in Christ, in our lives, and in our church. We give in proportion to what God has given us. One or two French fries out of 10 really isn't much at all. Neither are 10 or 11 fries out of 100. If someone told us he or she would give us $100,000 with the only condition being that we give the first $15,000 of it back, wouldn't we take the $85,000? If we recognize that God is the owner and giver of all our resources, returning a certain amount to Him is really not that much of a sacrifice, especially when we consider all that we've been given and all that we have left.

Giving is a joy when we do it in the right spirit. It all depends on whether we think of it as "what can I *spare*?" or "what can I *share*?" Generous and sacrificial giving is not an issue of money. Rather, it is a question of whether we believe that God is trustworthy. I can almost hear God saying, "Please pass the French fries!" (Douglas Scalise, *The Beacon,* Brewster Baptist Church, Nov., 1997).

**The "Matthew Effect."** Last night as I sat down to write checks and pay bills, there were three checks that I was able to write that brought me a great deal of pleasure. One was to my university, the other was to the seminary from which I graduated, and the third was to my church. As I wrote those checks, I also said a prayer of thanksgiving for all that I have been given by these three institutions. It gave me much joy to give something back to these places that have given me so much.

To give is to say "thanks." Being benevolent should be a common experience for every Christian. Benevolence is our response to Jesus' commandment to love others as He has loved us. When I wrote my check to First Presbyterian Church, I was reminded of all of those worthy people and organizations that are helped through the church's benevolence budget, which reaches out to individuals in countries throughout the world. It would take more space than is available here to identify all of the many areas and people that our church touches as it gives back to the community and world.

Soon after writing that check, I saw an article in *Forbes* magazine (Dec. 16, 1997) entitled, "Loosen Up a Bit, Folks." It was an excellent piece promoting charitable giving. One of the noteworthy things in this article was the fact that even though our government encourages charitable giving because of tax deductions, that incentive is not what motivates most people. The article indicated that the great majority of people contribute to a particular organization because of the worthiness of the goal of that organization.

The author stated, "the single most powerful force in giving, as in most human affairs, is an intimate association between giver and recipient. This is what is known as the "Matthew effect," from Matthew 6:21: 'where your treasure is, there is your heart also.' " It was good to read this in a non-religious periodical (Jeffrey Aiken, *Tidings,* First Presbyterian Church, Allentown, PA, Dec. 10, 1997).

---

**FOR YOUTH**

■ TOPIC: Joy from Giving

■ QUESTIONS: 1. In what ways do believers who are stingy in their giving reap sparingly? 2. In what ways does God enrich the lives of Christians who are generous in their giving? 3. What affect do you think your actions and attitudes have on unbelievers who might be interested in Christianity?

4. What are some ways you can further develop a pattern of giving generously and freely to the work of the Lord? 5. Why do you think encouragement is the best incentive to persuade believers to be generous in their giving to the church?

### ■ ILLUSTRATIONS:

**Had Good Cents to Help.** In 1989, three-year-old Nora Gross asked her father, Teddy, if they could take home a beggar. Wanting to affirm her concern, Teddy remembered that he and a neighbor kept cups of pennies on their dressers. He suggested that the two collect pennies. He took his idea of "harvesting pennies" to his place of worship, and soon everyone was collecting pennies. They raised $25,000, and *Common Cents* was born.

In 1992, New York City's public schools invited the program into the schools to help raise money for the victims of Hurricane Andrew. In three weeks, 200,000 children raised $100,000. Now the money raised is being used to clothe the homeless and purchase food for soup kitchens. Said one 14-year-old boy, "Some people think that one penny is just one cent, but if you put them together, you can help a lot of people." On that day when the child was interviewed, four and one-half tons of pennies were collected totaling over $16,000!

Paul also knew that taking small offerings and putting them together would aid the Christians in the Jerusalem church. All the believers working together would help a lot of impoverished Christians.

**Laundress Lauded.** The wrinkled Afro-American woman was 89 and a former laundress from Hattiesburg, Mississippi. But she has been hosted by the President of the United States, honored by television shows, Harvard University, and others, and fawned over by celebrities, politicians, and billionaire philanthropists. The reason is that Oseola McCarty saved a small fortune from her lifetime of menial toil and donated it all ($150,000) to the University of Southern Mississippi to provide scholarships to needy students. The woman who never finished the sixth grade and who spent most of her life over a wash pot and an ironing board wanted to help others. Now she is hailed as one of the purest examples of giving by the likes of Ted Turner. This is the kind of cheerful, generous, and sacrificial giving that Paul highlighted in 2 Corinthians.

**More Change Needed.** In the spring of 1998, the Treasury Department's Bureau of Engraving and Printing began testing a dollar bill that would not crumple. The bill is a polymer plastic. It would fold easily but could not be torn with fingers. It would also prevent counterfeiting, a growing problem with the advent of computer ink-jet printers. Another reason for creating this new bill is that it has greater strength than paper and would last four times as long as conventional paper money. This could result in a big savings for the Treasury Department.

The trouble is that the Department must work for the new bill's acceptance, both in a worldwide market and domestically. Bankers must accept it, potentially being forced to deal with three different designs for each currency denomination (the old style, the new style paper, and the plastic). It would also mean an expensive retooling of currency sorting and counting machines as well as vending machines. The Department is testing to see whether the plastic would be accepted and whether the public's attitude can be changed.

Regardless of whether the attitude about plastic money can be changed remains to be seen. Another attitude, though, also needs to be changed. People must learn to share their money. Paul addressed that attitude in 2 Corinthians and urged generous, sacrificial giving. Things have not changed much today. People are still reluctant to share. Nevertheless, giving produces both joy in the recipient and in the giver.

# LIVING IN THE FAITH

**BACKGROUND SCRIPTURE:** 2 Corinthians 13:1-13
**DEVOTIONAL READING:** Acts 4:32-37

**KEY VERSE:** Examine yourselves to see whether you are living in the faith. Test yourselves. Do you not realize that Jesus Christ is in you?—unless, indeed, you fail to meet the test!
2 Corinthians 13:5.

*KING JAMES VERSION*

2 CORINTHIANS 13:1 This is the third time I am coming to you. In the mouth of two or three witnesses shall every word be established.

2 I told you before, and foretell you, as if I were present, the second time; and being absent now I write to them which heretofore have sinned, and to all other, that, if I come again, I will not spare:

3 Since ye seek a proof of Christ speaking in me, which to you-ward is not weak, but is mighty in you.

4 For though he was crucified through weakness, yet he liveth by the power of God. For we also are weak in him, but we shall live with him by the power of God toward you.

5 Examine yourselves, whether ye be in the faith; prove your own selves. Know ye not your own selves, how that Jesus Christ is in you, except ye be reprobates?

6 But I trust that ye shall know that we are not reprobates.

7 Now I pray to God that ye do no evil; not that we should appear approved, but that ye should do that which is honest, though we be as reprobates.

8 For we can do nothing against the truth, but for the truth.

9 For we are glad, when we are weak, and ye are strong: and this also we wish, even your perfection.

10 Therefore I write these things being absent, lest being present I should use sharpness, according to the power which the Lord hath given me to edification, and not to destruction.

11 Finally, brethren, farewell. Be perfect, be of good comfort, be of one mind, live in peace; and the God of love and peace shall be with you.

12 Greet one another with an holy kiss.

13 All the saints salute you.

*NEW REVISED STANDARD VERSION*

2 CORINTHIANS 13:1 This is the third time I am coming to you. "Any charge must be sustained by the evidence of two or three witnesses." 2 I warned those who sinned previously and all the others, and I warn them now while absent, as I did when present on my second visit, that if I come again, I will not be lenient— 3 since you desire proof that Christ is speaking in me. He is not weak in dealing with you, but is powerful in you. 4 For he was crucified in weakness, but lives by the power of God. For we are weak in him, but in dealing with you we will live with him by the power of God.

5 Examine yourselves to see whether you are living in the faith. Test yourselves. Do you not realize that Jesus Christ is in you?—unless, indeed, you fail to meet the test! 6 I hope you will find out that we have not failed. 7 But we pray to God that you may not do anything wrong—not that we may appear to have met the test, but that you may do what is right, though we may seem to have failed. 8 For we cannot do anything against the truth, but only for the truth. 9 For we rejoice when we are weak and you are strong. This is what we pray for, that you may become perfect. 10 So I write these things while I am away from you, so that when I come, I may not have to be severe in using the authority that the Lord has given me for building up and not for tearing down.

11 Finally, brothers and sisters, farewell. Put things in order, listen to my appeal, agree with one another, live in peace; and the God of love and peace will be with you. 12 Greet one another with a holy kiss. All the saints greet you.

13 The grace of the Lord Jesus Christ, the love of God, and the communion of the Holy Spirit be with all of you.

13

| | | |
|---|---|---|
| *Monday, May 22* | 2 Corinthians 10:1-11 | *Paul Defends His Ministry* |
| *Tuesday, May 23* | 2 Corinthians 10:12-18 | *If You Boast, Boast in the Lord* |
| *Wednesday, May 24* | 2 Corinthians 11:1-15 | *Paul and the False Apostles* |
| *Thursday, May 25* | 2 Corinthians 11:16-29 | *Paul's Sufferings as an Apostle* |
| *Friday, May 26* | 2 Corinthians 12:1-10 | *Paul's Visions and Revelations* |
| *Saturday, May 27* | 2 Corinthians 12:11-21 | *Paul's Concern for the Corinthian Christians* |
| *Sunday, May 28* | 2 Corinthians 13:1-13 | *Live in Faith: Christ Is in You* |

## BACKGROUND

Paul planned to visit the believers in Corinth. But he was concerned that their sinfulness would lead to his and their embarrassment when he arrived in the city (12:20). The problems that he listed describe a congregation at war with itself. Most of them were sins the apostle had dealt with in his first letter to them.

That some of the people in the church had not repented of their wrongdoing would be a grave disappointment to Paul, for he had invested much time and effort in the church there. Yet the apostle unveiled his heart as he continued to reach out to the Corinthian believers, asking them to make things right with the Lord.

The renewal (or continuance) of disunity in the congregation at Corinth may have been the result of the intrusion of false apostles. Their erroneous teaching could have easily created the disorderly strife that Paul detailed in his letter. The apostle feared more than just finding the church in a state of disunity and division. Though he wanted to feel pride at the progress of his converts, he stated that he also was concerned about being humiliated by their ungodly practices (12:21). His disgrace from their unwillingness to repent would be a humbling experience that he preferred to avoid. So for the sake of their future time together, if for nothing else, the apostle asked those still engaged in sinful behavior to repent.

Paul felt genuine grief over those who continued to refuse his call to holiness. Apparently some of the Corinthian believers continued the same immoral practices they had participated in before they were converted. If they refused to repent, the apostle promised he would have to deal severely with them when he arrived in the city.

## NOTES ON THE PRINTED TEXT

In Deuteronomy 19:15, Moses prescribed that judicial cases not be decided on the basis of one witness, but that judges depend on the testimony of *two or three witnesses* before convicting anyone of a crime. In 2 Corinthians 13:1, Paul quoted this law. He meant that in dealing with the unrepentant people on his third visit, he would not rely on just one witness. There were an adequate number of people to confirm the offense before any discipline would be administered in the church.

Paul demonstrated to his readers the seriousness of his intentions. During his *second visit* (13:2), he had warned those who persisted in sin that he would deal severely with them unless they repented. He now wrote that on his third visit he would not spare these individuals; they would receive the discipline they deserved.

Paul took the reason for his impending stern behavior from the mouths of his opponents. Since they demanded proof of his apostolic authority, he would show it to them in the forcefulness of his corrective action. While Paul's opponents were seemingly unaffected by Christ's gentleness and meekness (see 10:1), they were impressed by displays of power. They had criticized the apostle's Christlike gentleness. Now they were about to come face-to-face with his Christlike power (13:3).

Paul described how both weakness and power worked in the life of Christ. When Jesus hung on the cross, it appeared that His life had ended in failure and futility. But the Cross, which seemed to epitomize weakness, became the focus of God's power, and Jesus' sacrifice served to reconcile humanity to God. The Resurrection further demonstrated the great might of the Lord, who is able to give new life to His people. The same weakness and power that worked in Jesus also operated through the life of Paul. If those at Corinth who persisted in sin did not repent, they would see that power demonstrated with force in the apostle's discipline (13:4).

Paul exhorted the Corinthians to examine and test themselves. Were they still Christians? Were they still obedient and trusting? He believed that they were, for he reminded them that Christ was with them. *Examine yourselves to see whether you are living in the faith. Test yourselves. Do you not realize that Jesus Christ is in you?—unless, indeed you fail to meet the test!* (13:5). If the Corinthians' self-examination indicated that they were not holding the faith, then Paul's efforts were a failure. Paul, though, was confident that they were faithful and that his ministry would be affirmed. *I hope you will find out that we have not failed* (13:6).

Paul prayed that the Corinthians would not need to be disciplined, but that they would do what was right. In this case, he wanted the offenders to repent of their sin. His ultimate goal was the spiritual well-being of his readers, not the vindication of his apostolic authority through the implementation of church discipline (13:7).

If Paul got to Corinth and found everything in order, there would be no need for him to exert his authority. Such a demonstration when the truth had already been established would not make sense (13:8). Though Paul was eager to vindicate himself, he would do it only if the situation demanded it. But it would be pointless if the offenders had turned back to the Lord.

Paul said that he would rejoice at the opportunity to be weak again in Corinth, for that would mean that the believers were strong. The strength of his readers would consist of repentance, moral goodness, and unity (13:9). The apostle hoped that by writing forcefully he would not have to deal forcefully with the Corinthians when he arrived in the city. His consistent purpose, whether he was absent or present, was to see his spiritual children grow in the Lord. The apostle's desire was not to be drawn into a power struggle with his adversaries. His prayerful concern was only for the edification of the church (13:10).

Paul closed his letter by giving the Corinthians a final encouragement to display the type of character that results from God's work in their lives. He urged them to strive to restore and maintain the unity of the church. Doing so would not only indicate the working of the Spirit in their lives, but also would lead to an enjoyable visit by the apostle (13:11).

After praying that *the God of love and peace will be with you* (13:11), Paul urged his readers to greet one another with a *holy kiss* (13:12). This was intended as a way to encourage harmony within the congregation. Paul also sent the greetings of *all the saints*, which referred to the Christians he was visiting at the time of writing. The apostle then prayed for the unity of the church, this time by appealing to the unity of the Trinity (13:13). Paul was confident that because of the grace of Christ, the love of the Father, and the fellowship of the Spirit, the church's best days still lay ahead.

## SUGGESTIONS TO TEACHERS

Have you ever felt ready to quit the church, or have you ever fantasized about trying to find a "perfect" congregation? Chances are that you and some of the members in your class have at least felt upset over what's going on in your church from time to time. It's not unusual to have fleeting thoughts of giving up on those who seem so difficult to live with in the community of faith! This week's lesson should resonate with you and your students in a meaningful way.

**1. STERN MEASURES.** Note Paul's emphasis on having an adequate number of witnesses to confirm the sinful behavior of an unrepentant believer before church discipline is enacted. In other words, don't rely on gossip, don't listen to rumors, and don't evaluate someone based on hearsay. If the persistent conduct of a church member is perceived to be harmful to the life of the congregation, have responsible, trusted leaders hear the testimony of several reliable persons. Also, handle criticism and accusations in a calm and reasonable manner.

**2. STRONG MASTER.** Though Paul had to endure unfair and false charges, he was gentle and forgiving toward his accusers. Point out to your students that gentleness and forgiveness must never be construed to mean weakness or naïveté. Christ's mercy is awesome in its ability to bring unity and harmony!

**3. SALVATION-MINDED.** *Examine yourselves* (13:5) Paul told the readers. In other words, the apostle urged them to test themselves to prove that they were in the faith. The apostle assumed that they would pass the test, and that in doing so they would prove that Christ lived in their hearts.

**4. SERENE MODEL.** What does it mean to *live in peace* (13:11)? Discuss the implications of this with the class members. How might you, they, and the rest of your church discover more fully God's *love and peace*?

| | |
|---|---|
| **FOR ADULTS** | ■ TOPIC: From Confrontation to Growth<br>■ QUESTIONS: 1. What warning did Paul issue to the members of the church at Corinth? 2. What was Paul's prayer for the Corinthian |

believers? 3. In what ways can you promote unity and Christlikeness among the members of your church? 4. Why do you think it is sometimes difficult to repent of persistent sins? 5. What are the foremost goals that your church seeks to achieve when it disciplines an unrepentant member of the congregation?

■ **ILLUSTRATIONS:**

**Imitation Faith.** Tourists throughout the years have visited the famous Acropolis, the ancient hilltop religious citadel in Athens. Thousands of people from all over the world have picked up marble rocks as souvenirs. So why hasn't the supply of rocks been exhausted over the years? Every few weeks a truckload of marble chunks from a quarry miles away is scattered around the Acropolis area. So tourists go home ecstatic with what they think are authentic pieces of ancient history.

We can be fooled by other kinds of imitations. Religious language and music, religious objects and services may woo us into imagining that we are experiencing a firsthand relationship with God when in reality we are simply going through empty routines. The possibility of pious deception should prompt some soul-searching. Our religous practices may be only imitations of the true heartfelt faith that the Lord wants from those who love Him.

**Was It You?**

• Did you speak to a new couple outside the church one recent Sunday morning, greeting them cheerily with "Good morning! I'm glad to see you today!"?

• Were you the greeter who welcomed the new couple with a firm handshake and a warm smile?

• Were you the usher who helped the new couple feel comfortable in choosing a place to sit?

• Were you the "pew neighbor" who learned the names of the new couple and made a point of introducing them after the service?

• Did you notice the new couple standing alone in Coffee Hour and take the lead in meeting them?

• Were you the person who made a follow-up visit and told the new couple about your church with enthusiasm?

• Did you invite the new couple to accompany you to a special event?

• Were you the one? If you were, you have helped you church build a reputation as a friendly congregation. (Adapted from the Paramount Baptist Church, Amarillo, Texas.)

**Definition of a Church.** Every congregation has some people whose lives do not come up to the moral standards that you expect. Every church also has at least a couple of members who seem to cause you or others problems at times. You may resent them because they seem to rebel against the authority of Christ. You may feel that you'd like to throw them out, or perhaps to walk away from the church. Here is where Parker Palmer has a marvelous definition of the church that you need to hear: It's "that place where the person you least want to live with always lives" *(The Company of Strangers)*. The confrontation that you may have might lead to spiritual growth for both you and the other person, especially when Christ's presence is known in your congregation.

**FOR YOUTH**

■ TOPIC: Growth from Confrontation

■ QUESTIONS: 1. How would Paul demonstrate the power of Christ to the unrepentant members of the Corinthian church? 2. What sort of visit did Paul want to have with the Corinthian believers when he saw them again? 3. How can God use your weaknesses, tragedies, and afflictions for His glory? 4. Why do you think it is always best to repent of persistent sin in your life? 5. How is your church strengthened when your fellow believers seek to promote unity and harmony among themselves?

■ **ILLUSTRATIONS:**

**Changed History.** *Braveheart* is a film about the life of William Wallace, the Scottish patriot who led his fellow citizens' insurrection against Edward I of England. Betrayed to Edward at Glasgow in 1305, Wallace was executed. His cries of freedom for Scotland motivated Robert the Bruce to continue the rebellion and eventually win Scotland's independence. Wallace's death changed the course of his nation's history.

Christ's death profoundly changed all of history and made it possible for each of us to be freed from sin. Consider the power of the crucified Christ. What seemed weak by human standards (namely, the death of Jesus on a cross) became the means for God's great power being demonstrated in the lives of believers.

**Intervened.** On July 29, 1945, the unescorted heavy cruiser, *Indianapolis,* was sailing across the Pacific from Guam to the Philippines, having just delivered the atomic bomb. It was torpedoed by a Japanese submarine and sank in 12 minutes.

Eight hundred men scrambled into the water as the distress signal was radioed. No one heard the calls for help and due to secrecy and a bureaucratic lapse, no one listed the ship as overdue. By August 2, only 320 men were left as a result of dehydration and shark attacks.

Adrian Marks, while flying his PBY5A Catalina, known as *Dumbo,* was summoned from Releliu when a flier spotted men in the water at 10 A.M. on August 2. Marks dropped three life rafts, but one broke when it hit the water. As the day dragged on, he grew more concerned for the survivors. Regulations forbade an open-sea landing. The seaplane was designed only for calm water landings, and the sea was high that day. Still, Marks polled the crew about whether they should try the dangerous landing. They all agreed with him to set the plane down.

The plane bounced 15 feet in the air as it hit the waves but seemed only slightly damaged. Marks and his crew picked up survivors, packing them two and three to a bunk and three deep in all the compartments. Shutting off the engines, men climbed onto the wings. Throughout the windy night men were cared for as best as possible. Finally the destroyer, *Cecil J. Doyle* arrived the following day. Mark's plane, being too damaged to fly, was sunk by the *Doyle.*

Marks knew what it meant to take action and intervene in a situation that could not be ignored. Paul also knew the risk of intervening. He also faced a situation that could not be ignored. Like Marks, Paul got involved, and his efforts helped to restore order and love to the Corinthian church.

**Now a Sour Sound.** In 1938, the von Trapp family fled Austria, for World War II was about to break out. (This was the family immortalized in the musical *The Sound of Music*). The family settled in the hills of Stowe, Vermont, and built an Austrian style lodge. When the lodge burned in 1980, it was rebuilt as a 93-room hotel. Later, 100 time-share units were constructed and an entire development of ski and walking trails were built. The family's finances, which had been incorporated since 1962 in the Trapp Family Lodge, grew as the 2200 acre resort flourished and royalties rolled in from *The Sound of Music*.

When Maria von Trapp died in 1987, her youngest son, Johannes, became president of the corporation. Discord began as factions within the family argued. A 1993 "blowup" resulted in Johannes being ousted as president. He won back control a year later and reorganized the company. His sister and the children of two brothers objected and cashed in their shares. The family business paid them each $2.5 million. They challenged, arguing that they were entitled to more. The Lamoille County Superior Court agreed and ordered the corporation to pay each 3 million in May, 1997. Johannes refused and appealed the verdict.

Like families, congregations sometimes fight. Discord causes resentments and accusations, which tear down, rather than build up, the congregation.

# NEW LIFE IN CHRIST

# LIVING IS CHRIST

**BACKGROUND SCRIPTURE:** Philippians 1:12-30
**DEVOTIONAL READING:** 1 Peter 1:3-9

**KEY VERSE:** For to me, living is Christ and dying is gain. Philippians 1:21.

*KING JAMES VERSION*

PHILIPPIANS 1:12 But I would ye should understand, brethren, that the things which happened unto me have fallen out rather unto the furtherance of the gospel;

13 So that my bonds in Christ are manifest in all the palace, and in all other places;

14 And many of the brethren in the Lord, waxing confident by my bonds, are much more bold to speak the word without fear.

15 Some indeed preach Christ even of envy and strife; and some also of good will:

16 The one preach Christ of contention, not sincerely, supposing to add affliction to my bonds:

17 But the other of love, knowing that I am set for the defence of the gospel.

18 What then? notwithstanding, every way, whether in pretence, or in truth, Christ is preached; and I therein do rejoice, yea, and will rejoice.

19 For I know that this shall turn to my salvation through your prayer, and the supply of the Spirit of Jesus Christ,

20 According to my earnest expectation and my hope, that in nothing I shall be ashamed, but that with all boldness, as always, so now also Christ shall be magnified in my body, whether it be by life, or by death.

21 For to me to live is Christ, and to die is gain.

22 But if I live in the flesh, this is the fruit of my labour: yet what I shall choose I wot not.

23 For I am in a strait betwixt two, having a desire to depart, and to be with Christ; which is far better:

24 Nevertheless to abide in the flesh is more needful for you.

25 And having this confidence, I know that I shall abide and continue with you all for your furtherance and joy of faith;

26 That your rejoicing may be more abundant in Jesus Christ for me by my coming to you again.

*NEW REVISED STANDARD VERSION*

PHILIPPIANS 1:12 I want you to know, beloved, that what has happened to me has actually helped to spread the gospel, 13 so that it has become known throughout the whole imperial guard and to everyone else that my imprisonment is for Christ; 14 and most of the brothers and sisters, having been made confident in the Lord by my imprisonment, dare to speak the word with greater boldness and without fear.

15 Some proclaim Christ from envy and rivalry, but others from goodwill. 16 These proclaim Christ out of love, knowing that I have been put here for the defense of the gospel; 17 the others proclaim Christ out of selfish ambition, not sincerely but intending to increase my suffering in my imprisonment. 18 What does it matter? Just this, that Christ is proclaimed in every way, whether out of false motives or true; and in that I rejoice.

Yes, and I will continue to rejoice, 19 for I know that through your prayers and the help of the Spirit of Jesus Christ this will turn out for my deliverance. 20 It is my eager expectation and hope that I will not be put to shame in any way, but that by my speaking with all boldness, Christ will be exalted now as always in my body, whether by life or by death. 21 For to me, living is Christ and dying is gain. 22 If I am to live in the flesh, that means fruitful labor for me; and I do not know which I prefer. 23 I am hard pressed between the two: my desire is to depart and be with Christ, for that is far better; 24 but to remain in the flesh is more necessary for you. 25 Since I am convinced of this, I know that I will remain and continue with all of you for your progress and joy in faith, 26 so that I may share abundantly in your boasting in Christ Jesus when I come to you again.

## BACKGROUND

Some of the most influential pieces of literature have been written by prisoners. For example, John Bunyan produced the classic *Pilgrim's Progress* during his 12 years in the Bedford dungeon. Dietrich Bonhoeffer smuggled out his famous *Letters and Papers from Prison* before his execution by the Nazis. Martin Luther King, Jr.'s *Letter from the Birmingham Jail* was influential in galvanizing the civil rights movement in America. The apostle Paul was the spiritual forerunner of those producing prison literature. At least four of the great evangelist-missionary's letters were issued during his first Roman imprisonment: Philippians, Ephesians, Colossians, and Philemon.

The Book of Acts tells us how Paul ended up under house arrest in Rome (21:1—28:31). Despite the advice of other Christians, Paul went to Jerusalem to deliver in person the special offering he had collected from Gentile congregations that he had established. The gift was intended to help destitute believers in the Holy City. Paul had been regarded with suspicion by many Jewish Christians there who clung to their ancient religious traditions. The relief offering demonstrated the love of Gentile Christians for their fellow Jewish believers. While in Jerusalem, Paul decided to visit the temple and worship, for he had never renounced his Jewish heritage. Perhaps he also wanted to show Jewish Christians who still prayed in the temple courts that he continued to feel a kinship with them.

Religious fanatics who frequented the temple had never forgotten or forgiven Paul for becoming a believer in Jesus and leading Jews to faith in Him. They had threatened the apostle and tried to undermine his evangelistic efforts throughout his ministry. When some of them saw him in the temple, they started a riot by accusing Paul of taking a Gentile into a forbidden area of the sanctuary.

A garrison of Roman soldiers took Paul into protective custody. He was later relocated to governmental headquarters in Caesarea for his own safety. The Roman governor heard the charges (all false) against Paul, and continued to hold him under arrest. Two years later, when a new governor was appointed, he held another hearing concerning Paul. The apostle, perhaps weary of the way his case had dragged on and confident of his rights as a Roman citizen, decided to appeal directly to the emperor in Rome. He thus was taken to the capital of the empire, and it is from there that he wrote a letter to the believers in Philippi.

# NOTES ON THE PRINTED TEXT

After receiving the disturbing news of Paul's arrest, the Philippians had inquired about his welfare. Knowing the unpleasant conditions and fearing that judgment was imminent, they expected the worst. Paul wrote to offer reassurance, and noted that the Gospel actually had been advanced. *I want you to know, beloved, that what has happened to me has actually helped to spread the gospel, so that it has become known throughout the whole imperial guard and to everyone else that my imprisonment is for Christ* (1:12-13). Paul had taken the opportunity to witness to the elite group of soldiers stationed in the city and who were required to guard him. These soldiers undoubtedly had spoken with their comrades about Paul and the Gospel he proclaimed.

Other Christians, encouraged by the apostle's example, became more bold in their efforts to evangelize the lost. *And most of the brothers and sisters, having been made confident in the Lord by my imprisonment, dare to speak the word with greater boldness and without fear* (1:14).

Paul also rejoiced that his rivals were confidently preaching. His imprisonment had given them the opportunity to promote themselves. Paul, though, was not upset, for he took comfort in knowing that Christ was being preached. *Some proclaim Christ from envy and rivalry, but others from goodwill. These proclaim Christ out of love, knowing that I have been put here for the defense of the gospel; the others proclaim Christ out of selfish ambition, not sincerely but intending to increase my suffering in my imprisonment. What does it matter? Just this, that Christ is proclaimed in every way, whether out of false motives or true; and in that I rejoice* (1:15-18).

Though the possibility of being executed was real, Paul remained confident in the Lord. The apostle's faith was sustained by the Philippians' prayers and Christ's support. *Yes, and I will continue to rejoice, for I know that through your prayers and the help of the Spirit of Jesus Christ this will turn out for my deliverance* (1:18-19). Whatever Rome's judgment, Paul hoped that his words and conduct would honor Christ. The apostle wanted to act courageously and boldly rather than cowardly. *It is my eager expectation and hope that I will not be put to shame in any way, but that by my speaking with all boldness, Christ will be exalted now as always in my body, whether by life or by death* (1:20).

Paul shared his thoughts with the believers in Philippi. It was hard for the apostle to decide whether he preferred to live or die. Living gave him the option to continue sharing Christ with the unsaved. Dying, though, released him from the physical and mental abuse of prison and allowed him to be with his Lord in heaven. *For to me, living is Christ and dying is gain. If I am to live in the flesh, that means fruitful labor for me; and I do not know which I prefer. I am hard pressed between the two: my desire is to depart and be with Christ, for that is far better; but to remain in the flesh is more necessary for you* (1:21-24). Paul's personal desire was death, though he recognized the ongoing need of the Philippians.

Paul reached a conclusion about the matter. He sensed that the Lord wanted him to continue laboring with the Philippians. There was no doubt or thought of suicide, only a committed pastor and preacher renewing his pledge to serve his fellow believers. *Since I am convinced of this, I know that I will remain and continue with all of you for your progress and joy in faith, so that I may share abundantly in your boasting in Christ Jesus when I come to you again* (1:25-26).

## SUGGESTIONS TO TEACHERS

How do you keep your faith when you're confined to a wheelchair, or facing life without your spouse after 30 years together, or reading still another letter rejecting your application for a job after being downsized and out of work for 18 months? Perhaps many in your class are healthy, happy, and comfortable, but eventually you and they will encounter times of hardship and sadness. The question will be this: How does a Christian handle these times? This week's lesson from Philippians will help prepare you and your class for these eventualities.

**1. PURPOSE IN IMPRISONMENT.** Paul's long stay in Caesarea and then in Rome must have seemed unjust and senseless. His plans to continue evangelizing the lost were thwarted. And there seemed to be no resolution or end to his incarceration. But Paul found a purpose even in the midst of these unfortunate circumstances. He preached to his guards, and he kept in touch with different churches by writing letters to them. Paul could testify that even in the poorest of situations God provided opportunities for him to serve and witness!

**2. PROCLAMATION OF CHRIST.** Even in prison cells or under house arrest, Paul discovered that he could proclaim the good news of Jesus Christ. Likewise, so may we find ways of sharing our faith in the midst of adverse circumstances. A physical ailment or handicap need not deter believers from demonstrating their faith, nor should any apparent "impossible" situation prevent them from showing Christ by word and example.

**3. PLEASURE IN HONORING CHRIST**. Paul was not sure whether he would win a release from the emperor or languish for years in prison. He was also uncertain about whether he would escape execution at the hands of Nero, the capricious ruler of the Roman Empire who eventually would show his disdain for Christians. Despite these ambiguities, Paul faced the future with equanimity, confident that his life was in the Lord's hands regardless of what might happen to him. Encourage your class members to consider how such a sense of calm and trust is possible for believers in turmoil.

**4. POSSIBILITY OF A VISIT.** If released from prison, Paul planned to visit the Philippian congregation. In the meantime, he intended to make every effort to proclaim Christ. The apostle knew that others not in prison were proclaiming Christ *from envy and rivalry* (1:15). But Paul wasn't bothered as long as Christ was being preached. The apostle took delight in realizing that the Gospel was being announced regardless of the motives of certain preachers. Spend a few moments discussing with your students the negative feelings some may have about pastors or churches who evangelize in ways that seem strange or improper.

---

| **FOR ADULTS** | ■ TOPIC: Living Is Christ<br>■ QUESTIONS: 1. What was it like for Paul under house arrest in Rome? 2. What attitude did Paul maintain while imprisoned in the |

capital of the empire? 3. Regardless of our circumstances, what constructive things can we do to serve the Lord? 4. How can we maintain an attitude of joy even when life seems dismal? 5. How can we be an encouragement to others during our times of difficulty?

---

■ **ILLUSTRATIONS:**

**Commitment.** In the Spring 1998 issue of *Leadership*, W. Frank Harrington related the story of three military recruiters who showed up to address a group of high school seniors. Each recruiter—representing the U.S. Army, Navy, and Marine Corps—was to have 15 minutes.

The Army and Navy recruiters took more time than they were allotted, so when it came time for the Marine to speak, he had just two minutes. He walked up and stood silent for a full sixty seconds, which was half of his time. Then he said this: "I doubt whether there are two or three of you in this room who could even cut it in the Marine Corps. But I want to see those two or three immediately in the dining hall when we are dismissed." The recruiter then turned and sat down. When he arrived in the dining hall, there was a crowd of students interested in learning more about the Marines.

The recruiter knew that commitment comes from appealing to the heroic dimension in every heart. It's that same type of heroism and commitment that was present in Paul's life. It also should be present in the life of every believer.

**Realistic Writings.** During the early days of World War II, the German Bishop of Hanover, Hans Lillje, was arrested and sentenced to solitary confinement in his house for his outspoken views against Hitler. A cordon of the Gestapo moved into the house, and Lillje's wife was moved to another location. The Gestapo was there to make sure that Lillje would not escape and ensure that no one brought aid to him.

The Bishop carried on his prayers and devotions as usual, and as a result converted the Gestapo agents. This crew was quickly replaced by another group, and the same thing happened, until Lillje was thrown into prison. Meanwhile, Lillje wrote frequently to his wife, and often quoted statements from the Bible. At first, these Scripture quotations were permitted, but later they were strictly censored on the grounds of being "too realistic," according to the Nazi authorities.

Bishop Lillje's experiences during the horrific days of the Nazi regime were reminiscent of Paul's time in the Philippi jail.

**Craving for More.** Ours is a culture that thrives and prospers on learned discontent. Relentless advertising campaigns on television and in the print media drive home the message that we cannot be satisfied with life until we buy that new car, have that svelte figure, and live in that prestigious neighborhood. Of course, once we have these things, there's always something else that lures us into discontentment. Having traded in the Chevy for the Volvo, we now crave the Lexus.

In his 1995 book entitled *How to Want What You Have*, psychologist Timothy Miller describes the syndrome as the insatiable craving for "More"—with a capital "M." The desire for more, he says, robs people of their satisfaction with what they have. Miller notes how some of his wealthy, successful patients suffer because no matter how high the economic rung they climb, they only see others still above them, not how far they've come. To help his distressed patients, Miller prescribes gratitude (among other things). He also challenges them to focus on what they have instead of what they may want but don't have.

It's no accident that this kind of advice is precisely what monks and mystics in the Christian tradition talk about as the liberation that comes from embracing poverty. By renouncing worldly goods, believers find the freedom to appreciate the many simple blessings that life has to offer. This reminds us that if our needs for food, shelter, and companionship are met, the rest is a bonanza (*Cape Cod Times,* Thursday, November 27, 1997).

**FOR YOUTH**

■ TOPIC: Hope during Hardship

■ QUESTIONS: 1. What brought about Paul's imprisonment in Rome? 2. What was Paul's motive in proclaiming the Gospel? 3. Why is God pleased when we share our faith with the unsaved? 4. How is it possible for us to maintain an attitude of hope even in seemingly hopeless circumstances? 5. How do you think God can use our trials to bring glory to His name?

■ **ILLUSTRATIONS:**

**Imprisoned Innocent.** Gordon J. Ragan, 22, languished for almost four years in a Pennsylvania prison, convicted of raping the wife of a University of Pennsylvania professor. However, he was innocent. He had been wrongly convicted of another person's crime. His innocence was discovered when another man admitted to committing the crime. The two men were so much alike that the victim and the two men's relatives had trouble telling them apart. Here was a young man who knew that he was innocent and had been unjustly imprisoned.

Throughout history, innocent people have been imprisoned. Paul was one of those people. Like Ragan, he could only hope that he would be freed. Yet Paul was aware that God was with him, regardless of whether he was in prison or free.

**Prayers at Death.** On April 26, 1998, John Gillette, a teacher at James W. Parker Middle School in Edinboro, Pennsylvania, was shot and killed by an eighth grader at the annual middle school graduation dance. Two days later, when the school reopened, 50 counselors were on hand to help students. All knew that Gillette, one of the most popular teachers, would never return. Students really did not know what to say and admitted this to others. Some simply asked for prayers.

These students were much like the Philippians. Because they knew that death would separate them from Paul, they also prayed for God's gracious intervention in his life. They were confident that the Lord would hear their prayers.

**Cornbread to Cadillacs.** She was a bride at 17 and a mother by 18. She stretched grocery money by living on red beans, rice, an occasional ham hock, and hot water cornbread. Divorced with two children, she dreamed of a car with air conditioning to dispel the heat of the hot Louisiana sun, especially as she watched her children suffer through the summers in the old red Ford.

Eventually Gayle Gaston moved from poverty to prosperity. She overcame adversity by selling Mary Kay Cosmetics and working her way up to eventually become the Executive Senior National Sales Director for the company. As Gaston speaks and motivates large numbers of her sales people, she often tells them about her initial misfortunes. She does this to show how these adversities helped her to grow as a person. In a similar manner, Paul never gave in to despair but used his trials to mature as a Christian and strengthen his resolve to serve the Lord.

# HAVING THE MIND OF CHRIST 2

**BACKGROUND SCRIPTURE:** Philippians 2:1-18
**DEVOTIONAL READING:** 2 Peter 3:8-18

**KEY VERSE:** Let the same mind be in you that was in Christ Jesus. Philippians 2:5.

## KING JAMES VERSION

PHILIPPIANS 2:1 If there be therefore any consolation in Christ, if any comfort of love, if any fellowship of the Spirit, if any bowels and mercies,

2 Fulfil ye my joy, that ye be likeminded, having the same love, being of one accord, of one mind.

3 Let nothing be done through strife or vainglory; but in lowliness of mind let each esteem other better than themselves.

4 Look not every man on his own things, but every man also on the things of others.

5 Let this mind be in you, which was also in Christ Jesus:

6 Who, being in the form of God, thought it not robbery to be equal with God:

7 But made himself of no reputation, and took upon him the form of a servant, and was made in the likeness of men:

8 And being found in fashion as a man, he humbled himself, and became obedient unto death, even the death of the cross.

9 Wherefore God also hath highly exalted him, and given him a name which is above every name:

10 That at the name of Jesus every knee should bow, of things in heaven, and things in earth, and things under the earth;

11 And that every tongue should confess that Jesus Christ is Lord, to the glory of God the Father.

12 Wherefore, my beloved, as ye have always obeyed, not as in my presence only, but now much more in my absence, work out your own salvation with fear and trembling.

13 For it is God which worketh in you both to will and to do of his good pleasure.

## NEW REVISED STANDARD VERSION

PHILIPPIANS 2:1 If then there is any encouragement in Christ, any consolation from love, any sharing in the Spirit, any compassion and sympathy, 2 make my joy complete: be of the same mind, having the same love, being in full accord and of one mind. 3 Do nothing from selfish ambition or conceit, but in humility regard others as better than yourselves. 4 Let each of you look not to your own interests, but to the interests of others. 5 Let the same mind be in you that was in Christ Jesus,

6 who, though he was in the form of God,
   did not regard equality with God
   as something to be exploited,
7 but emptied himself,
   taking the form of a slave,
   being born in human likeness.
And being found in human form,
8  he humbled himself
   and became obedient to the point of death—
   even death on a cross.
9 Therefore God also highly exalted him
   and gave him the name
   that is above every name,
10 so that at the name of Jesus
   every knee should bend,
   in heaven and on earth and under the earth,
11 and every tongue should confess
   that Jesus Christ is Lord,
   to the glory of God the Father.

12 Therefore, my beloved, just as you have always obeyed me, not only in my presence, but much more now in my absence, work out your own salvation with fear and trembling; 13 for it is God who is at work in you, enabling you both to will and to work for his good pleasure.

| | | |
|---|---|---|
| *Monday, June 5* | Philippians 2:1-11 | *Imitate Christ's Humility in Your Lives* |
| *Tuesday, June 6* | Philippians 2:12-18 | *Rejoice in One Another's Faithfulness* |
| *Wednesday, June 7* | Philippians 2:19-24 | *Timothy, a Faithful Servant of Christ* |
| *Thursday, June 8* | Philippians 2:25-30 | *Welcome Epaphroditus in Christ* |
| *Friday, June 9* | 1 Peter 3:8-12 | *Repay Evil with a Blessing* |
| *Saturday, June 10* | 1 Peter 3:13-22 | *Suffering for Doing Right* |
| *Sunday, June 11* | 2 Peter 1:1-11 | *You Are Participants in God's Blessings* |

## BACKGROUND

Like every congregation, the members of the church at Philippi sometimes showed a less-than-saintly side. Personal rivalries and human vanity cropped up. Relationships within the fellowship were not always as harmonious as they should have been. From this we see that the Philippians' biggest battle was not with their external circumstances but with those internal attitudes that can destroy unity.

One of the purposes in Paul's writing this letter was to remind the Philippian believers of what God had called them to be. The apostle told them that Jesus Christ was to be the model for everything they did, and that the Savior's sacrificial death on the cross was the key to understanding their calling. Just as Christ had willingly forsaken all dignity, all standing, all titles, and all rights in order to bring new life to humankind, so faithful followers were meant to live humbly and sacrificially for others.

To illustrate the principle of humility, Paul wrote a memorable piece about the incarnation of Christ (Phil. 2:6-11). Most scholars think that these verses were sung as a hymn in the early church. Whether Paul was the author or whether he was quoting from a worship song, this section contains magnificent poetry exalting the Savior. This hymn eloquently expresses the praise and gratitude every believer should feel toward Christ. The words echo the theme of the suffering Servant of the Lord, which is recorded in Isaiah 52—53. In this portion of Scripture we learn that the Servant willingly accepted pain and humiliation in obedience to the Lord. Christ's servanthood and sacrificial death accord Him the highest honor and praise.

## NOTES ON THE PRINTED TEXT

Disunity and discord threatened the Philippian church. Whether it was a result of factions involving two Christian women (Euodia and Syntyche; 4:2), or legalists who sought to impose the Mosaic law on Gentile believers, or simply dissatisfied people who felt Paul showed favoritism, the apostle was concerned. He said that if the Philippians truly wanted to please the Lord, they had to become a loving and harmonious fellowship bound together by God's Spirit. Paul did not urge them to agree on everything, but to develop a common attitude of faith, hope, and love. *If then there is any encouragement in Christ, any consolation from love, any sharing in the Spirit, any compassion and sympathy, make my joy complete: be of the same mind, having the same love, being in full accord and of one mind* (2:1-2).

Paul also mentioned conduct that the Philippians were to avoid. *Do nothing from selfish ambition or conceit, but in humility regard others as better than yourselves. Let each of you look not to your own interests, but to the interests of others* (2:3-4). Selfishness, conceit, and self-interest were to have no place in the Christian community. Rather, the Philippians were to adopt dignity, respect, and sacrificial service to others. The believers' goal in life was to become more like Christ. For example, they were to adopt His attitude of humility (2:5).

To clarify this point, Paul inserted a Christian hymn, which can be divided into three parts. Part one deals with Christ before His incarnation. We learn that Jesus was fully God and could have continued to retain all His rights, privileges, and honor as God the Son in heaven. *Who, though he was in the form of God, did not regard equality with God as something to be exploited* (2:6).

Part two of the hymn stresses Christ's servant-like existence and His obedience to the Father, even to the point of death. We learn that Jesus voluntarily set aside His heavenly privileges by entering our world as a human being and dying on the cross for our sins. *But emptied himself, taking the form of a slave, being born in human likeness. And being found in human form, he humbled himself and became obedient to the point of death—even death on a cross* (2:7-8).

Part three of the hymn emphasizes the Father's exaltation of His Son. The risen Christ received back His glory as the Lord of the universe. Paul said that one day Jesus' sovereignty will be acknowledged by everyone. *Therefore God also highly exalted him and gave him the name that is above every name, so that at the name of Jesus every knee should bend, in heaven and on earth and under the earth, and every tongue should confess that Jesus Christ is Lord, to the glory of God the Father* (2:9-11).

In light of these sublime truths, Paul appealed to the Philippians for obedience. He urged them to give full expression to their salvation through spiritual growth and development Paul promised that God would enable them to become more holy. *Therefore, my beloved, just as you have always obeyed me, not only in my presence, but much more now in my absence, work out your own salvation with fear and trembling; for it is God who is at work in you, enabling you both to will and to work for his good pleasure* (2:12-13).

## SUGGESTIONS TO TEACHERS

Nearly every week, another story of conflict within the Christian community emerges. Every religious tradition has been wracked with controversy, whether over questionable marriages, objectionable ordinations, charges of heresy, or differences in ideology. Likewise, multitudes of congregations are experiencing disagreements among members, ranging from anger over actions by the church officers to personal squabbles. Leaders in the congregation often spend lots of time trying to keep things patched together. Instead of attracting new members, many churches are seen as unattractive battlegrounds.

This week's lesson is not meant to be a time for class members to ventilate their frustrations. After all, they most likely already know the areas of discord in your church. Instead, the students need to learn afresh what it means to have a humble, Christlike attitude. A verse-by-verse study of this lesson's Scripture text will help greatly.

**1. MATURITY IN CARING.** Look carefully at Philippians 2:3, where Paul admonishes us to never act from *selfish ambition or conceit.* Isn't this the root of much of the conflict in every group, including the church? Discuss what it means to practice true humility and have a concern for the interests of others. Encourage the members of your class to consider when it is hardest for them to be humble, and to mentally note the names of those whom they find the hardest to love.

**2. MOTIVATION FOR SERVING.** The mind of Christ is what drives a believer's thinking and acting. This may be explained better to your students in the form of a question: "What would Jesus want me to do in this situation?"

**3. MODEL OF HUMILITY.** Devote some time to consider why Jesus humbled Himself, rather than seek glory and power. State that the cross summons Christ's followers to lay aside the prideful ways of the world and to adopt an attitude of humility and sacrifice.

**4. MINDFUL OF CALLING.** *Do all things without murmuring and arguing, so that you may be blameless and innocent, children of God* (2:14-15). Every church member is called to be part of the Lord's spiritual family. The family name and traditions must constantly be honored!

---

**FOR ADULTS**

■ TOPIC: Genuine Humility

■ QUESTIONS: 1. In what way did Jesus demonstrate true humility? 2. How did the Father honor the Son for His willingness to die on the cross for humanity's sin? 3. What encouragement in Christ have you recently experienced? 4. How does God's love, which He has shown to you in Christ, encourage you to be mindful of the needs of others? 5. In what ways has God recently worked in your life to help you become more Christlike?

■ ILLUSTRATIONS:

**True Humility.** Denver Broncos running back Terrell Davis is respected as one of the most self-effacing players in the National Football League (NFL). Unlike many athletes who promote their abilities and exhibit constant conceit, Davis shows true humility. For example, after the Super Bowl of 1998 between the Broncos and the Packers, Davis was named the game's most valuable player. But instead of going to the team party after Denver's victory, Terrell Davis went back to his hotel room so that he could spend time with his family. The next morning, the NFL told Davis that as a result of winning the award of Most Valuable Player, he could choose between two Ford cars as his prize. Davis was shocked. He had no idea that the award meant a car. What did Davis do? He let his brother decide which car to pick, and then Davis let his brother keep the car.

**Pentecost's Promise.** Today the church celebrates Pentecost, remembering the coming of the Holy Spirit to fulfill the promise of Jesus that He would send His power and presence upon *humble* followers. I am reminded of the time when Sir Ernest Shackleton, the explorer, was in the Antarctic. After reaching the South Pole in 1909, Shackleton and his men discovered that the ice was closing in on their ship. The group reached Elephant Island, but Shackleton was forced to order some of the party to remain there while he and a few others made a dash in a small boat to secure another ship. As the weather was worsening, Shackleton told those left on Elephant Island that he would come back for them. Then he sailed off.

After a monumental voyage in a boat, Shackleton procured another vessel and set off to rescue his stranded crew on Elephant Island. He tried several times to get back, but the weather drove him off repeatedly. Determined to rescue his men before the ice closed in again, he finally managed to get his new ship through the treacherous storms to the place where he had left behind many of his crew. To his surprise, he found that the men had the gear packed and were waiting on the beach when he steamed in. When he asked why they were so well prepared for his return, the crew told Lieutenant Shackleton, "When you left, you said that you would return and be with us. We were confident that you would keep your word and return to be with us."

Jesus promised His followers that though He would go away, He would soon send them the Comforter, namely, the Holy Spirit (John 14). At Pentecost, the disciples learned how Jesus fulfilled His promise. The Spirit's coming means that God is still guiding and controlling this world and our lives. Because we remember that Christ is still in charge, we may live with an attitude of humility.

**Vengeful Pride.** Arrogance is the opposite of humility. And a prideful way of living can lead to selfish and sometimes stupid decisions. Frederick W. Woolworth opened the first "Woolworth's 5 and 10 Cent Store" in Lancaster, Pennsylvania, in 1879, and later started a chain of "Five-and-Tens." He was denied a loan in his start-up years by the Metropolitan Life Insurance Company, and he never forgot the slight.

Years later, when he was a multi-millionaire, F. W. Woolworth began building his monument, the Woolworth Building, in New York City. By that time, the Metropolitan Life building was the tallest structure in the world. When the architect asked Woolworth how high he wanted his building to go, the old man bellowed, "Fifty feet higher than the Metropolitan tower!" The Woolworth Building on lower Broadway became the tallest structure for a time, but was later surpassed by others. Ironically, the company that was founded by F. W. Woolworth went bankrupt and the last store closed in New York in 1998.

---

### FOR YOUTH

■ **TOPIC:** Setting Aside Privileges

■ **QUESTIONS:** 1. Why do you think Paul urged the Philippian believers not to do anything from selfish ambition and conceit? 2. To what extent did Jesus humble Himself? 3. What are some ways that you, as a believer, can model the humble attitude of Christ? 4. How can you be an encouragement to your peers to live in a humble, Christlike way? 5. Why is it sometimes hard to put the needs of others first?

■ **ILLUSTRATIONS:**

**Examples.** During the late Medieval times, Francis of Assisi, the Italian monk who lived from 1182–1226, and who eventually became one of the world's best known monks, would send his fellow monks into the world with the statement, "Go everywhere and preach the Gospel. If you have to, use words." This may seem like a strange statement, but Francis knew that the best way to teach was by example. Followers of Christ are to provide a good example by exemplifying their Lord. Paul offered the example of Jesus Himself. What better way to preach the Gospel than to model a pattern of behavior that is based on the work and words of the Lord.

**Whom Do You Trust?** Who are the United States' most trusted professionals? The answer is not your pastor. It is the pharmacist! A 1997 CNN/USA TODAY/Gallup Poll showed that 69 percent of all Americans trusted the high honesty and ethical standards of their pharmacist above everyone else. The second most trusted individual was the local church pastor (listed at 59 percent), who ranked three percentage points ahead of medical doctors.

Local church pastors, as well as all believers, are to have the mind of Christ. All believers are to model principles of behavior consistent with the love and humility of the Savior. If this were to happen more often, I think that we would see a much higher level of trust.

**Followed Example.** The commencement speaker at Susqenita High School, which is located in Duncannon, Pennsylvania, spent the day scraping gum off the hardwood gym floor and then mopping it so that it would be spotless for the graduation exercises. He then returned hours later in a dark blue suit with a red tie and addressed the graduating class. When the speaker finished his address, in which he called for strong values, love for one another, and an ethic of hard work, there were wild cheers and applause.

The speaker was not the traditional teacher or community leader but 61-year-old Carl Rumbaugh, the high school custodian for 24 years. The senior class had selected him as their speaker because he was a mentor who had taken the time to get to know them. He cheered up the students when they were depressed, and spoke to them by name about their hobbies, studies, and problems. Many over the years had sought him out in the storeroom, which is fondly named "Carl's Closet," to speak privately with him. Students left the graduation ceremony promising to follow his principles of behavior in the years ahead.

In a similar manner, Paul called for new principles of behavior among the Christians in the church at Philippi. The apostle wanted them to live in harmony with one another, to heed the teaching of Scripture, and to be concerned for the needs of others. Above all, Paul urged his readers to let the humble example of Christ be reflected in every aspect of their life.

# PRESSING ON IN CHRIST

**BACKGROUND SCRIPTURE:** Philippians 3
**DEVOTIONAL READING:** Hebrews 10:19-25, 32-36

**3**

**KEY VERSE:** I press on toward the goal for the prize of the heavenly call of God in Christ Jesus. Philippians 3:14.

---

*KING JAMES VERSION*

PHILIPPIANS 3:7 But what things were gain to me, those I counted loss for Christ.

8 Yea doubtless, and I count all things but loss for the excellency of the knowledge of Christ Jesus my Lord: for whom I have suffered the loss of all things, and do count them but dung, that I may win Christ,

9 And be found in him, not having mine own righteousness, which is of the law, but that which is through the faith of Christ, the righteousness which is of God by faith:

10 That I may know him, and the power of his resurrection, and the fellowship of his sufferings, being made conformable unto his death;

11 If by any means I might attain unto the resurrection of the dead.

12 Not as though I had already attained, either were already perfect: but I follow after, if that I may apprehend that for which also I am apprehended of Christ Jesus.

13 Brethren, I count not myself to have apprehended: but this one thing I do, forgetting those things which are behind, and reaching forth unto those things which are before,

14 I press toward the mark for the prize of the high calling of God in Christ Jesus.

15 Let us therefore, as many as be perfect, be thus minded: and if in any thing ye be otherwise minded, God shall reveal even this unto you.

16 Nevertheless, whereto we have already attained, let us walk by the same rule, let us mind the same thing.

17 Brethren, be followers together of me, and mark them which walk so as ye have us for an ensample.

18 (For many walk, of whom I have told you often, and now tell you even weeping, that they are the enemies of the cross of Christ:

19 Whose end is destruction, whose God is their belly, and whose glory is in their shame, who mind earthly things.)

20 For our conversation is in heaven; from whence also we look for the Saviour, the Lord Jesus Christ:

21 Who shall change our vile body, that it may be fashioned like unto his glorious body, according to the working whereby he is able even to subdue all things unto himself.

*NEW REVISED STANDARD VERSION*

PHILIPPIANS 3:7 Yet whatever gains I had, these I have come to regard as loss because of Christ. 8 More than that, I regard everything as loss because of the surpassing value of knowing Christ Jesus my Lord. For his sake I have suffered the loss of all things, and I regard them as rubbish, in order that I may gain Christ 9 and be found in him, not having a righteousness of my own that comes from the law, but one that comes through faith in Christ, the righteousness from God based on faith. 10 I want to know Christ and the power of his resurrection and the sharing of his sufferings by becoming like him in his death, 11 if somehow I may attain the resurrection from the dead.

12 Not that I have already obtained this or have already reached the goal; but I press on to make it my own, because Christ Jesus has made me his own. 13 Beloved, I do not consider that I have made it my own; but this one thing I do: forgetting what lies behind and straining forward to what lies ahead, 14 I press on toward the goal for the prize of the heavenly call of God in Christ Jesus. 15 Let those of us then who are mature be of the same mind; and if you think differently about anything, this too God will reveal to you. 16 Only let us hold fast to what we have attained.

17 Brothers and sisters, join in imitating me, and observe those who live according to the example you have in us. 18 For many live as enemies of the cross of Christ; I have often told you of them, and now I tell you even with tears. 19 Their end is destruction; their god is the belly; and their glory is in their shame; their minds are set on earthly things. 20 But our citizenship is in heaven, and it is from there that we are expecting a Savior, the Lord Jesus Christ. 21 He will transform the body of our humiliation that it may be conformed to the body of his glory, by the power that also enables him to make all things subject to himself.

| | | |
|---|---|---|
| *Monday, June 12* | Philippians 3:1-6 | *Don't Be Led Astray!* |
| *Tuesday, June 13* | Philippians 3:7-11 | *The Ultimate Richness: Knowing Jesus Christ* |
| *Wednesday, June 14* | Philippians 3:12-16 | *Press On toward the Goal* |
| *Thursday, June 15* | Philippians 3:17—4:1 | *Our Citizenship Is in Heaven* |
| *Friday, June 16* | Hebrews 10:19-25 | *Encourage One Another in Christ Jesus* |
| *Saturday, June 17* | Hebrews 10:26-39 | *Hold Fast Your Confidence in Christ* |
| *Sunday, June 18* | Hebrews 12:1-13 | *Live a Disciplined Christian Life* |

## BACKGROUND

After founding a congregation in Philippi, Paul went to other cities to proclaim the Gospel. From its inception, the church that Paul had established in Philippi was a mixture of races, cultures, and social classes (though mostly poor). The first converts were an upper-class woman named Lydia (Acts 16:14-15), a middle-class Roman jailer (16:22-34), and perhaps a young slave girl who had been demon-possessed (16:16-18).

As the church grew, it maintained primarily a Gentile flavor, yet the less populous Jewish Christians exerted much influence over the fellowship. Part of the reason Paul wrote to the church in Philippi was to steady the new converts in their Christian practices. He knew that they would be subjected to pressures to veer from what he had taught them.

One such pressure came from a party known as the Judaizers, a group of ultra-conservative religious zealots who insisted that all the rules of Judaism had to be observed before anyone could be truly saved. This sect insisted on all male converts being circumcised and everyone observing the Jewish dietary laws. The legalists accused Paul of corrupting the Gospel by watering down its moral requirements, and they tried to undermine his ministry in many cities. Representatives from the circumcision party turned up in nearly all the churches Paul had started and demanded that the new Gentile converts take up all the trappings of the Old Testament law, if they were to call themselves true believers. This caused consternation and division in the young churches Paul had established. The apostle had to write to many of these congregations and remind them that their trust in Christ for salvation was sufficient.

In addition to pressures from the Judaizers, the Philippians were subjected to the strains of living in a pagan society. All believers found themselves surrounded by goals and values that were contrary to the objectives and ethics of the Gospel. Paul's letter to the Philippians was intended to encourage his fellow believers to persevere in the ways he had taught them.

The members of the congregation Paul founded in Philippi treated him with respect and generosity. But the same could not be said for some of the unsaved in the city. When we review the biblical record, we discover that Paul and his associates remained in Philippi after finding some women praying by the riverside one Sabbath. Paul shared the Gospel, and a woman named Lydia trusted in Christ for salvation. After she and her household were baptized, they became the nucleus of the Philippian church. Paul and Silas widened the fellowship through their evangelistic preaching (16:11-16).

Acts 16:16 records the events that led to Paul and Silas being severely beaten and jailed in Philippi. A slave girl exhibited by her owners on the streets each day apparently would fall into trances and scream words that the superstitious thought revealed their fortunes. The girl became a nuisance to Paul and his friends when she continually followed them and shrieked, *"These men are slaves of the Most High God, who proclaim to you a way of salvation"* (16:17). Paul, weary of the disruption that the demon-possessed girl was causing each day, expelled the evil spirit from her (16:18).

The slavegirl's owners then became enraged that they would no longer be able to make a lucrative income from her fortune-telling. They stirred up an angry crowd and accused Paul and Silas of being troublemakers. The mob dragged the two before the city magistrates, who ordered them to be beaten as punishment and thrown into prison. The jailer, taking no chances with the pair escaping, shackled their feet and left them bruised, bleeding, and hungry in the innermost cell of the compound (16:19-24).

About midnight a violent earthquake shook the foundations of the jail, which caused the doors of the prison to be opened and everyone's chains to become unfastened. In the events that followed, Paul and Silas led the jailer and his family to faith in Christ. The next day the missionaries were released from prison. After encouraging the new converts in Lydia's home, Paul and Silas departed (16:25-40).

## NOTES ON THE PRINTED TEXT

Paul warned the Philippians about the Judaizers, a legalistic group that hounded the apostle and insisted that believers had to be circumcised and keep the Mosaic law in order to be saved. Paul countered this teaching by using himself as an example of someone who had an impressive Jewish heritage and credentials (3:5-6). He then noted that God did not act like an accountant who listed moral credits and debits on a ledger. Paul declared that *whatever gains I had, these I have come to regard as loss because of Christ* (3:7). The things that the world lauded as commendable were far surpassed by the excellency of knowing Christ. *More than that, I regard everything as loss because of the surpassing value of knowing Christ Jesus my Lord* (3:8).

Paul wrote that he had no regrets in giving up all things to know Jesus more fully. Paul's attainments were mere refuse in comparison to the riches of Christ. *For his sake I have suffered the loss of all things, and I regard them as rubbish, in order that I may gain Christ and be found in him, not having a righteousness of my own that comes from the law, but one that comes through faith in Christ, the righteousness from God based on faith* (3:8-9).

Paul told the church in Philippi that his faith rested on the exalted Lord. The apostle was not ashamed to experience suffering for the sake of Christ, for Paul knew that one day Jesus would raise him from the dead. *I want to know Christ and the power of his resurrection and the sharing of his sufferings by becoming like him in his death, if somehow I may attain the resurrection from the dead* (3:10-11).

Paul humbly admitted that he had not reached his goal of fully knowing Christ. That's why the apostle pressed on to achieve that goal. Like a dedicated athlete, he strove to cross the finish line as he faithfully served the Lord. *Not that I have already obtained this or have already reached the goal; but I press on to make it my own, because Christ Jesus has made me his own* (3:12).

Paul could not obliterate the past from his memory, but he refused to let his past obstruct his progress toward the goal of becoming more Christlike. The apostle intently fixed his eyes on remaining faithful to Jesus to end of his life. *Beloved, I do not consider that I have made it my own; but this one thing I do: forgetting what lies behind and straining forward to what lies ahead, I press on toward the goal for the prize of the heavenly call of God in Christ Jesus* (3:13-14).

Though each believer in Philippi had a unique spiritual journey to make, they were all united in Christ. Paul urged his readers to stay in line spiritually and continue progressing in spiritual growth by the same principles he had taught them. *Let those of us then who are mature be of the same mind; and if you think differently about anything, this too God will reveal to you. Only let us hold fast to what we have attained* (3:15-16).

Paul directed the Philippians to model their behavior on his conduct. *Brothers and sisters, join in imitating me, and observe those who live according to the example you have in us* (3:17). The call to holy living was particularly urgent given the fact that some were casting shame on the Gospel by advocating gluttony and sexual immorality. These enemies of the cross had to be avoided (3:18-19).

The apostle reminded the Philippians that though they were in this world, they were not part of the world. *But our citizenship is in heaven, and it is from there that we are expecting a Savior, the Lord Jesus Christ. He will transform the body of our humiliation that it may be conformed to the body of his glory, by the power that also enables him to make all things subject to himself* (3:20-21).

## SUGGESTIONS TO TEACHERS

An old story relates how a church janitor was apparently able to accept the fact that every member of the congregation bossed him around. Someone asked the old fellow how he was able to take the pressures of so many people trying to tell him what to do. "Aw," he drawled, "I just put my mind in neutral and roll along without thinking."

The same thing might be said about the way many of us live as Christians. We just put our minds in neutral and roll on without thinking about what Jesus has taught us in His Word. Our culture gives us our orders, not Christ. This week's Scripture text shakes us by the lapels and tells us to think and behave as Christ's followers.

**1. FLEEING EVIL WORKERS.** Paul mentioned the legalists and the lovers of pedigrees and traditions. These are people who parade their titles and achievements. Their religion is a rule book that they have substituted for the Gospel. Have the members of your class consider what some of the pressures are that beset them and other Christians. When is it most difficult for the students to stand true for Christ?

**2. FORSAKING HUMAN CLAIMS.** Today, as in Paul's time, believers find themselves tempted to substitute human wisdom for the truth of the Gospel. For example, some congregations are "totally market driven," that is, anxious to please the public in order to grab a bigger share of the "market" Sadly, these churches think that success hinges on "giving people what they want," rather than urging them to become more Christlike.

**3. FORGETTING THE PAST.** The old phrase, "The Seven Last Words of the Church—'But we've always done it that way!'" may easily become a sacred mantra. We should not hastily abandon our religious traditions, but at the same time we must not worship them. Christians are to follow their risen Savior as He leads them onward into the future.

**4. FORGING ON TO THE END.** Paul undoubtedly was tempted to quit on occasion, but he refused. He knew that Jesus remained with him. Likewise, though we may feel like giving up and wanting to find a quiet spot to escape the toil of serving, we must forge on. We are sustained by Christ's strength, not our own. We have His example of persevering to the end and bringing glory to God.

---

| **FOR ADULTS** | ■ **TOPIC:** Striving to Be Christlike |
|---|---|

■ **QUESTIONS:** 1. What personal attainments did Paul willingly give up for the cause of Christ? 2. What goal did Paul press on to achieve? 3. Why should knowing Christ be your highest priority in life? 4. What difference has the power of Christ's resurrection made in your life? 5. What consolation is there in knowing that Jesus will one day return?

■ **ILLUSTRATIONS:**

**Don't Quit.** In his book entitled *Pastoral Grit: the Strength to Stand and to Stay,* Craig Brian Larson writes the following:

In 1972, NASA launched the exploratory space probe Pioneer 10. According to Leon Jaroff in *Time,* the satellite's primary mission was to reach Jupiter, photograph the planet and its moons, and beam data to earth about Jupiter's magnetic field, radiation belts, and atmosphere. Scientists regarded this as a bold plan, for at that time no earth satellite had ever gone beyond Mars, and they feared the asteroid belt would destroy the satellite before it could reach its target. But Pioneer 10 accomplished its mission and much, much more. Swinging past the giant planet in November 1973, Jupiter's immense gravity hurled Pioneer 10 at a higher rate of speed toward the edge of the solar system. At one billion miles from the sun, Pioneer 10 passed Saturn. At some two billion miles, it hurtled past Uranus; Neptune at nearly three billion miles; Pluto at almost four billion miles. By 1997, 25 years after its launch, Pioneer 10 was more than six billion miles from the sun. And despite that immense distance, Pioneer 10 continued to beam back radio signals to scientists on Earth. "Perhaps most remarkable," writes Jaroff, "those signals emanate from an 8-watt transmitter, which radiates about as much power as a bedroom night light, and takes more than nine hours to reach Earth." The Little Satellite That Could was not qualified to do what it did. Engineers designed Pioneer 10 with a useful life of just three years. But it kept going and going. By simple longevity, its tiny 8-watt transmitter radio accomplished more than anyone thought possible. So it is when we offer ourselves to serve the Lord. God can work even through someone with 8-watt abilities. God cannot work, however, through someone who quits.

**Christlike Behavior.** Abraham Lincoln was often harshly criticized and belittled. Even members of his cabinet made disparaging comments about him behind his back. Lincoln suffered silently under the barrage of slander. His nastiest critic was Edwin Stanton, whom he had named Secretary of War. After reports came to Lincoln of a particularly caustic set of comments Stanton had made in public about the President's shaggy appearance and backwoods origins, people expected Lincoln to give his cabinet secretary the dressing down he deserved. Someone finally asked Lincoln why he didn't get rid of such enemies as Stanton. Old Abe drawled, "Do I not get rid of my enemies when I make them my friends?" He insisted on speaking well of Stanton and all others who viciously attacked him, and ultimately won their respect.

**True Tourists.** Many years ago, an American traveler made a trip to Poland to visit the great spiritual leader in Judaism, Rabbi Hofetz Chaim. The American was astonished to find that the famous rabbi lived in a relatively bare place, in which his room contained only a plain table, one chair, and a few books. "Rabbi," the American visitor asked, "Where is your furniture?" Rabbi Chaim replied, "My furniture? Where is your furniture, my friend?" "But I am only a tourist, passing through," said the American. "So am I," answered the rabbi.

■ **TOPIC:** Press Ahead!

■ **QUESTIONS:** 1. Why would Paul willingly suffer the loss of all things for the cause of Christ? 2. What were the enemies of the cross guilty of doing? 3. If you were to take stock of your life, what would eternally count and what would not? 4. In what ways can you encourage your peers to become followers of Christ? 5. In what ways do you think God and His purposes are served by the life you are pursuing?

■ **ILLUSTRATIONS:**

**Pressed on for Years.** On July 14, 1986, Dr. Robert Ballard of the Woods Hole Oceanographic Institution peered out of a porthole of the three-man submersible, Alvin, and looked at the remains of the sunken liner, Titanic, on the muddy ocean floor. The experience was a culmination of years of dreaming and planning. The effort began in 1973, when Ballard proposed using the wreck as a subject for undersea photography. For years he was unable to secure funding for the project. However, during that time, he developed the Argo, a deep-towed remotely controlled camera sled, as well as the Jason, a robot submarine that carried lights and cameras. In 1985, the U.S. Navy agreed to fund a three-week test of the Argo. The mission was a success and prompted a second mission the following year. Ballard is someone who pressed on ahead for years. Discouragement and setbacks did not deter his determination. Paul also was not someone to let setbacks deter him.

**Unfocused.** Abel Anton was leading all of the runners in the London Marathon as he headed toward the finish line on Sunday, April 28, 1998. Confident of victory, he began nodding and waving, acknowledging the crowd of well-wishers who cheered him on. As he did so, he took his eyes off of the finish line and the finish clock. While he won the race, his lack of focus cost him a record time (by 2 seconds) and losing the bonus of $25,000 for failing to break the existing record!

Using the image of a runner, Paul reminded the Philippians of the importance of pressing on toward the goal of growing in Christlikeness. Believers must stay focused on the Savior, or they too will make costly eternal blunders in life.

**God of the Belly?** As you read Paul's line, *their god is the belly* (3:19), consider that America is the nation with the heaviest people on earth. Our leading health problem is obesity. The government has issued new guidelines to thin down the populace. This fact has also prompted some religious traditions to urge their pastors to focus on the old sin of gluttony, or excessive eating and drinking. Paul issued a similar warning to the congregation in Philippi. The apostle reminded his readers not to abuse their bodies with excessive food. Rather, they were to imitate him and practice moderation and concern for others.

# REJOICING IN CHRIST

**BACKGROUND SCRIPTURE:** Philippians 4:4-20
**DEVOTIONAL READING:** 1 Thessalonians 1:2-10

**KEY VERSE:** Rejoice in the Lord always; again I will say, Rejoice. Philippians 4:4.

*KING JAMES VERSION*

PHILIPPIANS 4:4 Rejoice in the Lord alway: and again I say, Rejoice.

5 Let your moderation be known unto all men. The Lord is at hand.

6 Be careful for nothing; but in every thing by prayer and supplication with thanksgiving let your requests be made known unto God.

7 And the peace of God, which passeth all understanding, shall keep your hearts and minds through Christ Jesus.

8 Finally, brethren, whatsoever things are true, whatsoever things are honest, whatsoever things are just, whatsoever things are pure, whatsoever things are lovely, whatsoever things are of good report; if there be any virtue, and if there be any praise, think on these things.

9 Those things, which ye have both learned, and received, and heard, and seen in me, do: and the God of peace shall be with you.

10 But I rejoiced in the Lord greatly, that now at the last your care of me hath flourished again; wherein ye were also careful, but ye lacked opportunity.

11 Not that I speak in respect of want: for I have learned, in whatsoever state I am, therewith to be content.

12 I know both how to be abased, and I know how to abound: every where and in all things I am instructed both to be full and to be hungry, both to abound and to suffer need.

13 I can do all things through Christ which strengtheneth me.

14 Notwithstanding ye have well done, that ye did communicate with my affliction.

15 Now ye Philippians know also, that in the beginning of the gospel, when I departed from Macedonia, no church communicated with me as concerning giving and receiving, but ye only.

16 For even in Thessalonica ye sent once and again unto my necessity.

17 Not because I desire a gift: but I desire fruit that may abound to your account.

18 But I have all, and abound: I am full, having received of Epaphroditus the things which were sent from you, an odour of a sweet smell, a sacrifice acceptable, wellpleasing to God.

*NEW REVISED STANDARD VERSION*

PHILIPPIANS 4:4 Rejoice in the Lord always; again I will say, Rejoice. 5 Let your gentleness be known to everyone. The Lord is near. 6 Do not worry about anything, but in everything by prayer and supplication with thanksgiving let your requests be made known to God. 7 And the peace of God, which surpasses all understanding, will guard your hearts and your minds in Christ Jesus.

8 Finally, beloved, whatever is true, whatever is honorable, whatever is just, whatever is pure, whatever is pleasing, whatever is commendable, if there is any excellence and if there is anything worthy of praise, think about these things. 9 Keep on doing the things that you have learned and received and heard and seen in me, and the God of peace will be with you.

10 I rejoice in the Lord greatly that now at last you have revived your concern for me; indeed, you were concerned for me, but had no opportunity to show it. 11 Not that I am referring to being in need; for I have learned to be content with whatever I have. 12 I know what it is to have little, and I know what it is to have plenty. In any and all circumstances I have learned the secret of being well-fed and of going hungry, of having plenty and of being in need. 13 I can do all things through him who strengthens me. 14 In any case, it was kind of you to share my distress.

15 You Philippians indeed know that in the early days of the gospel, when I left Macedonia, no church shared with me in the matter of giving and receiving, except you alone. 16 For even when I was in Thessalonica, you sent me help for my needs more than once. 17 Not that I seek the gift, but I seek the profit that accumulates to your account. 18 I have been paid in full and have more than enough; I am fully satisfied, now that I have received from Epaphroditus the gifts you sent, a fragrant offering, a sacrifice acceptable and pleasing to God.

| | | |
|---|---|---|
| *Monday, June 19* | Philippians 4:2-7 | *Rejoice, and Be Gentle with One Another* |
| *Tuesday, June 20* | Philippians 4:8-14 | *Keep on Keeping On in Christ* |
| *Wednesday, June 21* | Philippians 4:15-23 | *Paul's Thanks for the Philippian Church* |
| *Thursday, June 22* | Acts 2:43-47 | *Life among the Early Believers* |
| *Friday, June 23* | 1 Thessalonians 1:1-10 | *Paul's Thanks for the Thessalonian Church* |
| *Saturday, June 24* | 1 Thessalonians 4:1-12 | *Lives Pleasing to God* |
| *Sunday, June 25* | 3 John 1-8 | *Faithfulness Brings Great Joy* |

## BACKGROUND

When you read Paul's letter to the Philippian church, you sense that the apostle felt closer to that congregation than any other. He certainly enjoyed a harmonious relationship with that group. Unlike the contentious Corinthians or the rebellious Galatians and other problem-filled daughter churches, the group of believers at Philippi remained loyal and supportive of Paul, and he had a special place in his heart for them.

Paul had several reasons for writing this letter. He wanted to express his thanks for the monetary gift that the Philippians had given to him (4:10-18). The apostle also wanted his readers to know why he decided to send Epaphroditus [e-paff-roh-DIE-tuss] back to them. Paul did not want the Philippians to think that their service to the apostle had been unsatisfactory (2:25-26). Furthermore, Paul wanted to inform his readers about his circumstances in Rome (1:12-26). Moreover, the apostle sought to exhort the Philippians to unity (2:1-2; 4:2). Finally, Paul wrote to warn his readers against false teachers (3:1—4:1).

The most prominent theme of the apostle's letter is joy, namely, delight in serving Christ. The general tone of the epistle reflects Paul's gratitude toward the Philippians and his joy in God. This remained true despite the difficult circumstances the apostle faced.

Another key theme is the mutual partnership believers have in the ministry of the Gospel. For example, the Philippians were actively involved in Paul's work by financially and prayerfully supporting him. The apostle exhorted them to not only abound in their love for him but also to experience more of God so that they could grow into a mature understanding of His ways.

As one studies this epistle, one notices an emphasis on Paul's affection for his readers, the sovereignty of the triune God, the superlative example of Christ's humility, justification through faith in Christ, and the importance of the Christ-centered life for the believer. Paul stressed the importance of identification with Christ in His death and resurrection. The apostle underscored the necessity of believers endeavoring to grow in Christlikeness. They can do so, confident that the power of God is at work within them to make it a reality.

# NOTES ON THE PRINTED TEXT

Paul's letter drew to a close with some final exhortations. *Rejoice in the Lord always; again I will say, Rejoice* (4:4). The apostle was urging the Philippians to be joyous on a regular basis. Their joy was to be based on what Christ did for them at Calvary. That foundation was also the basis for a second exhortation. *Let your gentleness be known to everyone. The Lord is near* (4:5). Despite the presence of opposition and persecution, Christians were to deal fairly with others.

Paul urged the believers in Philippi not to be nervous or concerned for their own well being. Rather, they were to be fervent in prayer. *Do not worry about anything, but in everything by prayer and supplication with thanksgiving let your requests be made known to God* (4:6). The Philippians could give their problems to God, for they knew that He was like a sentry standing guard over their thoughts and emotions. His continual presence was the basis of their protection, preservation, and peace. *And the peace of God which surpasses all understanding, will guard your hearts and your minds in Christ Jesus* (4:7).

Paul encouraged his readers to cultivate and practice virtues that were extolled in Scripture. Doing so would bring glory to God and honor the name of Christ. For instance, the Philippians were to be truthful, morally good, upright, and living in a decent and praiseworthy manner. *Finally, beloved, whatever is true, whatever is honorable, whatever is just, whatever is pure, whatever is pleasing, whatever is commendable, if there is any excellence and if there is anything worthy of praise, think about these things* (4:8).

These were qualities evident in the lives of those who claimed to be citizens of God's kingdom. These were also virtues that Paul himself had stressed. The faithful were to live by the example that he had set for them. *Keep on doing the things that you have learned and received and heard and seen in me, and the God of peace will be with you* (4:9). Scripture teaches that God is peace (Rom. 16:20), makes peace with sinners through Christ (2 Cor. 5:18-20), and can give perfect peace in times of trouble (Phil. 4:7).

Paul thanked the Philippian church for the financial gift that Epaphroditus had brought with him. To the overjoyed apostle it was another example of the congregation's love reviving, or blossoming like a plant in the spring. *I rejoice in the Lord greatly that now at last you have revived your concern for me; indeed, you were concerned for me, but had no opportunity to show it* (4:10).

While thankful, Paul also wrote that he did not need the gift. Despite his circumstances, he found contentment in Jesus Christ. God ultimately was the source of the apostle's strength. *Not that I am referring to being in need; for I have learned to be content with whatever I have. I know what it is to have little, and I know what it is to have plenty. In any and all circumstances I have learned the secret of being well-fed and of going hungry, of having plenty and of being in need. I can do all things through him who strengthens me* (4:11-13).

Despite Paul's ability to live in any situation, he expressed his gratitude for the church's kindness and support. He added a word of clarification so that his readers would not think he was ungrateful for their most recent gift. *In any case, it was kind of you to share my distress* (4:14).

Paul reminded the Philippians of their relationship with him. Their supportive partnership began when he departed for Thessalonica and the church had sent several generous gifts to aid his efforts. *You Philippians indeed know that in the early days of the gospel, when I left Macedonia, no church shared with me in the matter of giving and receiving, except you alone. For even when I was in Thessalonica, you sent me help for my needs more than once* (4:15-16).

Though Paul did not need the monetary gifts, he was thankful for them. Using the vocabulary of commerce and business, Paul noted that his readers' generosity was producing spiritual profit just as money deposited in a bank account accrues interest. By giving to Paul so generously, the Philippians had offered themselves as a gift to God. *Not that I seek the gift, but I seek the profit that accumulates to your account. I have been paid in full and have more than enough; I am fully satisfied, now that I have received from Epaphroditus the gifts you sent, a fragrant offering, a sacrifice acceptable and pleasing to God* (4:17-18). Paul reassured his readers that God would give increase to them in proportion to His infinite resources (4:19).

## SUGGESTIONS TO TEACHERS

Some have called this the "Prozac Generation." Coping with life at the close of this frenetic century pushes many to lean on drugs, legal and illegal. Our movies, televisions, novels, and newspapers remind us that we do not live in an age noted for joy. The pervading sense of despair explains why suicide is the second-leading cause of death among our youth.

Paul's times were also filled with anxiety and depression. Life was grim for many. And the aging apostle, now imprisoned with no certainty of release, and confronted every day with the possibility of being executed, had all the reasons imaginable to sink into feelings of hopelessness and toss at night with anxiety. But he radiated a joy that came from his relationship with Christ. The apostle's concluding portion of this letter offers us insights into how our faith sustains us in the face of whatever life throws at us.

**1. SOURCE OF PEACE.** Christ's people may rejoice, for He lives. Christ provides spiritual strength; thus, His people have hope. In light of these truths, His followers should not let worries overwhelm them. Spend some time discussing Philippians 4:4-7, and consider how prayer enables believers to rise above anxiety. Note that the petitions of believers include expressions of gratitude for God's past mercies and abiding presence.

**2. STUDY OF THE BEST.** Paul advised a disciplining of the mind, whereby believers focus their thinking on whatever is true, honorable, just, and pure (4:8).

Just as computer buffs say "Garbage in, garbage out" in reference to botched-up programming, Christians might also use the phrase in reference to living. When the garbage of violence, resentments, narcissistic pleasure, and greedy consumption are the main thoughts in a person's life, it produces wretched results. The best option is to cultivate a joy-filled and serene response to life's problems.

**3. SECRET OF CONTENTMENT.** Dwell at length on the rich meaning of Paul's words in 4:10-13. We *can do all things*—not just some things—through Christ, who strengthens us. This remains true despite hunger, loss, loneliness, or hurting of any kind!

**4. SENSE OF GRATITUDE.** Paul's letter to the Philippians was sent as a "thank-you note" to the caring and generous congregation in Philippi. The apostle radiated a sense of appreciation for his readers' thoughtfulness, and, most of all, for Christ's abiding mercy. Do the members of your class have a daily "attitude of gratitude" for their blessings? Giving thanks is not confined to the last Thursday of November, but should be celebrated every day!

---

**FOR ADULTS**

■ TOPIC: Deep Joy

■ QUESTIONS: 1. What does it mean to be joyful in the Lord, and how is this possible in difficult circumstances? 2. In what way had the Philippians been generous to Paul? 3. What are some worries that you can give to God in prayer? 4. In what ways has God's peace calmed your heart in times of uncertainty? 5. Whom might you console with the good news of Jesus' comforting presence?

■ ILLUSTRATIONS:

**Source of Joy.** Years ago in Maine there lived a minister who conducted a weekly radio program that brought hope, help, and cheer to many listeners. Few of his listeners, however, knew about this man's personal predicament, namely, that he had been bedridden for 14 years, and also that he was blind. In a letter to a friend he wrote, "Thank God, the anchor holds. I can no longer move, but I can pray and praise."

**Psychiatric Disorder?** Some British psychiatrists claim that happiness should be classified as a psychiatric disorder. Why? Because, they claim, so many people feel they should be happy but are not. The psychiatrists argue that since happiness exists in the lives of so few persons, it should be called an abnormal condition, or even a major disorder. The March, 1996 journal, *Science*, also wrote that the notion of happiness threatens mental health.

The deep joy promised by Christ and described in Paul's letter to the Philippians is not the happiness of a disordered life that should be regarded as some type of mental illness. And the joy of Christ's people is not a shallow, self-centered feeling of euphoria. The joyous people who mirror Christ's deep inner delight, radiate contentment and trust in the Lord in all circumstances.

**Definition of an Appraiser.** During a visit to Grandma's and Grandpa's, the two daughters of Jennifer Breeding of Whiteman AFC, Missouri, watched from the breakfast table as a man came to the back door. When the visitor left, Grandpa explained that he was an appraiser. "What's an appraiser?" the younger child asked. Before Grandpa had a chance to explain, the older sister quickly cleared up the matter. "He's a praiser. He goes to church every Sunday!" (Reprinted from *Sing,* June, 1995.)

---

**FOR YOUTH**

■ **TOPIC:** Rejoicing in Christ

■ **QUESTIONS:** 1. What things did Paul want the Philippians to think about? 2. What was Paul's attitude toward the monetary gift he had received from his readers? 3. In what ways can you show the gentleness of Christ to your peers? 4. What are some commendable things God might give you the strength to do? 5. What are some of your pressing needs that you can ask God to meet?

■ **ILLUSTRATIONS:**

**Freely Gives.** Sixteen-year-old Tim McKenzie of Pittsburgh is one youth who understands the importance of giving without expecting to receive. Tim works with the East Liberty Concerned Citizens Corp as a volunteer. One project found him involved with the Operation Picket Fence Program cleaning up his neighborhood and planting flowers and vegetables on vacant lots. He gives his time in Operation Hammer, a youth program that focuses on public safety, crime prevention, education, and life skills. Tim works with young people on their reading, writing, and art work. He also shares his energies as a mentor at a year-round after school program. He moreover works with a breakfast and lunch program at the local community center. Furthermore, this young man participates in the National Night Out program as well as other similar projects.

Here is a person who demonstrates amazing commitment to his community through his giving of his time and energy. Tim's generosity of spirit reflects the extraordinary giving that Paul described in his letter and that should characterize us as followers of Christ.

**Generosity.** In the December 24, 1995 issue of the *Chicago Tribune Magazine,* Anne Keegan wrote an article entitled "Blue Christmas." It was a collection of Christmas stories told by Chicago police officers. One was the story of George White.

George lived in a rented room at the YMCA. He had one set of clothes, shoes wrapped with rubber bands to keep the soles from flopping, and a threadbare black overcoat. He spent his mornings napping in an old metal chair in the back of the 18th District office.

Two officers, Kitowski and Mitch, took an interest in the old man, occasionally slipping him a few bucks. They found out that Billy the Greek over at a local grill gave him a free hot breakfast every morning. The two policemen and their families decided to have George as their guest for Christmas dinner. They gave him presents, which he unwrapped carefully.

As the two policemen drove George back to the YMCA, he asked, "Are these presents really mine to keep?" They assured him they were. "Then we must stop at the local grill before I go home," he said. With that, George began rewrapping his presents.

When the three men walked into the grill, Billy the Greek was there as always. "You've been good to me, Billy," said George. "Now I can be good to you. Merry Christmas." George gave all his presents away on the spot. Generosity is natural when a grateful attitude prevails.

**Don't Worry.** Several years ago pop singer Bobby McFerrin sang a tune that captured the interest of the nation. The refrain chanted, "Don't worry, be happy!" People of all ages shared these words with one another. As sentimental as the lyrics were, no one truly believed the lines.

Paul, though, urged believers not to be anxious. The apostle was talking about nervous, doubt-filled concerns. His appeal was based on what Christ did for us at Calvary, not mere sentimentality. Rather than repeat an empty slogan, Paul reminded his readers that God Himself stood guard over their lives. This should encourage us to place our confidence and trust in Him.

# CALLED TO SPIRITUAL BLESSINGS IN CHRIST

**BACKGROUND SCRIPTURE:** EPHESIANS 1
**DEVOTIONAL READING:** ROMANS 1:8-17

**KEY VERSE:** Blessed be the God and Father of our Lord Jesus Christ, who has blessed us in Christ with every spiritual blessing in the heavenly places. Ephesians 1:3.

*KING JAMES VERSION*

EPHESIANS 1:1 Paul, an apostle of Jesus Christ by the will of God, to the saints which are at Ephesus, and to the faithful in Christ Jesus:

2 Grace be to you, and peace, from God our Father, and from the Lord Jesus Christ.

3 Blessed be the God and Father of our Lord Jesus Christ, who hath blessed us with all spiritual blessings in heavenly places in Christ:

4 According as he hath chosen us in him before the foundation of the world, that we should be holy and without blame before him in love:

5 Having predestinated us unto the adoption of children by Jesus Christ to himself, according to the good pleasure of his will,

6 To the praise of the glory of his grace, wherein he hath made us accepted in the beloved.

7 In whom we have redemption through his blood, the forgiveness of sins, according to the riches of his grace;

8 Wherein he hath abounded toward us in all wisdom and prudence;

9 Having made known unto us the mystery of his will, according to his good pleasure which he hath purposed in himself:

10 That in the dispensation of the fulness of times he might gather together in one all things in Christ, both which are in heaven, and which are on earth; even in him:

11 In whom also we have obtained an inheritance, being predestinated according to the purpose of him who worketh all things after the counsel of his own will:

12 That we should be to the praise of his glory, who first trusted in Christ.

13 In whom ye also trusted, after that ye heard the word of truth, the gospel of your salvation: in whom also after that ye believed, ye were sealed with that holy Spirit of promise,

14 Which is the earnest of our inheritance until the redemption of the purchased possession, unto the praise of his glory.

*NEW REVISED STANDARD VERSION*

EPHESIANS 1:1 Paul, an apostle of Christ Jesus by the will of God,

To the saints who are in Ephesus and are faithful in Christ Jesus:

2 Grace to you and peace from God our Father and the Lord Jesus Christ.

3 Blessed be the God and Father of our Lord Jesus Christ, who has blessed us in Christ with every spiritual blessing in the heavenly places, 4 just as he chose us in Christ before the foundation of the world to be holy and blameless before him in love. 5 He destined us for adoption as his children through Jesus Christ, according to the good pleasure of his will, 6 to the praise of his glorious grace that he freely bestowed on us in the Beloved. 7 In him we have redemption through his blood, the forgiveness of our trespasses, according to the riches of his grace 8 that he lavished on us. With all wisdom and insight 9 he has made known to us the mystery of his will, according to his good pleasure that he set forth in Christ, 10 as a plan for the fullness of time, to gather up all things in him, things in heaven and things on earth. 11 In Christ we have also obtained an inheritance, having been destined according to the purpose of him who accomplishes all things according to his counsel and will, 12 so that we, who were the first to set our hope on Christ, might live for the praise of his glory. 13 In him you also, when you had heard the word of truth, the gospel of your salvation, and had believed in him, were marked with the seal of the promised Holy Spirit; 14 this is the pledge of our inheritance toward redemption as God's own people, to the praise of his glory.

## Home Bible Readings

## Background

We continue this quarter's study of Paul's prison letters by turning to Ephesians for the next five lessons. We quickly discover what countless others have learned, namely, that Ephesians is one of the greatest theological and devotional writings we will ever find. This piece of literature sums up Paul's thinking about God's intentions for the universe, the work of Jesus Christ, the place of the church, and the responsibilities of believers.

Many Bibles list this book as "The Letter of Paul to the Ephesians," but scholars remind us that the earliest Greek manuscripts do not have the words "in Ephesus" in the opening verse. All of Paul's other letters give the name of the recipient at the beginning of the document. Only later did the name of the congregation in Ephesus become attached to this letter. Perhaps Paul sent it to the Ephesian church, or perhaps he dispatched it as a circular letter for all the churches in the area of Ephesus. But this point need not concern us, for the lessons from this outstanding portion of God's Word are not affected by the unanswered question about the original destination of the epistle.

Scholars also point out the strong similarities between Ephesians and Colossians. This prompts them to think that these two letters were written about the same time. Next month, we will look at Colossians and find that Paul expanded on some of the ideas he presented in Ephesians.

From a technical viewpoint Ephesians is not a letter in the sense of Philippians and 1 and 2 Corinthians, for there is no mention of specific persons or problems in Ephesus. In fact, this portion of the New Testament is more like a treatise. This point in no way diminishes the value of the document. In fact, Ephesians may be seen as a special communiqué from Paul to every congregation and every Christian today, as well to those in Asia Minor in the first century!

## Notes on the Printed Text

Most scholars believe that Ephesians was addressed primarily to Gentile converts who were joining the church in huge numbers. With them came an easy living moral code that was based on a misunderstanding of Paul's teachings about Christian freedom. In an effort to curb the false notions, Paul began his letter by noting his authority as *an apostle of Christ Jesus by the will of God* (1:1). Paul next mentioned the recipients in Ephesus by describing them as the saints and faithful followers of Christ. In other words, they had been set apart as God's holy people. Paul then included a standard prayer greeting in his letter. *Grace to you and peace from God our Father and the Lord Jesus Christ* (1:2).

The apostle outlined the truths of the salvation that the Ephesians had through faith in Christ. It all began with God, who chose them before time ever began to praise Him and do His will. In other words, the Lord eternally planned to liberate the Ephesian Christians from sin so that they might be free to serve Him in love. *Blessed be the God and Father of our Lord Jesus Christ, who has blessed us in Christ with every spiritual blessing in the heavenly places, just as he chose us in Christ before the foundation of the world to be holy and blameless before him in love* (1:3-4).

In His grace, God adopted the believers in Ephesus into His spiritual family. The Lord made them His children so that they would be inwardly transformed after the image of Christ. They received not just Christ's eternal riches but also the blessings associated with trusting in Him. *He destined us for adoption as his children through Jesus Christ, according to the good pleasure of his will, to the praise of his glorious grace that he freely bestowed on us in the Beloved* (1:5-6)

Paul noted that Christ, through His sacrificial death on the cross, bought us from our slavery to sin. God's grace makes it possible for us to have redemption and forgiveness in Christ. *In him we have redemption through his blood, the forgiveness of our trespasses, according to the riches of his grace that he lavished on us* (1:7-8). Of course, redemption was only part of God's plan. His goal was to place all things in the universe under the lordship of Christ. *With all wisdom and insight he has made known to us the mystery of his will, according to his good pleasure that he set forth in Christ, as a plan for the fullness of time, to gather up all things in him, things in heaven and things on earth* (1:8-10).

The message of redemption was not restricted to the Gentiles. Paul noted that unsaved Jews were also trusting in Christ for salvation and becoming heirs of His eternal riches. In fact, the Jews were the first to trust in Christ and work and witness for God. *In Christ we have also obtained an inheritance, having been destined according to the purpose of him who accomplishes all things according to his counsel and will, so that we who were the first to set our hope on Christ, might live for the praise of his glory* (1:11-12).

Paul noted that when the Ephesians heard the Gospel proclaimed, they put their faith in Christ. God, in turn, sealed them with the Holy Spirit as the guarantee of their eternal inheritance. The permanent presence of the Spirit indicated that they belonged to God and existed to do His will. *In him you also, when you heard the word of truth, the gospel of your salvation, and had believed in him, were marked with the seal of the promised Holy Spirit; this is the pledge of our inheritance toward redemption as God's own people, to the praise of his glory* (1:13-14).

In describing the Holy Spirit as a *pledge* (1:14), the apostle used a business term. It denoted a down payment on a purchase that guaranteed that full payment would be made later. Archaeologists have found examples of a woman who sold a cow and who received a guarantee of 1,000 drachmas in advance. Believers have received the Holy Spirit as the pledge, or guarantee, of their future salvation.

## SUGGESTIONS TO TEACHERS

Suppose each person in your class were asked to describe God's master plan for the universe. How do you think they would respond? Undoubtedly, they would find such a question mindboggling. But occasionally we need to take time to ponder such deep questions. It is here that Ephesians offers us superb insights into God's intentions for humankind and the universe.

**1. PEOPLE.** Paul opened this great tract with reminders of who Christians should understand themselves to be. Terms such as *saints* and statements such as *God . . . has blessed us . . . chose us . . . destined us for adoption* (1:1-5) make it clear that believers in Christ have a special standing before the Creator. Take time to delve into the significance of each of these truths.

**2. PURPOSE.** We are given mercy and new life. In His unconditional love, God has chosen us to be saved. This special standing is not because we are nicer, smarter, or more attractive than anyone else. Rather, God made us the recipients of His goodness and grace in Christ so that we might carry out His work in the world.

**3. PLAN.** God has a plan in mind for us and for the rest of creation. In fact, He has fully disclosed *the mystery of his will* (1:9) through the Savior. It is God's eternal plan to bring all things under the lordship of Christ. This means that believing Gentiles are now heirs with saved Jews of the spiritual blessings available through faith in Christ. The church is a community where God's power to reconcile people to Himself is experienced and shared in transformed relationships

**4. PRESENCE.** Paul insisted that all this would come to pass because God has given us a *pledge of our inheritance* (1:14). In the midst of the world's pessimism about God, life, and the future, the Lord makes a solemn promise that is backed by the presence of His Spirit.

**5. POWER.** God's power is immeasurable. Even now we experience His power to make us more like Jesus Christ. Devote some time to examine the meaning of the cross and resurrection, and Paul's exalted view of the person of Jesus Christ, as indicated in 1:19-23.

**FOR ADULTS**

■ **TOPIC:** Claim Your Spiritual Blessings

■ **QUESTIONS:** 1. How did God choose us in Christ? 2. What is the source of our eternal redemption? 3. What are some of the many spiritual blessings from God that you have recently experienced? 4. How has your eternal inheritance in Christ made a difference in your life? 5. How might you give praise to God for all that He has done for you in Christ?

■ **ILLUSTRATIONS:**

**A Critique of New Age Spirituality.** Paul called upon his readers (including us) to claim our blessings in Jesus Christ. This becomes even more imperative when we consider the critique that British sociologist of religion David Martin gave concerning New Age spirituality. He stated the following (*Times Literary Supplement*, August 29, 1997):

> Nearly every bookstore today has a section given over to "spirituality." Spirituality is one of those words, like metaphysics and mysticism, that retain serious connotations but have looser usages referring to the psychic junk-shop. This is where a popular semi-educated mentality browses over science fiction television and cinematic fantasy about Ascended Masters and menacing Aliens, the offerings of Sunday-supplement astrology, spiritual travelogues among the arcane and exotic, and alternative therapies, as well as pseudo-scholarly forays into the world of the gospels, the Gnostics, and the Dead Sea Scrolls. All this can be complemented by down-market appropriations of words like "indeterminacy," "model," "trauma," "relativism," and other vague echoes from serious critiques of objectivity, positivism, and the concepts of truth and factuality. At the wackier margin lie notions like "identity-based knowledge," according to which individuals or groups each tell equally "authentic" stories, as well as abuse of science as masculine, egobased, ethnocentric, and exploitative. In short, located here is a riotous unreason at least as virulent as the crass scientism that dismisses all signals of transcendence as mere superstition on a par with the tooth fairy. . . . The United States is a land of exuberant religiosity, where seven persons in ten believe in angels, five in ten in UFOs, and three in ten in reincarnation and communication with the dead. Beyond that, a residue of Protestantism encourages do-it-yourself spiritual technology and individual experiment. . . . For New Agers, all truths are equal except the dogma that some truths are more equal than others. Where orthodox Christianity requires deliverance from evil into saving faith, New Agers seek out pathways where the innate goodness of humankind may flower in mutual harmony and respect for others and nature. Worship is otiose when all you need is to adore your own divine humanity.

**Insight of a Novelist.** An old adage says, "When people cease to believe in something, they do not believe in nothing; rather, they believe in anything." Is not this the way we could describe the thinking of many persons in our days? When people cease to claim their spiritual blessings through Christ, they accept any claim made by any charlatan cult leader.

**More Than Speculation.** A newspaper reporter approached Richard Mouw, president of Fuller Theological Seminary, and asked him what the theological implications were when scientists announced that there was the possibility of discovering life in a rock from Mars. Mouw could have cited philosophical speculations from many sources through history and indulged in a windy discourse. Instead, he quoted a couple of lines from the familiar hymn, "How Great Thou Art." Mouw quietly said, "O Lord my God! When I in awesome wonder consider all the worlds thy hands have made." The seminary president realized that Christians should never feel threatened by the possibility of life on Mars or on any other planet in the universe. Richard Mouw, like Paul in his Letter to the Ephesians, affirmed that Christ is Lord of everything in the universe!

---

■ TOPIC: That's the Spirit!
■ QUESTIONS: 1. What is God's eternal plan for all believers?
2. What sort of inheritance do all believers have through faith in Christ? 3. From what sorts of sins have you found forgiveness in Christ? 4. In what ways can you use your life to bring glory to God? 5. How has the presence of the Spirit made a difference in your life as a believer?

■ ILLUSTRATIONS:
**Experienced Forgiveness.** The three teenage girls murdered in 1998 by a 14 year old in West Paducah, Kentucky, had not yet been buried when the students of the Christian prayer group announced to the boy, "We forgive you." While there is no record of the young man's response, the students felt that giving immediate forgiveness was important.

How do you feel about this? What does the Bible say? In Ephesians, we learn that the sacrifice of Christ makes it possible for God to forgive us. Thus as His spiritual children, we should display our gratitude for what the Lord has done by freely forgiving others who have wronged us.

**Different Approaches.** Do you remember the classic film, *The Wizard of Oz*? Dorothy wanted to return from Oz to Kansas and be reconciled to Auntie Em and the rest of the farm family. She approached the Wizard, who had set himself up to be terrifying and unapproachable. The great Wizard of Oz wanted people to stay away from him and made it difficult for people to gain a personal audience with him. In addition, his help came at a price. In Dorothy's case, she had to bring back the broomstick of the wicked witch.

Do not mistake the wizard's approach to that of God's. Contrast the wizard's approach with how Paul describes God's actions. The Lord wants to reconcile us to Himself through Christ. In fact, God freely acted to redeem us through the sacrifice of His Son. Think about it—God's own Son became the sacrifice for our sin. The presence of the Spirit in our life is the reminder of what God has done for us in the past, what He is doing in the present, and what He will do for us in future. As a result, we should praise the Lord for the redemption and hope that He has provided us through faith in Christ.

**Seduced.** Teens are being seduced to gamble in the hope of winning large financial prizes. They are enticed by the possibility of obtaining material possessions that they think they need. Youth spend almost one billion dollars per year on gambling. Studies now suggest that teens are twice as likely to become compulsive gamblers, joining the 1.3 million (or seven percent of the population) already classified as compulsive gamblers. Sports betting is particularly rampant in high schools, reports Durant F. Jacobs, a professor of psychiatry at Loma Linda University Medical School and an authority on teenage gambling. The lure of big money is simply too much for many youth to resist.

Most youth want material things and do not consider the need to plan or safeguard for their future. However, the future is not made by gambling. Children end up owing thousands of dollars that can legally be collected from parents by forcing them to drain bank accounts, take out second mortgages, sell homes, or cash in retirement accounts.

Let this be a sobering reminder that the future lies with Christ. He alone is the source of eternal riches, and He alone can give us a heavenly inheritance.

# CALLED TO ONENESS IN CHRIST

**BACKGROUND SCRIPTURE:** Ephesians 2
**DEVOTIONAL READING:** John 17:1-11, 20-23

**KEY VERSE:** You are no longer strangers and aliens, but you are citizens with the saints and also members of the household of God. Ephesians 2:19.

*KING JAMES VERSION*

EPHESIANS 2:8 For by grace are ye saved through faith; and that not of yourselves: it is the gift of God:

9 Not of works, lest any man should boast.

10 For we are his workmanship, created in Christ Jesus unto good works, which God hath before ordained that we should walk in them.

11 Wherefore remember, that ye being in time past Gentiles in the flesh, who are called Uncircumcision by that which is called the Circumcision in the flesh made by hands;

12 That at that time ye were without Christ, being aliens from the commonwealth of Israel, and strangers from the covenants of promise, having no hope, and without God in the world:

13 But now in Christ Jesus ye who sometimes were far off are made nigh by the blood of Christ.

14 For he is our peace, who hath made both one, and hath broken down the middle wall of partition between us;

15 Having abolished in his flesh the enmity, even the law of commandments contained in ordinances; for to make in himself of twain one new man, so making peace;

16 And that he might reconcile both unto God in one body by the cross, having slain the enmity thereby:

17 And came and preached peace to you which were afar off, and to them that were nigh.

18 For through him we both have access by one Spirit unto the Father.

19 Now therefore ye are no more strangers and foreigners, but fellowcitizens with the saints, and of the household of God;

20 And are built upon the foundation of the apostles and prophets, Jesus Christ himself being the chief corner stone;

21 In whom all the building fitly framed together groweth unto an holy temple in the Lord:

22 In whom ye also are builded together for an habitation of God through the Spirit.

*NEW REVISED STANDARD VERSION*

EPHESIANS 2:8 For by grace you have been saved through faith, and this is not your own doing; it is the gift of God— 9 not the result of works, so that no one may boast. 10 For we are what he has made us, created in Christ Jesus for good works, which God prepared beforehand to be our way of life.

11 So then, remember that at one time you Gentiles by birth, called "the uncircumcision" by those who are called "the circumcision"—a physical circumcision made in the flesh by human hands— 12 remember that you were at that time without Christ, being aliens from the commonwealth of Israel, and strangers to the covenants of promise, having no hope and without God in the world. 13 But now in Christ Jesus you who once were far off have been brought near by the blood of Christ. 14 For he is our peace; in his flesh he has made both groups into one and has broken down the dividing wall, that is, the hostility between us. 15 He has abolished the law with its commandments and ordinances, that he might create in himself one new humanity in place of the two, thus making peace, 16 and might reconcile both groups to God in one body through the cross, thus putting to death that hostility through it. 17 So he came and proclaimed peace to you who were far off and peace to those who were near; 18 for through him both of us have access in one Spirit to the Father. 19 So then you are no longer strangers and aliens, but you are citizens with the saints and also members of the household of God, 20 built upon the foundation of the apostles and prophets, with Christ Jesus himself as the cornerstone. 21 In him the whole structure is joined together and grows into a holy temple in the Lord; 22 in whom you also are built together spiritually into a dwelling place for God.

6

| *Monday, July 3* | Ephesians 2:1-10 | *Saved and Made Alive by Grace* |
| *Tuesday, July 4* | Ephesians 2:11-16 | *One Body in Jesus Christ* |
| *Wednesday, July 5* | Ephesians 2:17-22 | *God Dwells in You* |
| *Thursday, July 6* | John 17:1-6 | *Jesus Commits Disciples to God's Care* |
| *Friday, July 7* | John 17:7-13 | *Jesus Prays for the Disciples' Protection* |
| *Saturday, July 8* | John 17:14-21 | *Jesus Prays for the Disciples' Unity* |
| *Sunday, July 9* | John 17:22-26 | *May God's Love Be in Christ's Disciples* |

## BACKGROUND

The general nature of Ephesians makes it difficult to determine the specific circumstances that gave rise to the epistle. Nevertheless, it is clear that the recipients were Gentiles (3:1) who were estranged from citizenship in the kingdom of Israel (2:11). Now, thanks to the gracious gift of God, they enjoyed the spiritual blessings that come through faith in Christ.

It is likely that Priscilla and Aquila first brought the Gospel to Ephesus (Acts 18:26), and that Paul most likely left them there as he continued on his second missionary journey (18:18-19). The city was located at the intersection of several major trade routes and became a vital commercial, political, and educational center of the Roman empire. Ephesus was perhaps best known for its magnificent temple of Artemis, or Diana, one of the seven wonders of the ancient world.

Most importantly, Ephesus figured prominently and dramatically in early church history, for Paul used the city as a base for his missionary work in that region. In fact, on the apostle's third missionary journey, he spent three years there (20:31). So many people in Ephesus turned to Christ and renounced their pagan ways that some local craftsmen started a riot because the Gospel threatened their trade of making and selling idols (see chap. 19). Paul's affectionate ties with this church are evident by his farewell speech to its elders (20:16-38).

Paul's letter to the Ephesians has been called "The Heavenly Epistle" and "The Alps of the New Testament." In it the apostle takes the reader from the depths of ruin to the heights of redemption. And the focus of this letter is the mystery of the church. (A mystery is a previously unrevealed divine truth that God has now disclosed in Christ; 3:5, 9).

One learns from Ephesians that the church is a community where God's power to reconcile people to Himself is experienced and shared in transformed relationships (2:1-10; 4:1-16; 4:32—5:2; 5:22—6:9). It is a new temple, a building of people, grounded in the sure revelation of what God has done in history (2:19-22; 3:17-19). The church is an organism where power and authority are exercised after the pattern of Christ (1:22; 5:25-27), and its stewardship is a means of serving Him (4:11-16; 5:22—6:9). The church is an outpost in a dark world (5:3-17), looking for the day of final redemption. Above all, the church is the bride preparing for the approach of her Lord (5:22-32).

Paul continued to describe the purpose of humanity, in particular the church. He reminded his readers that their salvation came not through their own efforts, but through God's initiative. *For by grace you have been saved through faith, and this is not your own doing; it is the gift of God—not the results of works, so that no one may boast* (2:8-9). Paul taught that salvation was God's free gift. No human effort or work could earn redemption.

As a result of trusting in Christ, believers were supposed to act differently. Their new life was expressed in positive, caring, and loving actions. As the Lord's new creation, the body of Christ was to demonstrate concern and compassion through its works. *For we are what he has made us, created in Christ Jesus for good works, which God prepared beforehand to be our way of life* (2:10).

Paul recalled how the Gentile readers of his letter used to live before they got saved. They had existed outside of God's covenant, which is symbolized by circumcision. They had no hope of a Messiah, and they had no citizenship within the elect nation of Israel. In fact, they had no prospect for being redeemed. *So then, remember that at one time you Gentiles by birth, called the "uncircumcision" by those who are called "the circumcision"—a physical circumcision made in the flesh by human hands—remember that you were at that time without Christ, being aliens from the commonwealth of Israel, and strangers to the covenants of promise, having no hope and without God in the world* (2:11-12).

Through faith in Christ, believing Gentiles (and Jews) had access to the Father. *But now in Christ Jesus you who once were far off have been brought near by the blood of Christ* (2:13). In fact, through Christ saved Gentiles were brought into the community of faith as equals with saved Jews. What had once been two separate cultures and religions were unified in Christ. Perhaps Paul had in mind the gateway leading from the Court of the Gentiles into the Court of Israel in the Jerusalem temple. There warning signs were posted stating that any non-Jew who entered the hallowed precincts of the sanctuary would be killed. *For he is our peace; in his flesh he has made both groups into one and has broken down the dividing wall, that is, the hostility between us* (2:14).

One of the greatest barriers between the Gentiles and Jews was the Mosaic law. Through His death, Christ abolished the Old Testament ceremonial laws, feasts, and sacrifices in order to promote peace and unity between believing Jews and Gentiles. *He has abolished the law with its commandments and ordinances, that he might create in himself one new humanity in place of the two, thus making peace, and might reconcile both groups to God in one body through the cross, thus putting to death that hostility through it* (2:15-16).

Paul noted that the reconciliation of believing Jews and Gentiles was made possible through faith in Christ. His atoning sacrifice at Calvary made peace with God and with one another as well as mutual access to God possible. *So he came and proclaimed peace to you who were far off and peace to those who were near;*

*for through him both of us have access in one Spirit to the Father* (2:17-18).

Christ's saving work united two previously separated groups into one spiritual family, the church. Every member was equal and enjoyed the same eternal privileges. The apostles and prophets were the foundation of the church, and Christ was the cornerstone. In Him believers became a spiritual body of redeemed individuals in whom the Spirit took up permanent residence. *So then you are no longer strangers and aliens, but you are citizens with the saints and also members of the household of God, built upon the foundation of the apostles and prophets, with Christ Jesus himself as the cornerstone. In him the whole structure is joined together and grows into a holy temple in the Lord; in whom you also are built together spiritually into a dwelling place for God* (2:19-22).

## SUGGESTIONS TO TEACHERS

Every newscast seems to report brokenness. Bosnia: Serbs versus Croats versus Muslims; Rwanda: Hutus versus Tutsis; Middle East: Israelis versus Palestinians; Northern Ireland: Protestant militants versus Catholic militants; Cyprus: Turks versus Greeks; inner-city ghettos in America: young jobless males versus society and authority. Or glance at most major denominations, some of which are verging on schism. Broken relationships surface in religious groups as well as in ethnic groups. This week's lesson is a "must" to encourage your students to heed Christ's call to oneness in Him.

**1. NOW ALIVE.** Paul stated that we were once spiritually dead, but now have been given new life in Christ. In a sense, we are the Easter people! We are not among those obsessed by destruction or resigned to hopelessness. Because of Christ's resurrection, we have the hope of one day being raised from the dead.

**2. NOW ACCEPTED.** Once we were separated from Christ and alienated from God. Formerly we were strangers to the covenants and promises of the Lord. But now through Christ we are accepted and affirmed as God's beloved.

**3. NOW ALLIED.** Have the class consider some of the ways Paul described the new oneness they have in Christ: the walls of hostility dividing us have been broken; there is one new humanity instead of two; and we are members of God's household. Christ's people should never see each other as adversaries but as allies.

**4. NOW AFFECTED.** Through Christ, believers become a living temple housing God's presence. Do others in your community see the corporate life of your congregation as a manifestation of Christ's goodness?

---

**FOR ADULTS** ■ **TOPIC:** Claim Your New Status

■ **QUESTIONS:** 1. What is the basis for the believers' salvation in Christ? 2. For what purpose has God created us in Christ? 3. In what ways has the peace of Christ made a difference in your life as a believer? 4. How should being a part of the body of Christ transform your relationships with others? 5. How might you encourage other believers with the truth that they are a spiritual temple of God in whom the Spirit dwells?

### ■ ILLUSTRATIONS:

**The Healthy Forest.** We sometimes mistakenly imagine a great hardwood sending down roots deep into the soil. But naturalists point out that a healthy tree is one whose roots go sideways, not deep down. And the roots don't just protect that one tree, but rather are woven together with the roots of other trees in order to hold up the entire forest. Like a healthy growth of trees in a forest, Christ's people do not consider merely protecting themselves. They realize that the loneliness, meaninglessness, and alienation in the world stem from the refusal of people to relate to God and to one another. Indulging in self-interest and self-preservation produces an unstable person who, like a poorly rooted tree, will be weak and easily toppled. Believers must be rooted together in Christ!

**Door of Reconciliation.** In the ancient cathedral of Saint Patrick, in Dublin, Ireland, the Medieval Chapter House has an old door with a strange hole in it. Visitors to the west end of the nave of the cathedral see the hole in the door of the Medieval Chapter House, and wonder why it is there. It seems that in 1492, two noblemen, the Earl of Ormond and the Earl of Kildare, were sworn enemies. The Earl of Ormond, feeling that his life was in danger, fled to the cathedral and took refuge in the Medieval Chapter House behind the great bolted door.

The Earl of Kildare finally realized that he would have to take the initiative and offer reconciliation. He went to the door and called to the man with whom he had been alienated. Finally, to prove that he meant as a Christian to live in peace with the Earl of Ormond, the Earl of Kildare cut a hole in the door and stretched his arm out through the hole to grasp the hand of the man within the Chapter House who was separated from him. The two became reconciled. The door is known as "the door of reconciliation." God broke through the barriers separating us from Him and one another. He calls us, in turn, to be agents of reconciliation with all from whom we are separated.

**Reunited.** Ken Burns, in his book entitled *The Civil War*, notes that in 1913, the Federal government held a fiftieth anniversary reunion at Gettysburg. It lasted three days. Thousands of survivors camped in the old battlefield, swapped stories, and looked up comrades.

The climax of the gathering was a reenactment of Pickett's Charge. Thousands of spectators gathered to watch as the Union veterans took their positions on Cemetery Ridge, and waited as their old adversaries emerged from the woods on Seminary Ridge and started forward toward them across the long, flat fields. Philip Myers, who witnessed the event as an 18 year old, wrote, "We could see not rifles and bayonets but canes and crutches. We soon could distinguish the more agile ones aiding those less able to maintain their places in the ranks."

As the men neared the northern line, they broke into one final, defiant rebel yell. At the sound, "after half a century of silence, a moan, a sigh, a gigantic gasp of unbelief" rose from the Union men on cemetery Ridge. "It was then," wrote Myers, "that the Yankees, unable to restrain themselves longer, burst from behind the stone wall, and flung themselves upon their former enemies . . . not in mortal combat, but reunited in brotherly love and affection."

This is a wonderful example of the love and forgiveness that can exist among believers in Christ.

---

**FOR YOUTH**

■ TOPIC: All for One!

■ QUESTIONS: 1. In what ways were Gentiles alienated from Jews? 2. How has Christ made peace possible for believing Jews and Gentiles? 3. What are some good works that God is calling you to do as a Christian? 4. How has your way of life been transformed by the peace of God that is found in Christ? 5. How might the hope that you have in Christ be a source of encouragement in times of difficulty?

■ ILLUSTRATIONS:

**Call for Unity.** In the spring of 1997, Pope John Paul II journeyed to Poland for an 11-day trip. In Gniezno, the Pontiff spoke to the presidents of seven central and east European countries. After describing the tragic breakup of Yugoslavia, the Albanian crisis, and the massacres in Bosnia, the pope called upon the leaders to push for unity. The "invisible wall" of fear, aggressiveness, and prejudice had to be destroyed, he announced. Centuries earlier the apostle Paul, spoke about a wall being destroyed and called for unity and harmony among believers in Christ.

**God's Grace.** In an interview with *Today's Christian Woman*, author Gwen Shamblin told this story:

> The girls at the horse barn next door are sweet, but they kept wanting our collies, Chaucer and Virginia, to come over. I told them, "I don't know about letting them come across the fence 'cause they might get confused. But as long as you don't feed them, it's fine." Soon I had no dogs. They were over at the barn every day, living the high life. I'd call them home, but they wouldn't come. . . . Eventually I realized the problem was that our dogs no longer knew who their master was. So a silent war was declared that day. I had to lift Chaucer and carry him home from the barn. We put our dogs on leashes. Then I fussed at Chaucer and Virginia when they were over there, and loved them when they were at home. Then we'd unleash them, test them, find them back over at the barn, and have to

repeat the process. But finally we got their hearts back home. . . . Did I want those dogs because of their work? No! They bark at the wrong people. They bark at cars leaving, not coming. They slobber all over me and my company. They're completely in the way. They steal the cat food. They're trouble, but they're still precious to me, and I adore them.

We're precious in God's sight, and He pursues us. This is the nature of His grace toward us in Christ.

**Drastic Changes.** When Phil and Florence became engaged in 1961, a friend spoke with Phil to offer 10 reasons why he should not get married. The first reason was that Florence was black and that Phil was white. Even the pastor of Phil's Southern Baptist church had said that God disapproved of his interracial union. Phil's mother cried. Despite all the pressure, Phil and Florence married and thus joined a group of interracial couples who made up less than one percent of the population in the 1960s. The marriage of Phil and Florence has endured, for it is based on commitment to the Lord and to one another. They have a loving, stable union. In fact, they say that they feel closer to each other now than when they were married nearly 40 years ago.

Today, decades later, a dramatic change has occurred in our nation, according to a 1998 U.S. Census Bureau report. Over 3 percent of marriages are interracial. The most telling statistic is the public's acceptance of mixed-race marriages. Now interracial couples thrive. Few now draw stares or disparaging remarks. Another wall—a racial one—has crumbled in America.

# CALLED TO USE YOUR SPIRITUAL GIFTS

**BACKGROUND SCRIPTURE:** Ephesians 4:1-16
**DEVOTIONAL READING:** Ephesians 3:14-21

---

**KEY VERSE:** Each of us was given grace according to the measure of Christ's gift. Ephesians 4:7.

---

*KING JAMES VERSION*

EPHESIANS 4:1 I therefore, the prisoner of the Lord, beseech you that ye walk worthy of the vocation wherewith ye are called,

2 With all lowliness and meekness, with longsuffering, forbearing one another in love;

3 Endeavouring to keep the unity of the Spirit in the bond of peace.

4 There is one body, and one Spirit, even as ye are called in one hope of your calling;

5 One Lord, one faith, one baptism,

6 One God and Father of all, who is above all, and through all, and in you all.

7 But unto every one of us is given grace according to the measure of the gift of Christ.

8 Wherefore he saith, When he ascended up on high, he led captivity captive, and gave gifts unto men.

9 (Now that he ascended, what is it but that he also descended first into the lower parts of the earth?

10 He that descended is the same also that ascended up far above all heavens, that he might fill all things.)

11 And he gave some, apostles; and some, prophets; and some, evangelists; and some, pastors and teachers;

12 For the perfecting of the saints, for the work of the ministry, for the edifying of the body of Christ:

13 Till we all come in the unity of the faith, and of the knowledge of the Son of God, unto a perfect man, unto the measure of the stature of the fulness of Christ:

14 That we henceforth be no more children, tossed to and fro, and carried about with every wind of doctrine, by the sleight of men, and cunning craftiness, whereby they lie in wait to deceive;

15 But speaking the truth in love, may grow up into him in all things, which is the head, even Christ:

16 From whom the whole body fitly joined together and compacted by that which every joint supplieth, according to the effectual working in the measure of every part, maketh increase of the body unto the edifying of itself in love.

*NEW REVISED STANDARD VERSION*

EPHESIANS 4:1 I therefore, the prisoner in the Lord, beg you to lead a life worthy of the calling to which you have been called, 2 with all humility and gentleness, with patience, bearing with one another in love, 3 making every effort to maintain the unity of the Spirit in the bond of peace. 4 There is one body and one Spirit, just as you were called to the one hope of your calling, 5 one Lord, one faith, one baptism, 6 one God and Father of all, who is above all and through all and in all.

7 But each of us was given grace according to the measure of Christ's gift. 8 Therefore it is said,

"When he ascended on high he made captivity itself a captive;

he gave gifts to his people."

9 (When it says, "He ascended," what does it mean but that he had also descended into the lower parts of the earth? 10 He who descended is the same one who ascended far above all the heavens, so that he might fill all things.) 11 The gifts he gave were that some would be apostles, some prophets, some evangelists, some pastors and teachers, 12 to equip the saints for the work of ministry, for building up the body of Christ, 13 until all of us come to the unity of the faith and of the knowledge of the Son of God, to maturity, to the measure of the full stature of Christ. 14 We must no longer be children, tossed to and fro and blown about by every wind of doctrine, by people's trickery, by their craftiness in deceitful scheming. 15 But speaking the truth in love, we must grow up in every way into him who is the head, into Christ, 16 from whom the whole body, joined and knit together by every ligament with which it is equipped, as each part is working properly, promotes the body's growth in building itself up in love.

| | | |
|---|---|---|
| *Monday, July 10* | Ephesians 3:1-6 | *Gentiles Are Fellow Heirs in Christ* |
| *Tuesday, July 11* | Ephesians 3:7-13 | *Gentiles Receive the Gospel's Riches* |
| *Wednesday, July 12* | Ephesians 3:14-21 | *Paul Prays for the Ephesian Christians* |
| *Thursday, July 13* | Ephesians 4:1-10 | *Unity in the Body of Christ* |
| *Friday, July 14* | Ephesians 4:11-16 | *Grow to Maturity in Christ Jesus* |
| *Saturday, July 15* | Ephesians 4:17-24 | *Live in Righteousness and Holiness* |
| *Sunday, July 16* | Ephesians 4:25-32 | *Live a New Life in Christ* |

## BACKGROUND

The congregations started by Paul tended to be in large Greek-speaking cities where a pagan culture flourished. In most cases the morality and customs of Jerusalem and the Jewish villages of Palestine were nonexistent in these metropolitan centers. Though Paul usually evangelized first in the synagogues of the cities where there was a Jewish community, he almost always was thrown out by agitated fanatics. And while the apostle led many Jews to faith in Jesus, the majority of his converts came from a pagan background.

These new believers often found it difficult to shed their old ways and attitudes. After all, they continued to live, work, and socialize in the same places as before their conversions, and they found themselves immersed in the outlook of the morally loose Mediterranean world. This was a society in which one's place in the pecking order was defined, and in which many people tried to exploit and manipulate those below them. Sadly, this thinking crept into the behavior of many in the congregations Paul had established. Leaders often ignored Jesus' humble style of servant leadership, and instead were bossy and insolent. Believers with supposedly insignificant spiritual abilities were sometimes dismissed as unimportant by those inflated with pride.

Paul often wrote to his Christian friends that such high-and-mighty ways were antithetical to the Gospel of Christ. In the Letter to the Ephesians, Paul stressed that God has bestowed special abilities on every Christian. The spiritual gifts of each believer were indispensable for the well-being of the church and for Christ's ministry to the world.

## NOTES ON THE PRINTED TEXT

There is a distinct change in tone and theme between Ephesians 1—3 and chapters 4—6. In the first half of the letter, Paul focused on the truths of the Christian faith. But in the second half, he discussed the practical application of those truths to the Christian life.

*I therefore, the prisoner in the Lord, beg you to lead a life worthy of the calling to which you have been called* (4:1). Paul summoned believers to live in a way that was worthy of Christ. The imprisoned apostle urged his readers to practice humility, gentleness, patience, and love (4:2). Paul asked the Ephesian Christians not to seek their own advancement or prominence. Instead, love, toleration (even of insults), courtesy, and patience were to be exhibited. The apostle's goal was to promote unity and peace within the church: *making every effort to maintain the unity of the Spirit in the bond of peace* (4:3).

Paul described the unity of the Spirit by using what may have been an old creed or confession of the Christian faith. Some have suggested that it was recited at baptismal ceremonies. *There is one body and one Spirit, just as you were called to the one hope of your calling, one Lord, one faith, one baptism, one God and Father of all, who is above all and through all and in all* (4:4-6).

Paul moved from the subject of the unity of all believers to the uniqueness of each one. Based on the redeeming work of Christ, the Father freely bestows on every believer special abilities. They are to use these spiritual gifts for the betterment of the church. *But each of us was given grace according to the measure of Christ's gift* (4:7).

Paul quoted from Psalm 68:18 to stress that God's grace was evident in Jesus' coming to earth. He died on the cross, rose from the dead, and then ascended into heaven. He alone has the right to rule the universe and the church, and to bestow gifts of grace on His followers. *Therefore it is said, "When he ascended on high he made captivity itself a captive; he gave gifts to his people. (When it says, "He ascended," what does it mean but that he had also descended into the lower parts of the earth? He who descended is the same one who ascended far above all the heavens, so that he might fill all things)* (Eph. 4:8-10).

Paul next listed some of the gifts that Christ gave to the Church. *Some would be apostles, some prophets, some evangelists, some pastors and teachers, to equip the saints for the work of ministry, for building up the body of Christ, until all of us come to the unity of the faith and of the knowledge of the Son of God, the maturity, to the measure of the full stature of Christ* (4:11-13). God used such believers as apostles, prophets, and evangelists to proclaim the Gospel, lead the lost to faith, and establish local churches. And God used such believers as pastors and teachers to give believers further instruction in the faith.

Notice the various stages of growth delineated by Paul in 4:12-13. Gifted leaders were responsible to *equip the saints*. They in turn were to do the work of the *ministry*. As a result, *the body of Christ* would be built up. Through this ongoing process maturity, love, and truth would be established. In the absence of such efforts, new converts would remain spiritually immature and would be easy targets for spiritual frauds. That is why Paul urged his readers to *no longer be children, tossed to and fro and blown about by every wind of doctrine, by people's trickery, by their craftiness in deceitful scheming* (4:14).

Under the lordship of Christ, His spiritual body is fitted together perfectly. As each part does its own special task, it helps the other members of the body to grow. Consequently, the whole body remains healthy, and it grows into the fullness of the love of Christ (4:15-16). Thus every part is essential to the body's full growth. There are no insignificant members of the church (1 Cor. 12:14-27). In the Savior's eyes every believer serves a good and valued purpose in His body.

## SUGGESTIONS TO TEACHERS

Unlike other human organizations, the church is not intended to have a pecking order of members. Clubs, companies, and other collections of people create lists of who's more important than others and whose abilities count more than others. This is not to be true among Christians in the church. This week's lesson should challenge your students to appreciate each other's spiritual gifts and to value what they do in the church.

**1. HUMILITY IN CALLING.** Ephesians 4 opens with a reminder that believers should not be inflated with pride. Paul noted that all of us are saved by God's grace and are called to serve Him, regardless of where we live and work. Belonging to Jesus means reflecting the humility of the Savior in one's life. For example, your students should make allowance for each other's faults because of their mutual love for one another.

**2. UNITY IN FAITH.** Paul often referred to the Church as the spiritual Body of Christ. The idea is that the Spirit has joined individual believers to the Savior. They are to live in unity because they belong to the same body, share the same Spirit, and look with anticipation to the same glorious future. In an era of unrepressed individualism and unrepentant narcissism, we have been taught to insist on getting "our way." Solitary religion (namely, "I can worship by myself when I feel like it, and I don't need others!") is becoming the norm. But Christians have been called to unity.

**3. DIVERSITY OF GIFTS.** Be sure to stress the following points with the members of your class: (a) God has given every believer some kind of spiritual gift; (b) each gift is necessary for the well-being of the church; (c) no one's gift is superior to or more important than the others; (d) no one's gift is identical to that of anyone else; and, (3) every gift is given to build up the Body of Christ. Above all, try to help each student identify and affirm the unique abilities of every other class member.

**4. CHARITY TOWARD EACH OTHER.** In celebrating the oneness of Christ's people, there is no place ever for pride or pecking orders. Christian love, when translated into action, means a mutual respect and sensitivity for others.

**FOR ADULTS**

■ TOPIC: Claim Your Ministry

■ QUESTIONS: 1. What were some of the virtues that Paul urged his readers to display? 2. What were some of the spiritual gifts that Christ bestowed on the church? 3. What are some ways that you can promote peace within your church? 4. How might you use your spiritual gifts to build up your church? 5. What can you do to affirm the spiritual gifts of other believers?

■ **ILLUSTRATIONS:**

**Interconnected, Interdependent.** Paul used a metaphor that has immense meaning: the Church is the Body of Christ, and each person is an integral part of that Body. The Lord uses His followers to manifest His presence and do His work in the world.

But there is more. A body is an organic entity. A human body, as Paul reminded us, is composed of amazing interrelated and interacting parts. Each is necessary for the well-being of the organism. One's body is more than merely a collection of bones, tissues, and organs. Rather, it is a system in which everything is interconnected and needed. If one part is hurting, other parts are affected.

Years ago, I injured my right shoulder in sports, and finally had to have surgery and a cast for many weeks. I learned that it was not simply the shoulder that was affected, but also my arm, elbow, wrist, hand, and fingers. Even my neck experienced pain, discomfort, and inability to function properly. Each member of my body was dependent on the other. Hurt and dislocation in one part caused difficulties in all other parts, and my body could not operate normally. Likewise in the Body of Christ, each part is indispensable for the full and healthy operation of the whole.

Each of us is part of the Church. And each of us is as indispensable as any other follower of the Lord. Without one other, the Church is weakened, less healthy, and unproductive.

**Just Suppose.** Just suppose that your church membership was good only for one year at a time and that its renewal depended upon your faithfulness in attendance, stewardship, and service. Would you retain your membership? Just suppose that the membership was limited to those who could give a valid written excuse for absences. Would your absences be acceptable? Just suppose that some parents could look into the future and see the dreadful results of neglecting to come with their children to Sunday school and worship. Would they be different parents?

Just suppose that people were as enthusiastic about church events as they are about sporting events. Would there not be a marked difference in the life of the church? Just suppose that you were called upon to explain why your church should continue your name on its membership roll. Could you do it? Just suppose that every member of the church attended as often as you. Would we need more seating, or would the building be closed and put up for sale?

Suppose then that we stop supposing and renew our dedication to the high calling of Jesus Christ. Our attendance and stewardship would increase sharply. This is something for all of us to think about.

**Lesson from the Lighthouse.** The powerful beam from any of the lighthouses along the coasts of North America is caused not simply by a strong electric light. The secret of the brilliant glow is the carefully constructed reflector. This device consists of hundreds of highly-polished mirrors. Each small one is mounted at a specific angle so that the lamp will be reflected in a way that accentuates the light. The banks of mirrors are positioned to increase the range and intensity of the source of the light.

Your congregation could be compared to a lighthouse. The members are to be like individual mirrors that reflect the source of the light, Jesus Christ. They must remain united in order to cast a powerful beam that pierces through the world's darkness and offers guidance, truth, and hope to people who are lost in sin.

---

**FOR YOUTH**

■ TOPIC: Use Your Gifts!
■ QUESTIONS: 1. In what ways are believers spiritually united to one another? 2. Why did God gave spiritual gifts to believers? 3. What are some ways that God has spiritually gifted you? 4. How might you use your special abilities to bring glory to God? 5. What happens when you and others in your church choose to operate for the good of the congregation?

■ ILLUSTRATIONS:

**Called to Oneness of Purpose.** In January 1998, Pope John Paul II visited Cuba for five days. "The Pope of the Young," as he was dubbed, celebrated a special mass at Camaguey's Plaza Ignacio Agramonte (which is 400 miles east of Havana) for Cuba's young people. The church leader called them to develop values, be honest and virtuous in their relationships, and be hospitable to everyone. They were to be bold in truth, courageous in freedom, generous in love, and invincible in hope. Finally, they were to work together enthusiastically to overcome all setbacks and limitations. Long before the pope, the apostle Paul urged his new converts to recognize the value of working together in building up the body of Christ.

**Seemed to Have It All.** Edward, age 21, was a Lehigh University senior. As a business administration and accounting major, he had already accepted a position with the New York City accounting firm of Arthur Anderson, where his older brother worked. Edward's past included varsity letters in soccer and lacrosse. He had participated in soccer's National Youth Challenge Cup, and he had helped lead the Pittsburgh Strikers to a national championship. A fraternity man from a well-to-do family, he was popular at school.

However, on Friday night, November 7, 1997, Edward hanged himself from the fire escape of the Phi Delta Gamma fraternity house. A sparkling past and a promising future suddenly ended. His soccer coach summed up everyone's thoughts when he stated that no one expected the suicide to happen, especially to a young person who seemed to have everything going for him.

Edward is only one of many youth who feel that death is the answer to their problems. He probably never experienced the comfort and love that the church could offer.

**No "I" in Team.** High school coaches have the slogan *There is No "I" in Team* on posters and T-shirts. The point is to build a team spirit and remind players that no one is more significant than the others. Winning demands a team effort.

In football and baseball, even a franchise player cannot win a title. These are genuinely team sports. Every one must work together if that particular team is to win and make the playoffs. The same principle is true in the church. Everyone must work together by using their gifts, especially if the church is to achieve its goal of bringing glory to God.

# CALLED TO RESPONSIBLE LIVING

**BACKGROUND SCRIPTURE:** Ephesians 5:1—6:4
**DEVOTIONAL READING:** Ephesians 5:6-20

**KEY VERSE:** Be subject to one another out of reverence for Christ. Ephesians 5:21.

*KING JAMES VERSION*

EPHESIANS 5:1 Be ye therefore followers of God, as dear children;

2 And walk in love, as Christ also hath loved us, and hath given himself for us an offering and a sacrifice to God for a sweetsmelling savour.

3 But fornication, and all uncleanness, or covetousness, let it not be once named among you, as becometh saints;

4 Neither filthiness, nor foolish talking, nor jesting, which are not convenient: but rather giving of thanks.

5 For this ye know, that no whoremonger, nor unclean person, nor covetous man, who is an idolater, hath any inheritance in the kingdom of Christ and of God. . . .

21 Submitting yourselves one to another in the fear of God.

22 Wives, submit yourselves unto your own husbands, as unto the Lord.

23 For the husband is the head of the wife, even as Christ is the head of the church: and he is the saviour of the body.

24 Therefore as the church is subject unto Christ, so let the wives be to their own husbands in every thing.

25 Husbands, love your wives, even as Christ also loved the church, and gave himself for it;

26 That he might sanctify and cleanse it with the washing of water by the word,

27 That he might present it to himself a glorious church, not having spot, or wrinkle, or any such thing; but that it should be holy and without blemish.

28 So ought men to love their wives as their own bodies. He that loveth his wife loveth himself.

29 For no man ever yet hated his own flesh; but nourisheth and cherisheth it, even as the Lord the church: . . .

6:1 Children, obey your parents in the Lord: for this is right.

2 Honour thy father and mother; which is the first commandment with promise;

3 That it may be well with thee, and thou mayest live long on the earth.

4 And, ye fathers, provoke not your children to wrath: but bring them up in the nurture and admonition of the Lord.

*NEW REVISED STANDARD VERSION*

EPHESIANS 5:1 Therefore be imitators of God, as beloved children, 2 and live in love, as Christ loved us and gave himself up for us, a fragrant offering and sacrifice to God.

3 But fornication and impurity of any kind, or greed, must not even be mentioned among you, as is proper among saints. 4 Entirely out of place is obscene, silly, and vulgar talk; but instead, let there be thanksgiving. 5 Be sure of this, that no fornicator or impure person, or one who is greedy (that is, an idolater), has any inheritance in the kingdom of Christ and of God. . . .

5:21 Be subject to one another out of reverence for Christ.

22 Wives, be subject to your husbands as you are to the Lord. 23 For the husband is the head of the wife just as Christ is the head of the church, the body of which he is the Savior. 24 Just as the church is subject to Christ, so also wives ought to be, in everything, to their husbands.

25 Husbands, love your wives, just as Christ loved the church and gave himself up for her, 26 in order to make her holy by cleansing her with the washing of water by the word, 27 so as to present the church to himself in splendor, without a spot or wrinkle or anything of the kind—yes, so that she may be holy and without blemish. 28 In the same way, husbands should love their wives as they do their own bodies. He who loves his wife loves himself. 29 For no one ever hates his own body, but he nourishes and tenderly cares for it, just as Christ does for the church, . . .

6:1 Children, obey your parents in the Lord, for this is right. 2 "Honor your father and mother"—this is the first commandment with a promise: 3 "so that it may be well with you and you may live long on the earth."

4 And, fathers, do not provoke your children to anger, but bring them up in the discipline and instruction of the Lord.

| Monday, July 17 | Ephesians 5:1-5 | *Turn Your Backs on Pagan Ways* |
| *Tuesday, July 18* | Ephesians 5:6-14 | *Live as Children of the Light* |
| *Wednesday, July 19* | Ephesians 5:15-20 | *Serve and Worship with Thanks* |
| *Thursday, July 20* | Ephesians 5:21-27 | *Words for Christians in Families* |
| *Friday, July 21* | Ephesians 5:28-33 | *Love as Christ Loved the Church* |
| *Saturday, July 22* | Ephesians 6:1-9 | *Treat Everyone with Love and Respect* |
| *Sunday, July 23* | Luke 6:43-49 | *Hear God's Word, and Obey* |

## BACKGROUND

The Letter to the Ephesians deals with matters of belief and also matters of behavior. Paul wrote about doctrine in the first portion of this tract (chaps. 1—3). After he wrote his sublime words about God's purpose through Jesus Christ and the call of the church to work with the Creator in carrying out that purpose, Paul turned to the ethical responsibilities of all who carry the name of Christ. Beginning in chapter 4 and continuing through chapter 6, the apostle gave detailed instructions about how Christians were to act.

One of the problems that Paul encountered on many occasions among his Gentile converts was their inclination to continue in their casual pagan-world morality. These members of the church had no grounding in the Ten Commandments or the morals of Judaism. Many had misunderstood Paul's teachings about God's grace. Hearing that it was not necessary for them to be circumcised or observe certain eating rules to be saved, many newly-baptized former pagans assumed that there were no restraints or rules to follow. They felt that they were independent of Israel and the basic morality of Judaism. Some were even critical of Jewish believers for insisting on high ethical standards, especially in matters of sex and marriage.

Paul had to remind his new Gentile converts, especially those who were indifferent and forgetful about their spiritual roots in Judaism, that Christ's people were expected to reflect their Lord in their behavior. In Paul's writings, he emphatically and repeatedly warned that believers could not ignore the basic ethical requirements of Scripture. Members of Christ's community belonged to the Savior and were called to responsible living in their daily personal activities, whether it be in their homes or in their places of work.

Like Paul's other letters, Ephesians contains three elements. First, there is an *autobiographical* aspect. In other words, the apostle gave us information about himself, particularly concerning his ministry to the church. Second, there is a *didactic* aspect. In other words, Paul used this epistle to teach his readers what to believe and how to act. The letter contains theological and ethical interpretations that helped to form the foundation of the Christian faith. Third, there is an *apologetic* aspect. In other words, Paul used this letter to defend a true understanding of the Gospel and to guard the church against heresy.

## NOTES ON THE PRINTED TEXT

Paul offered practical statements on Christian living. Along with the guidelines he also offered a pattern to follow. *Therefore be imitators of God, as beloved children, and live in love, as Christ loved us and gave himself up for us, a fragrant offering and sacrifice to God* (5:1-2). Believers, as God's children, were to imitate the Savior's example of sacrificial love. Their lives were to reflect their commitment to Christ in terms of a higher morality. *But fornication and impurity of any kind, or greed, must not even be mentioned among you, as is proper among saints* (5:3). Sex outside of marriage, lust, and any other form of immorality were not to be practiced or advocated by God's people. Indecent speech and dirty insinuations or jokes were not to be spoken by Christians. *Entirely out of place is obscene, silly, and vulgar talk; but instead, let there be thanksgiving* (5:4).

Should these ethical guidelines fail to sway his readers, Paul offered a stern reminder. *Be sure of this, that no fornicator or impure person, or one who is greedy (that is, an idolater), has any inheritance in the kingdom of Christ and of God* (5:5). Those who were sexually immoral showed by their attitudes and actions that they did not care about eternal life in God's kingdom. Thus it was imperative for the apostle's readers to renounce their ungodly ways (5:6-20).

Paul next turned his attention to the Christian household. The apostle advocated the display of mutual love and respect. Every family member was to subordinate their own interests to those of their loved ones. *Be subject to one another out of reverence for Christ* (5:21).

The apostle first addressed the wives. *Wives, be subject to your husbands as you are to the Lord* (5:22). Paul was not urging wives to be doormats for their husbands, especially to those who acted like an irrational tyrant. After all, Christianity had elevated the status of women in society. Their obedience and commitment to the Lord was the basis for their relationship with their husband. Harmony and love between a husband and wife would prevail when both partners had a strong relationship with Christ and were mutually concerned for the happiness of the other. *For the husband is the head of the wife just as Christ is the head of the church, the body of which he is the Savior. Just as the church is subject to Christ, so also wives ought to be, in everything, to their husbands* (5:23-24).

The husbands were not to be selfish or demanding despots. Rather, a Christian husband was to love his wife completely, unconditionally, and sacrificially. Christ's love for the Church was the example to follow. *Husbands, love your wives, just as Christ loved the church and gave himself up for her, in order to make her holy by cleaning her with the washing of water by the word, so as to present the church to himself in splendor, without a spot or wrinkle or anything of the kind—yes, so that she may be holy and without blemish* (5:25-27).

Paul stated that just as a man cared for his own body, so too he was to care for his wife. A husband provided himself with nourishment, warmth, protection, and comfort; likewise, he must care for his wife, just as Christ did for the church. *In the same way, husbands should love the wives as they do their own bodies. He who loves his wife loves himself. For no one ever hates his own body, but he nourishes and tenderly cares for it, just as Christ does for the church* (5:28-29).

Husbands and wives were not the only family members who were to mutually love and respect each other. Children of all ages were also to honor their parents. *Children, obey your parents in the Lord, for this is right* (6:1). Paul backed his call for respect and care by quoting the fifth commandment and reminding his readers of the promise. *"Honor your father and mother"—this is the first commandment with a promise: "so that it may be well with you and you may live long on the earth"* (6:2-3).

The apostle then made a comment to fathers. *And, fathers, do not provoke your children to anger, but bring them up in the discipline and instruction of the Lord* (6:4). Fathers were not to exasperate their children with unreasonable demands. Instead, they were to love and care for their children. In addition, fathers were responsible for teaching their children about Jesus Christ.

## SUGGESTIONS TO TEACHERS

When a retired couple from a Chicago suburb won $195 million in the 1998 Powerball lottery jackpot, several newspapers asked readers what they'd do if they had been like the Illinois winners, who now had a lot of money to spend. Most said, in effect, "Spend!" A typical response was given by Christine Hanna of Hyannis, Massachusetts. "What would I do with $195 million? Start spending it!" Hanna added, "I'd take a trip around the world. Then I'd buy a Caribbean island." Society's attitude of "Look after me!" had spoken again.

Paul in Ephesians urged Christ's people to live responsibly in every area of their lives, including the workplace, the home, and the social group. The apostle pointed out that responsible living starts with imitating God and sacrificing for others. Self-indulgence, self-interest and self-gratification are ruled out.

**1. TALK.** Responsibility applies even in a believer's talk. Dwell for a time on 5:3-14, where Christians are advised to avoid using words or participating in conversations in which obscene topics are relished. Paul urged believers to stay away from those whose speech and interests center on lust, greed, and all matters that degrade people.

**2. WARNINGS.** Paul knew that giving in to thoughts of immorality could tug a person into destructive ways and apart from Christ. Thus the apostle warned his readers to be wary every waking hour of the clutches of evil. Be sure to focus on 5:15-20, which stresses the importance of maintaining private or personal devotions and regular public worship with one's congregation.

**3. WISDOM.** Daily living by responsible believers means a careful use of time. Discuss some of the most helpful ways believers can use disposable hours.

**4. WAYS.** Paul discussed the responsibilities of husbands and wives to one another (5:21-33). The important point to emphasize is mutual caring. If your class is made up of married persons or people of marriage age, you will want to let this portion of the lesson take the major part of the class time for discussion. Examine and allow comments on these verses.

**5. WARMTH.** Paul gave a word to parents and children. In a society where family life is crumbling, the apostle's admonitions on responsible living are wise to follow.

---

**FOR ADULTS**

■ TOPIC: Claim Your Responsibilities

■ QUESTIONS: 1. Why do you think Paul underscored the importance of living in love? 2. How can the love of Christ transform the various family relationships that the apostle mentioned? 3. How detrimental would obscene stories and coarse jokes be to your family and work relationships? 4. In what ways can you submit to your loved ones out of reverence for Christ? 5. How might you show the love of Christ to your loved ones?

■ **ILLUSTRATIONS:**

**Concrete Love.** The story is told of a child psychologist who spent a long afternoon constructing a new driveway at his home. Just after he smoothed the surface of the newly-poured concrete, his small children chased a ball across the driveway, leaving deep footprints. The man yelled at them with harshly angry words. His wife yelled back, "You're a psychologist who's supposed to love children." The fuming man shouted, "I love children in the abstract, not in the concrete!"

It's easy to laugh at this incident and raise our eyebrows at the doctor's play on words, but the story has the ring of truth from which we can learn. While we agree in principle with the concept of self-giving love, we may often find ourselves failing to express it to the people we care about deeply. As a mere theory, love isn't worth much. But as expressed in daily actions, it is the greatest gift that one can offer to others. When the careless footprints of others are left in our lives, people can see whether our love exists in the abstract or in the concrete.

**Blessed Are the Parents.** Blessed are the parents who make their peace with spilled milk and mud, for of such is the kingdom of childhood. Blessed are the parents who refuse to compare their children with others, for precious to each is the rhythm of his or her own growth. Blessed are the fathers and mothers who have learned to laugh, for it is the music of the child's world. Blessed are those parents who understand the goodness of time, for they make it not a sword that kills growth, but a shield to protect and guide their children.

Blessed are those parents who accept the awkwardness of their growing children, letting each one grow at his or her own speed. Blessed are the parents who can say "no" without anger, for comforting to the child is the security of a firm decision. Blessed are the parents who are teachable, for knowledge brings understanding and understanding brings love. Blessed are the parents who love their children in the midst of a hostile world, for love is the greatest of all gifts (author unknown).

**More than Computers.** "Computers are going to be central to our children's lives, and that knowledge will be essential to them as adults, but I think it's just like television. When parents aren't watching, the computer becomes a baby-sitter; it gives them an excuse not to interact with their own children. With two-career families, parents are spending something like a third less time with their children than they were 30 years ago. Also, we've oversold computers. Parents say, 'Hey, they're learning all about computers,' but we find kids substituting knowledge for values. They don't have to empathize with other children; they just have to learn to use this 'wonderful machine' " (Edward Zigler, Sterling Professor of Psychology, Yale University).

**FOR YOUTH**

■ TOPIC: A Place for Me!

■ QUESTIONS: 1. What example did Christ leave us in terms of loving others? 2. Why do you think Paul urged his readers not to let any form of sexual immorality, impurity, or greed exist among them? 3. What are some ways that you can show honor and love to your parents? 4. How might you encourage your peers to do the same thing? 5. How do you think your parents would respond to your displays of respect and love?

■ ILLUSTRATIONS:

**The Product of Broken Homes.** Epidemiologists from the Harvard School of Public Health collected and analyzed data from more than 2,500 children between the ages of six and eleven. They concluded that there was a direct link between the family and the child's need for medical and psychological help. Children from a single-parent family were twice as likely to need treatment for mental health problems as compared to those from a two-parent family. Nineteen centuries before such studies were done, Paul counseled his readers to live responsibly in their families. Believers were to submit to and care for one another.

**Why Get Married?** While educators, clergy, doctors, and a host of other professionals all agree that youth lack the experience to prepare themselves for marriage and parenthood, one reason might be their homelife. Given the large numbers of individuals cohabiting outside the covenant of marriage, many youth wonder whether marriage is even necessary. A study done at Pennsylvania State University concluded that cohabitation actually increases hostility to marriage.

Sociologists William G. Axinn and Jennifer S. Bates analyzed data collected over 23 years and wrote that the longer a child lives in a sexual cohabiting agreement, the less likely he or she will be to endorse marriage and the family.

Paul described the ideal family as having a married mother and father. He outlined the responsibilities of each in his letter to the Ephesians. The apostle's intent seems to have been to prepare every member of the family for their responsibilities in life.

**The Cry for Love.** A father sat at his desk working on the family's monthly bills when his young son announced, "Dad, because this is your birthday and you're 55 years old, I'm going to give you 55 kisses, one for each year!" When the boy started making good on his proimise the father exclaimed, "Oh, Andrew, don't do it now; I'm too busy!"

The young boy fell silent as tears welled up in his big blue eyes. Apologetically the father said, "You can finish later." But the boy looked down and quietly walked away, disappointment written all over his face. Later that evening the father said, "Come and finish the kisses now, Andrew." But the boy didn't respond.

A short time after this incident the boy passed away in an accident His heartbroken father wrote, "If only I could tell him how much I regret my thoughtless words, and could be assured that he knows how much my heart is aching."

If we are too busy to give and receive love, we are too busy. Nothing is more important than responding with love to the cry for love from those who are near and precious to us.

# CALLED TO STAND FIRM

**BACKGROUND SCRIPTURE:** Ephesians 6:10-24
**DEVOTIONAL READING:** John 14:15-27

**KEY VERSE:** Be strong in the Lord and in the strength of his power. Ephesians 6:10.

*KING JAMES VERSION*

EPHESIANS 6:10 Finally, my brethren, be strong in the Lord, and in the power of his might.

11 Put on the whole armour of God, that ye may be able to stand against the wiles of the devil.

12 For we wrestle not against flesh and blood, but against principalities, against powers, against the rulers of the darkness of this world, against spiritual wickedness in high places.

13 Wherefore take unto you the whole armour of God, that ye may be able to withstand in the evil day, and having done all, to stand.

14 Stand therefore, having your loins girt about with truth, and having on the breastplate of righteousness;

15 And your feet shod with the preparation of the gospel of peace;

16 Above all, taking the shield of faith, wherewith ye shall be able to quench all the fiery darts of the wicked.

17 And take the helmet of salvation, and the sword of the Spirit, which is the word of God:

18 Praying always with all prayer and supplication in the Spirit, and watching thereunto with all perseverance and supplication for all saints;

19 And for me, that utterance may be given unto me, that I may open my mouth boldly, to make known the mystery of the gospel,

20 For which I am an ambassador in bonds: that therein I may speak boldly, as I ought to speak.

21 But that ye also may know my affairs, and how I do, Tychicus, a beloved brother and faithful minister in the Lord, shall make known to you all things:

22 Whom I have sent unto you for the same purpose, that ye might know our affairs, and that he might comfort your hearts.

23 Peace be to the brethren, and love with faith, from God the Father and the Lord Jesus Christ.

24 Grace be with all them that love our Lord Jesus Christ in sincerity. Amen.

*NEW REVISED STANDARD VERSION*

EPHESIANS 6:10 Finally, be strong in the Lord and in the strength of his power. 11 Put on the whole armor of God, so that you may be able to stand against the wiles of the devil. 12 For our struggle is not against enemies of blood and flesh, but against the rulers, against the authorities, against the cosmic powers of this present darkness, against the spiritual forces of evil in the heavenly places. 13 Therefore take up the whole armor of God, so that you may be able to withstand on that evil day, and having done everything, to stand firm. 14 Stand therefore, and fasten the belt of truth around your waist, and put on the breastplate of righteousness. 15 As shoes for your feet put on whatever will make you ready to proclaim the gospel of peace. 16 With all of these, take the shield of faith, with which you will be able to quench all the flaming arrows of the evil one. 17 Take the helmet of salvation, and the sword of the Spirit, which is the word of God.

18 Pray in the Spirit at all times in every prayer and supplication. To that end keep alert and always persevere in supplication for all the saints. 19 Pray also for me, so that when I speak, a message may be given to me to make known with boldness the mystery of the gospel, 20 for which I am an ambassador in chains. Pray that I may declare it boldly, as I must speak. 21 So that you also may know how I am and what I am doing, Tychicus will tell you everything. He is a dear brother and a faithful minister in the Lord. 22 I am sending him to you for this very purpose, to let you know how we are, and to encourage your hearts.

23 Peace be to the whole community, and love with faith, from God the Father and the Lord Jesus Christ. 24 Grace be with all who have an undying love for our Lord Jesus Christ.

| | | |
|---|---|---|
| *Monday, July 24* | Ephesians 6:10-15 | *Be Strong in the Lord* |
| *Tuesday, July 25* | Ephesians 6:16-20 | *Pray Always in the Lord's Spirit* |
| *Wednesday, July 26* | Ephesians 6:21-24 | *Grace, Peace, and Love from God* |
| *Thursday, July 27* | John 14:15-27 | *God's Spirit Will Strengthen You* |
| *Friday, July 28* | John 15:1-11 | *Abide in Christ, and Bear Fruit* |
| *Saturday, July 29* | John 15:12-27 | *We Are Chosen by Christ* |
| *Sunday, July 30* | John 16:16-24 | *Your Pain Will Turn to Rejoicing* |

## BACKGROUND

Paul never had any illusions about the power of evil in the world. He neither indulged in idle speculation about the source of evil nor spun philosophical explanations about the dark side of human behavior. Paul knew that evil was real and that evil powers were assailing God's people constantly.

Paul was acutely aware that these destructive forces were stronger than any human powers. In fact, the apostle thought of Christianity's battle against these threatening powers in terms of the hand-to-hand combat and as a fight to the finish that front-line soldiers face against a fierce enemy.

Paul wrote the Letter to the Ephesians while imprisoned in Rome. We know from the apostle's reference to sharing the Good News to the soldiers guarding him—namely, the elite imperial guard that he referred to in Philippians 1:13—that Paul had close contact with the military. Perhaps he had watched the soldiers looking after their equipment and going through continuous training exercises. He undoubtedly knew that the secret of the Roman army was a well-trained, well-equipped, and well-prepared soldier. The apostle recognized the need for discipline, physical fitness, good defensive gear, and excellent weapons.

The military metaphors suggested by the presence of the Roman soldiers around Paul's prison were ideal for describing the way that Christians had to prepare themselves for battle against the pervasive and superhuman forces of evil. Just as the members in the crack Praetorian Guard regiment drilled and conditioned themselves to be ready to fight the enemy at any time, so too Christians must be prepared for the assaults of the evil one and his demonic cohorts.

## NOTES ON THE PRINTED TEXT

Paul, ever a realist, knew that life was not easy and idyllic. Life was a battle for every Christian. Knowing that his readers were under fire each day, the apostle urged, *Finally, be strong in the Lord and in the strength of his power* (6:10). The Ephesians were literally "to be made strong" or "empowered" by the Lord. His might would enable them to face the enemies of the faith.

Not only were believers empowered, but also they were to be equipped. The church was to outfit itself for battle. *Put on the whole armor of God, so that you may be able to stand against the wiles of the devil* (6:11). The battle was not only against the unsaved, but also against the devil. Paul did not underestimate the opposition. The apostle knew that the evil one sought to extend the dominion of darkness everywhere! *For our struggle is not against enemies of blood and flesh, but against the rulers, against the authorities, against the cosmic powers of this present darkness, against the spiritual forces of evil in the heavenly places* (6:12).

Paul urged the Ephesian Christians to equip themselves for spiritual battle so that they could stand, fight, and prevail against the enemy. *Therefore take up the whole armor of God, so that you may be able to withstand on that evil day, and having done everything, to stand firm* (6:13).

Paul's model was a battle-ready Roman soldier. (Some commentators suggest that the apostle was describing the soldier who was chained to him.) *Stand therefore, and fasten the belt of truth around your waist, and put on the breastplate of righteousness* (6:14). The Roman soldier wore a short sleeved wool shirt called a *tunica militaris*. It was short in length to enable maximum mobility. The soldier wore a leather belt called a *cingulum militare*. It was a sign of preparedness indicating that the soldier was ready for action. The believer, too, was to be ready for action. The soldier also wore a sleeveless, hardened leather corset, which was reinforced with strips of metal that ran from the neck down to the tops of the hips. In close combat, it protected the soldier's vital organs. The believers' defense, or protection, was an upright moral life.

To march, a soldier needed foot protection. The soldier wore a heavy leather sandal that was studded with hobnails and was laced with leather thongs, which ran up to the top of the soldier's shin. Archaeologists have excavated some of these sandals, which attests to their durability! Christians were to be shod in whatever enabled them to proclaim God's message of peace and reconciliation to the lost. *As shoes for your feet put on whatever will make you ready to proclaim the gospel of peace* (6:15).

One of the most feared weapons encountered by foot soldiers was the flaming arrow. Dipped in burning pitch, it could kill or set clothing or baggage on fire. To counter this threat, Roman soldiers carried a large quadrangular shield called a *scutum*. It was about 4 feet by 2 feet. The shield was constructed of thin sheets of wood glued together, covered with decorated leather (often the soldier's commanding centurion's name was written on it), and bound on the edges with iron. The shield was the soldier's defense against flaming arrows, particularly when the leather was dampened. A Christian's faith provided protection against the flaming arrows of the devil. *With all of these, take the shield of faith, with which you will be able to quench all the flaming arrows of the evil one* (6:16).

Roman soldiers had two other pieces of equipment. The bronze helmet with its hinged cheek guards was formed around an iron skull plate that extended down the back of the neck, providing additional protection. Believers were protected from past and future sins by their salvation through faith in Christ. The Roman soldier's chief weapon was a two-foot long sword, which was fitted with a corrugated handle grip. Believers were enabled to be on the offense or defense through God's Word. *Take the helmet of salvation, and the sword of the Spirit, which is the word of God* (6:17).

Good soldiers had additional equipment in their armory. The Christians' armory included *prayer and supplication* (6:18). Paul asked his readers to *keep alert* and *persevere*, lest the church be caught unprepared and off guard. Believers were to rely on the Spirit for support and ask for the help of other Christians (6:19). Paul ended his letter by expressing his desire to continue sharing the Gospel, for which he was presently imprisoned (6:19-24).

## SUGGESTIONS TO TEACHERS

Possibly you or some members of your class served in the military. Part of basic training and continuing service in any branch of the armed forces is physical fitness. In addition, constant upgrading of skills in using weapons and equipment is done. From the Roman army of ancient times down to your local unit of the National Guard, battle preparedness has always required capable, committed personnel. Paul used the military metaphor to call for a state of alertness and readiness on the part of every Christian. Ephesians 6:10-24 contains commands that we must heed every day.

**1. THE WAR.** Paul compared the situation in which Christians must exist to waging all-out war. The enemy is relentless and presses to crush us. Our opponent is the devil and the forces of darkness. Urge the members of your class to take seriously the onslaught of evil forces in the world. Those vicious diabolic powers are constantly on the offensive and threaten to overwhelm us. Discuss with the class how God's community is engaged in warfare against a ruthless foe. Explain that evil takes many forms, such as greed, immorality, violence, and injustice. Also note that evil is organized in many ways in society.

**2. THE EQUIPMENT.** Take plenty of time to go over the battle gear that Paul listed in 6:13-17. The complete armor of Roman soldiers consisted of equipment for both their defense and offense. Paul likewise saw well-prepared Christians as being prepared to strap on heavenly gear to protect themselves against the powers of darkness. The apostle also urged Christ's people to know how to use the weaponry they had from God to defeat the evil one.

**3. THE INSTRUCTIONS.** Paul underscored the importance of prayer in the fight against Satan. When believers are fervent in prayer, they are able to persevere against desperate odds. Remind the students that prayer is more than whimpering requests or an occasional casual nod to God. Prayer demands the same level of dedication as the toughening exercise of boot camp and daily calisthenics and serious workouts. Prayer calls for the same serious effort as learning and perfecting skills with sophisticated weaponry. A genuine prayer life is essential for anyone sworn into the service of Christ, who is the Commander-in-Chief of the Church.

Perhaps some members of your class are into physical fitness. Jogging, working out at a health club, conditioning one's self on an exercise machine, or simply walking every day has become an important part of many people's routine. Physicians, of course, recommend regular physical activity for healthy bodies. But what about spiritual workouts? What are you and your class members doing to keep fit as committed followers of Christ? This week's lesson is a summons to get in spiritual shape.

---

**FOR ADULTS**

■ **TOPIC:** Claim Your Power Base

■ **QUESTIONS:** 1. Why did Paul urge believers to be strong in the Lord, especially as they faced the spiritual enemy in battle? 2. Why was the whole armor of God needed to wage war against the forces of darkness? 3. What are some encounters that you have had with the forces of darkness? 4. How has prayer made a difference for you in those situations? 5. How has God's spiritual provisions enabled you to overcome the evil one?

■ **ILLUSTRATIONS:**

**Nothing Else Needed.** The late Mother Teresa once met with a group of Catholic Sisters who were heading convents from various places in the western world. These Mother Superiors came from many different Roman Catholic Orders, but all were apparently representing religious houses that had been losing members and gaining few new ones. During a question period following Mother Teresa's presentation, one America nun spoke for many by asking how Mother Teresa's order of the Missionaries of Charity was attracting hundreds of women each year.

"I give them Jesus," answered Mother Teresa. The American woman persisted, and asked whether Mother Teresa's nuns didn't object to wearing habits and how Mother Teresa managed to have these sisters adhere to the rules of the order. "I give them Jesus," Mother Teresa again replied. Slightly impatient, the questioner from North America demanded that the saintly leader from Calcutta be more specific. "I give them Jesus," Mother Teresa quietly repeated. The woman pushed on by inquiring, "Mother we are all aware of your fine work, but I want to know about something else." "I give them Jesus. There is nothing else."

**The Real Game of Life.** There is an apocryphal story of a conversation baseball slugger Ted Williams once had with golfer Sam Snead. "Look," Williams needled Snead, "you use a club with a flat hitting surface and belt a stationary object. What's tough about that? I gotta stand up there with a round bat and hit a ball that is traveling at me 110 miles an hour—and curving." Snead responded, "Yeah, Ted, but you don't have to go up in the stands and play all your foul balls." Paul, who loved a sports metaphor, would have stated that life is having to go in the stands and play all your foul balls!

**Listened and Stood Firm.** Paul's letter to the Ephesians was John Calvin's favorite epistle. Calvin's book of sermons on Ephesians was what John Knox wanted read to him most frequently when he suffered from his final illness. The doughty old Scottish reformer faced enemies throughout his career, especially as he strove to build Christ's teachings into the life of Scotland. The final enemy was Knox's impending death. As he lay in his bed weak and in pain in his humble room on Edinburgh's High Street, the words from Ephesians reminded Knox that his sole power base was the risen, living Lord. When Knox died, the Earl of Morton correctly remarked, "Here was one who feared the face of no person."

---

**FOR YOUTH**

■ TOPIC: Stand Firm!

■ QUESTIONS: 1. What are the functions of the various pieces of spiritual weaponry that Paul mentioned? 2. Why did Paul ask for prayer, especially as he boldly proclaimed the Gospel? 3. What are some spiritual struggles currently in your life? 4. How can the whole armor of God enable you to overcome these difficulties? 5. How might you encourage other believers to make full use of God's spiritual armor?

■ ILLUSTRATIONS:

**Shoe-In.** Two thousand delegates convened at Grove City College for the Western Pennsylvania United Methodist Annual Conference on June 11, 1998. They gathered to debate several issues, some of which were controversial. But one item seemed to unite the delegates, namely, their shoes! A semi-trailer containing over 30,000 pairs of shoes sat in the parking lot. A second trailer was added so that eventually 44,000 African children would have athletic shoes in which to walk and run. At the conclusion of the conference, the shoes were to be blessed at a special service.

A program begun by the United Methodist Council of Bishops sought the shoes. Realizing that many African children die from cuts received from debris in the war zones, or from fleeing advancing armies, or from parasites in the refugee camps, all from infections picked up while going barefoot, the bishops had called for the footwear. Churches responded immediately and enthusiastically. An 85-year-old man managed to get the Converse Company to donate 500 pairs. One family gave their income tax refund check. Sunday school classes collected money.

Paul urged his followers to put on the shoes of the gospel of peace. Here is one religious group's effort to put on those shoes. It is a fine demonstration of the compassion and care of Christ in a way that is relevant and tangible.

**Concerned about the Devil.** Faith Willard's children no longer attend public school in Mount Lebanon, Pennsylvania. In September, 1997, she pulled her two daughters out of school and began to teach them at home. At the same time she presented a petition signed by 150 residents asking the school district to change the mascot, complaining that it was satanic. Faith believed that the Mount Lebanon Blue Devil promoted satanism and was actually advancing the cause of evil in the public school. Though the school board refused and the local chapter of the American Civil Liberties Union would not take her case, Willard stood firm. She would teach her children at home rather than let them experience what she believed were the flaming missiles of the evil one.

You may smile at the story, but here is a woman who is serious about wanting to shield her daughters from the forces of darkness.

**Source of Support.** A January 1998 study released by the National Institute on Alcohol Abuse and Alcoholism (the largest study on alcohol ever conducted) interviewed 40,000 individuals. It concluded that teens who began drinking before the age of 14 were 4 times more likely to become alcoholics in later life than those who waited until 21 years of age to begin drinking. The chances of becoming an alcoholic dropped 14 percent for each year a person put off drinking. Still, the statistics were staggering. Over one-third of American high school students got drunk at least every other month, and almost 90 percent of all high school students had tried alcohol. Of those who had drinking problems, the reason most cited for beginning to drink was support. Alcohol was the chemical crutch that enabled the teens to get through life.

Paul offered no crutch. Rather, he offered believers the armor of God to enable them to live for Him. We must heed the apostle's summons to use the Lord's provisions to win the battle against the forces of darkness.

# THE SUPREMACY OF CHRIST

**BACKGROUND SCRIPTURE:** Colossians 1
**DEVOTIONAL READING:** John 1:1-5, 9-18

**KEY VERSE:** In Christ all the fullness of God was pleased to dwell, and through him God was pleased to reconcile to himself all things. Colossians 1:19-20.

*KING JAMES VERSION*

COLOSSIANS 1:15 Who is the image of the invisible God, the firstborn of every creature:

16 For by him were all things created, that are in heaven, and that are in earth, visible and invisible, whether they be thrones, or dominions, or principalities, or powers: all things were created by him, and for him:

17 And he is before all things, and by him all things consist.

18 And he is the head of the body, the church: who is the beginning, the firstborn from the dead; that in all things he might have the preeminence.

19 For it pleased the Father that in him should all fulness dwell;

20 And, having made peace through the blood of his cross, by him to reconcile all things unto himself; by him, I say, whether they be things in earth, or things in heaven.

21 And you, that were sometime alienated and enemies in your mind by wicked works, yet now hath he reconciled

22 In the body of his flesh through death, to present you holy and unblameable and unreproveable in his sight:

23 If ye continue in the faith grounded and settled, and be not moved away from the hope of the gospel, which ye have heard, and which was preached to every creature which is under heaven; whereof I Paul am made a minister;

24 Who now rejoice in my sufferings for you, and fill up that which is behind of the afflictions of Christ in my flesh for his body's sake, which is the church:

25 Whereof I am made a minister, according to the dispensation of God which is given to me for you, to fulfil the word of God;

26 Even the mystery which hath been hid from ages and from generations, but now is made manifest to his saints:

27 To whom God would make known what is the riches of the glory of this mystery among the Gentiles;

which is Christ in you, the hope of glory:

28 Whom we preach, warning every man, and teaching every man in all wisdom; that we may present every man perfect in Christ Jesus.

*NEW REVISED STANDARD VERSION*

COLOSSIANS 1:15 He is the image of the invisible God, the firstborn of all creation; 16 for in him all things in heaven and on earth were created, things visible and invisible, whether thrones or dominions or rulers or powers—all things have been created through him and for him. 17 He himself is before all things, and in him all things hold together. 18 He is the head of the body, the church; he is the beginning, the firstborn from the dead, so that he might come to have first place in everything. 19 For in him all the fullness of God was pleased to dwell, 20 and through him God was pleased to reconcile to himself all things, whether on earth or in heaven, by making peace through the blood of his cross.

21 And you who were once estranged and hostile in mind, doing evil deeds, 22 he has now reconciled in his fleshly body through death, so as to present you holy and blameless and irreproachable before him— 23 provided that you continue securely established and steadfast in the faith, without shifting from the hope promised by the gospel that you heard, which has been proclaimed to every creature under heaven. I, Paul, became a servant of this gospel.

24 I am now rejoicing in my sufferings for your sake, and in my flesh I am completing what is lacking in Christ's afflictions for the sake of his body, that is, the church. 25 I became its servant according to God's commission that was given to me for you, to make the word of God fully known, 26 the mystery that has been hidden throughout the ages and generations but has now been revealed to his saints. 27 To them God chose to make known how great among the Gentiles are the riches of the glory of this mystery, which is Christ in you, the hope of glory. 28 It is he whom we proclaim, warning everyone and teaching everyone in all wisdom, so that we may present everyone mature in Christ.

10

## HOME BIBLE READINGS

## BACKGROUND

This week we begin the final portion of this quarter's lessons concerning the letters that Paul wrote during his first Roman imprisonment. Paul's letter to the Colossians, which is our focus for the next three lessons, is similar to Ephesians in many respects. The strong connection between these two epistles convinces scholars that they were written at about the same time. Some think that Colossians was an expansion of Paul's ideas in Ephesians, or, perhaps that Colossians might have been written first and then Ephesians thereafter.

Ephesians, we have seen, was probably intended as a sort of general tract or treatise to the cluster of congregations in the area around Ephesus. Colossians, on the other hand, was addressed to a particular church in a specific city. Though both letters contain many of the same ideas, Paul's epistle to the Colossians deals with specific issues that believers in the city were facing.

Colosse was located in the Roman province of Asia (modern Turkey) in the Lycus River Valley about 100 miles east of Ephesus. As early as the fifth century B.C., Colosse was known as a prosperous city, but by the beginning of the Christian era, it was eclipsed by neighboring towns. Though Colosse was increasingly overshadowed by other nearby cities, it retained considerable importance into the next several centuries.

There is no record that Paul ever visited Colosse. The congregation apparently grew up under the leadership of Epaphras [EPP-uh-fruss] (Col. 1:7; 4:12) and Archippus (Col. 4:17; Philem. 2). Colosse's population was mainly Gentile. Yet there was also a large Jewish settlement dating from the days of Antiochus [an-TIE-uh-kuss] the Great (223-187 B.C.). The city's mixed population of Jews and Gentiles manifested itself both in the composition of the church and in the heresy that plagued it. To combat this problem, Paul wrote a letter in which he extolled the supremacy and sufficiency of Christ.

## NOTES ON THE PRINTED TEXT

Note that in Ephesians the emphasis is on the dignity of Church, which is the Body of Christ; in Colossians the emphasis is on the deity of Christ, who is the Head of that Body. Ephesians considers the Church's oneness with Christ; Colossians considers the church's completeness in Christ. Ephesians speaks of the Christian being in Christ; Colossians speaks of Christ being in the Christian.

Christ *is the image of the invisible God, the firstborn of all creation* (1:15). This means that Jesus is the exact likeness of God (Heb. 1:3). In fact, He existed in the same form as God (Phil. 2:6). Christ is also first in rank over all creation, *for in him all things in heaven and on earth were created, things visible and invisible, whether thrones or dominions or rulers or powers—all things have been created through him and for him* (Col. 1:16). Christ not only is eternal in His existence, but also He unites and sustains everything in the universe. *He himself is before all things, and in him all things hold together* (1:17).

Just as the human body is controlled from the brain, so too Christ controls every part of the Church, giving it life and direction. *He is the head of the body, the church (1:18).* Christ is supreme over life and death, for He is the first of all who will rise from the dead. *He is the beginning, the firstborn from the dead, so that he might come to have first place in everything.*

Paul asserted that all the divine powers and attributes completely dwell in Christ alone. For this reason the Father was pleased to remove the ill-will between Himself and the human race through Christ. The implication is staggering. All things in the universe will one day be subdued to the Father through the Son (Phil. 2:9-11). *For in him all the fullness of God was pleased to dwell, and through him God was pleased to reconcile to himself all things, whether on earth or in heaven, by making peace through the blood of his cross* (Col. 1:19-20).

It would be wrong to assume that all people are automatically saved. Rather, they must trust in Christ for salvation. This included the Colossians, who were once far away from God. Through Jesus' work on the cross, their estranged relationship with God was restored. Now they could stand holy and blameless in His presence because of what Christ had done on the cross (1:21-22).

Paul reminded the Colossians of their moral responsibility before God. They were not to drift complacently, but rather were to remain unwavering in their commitment to Christ. They would spiritually flourish, provided they stood firm in the truth of the Gospel. Paul urged his readers not to drift away from the hope of salvation they had in Christ. This is the message that Paul preached throughout the Roman empire as God's appointed servant (1:23).

Paul noted that though he suffered for the cause of Christ, his afflictions were worth it for the long-term good of the Church (1:24). The apostle had the God-given responsibility to proclaim the Good News to the Gentiles (1:25). The Gospel was a mystery in the sense that it was previously unrevealed but now had been disclosed by God in Christ through believers (1:26). The wonderful truth is that the Savior now lives in Gentile (as well as Jewish) believers (1:27).

Paul and his associates spared no effort to make this truth known to others (1:28). The apostle explained to his readers that in order for them to enjoy the favor and acceptance of God, they needed to trust in Christ. He, and only He, could reconcile them to God. The reason is that God accepted them by virtue of their spiritual union with Christ in His death and resurrection.

## SUGGESTIONS TO TEACHERS

Christians are sometimes tempted to downplay the significance of Christ. This tendency can come in the form of not wanting to appear arrogant when discussing other religions. Or believers may deemphasize the importance of trusting in Jesus for salvation. Some so-called Christians completely set aside the teachings of the Bible and devote themselves to pagan religions in order to find answers to life's challenges. This week's lesson is a needed reminder of the supremacy and sufficiency of Christ. As you work through the Scripture text, be sure to note these points about the Savior.

**1. THE CARING REDEEMER OF ALL HUMANS.** Jesus is preeminent in the universe, and only He is able to free people from the destructive grip of sin and self. Only Christ is able to reconcile people to God and to one another. It is only through faith in Christ that we can enjoy enduring love and fellowship with the Father.

**2. THE EXACT REPRESENTATION OF THE DIVINE.** Paul used vivid language to describe the person and the work of Christ. Jesus is the visible image of the invisible God. Christ existed before God made anything at all, and He is supreme over all creation. In fact, Jesus is the One through whom God created everything in heaven and on earth. Any scaled-down portrayals of Jesus are paltry and puny in comparison to Paul's mighty claims about Him!

**3. THE COMPLETE REVELATION OF THE CREATOR'S PURPOSE.** Paul declared that Christ is the Head of the church, which is His body. He is also the first of all who will rise from the dead, and thus He rightly is preeminent in all things. Through Him the Father has unveiled His plan for all humanity and will bring to pass His eternal purpose.

**4. THE CONSTANT RECONCILER BETWEEN GOD AND HUMAN-ITY.** When Adam and Eve sinned, the relationship of themselves and their descendants to God was drastically changed. Only the God-man, Jesus Christ, could bring about reconciliation. Through faith in Christ, people can experience a new and right relationship with God. The work of the Redeemer permits God to welcome us into His holy, loving presence.

---

**FOR ADULTS**

■ **TOPIC:** The Source of Life

■ **QUESTIONS:** 1. What does Paul say about the person and work of Christ? 2. What is the nature of the relationship between Christ and the Church? 3. How does the knowledge of Christ's divinity encourage you to worship and serve Him? 4. In what ways has the Gospel transformed your life? 5. Whom might you tell the wonderful news about salvation in Christ?

**Received Eternal Life.** Art Monk has the National Football League's record for the most catches in a career: 934 catches altogether. He is also the athlete with the most consecutive games with a catch: 880 in all. Monk played in three Super Bowl championship games. But the great athlete testifies that midway through his spectacular career, he felt an emptiness and loneliness. "I had everything I wanted," he states, "and yet I still felt that something was missing."

In 1987, Monk began attending a Bible study. This prompted him to sense that he needed to commit his life to Jesus Christ. The verses from 1 Timothy 1:15-16 seemed addressed to him. Paul declared that Christ was the source of true living for everyone, including a great athlete. *Christ Jesus came into the world to save sinners—of whom I am the foremost. But for that very reason I received mercy, so that in me, as the foremost, Jesus Christ might display the utmost patience, making me an example to those who would come to believe in him for eternal life.*

Art Monk made a personal entrustment of his life to Christ. He announces today that his life has changed because Christ is the source and center of all his being.

**Lifts the Person Up.** A man fell into a pit and couldn't get himself out. A subjective person came along and said, "I feel for you down there." An objective person came along and said, "It's logical that someone would fall down there." A legalist said, "Only bad people fall into a pit." A mathematician calculated how the man fell into the pit. A news reporter wanted an exclusive story on the pit. A radical said, "You deserve your pit." A federal agent asked whether the man was paying taxes on the pit. A self-pitying person said, "You haven't seen anything until you've seen my pit." A religious person said, "Just confess that you're not in a pit." An optimist said, "Things could be worse." A pessimist said, "Things will get worse." Jesus, seeing the man, took him by the hand and lifted him out of the pit! (David Gibbs, adapting an idea from Barbara Johnson, in *Homiletics* July/Sept. 1997.)

**Now We Know.** When he was only 13 years old, violinist Yehudi Menuhin was invited to perform with the Berlin Philharmonic Symphony Orchestra. With several distinguished people in the audience listening to him, the young boy played some of the most difficult pieces by Beethoven, Bach, and Brahms.

The response of the audience was so impassioned that the management called in the police in case crowd control was needed. Albert Einstein, who had listened with delight to the young musician, circumvented the authorities by running across the stage and back to Yehudi's dressing room. He hugged the young violinist and exclaimed, "Now I know there is a God in heaven!"

While beautiful music does indeed bear witness to God's character, He has given us many other signs pointing to His existence. It takes God's revelation of

Himself in Jesus Christ (Col. 1:15, 19). Only through the Son are we able to know what the Father is like. When we understand who Jesus really is, we are prompted to exclaim, "Now we know there is a God in heaven!"

---

<table>
<tr><td rowspan="2">FOR YOUTH</td><td>■ TOPIC: The Image of God</td></tr>
<tr><td>■ QUESTIONS: 1. Through whom did God bring the creation into existence?</td></tr>
</table>

2. What is the basis for the reconciliation of believers with God? 3. What are some of the things that Christ has given you for which you can thank Him in prayer? 4. How should Christ's lordship over all creation change your perspective on the circumstances of life? 5. How has the message of the Gospel transformed your relationship with others?

■ **ILLUSTRATIONS:**

**Who Comes First?** It was Game 1 of the Stanley Cup Finals. Leslie Wills' beloved Detroit Red Wings were to play the Washington Capitals at Joe Louis Arena on Tuesday, June 9, 1998. Pregnant Leslie went into labor. She told her husband, David, to take her to the game, not the hospital. The Red Wings came first! After the game, which Leslie's Red Wings won 2-1, David rushed Leslie to the hospital. There she delivered their daughter, Noelle.

What comes first in your life? Is it your favorite team, a hobby, a job, or money? Or does the Lord come first? Paul described the supremacy of Christ to the Colossians. In Paul's thinking, Christ came first!

**Aspiring to Greatness.** In my community many years ago there was a young man named Bill who was a great football running back at the former Lee Edwards High School. When game time arrived on Fridays, the crowds would pour out to watch Bill almost single-handedly defeat the opponents.

Bill's younger brother, Charlie, didn't play football. Why try? Who could ever live up to his older brother's greatness? Charlie would languish in Bill's shadow. It seemed easier not even to make the effort. However, a wise football coach named Lee Stone went to Charlie and said, "Son, I think you have the speed and skills to play this game. Why don't you try out for the team?" After some cajoling and encouraging, the coach convinced the reticent younger brother to give it a shot. The rest is history. Charlie "Choo Choo" Justice went on to become an All-American at the University of North Carolina and one of the leading rushers and scorers in the history of the Washington Redskins.

God is still in the business of doing what seems most unlikely. Paul reminded his readers that not many of them were wise in the world's eyes, or powerful, or even wealthy (1 Cor. 1:26). Nevertheless, the Lord redeemed them for His glory. Who is to say what God can do with unlikely folks, if He so chooses? Though our dreams may seem foolish to the world (vs. 27), in God's hands they can become tomorrow's realities. Don't give up on yourself or on God's power to make something exciting out of your life (vs. 28).

**God's Good Gifts.** There are some folks out there with major hang-ups about God. They say that He's mean, hateful, and vindictive. And they warn that God's out to get you. It's true. God is out to get you. But the hunt isn't vindictive. The first desire of God's heart is to spiritually bless you. His blessings are His good gifts to you (Jas. 1:17). If you have not experienced His abundance, perhaps it's because you haven't asked for it (4:2).

# A COMPLETE LIFE IN CHRIST

**BACKGROUND SCRIPTURE:** Colossians 2:6-19
**DEVOTIONAL READING:** Romans 8:31-39

**KEY VERSE:** As you therefore have received Christ Jesus the Lord, continue to live your lives in him, rooted and built up in him and established in the faith. Colossians 2:6-7.

*KING JAMES VERSION*

COLOSSIANS 2:6 As ye have therefore received Christ Jesus the Lord, so walk ye in him:

7 Rooted and built up in him, and stablished in the faith, as ye have been taught, abounding therein with thanksgiving.

8 Beware lest any man spoil you through philosophy and vain deceit, after the tradition of men, after the rudiments of the world, and not after Christ.

9 For in him dwelleth all the fulness of the Godhead bodily.

10 And ye are complete in him, which is the head of all principality and power:

11 In whom also ye are circumcised with the circumcision made without hands, in putting off the body of the sins of the flesh by the circumcision of Christ:

12 Buried with him in baptism, wherein also ye are risen with him through the faith of the operation of God, who hath raised him from the dead.

13 And you, being dead in your sins and the uncircumcision of your flesh, hath he quickened together with him, having forgiven you all trespasses;

14 Blotting out the handwriting of ordinances that was against us, which was contrary to us, and took it out of the way, nailing it to his cross;

15 And having spoiled principalities and powers, he made a shew of them openly, triumphing over them in it.

16 Let no man therefore judge you in meat, or in drink, or in respect of an holyday, or of the new moon, or of the sabbath days:

17 Which are a shadow of things to come; but the body is of Christ.

18 Let no man beguile you of your reward in a voluntary humility and worshipping of angels, intruding into those things which he hath not seen, vainly puffed up by his fleshly mind,

19 And not holding the Head, from which all the body by joints and bands having nourishment ministered, and knit together, increaseth with the increase of God.

*NEW REVISED STANDARD VERSION*

COLOSSIANS 2:6 As you therefore have received Christ Jesus the Lord, continue to live your lives in him, 7 rooted and built up in him and established in the faith, just as you were taught, abounding in thanksgiving.

8 See to it that no one takes you captive through philosophy and empty deceit, according to human tradition, according to the elemental spirits of the universe, and not according to Christ. 9 For in him the whole fullness of deity dwells bodily, 10 and you have come to fullness in him, who is the head of every ruler and authority. 11 In him also you were circumcised with a spiritual circumcision, by putting off the body of the flesh in the circumcision of Christ; 12 when you were buried with him in baptism, you were also raised with him through faith in the power of God, who raised him from the dead. 13 And when you were dead in trespasses and the uncircumcision of your flesh, God made you alive together with him, when he forgave us all our trespasses, 14 erasing the record that stood against us with its legal demands. He set this aside, nailing it to the cross. 15 He disarmed the rulers and authorities and made a public example of them, triumphing over them in it.

16 Therefore do not let anyone condemn you in matters of food and drink or of observing festivals, new moons, or sabbaths. 17 These are only a shadow of what is to come, but the substance belongs to Christ. 18 Do not let anyone disqualify you, insisting on self-abasement and worship of angels, dwelling on visions, puffed up without cause by a human way of thinking, 19 and not holding fast to the head, from whom the whole body, nourished and held together by its ligaments and sinews, grows with a growth that is from God.

## HOME BIBLE READINGS

## BACKGROUND

The Letter to the Colossians indicates that false teaching had taken root in the city. This teaching combined Jewish observances (2:16) and pagan speculation (2:8). It is possible that this resulted in an early form of Gnosticism [NAHS-tih-cihz-uhm]. This term designates any of a variety of heretical movements in the early Christian centuries (especially the second century A.D.) that mingled ideas from Greek philosophy, oriental mysticism, and Christianity. In the Gnostic system, the physical body was regarded as evil. Adherents also emphasized salvation through intuitive, secret knowledge rather than through faith in Christ. (The Greek word for "knowledge" is *gnosis* [NO-siss].)

The heresy at Colosse pretended to add to or improve upon the Gospel that had come from Paul. Some of the additions noted by Paul included an undue emphasis on observing feasts and observances (some of which were related to astrology; 2:16), in addition to keeping a list of rules (2:20-21). These practices were then included within a philosophy in which angels played a leading role (2:18). These pagan notions were filled with laws and rituals that supposedly had to be observed in order to achieve divine acceptance. Far from being advanced, profound knowledge, these notions were simplistic and immature.

In response to this threat, Paul emphasized the sufficiency and supremacy of Christ. He and only He could save believing sinners. The reason is that God had already accepted them by virtue of their spiritual union with Christ in His death and resurrection. The apostle also stressed that while there was still a level of spiritual maturity his readers needed to attain (1:22-23, 28), they were already complete in Christ (2:10).

## NOTES ON THE PRINTED TEXT

Paul's tract to the Colossians underscores the importance of being correct in what we believe. For instance in 2:6, Paul reminded his readers that their entrance into salvation was by faith in Christ. Likewise, their continued acceptance before God and growth in grace would be through the Savior. That's why the apostle urged the Colossians to let the roots of their spiritual life grow down into Christ and draw up nourishment from Him. This would enable them to grow in their faith and become strong in the truths they had learned (2:7).

Tragically, religious frauds had misled the Colossians with empty philosophy and overblown notions, all of which came from human thinking and the world's diabolic forces, rather than Christ (2:8). If Paul's readers wanted to know the truth in all its abundance, they needed to rivet their attention on the Savior, for in Him the fullness of God dwells in bodily form (2:9). They did not need to add anything to Christ, for they were spiritually complete through their union with Him (2:10). No one else could replace Him, for He is Lord over every ruler and authority in the universe.

Evidently some of the heretics in Colosse had urged Paul's readers to be circumcised in order to get right with God. The apostle countered this incorrect teaching by stating that when his readers trusted in Christ for salvation, they were *circumcised* (2:11). By this the apostle did not mean a surgical operation; rather, he was referring to a spiritual change in which the Lord put off the *body of the flesh*. Paul's teaching was consistent with that of the Old Testament, in which circumcision symbolized humanity's need for cleansing of the heart (Deut. 10:16; 30:6; Jer. 4:4).

When people trust in Jesus, they become members of God's family (John 1:12) and are joined to Christ's spiritual body (1 Cor. 12:13). The ceremony of baptism symbolizes the inner transforming work of God in their life. It's as if they were buried with Christ when they were baptized (Col. 2:12). And through faith in Him they were raised to new life. The same divine power that raised Jesus from the dead is also at work in believers to enable them to grow in holiness and grace.

Paul spared no words to describe the sinful state in which the readers once existed. They were as good as dead in terms of their relationship with God. Their sinful nature prompted them to violate His will time after time. But God, in His mercy, made them alive through faith in Christ. The Lord also forgave all their sins (2:13). He canceled the record containing all the charges that had been brought against the Colossians. Metaphorically speaking, the Lord nailed the sins of humanity to the cross of Christ so that the guilt and punishment associated with these transgressions would be wiped out (2:14).

The ramifications of Christ's atoning sacrifice went far beyond humanity. Through Jesus' crucifixion, God disarmed the evil rulers and authorities. The Lord publicly shamed them by the victory He won through the cross of Christ (2:15). In light of what Jesus had done, nothing else needed to be added to the believer's salvation.

Paul urged his readers not to let anyone condemn them *in matters of food and drink or of observing festivals, new moons, or sabbaths* (2:16). Why? The apostle explained that these rules were only shadows pointing to Christ. Since Jesus—the reality of all things—has come, the shadows are not needed anymore (Heb. 8:5; 10:1).

The Colossians were not to let anyone condemn them by insisting on self-denial, as if this was needed to win God's favor. Similarly, the Colossians were to resist all forms of pressure to worship angels, as if they were needed to approach God (Col. 2:18). Through faith in Christ, believers are made right with God and can come before Him in worship, prayer, and praise.

Paul said that his Christian friends in Colosse were joined to the Savior, who is the Head of the Church, His spiritual body. Their growth and development came as a result of being united to Him by faith (2:19). The religious charlatans, however, were alienated from Christ. This was true, even though they asserted being humble and spiritual, and even though they claimed to see visions from God.

## SUGGESTIONS TO TEACHERS

Ask the members of your class to note some of the superstitions that people commonly have. These might include lucky charms carried in a purse or pocket, avoiding certain numbers, or wearing a certain article for good luck. The students might mention such practices as following astrology, or playing the lottery in the secret hope of coming up with the winning combination of digits. All these may seem like harmless and innocent fun, but they reflect something far less than full trust in Christ!

**1. REJECTING SUPERSTITION.** This week's lesson teaches that our lives are in the hands of the God, who has come to us in love in the person of Jesus Christ. Life is not controlled by strange, capricious forces that can be manipulated. All superstitions are basically attempts to control unknown powers that are believed to direct the affairs of humans. Christians know that their lives are not ruled by blind fate, Lady Luck, power crystals, the planets, and so on. This is God's world and He reigns supreme over it!

**2. RELYING ON THE SAVIOR.** The Colossians believed that they had to tack on other ideas and observances to their faith in Christ. Supposedly He alone could not bring them closer to God. Paul's letter makes it clear that trusting in the saving power of Christ is sufficient. We need no extras—such as asceticism, fancy homemade rituals, or lists of rules—to bring us into God's presence.

**3. REMEMBERING OUR BAPTISM.** Paul urged his readers to keep their identity as Christians by remembering that they had been baptized. Discuss what baptism means for the students and your church. Remind the class that baptism is more than being dubbed with a name. It is signifies one's spiritual union to Jesus Christ for the rest of one's life!

**4. REJOICING IN THE FREEDOM THAT CHRIST BRINGS.** Any idea, belief, or practice in the name of religion that fails to honor and reflect Christ is suspect. Paul warned his fellow Christians against those who, in the name of religion, try to shackle believers with ways that diminish the sufficiency and supremacy of the Lord. Colossians 2:16-19 enumerates some of these practices. Explain that faith in Jesus must never be compromised by thinking that other observances are needed for salvation.

■ TOPIC: The Fullness of Life

■ QUESTIONS: 1. Why is faith in Christ central to the salvation of believers? 2. In what way is Christ dishonored when people insist that they must observe certain rules or ceremonies in order to be right with God? 3. How might you use God's Word to grow stronger in your faith? 4. What can you do to allow your life to overflow with thanksgiving to God for all He has done for you in Christ? 5. How has your life changed since trusting in Christ?

■ ILLUSTRATIONS:

**Missing the Target.** Charlie Brown was doing some target shooting one day with his bow and arrows. He would pull the string back as far as he could and then let the arrow fly into the fence. Then he would run over to the fence with a piece of chalk and draw a target around the arrows.

Lucy soon showed up, saw what he was doing, and became hysterical. "That's not the way to practice!" she shouted. "You're supposed to draw the target and then shoot at it!" But an unrepentant Charlie Brown dismissed her criticism by saying, "If you do it my way, you never miss!"

The church at Colosse believed and practiced much like Charlie Brown. Paul caught those early Christians drawing bull's eyes around their "best shots." They did what they thought were the right things. They supposedly lived their lives the right way, followed all the rules, and even boasted about the quality of their spiritual gifts. But Paul pointed out that they were really missing the mark, especially if Christ wasn't their aim. Apart from Him their lives were off target.

**Superstitions in the Real Estate Market.** In an often devilishly mercurial real estate market, a growing number of homesellers think that the secret to success is to call on a higher power. For instance, many homeowners believe in Saint Joseph as the unofficial "good luck charm" of real estate. People all over the country have followed the practice of burying a statue of Saint Joseph in their yard to get a house sold quickly, and there are many stories about the practice allegedly working like a charm even after houses have failed to sell for two or three years.

"It's about hope and believing in a higher power," says Donna Schultze, a real estate broker and licensed appraiser with Re/Max Liberty in Marstons Mills, who reputedly had firsthand success with a statue. She asserts, "Saint Joseph does give people hope, and sometimes that's all you need. Some people are so desperate to sell their house that they'd probably do eye of newt. It's about hope and having faith in things."

Schultze's story involves a Marstons Mills house that had been through three different brokers over three years. "When I got it, I decided we needed a little extra push," she says. So she went and bought a Saint Joseph's statue. When she told the owner, he said his mother gave him one, too. Thus, two Saint Joseph statues were buried there. Within two weeks, the house sold.

This practice has become so commonplace that there are Saint Joseph kits that real estate agents can buy at conventions and trade shows and that are sold by Hallmark through a trade catalog. The box for the Saint Joseph Home Sale Practice Kit is decorated with a drawing of an icon standing near a real-estate sign with a "SOLD" notice printed across it. The box contains a plastic statue, a prayer card, and introductory material on how and why to use the figure. The statues come separately or in sets of six at a discount price. "Faith can move mountains and homes!" reads the statue's packing (Kathi Scrizzi Driscoll, *Cape Cod Times*, March 8, 1998).

**Prison Music Lady.** Millicent Gordon is known as "The Music Lady" in the 16-story Western Youth Institution near Morganton, North Carolina, a penitentiary holding tough young men convicted of murder, rape, armed robbery, and every other crime in the book. Mrs. Gordon regularly visits the forbidding looking cell-blocks to teach music. For over 15 years, she has worked at the prison after a career of giving music lessons and directing church choirs. A devout Christian, Mrs. Gordon states that teaching music at this state institution is her calling from God. She adds that this ministry is the most fulfilling time in her life.

As if making a difference in the lives of the young men she regularly visits isn't enough, this grandmotherly-looking woman began a volunteer program involving others. In 1992, Project Together, Millicent Gordon's brainchild, began to involve older adults with talents and experience in the arts to go among young inmates. Today, a large group of senior citizens offer their services to teach art, music, and writing. Project Together has been taken up by other communities. Both the young men behind bars and the oldsters with talents agree that Mrs. Gordon's inspiration has made a difference in the lives of everyone, both prisoners and teachers. Millicent Gordon knows the fullness of life that Christ brings, and in turn shares it in a significant way with others.

| **FOR YOUTH** | ■ TOPIC: A Full Life in Christ<br>■ QUESTIONS: 1. What is the spiritual condition of people before they trust in Christ? 2. Why is remaining joined to Christ by faith |

important for spiritual growth? 3. What can you do to support new Christians in their walk with the Lord? 4. How might you affirm to others the confidence you have in the saving work of Christ? 5. How has your relationship with Christ changed the focus of your life?

■ **ILLUSTRATIONS:**

**Initiated.** While the high school code of behavior specifically ruled out any hazing, most of the sports teams had some simple rite of initiation. For the soccer team, it began on the first day of practice. All freshmen were expected to set up and take down the portable goals on the practice field, an effort that required the boys to hustle to the field ten minutes earlier than the rest of the team. They also had to do the bidding of the seniors. Finally, tradition dictated a "buzz" haircut before the first August scrimmage. Still, year after year, the freshmen boys complied, even though most deeply resented what transpired. Like these soccer players, other youth have experienced dubious rituals and initiations. Paul cautioned the church against such morally questionable practices.

**Whom Do You Lean On?** One of 1997's best sellers was Richard Carlson's *Don't Sweat the Small Stuff . . . and It's All Small Stuff*. In the book, the self-realization author stresses how to escape nagging doubts and worries. Supposedly you, as the reader, have that power to do whatever you want alone.

Long before Carlson, Paul wrote to the Colossians that they could escape their nagging worries. However, believers do not achieve freedom from worry in their own strength. The power to conquer comes from without, not within. They do not walk alone; rather, Jesus remains with them every step of the way. Paul declared that Christ is preeminent over all things. He also rules over all earthy authorities, even those who often cause us to be filled with anxiety.

**Captured But Freed.** Pittsburgh Police were called to the home of a hysterical person named Kate on March 12, 1998. However, the call was far from the typical domestic dispute. Kate maintained that her husband, Benjamin, was holding her captive. The officers walked to the door and easily unlocked it. They showed her that the door was unlocked. Kate persisted, stating that the locks were not preventing her escape. Her husband had cast a spell on the locks and windows. She took the bewildered officers downstairs to the basement and showed them an altar, a live chicken, and ceremonial priest's garb. The bloody altar contained the head and body parts of a pigeon. Supervisors were summoned. Benjamin arrived home and admitted to the Caribbean-West African spell. He was angry with Kate and was punishing her. Benjamin was arrested for simple assault by menacing and terroristic threats, and Kate was freed.

It could be said that Kate had been taken captive by philosophies and empty deceit, namely, those of human tradition. Paul reminded the Colossians that Christ was their ultimate authority. Jesus is God in the flesh. Every believer is joined to Him through faith. In union with Him, they belonged to God, who is sovereign over all the forces of the universe.

# THE WAY TO RIGHTEOUSNESS

**BACKGROUND SCRIPTURE:** Colossians 3:1-17
**DEVOTIONAL READING:** Mark 12:28-34

**KEY VERSE:** Whatever you do, in word or deed, do everything in the name of the Lord Jesus, giving thanks to God the Father through him. Colossians 3:17.

*KING JAMES VERSION*

COLOSSIANS 3:1 If ye then be risen with Christ, seek those things which are above, where Christ sitteth on the right hand of God.

2 Set your affection on things above, not on things on the earth.

3 For ye are dead, and your life is hid with Christ in God. . . .

5 Mortify therefore your members which are upon the earth; fornication, uncleanness, inordinate affection, evil concupiscence, and covetousness, which is idolatry:

6 For which things' sake the wrath of God cometh on the children of disobedience:

7 In the which ye also walked some time, when ye lived in them.

8 But now ye also put off all these; anger, wrath, malice, blasphemy, filthy communication out of your mouth.

9 Lie not one to another, seeing that ye have put off the old man with his deeds;

10 And have put on the new man, which is renewed in knowledge after the image of him that created him:

11 Where there is neither Greek nor Jew, circumcision nor uncircumcision, Barbarian, Scythian, bond nor free: but Christ is all, and in all.

12 Put on therefore, as the elect of God, holy and beloved, bowels of mercies, kindness, humbleness of mind, meekness, longsuffering;

13 Forbearing one another, and forgiving one another, if any man have a quarrel against any: even as Christ forgave you, so also do ye.

14 And above all these things put on charity, which is the bond of perfectness.

15 And let the peace of God rule in your hearts, to the which also ye are called in one body; and be ye thankful.

16 Let the word of Christ dwell in you richly in all wisdom; teaching and admonishing one another in psalms and hymns and spiritual songs, singing with grace in your hearts to the Lord.

17 And whatsoever ye do in word or deed, do all in the name of the Lord Jesus, giving thanks to God and the Father by him.

*NEW REVISED STANDARD VERSION*

COLOSSIANS 3:1 So if you have been raised with Christ, seek the things that are above, where Christ is, seated at the right hand of God. 2 Set your minds on things that are above, not on things that are on earth, 3 for you have died, and your life is hidden with Christ in God. . . .

5 Put to death, therefore, whatever in you is earthly: fornication, impurity, passion, evil desire, and greed (which is idolatry). 6 On account of these the wrath of God is coming on those who are disobedient. 7 These are the ways you also once followed, when you were living that life. 8 But now you must get rid of all such things—anger, wrath, malice, slander, and abusive language from your mouth. 9 Do not lie to one another, seeing that you have stripped off the old self with its practices 10 and have clothed yourselves with the new self, which is being renewed in knowledge according to the image of its creator. 11 In that renewal there is no longer Greek and Jew, circumcised and uncircumcised, barbarian, Scythian, slave and free; but Christ is all and in all!

12 As God's chosen ones, holy and beloved, clothe yourselves with compassion, kindness, humility, meekness, and patience. 13 Bear with one another and, if anyone has a complaint against another, forgive each other; just as the Lord has forgiven you, so you also must forgive. 14 Above all, clothe yourselves with love, which binds everything together in perfect harmony. 15 And let the peace of Christ rule in your hearts, to which indeed you were called in the one body. And be thankful. 16 Let the word of Christ dwell in you richly; teach and admonish one another in all wisdom; and with gratitude in your hearts sing psalms, hymns, and spiritual songs to God. 17 And whatever you do, in word or deed, do everything in the name of the Lord Jesus, giving thanks to God the Father through him.

12

## BACKGROUND

Paul had heard about the dangerous theories being spread among the Colossian Christians. The religious frauds were saying that Jesus Christ was not enough, but that believers needed something more to be right with God. Their supplements to the Gospel were unnecessary, and they demoted Jesus to a minor role in salvation. Paul knew that these errors would wreak havoc among the Colossians. That's why he underscored the uniqueness and sufficiency of Christ for everyone's salvation.

Jesus answers all our spiritual needs and satisfies all our deepest longings for knowing God. There is no point in seeking truths in esoteric philosophical speculation. There is no need to try to make contact with angels for help in getting saved. There is no need to invent secret rituals or devise elaborate ceremonies. There is no reward in self-made holiness through rigorous asceticism. There is no point in searching for insights through self-induced mystical trances. There is no need to tremble before the stars and planets in the night sky, imagining that these will determine one's future. There is no hope in studying the occult or being absorbed in astrology. Jesus Christ is supreme, and He is sufficient. He brings freedom, whereas anything else enslaves.

Paul might have written to believers in a somewhat unimportant city in the Roman empire. But his epistle to the Colossians remains one of the most significant expositions of how Christ is above all!

## NOTES ON THE PRINTED TEXT

Paul urged his readers to live as members of the community of the resurrected Lord. Their conduct was to reflect their faith. Since they had been raised with Christ to new life, believers were to live in a worthwhile manner. *So if you have been raised with Christ, seek the things that are above, where Christ is, seated at the right hand of God* (3:1).

The apostle urged the believers in Colosse to fill their thoughts with the things of heaven, for this was their eternal home. After all, through faith in Christ, they were united with His death, burial, and resurrection. *Set your minds on things that are above, not on things that are on earth, for you have died, and your life is hidden with Christ in God* (3:2-3). Paul further noted that at Christ's return, all believers would share in His glory. *When Christ who is your life is revealed, then you also will be revealed with him in glory* (3:4).

Christian commitment must be lived! People are declared righteous by faith, and they demonstrate the reality of their right standing before God through holy living. That is why Paul urged the Colossians to *put to death . . . whatever in you is earthly* (3:5). Paul mentioned five vices. *Fornication* referred to any sexual relationship outside the marriage bond, but the term was often used for premarital sex. *Impurity* was any moral uncleanness. *Passion* was any desire that led to sexual affairs or perversion. *Greed*, which is the only non-sexual vice mentioned by Paul, referred to a obsession to amass things. Because greed leads people to trust in material goods rather than God, Paul said that it was idolatry.

Paul noted that God's judgment was the consequence of these vices. *On account of these the wrath of God is coming on those who are disobedient* (3:6). The apostle also declared that the believers in Colosse used to live this way (3:7). However, that all changed when they trusted in Christ for salvation.

Paul mentioned five other sins that were also to be avoided. Left unchecked, these vices would destroy the unity and trust of believers. *But now you must get rid of all such things—anger, wrath, malice, slander, and abusive language from your mouth. Do not lie to one another, seeing that you have stripped off the old self with its practices and have clothed yourselves with the new self, which is being renewed in knowledge according to the image of its creator* (3:8-10). All these deplorable attributes were to be discarded. In place of them, the believer was to follow the example of Christ.

God's people were to make no distinctions or divisions based on nationalities, social standing, or religious background, for Christ united all peoples, even the non-Greek barbarians and the Scythians, who were considered animals in Paul's day. *In that renewal there is no longer Greek and Jew, circumcised and uncircumcised, barbarian, Scythian, slave and free; but Christ is all and in all* (3:11).

The apostle then wrote that *as God's chosen ones, holy and beloved, clothe yourselves with compassion, kindness, humility, meekness, and patience* (3:12). Believers were to exhibit heartfelt concern for others. In addition, they were not to hold a grudge against others, for they were called to forgive as Christ forgave. *Bear with one another and, if anyone has a complaint against another, forgive each other; just as the Lord has forgiven you, so you also must forgive* (3:13).

Paul urged the Colossians to practice love, for this was the distinctive Christian quality that fostered unity among believers. *Above all, clothe yourselves with love, which binds everything together in perfect harmony* (3:14). So concerned for unity was Paul that he reminded the Colossians not to let anything threaten the harmony of the church. The apostle also reminded his readers to be thankful. *And let the peace of Christ rule in your hearts, to which indeed you were called in the one body. And be thankful* (3:15).

Paul admonished the believers in Colosse to teach and share their faith. In addition, their faith was to be expressed through music. *Let the word of Christ dwell in you richly; teach and admonish one another in all wisdom; and with gratitude in your hearts sing psalms, hymns, and spiritual songs to God* (3:16). Finally, Paul exhorted the believers to show gratitude to God in every circumstance. *And whatever you do, in word or deed, do everything in the name of the Lord Jesus, giving thanks to God the Father through him* (3:17).

## SUGGESTIONS TO TEACHERS

We have had a spate of publicity about the way advertisers target youth. One ad was finally banned after it proved too effective in persuading teenagers to smoke. Many parents of adolescents know that only name-brand shoes and clothes are acceptable in the youth culture of today. And yet the over-used phrase "peer pressure" also applies to the rest of the population. Perhaps even more, what could be labeled "culture pressure" influences what we think and how we act as well as what we buy and how we live. Paul's words to the Colossians have just as much meaning for us as they did for believers in the first century A.D.

**1. LOOKING UP TO CHRIST.** Paul urged believers to ask themselves, "What is your outlook on life? What is your view of yourself? Do you have any idea of what life and society can be like under the lordship of Christ?" Paul then called upon his readers to get a perspective based on understanding who Jesus is, what He has done, and what He can do for them.

**2. LEAVING EARTHLY WAYS.** Have the class go through the inventory of destructive ways mentioned in Colossians 3:5-9. In our generation, where we're told that "anything goes" and "it's my life, and I can do as I please," Christ's people are called to holy living.

**3. LIVING AS THE NEW CREATION IN CHRIST.** Anyone who trusts in Christ for salvation is morally transformed. This results in new and different patterns of behavior. Invite you students to discuss at length the changes that God wants to bring about in their lives through Christ.

**4. LINKING CONDUCT WITH CHRIST.** Colossians 3:17 sums up nicely what is expected of each of us: *Whatever you do, in word or deed, do everything in the name of the Lord Jesus, giving thanks to God the Father through him.* Conduct that is consistent with Christ's life and an attitude of thankfulness before God is the way to meaningful living!

**FOR ADULTS**

■ **TOPIC:** The Way of Life

■ **QUESTIONS:** 1. What does it mean to be raised with Christ? 2. In what way do believers put to death the vices mentioned by Paul? 3. What are some former vices in your life that you have been freed from through faith in Christ? 4. What are some tangible ways that you can show the love of

Christ to others? 5. How can studying and applying the teachings of Christ fill your heart with wisdom?

■ ILLUSTRATIONS:

**Testimony of Harry McCann.** Twenty years ago I had a serious "accident." Someone planted a bomb below my car, which was outside my jeweler's shop in Antrim, my hometown. Whether it was a loyalist or republican attack was never discovered. No group ever acknowledged responsibility for the crime. I lost both my legs and suffered severe abdominal injuries. Both my eardrums were perforated, and my face and hands were lacerated.

I have two indelible memories of that day. One is of recovering consciousness momentarily before the ambulance arrived and looking up into the face of a neighbor, Francis Cooney, and finding myself saying, "May God forgive the people who did this to me." The other is regaining consciousness as I was being rushed to the hospital in the ambulance and faintly hearing these words coming from my lips repeatedly: "Father, forgive them, for they do not know what they are doing."

That could only have been the grace of God at work in me. It had to be an on-the-spot, God-given grace, for I had not previously been a forgiving kind of person at all. But now I had no feelings of anger, hatred, or revenge. Nor did I have resentment through all the tortuously slow and painful process of physical healing and rehabilitation that followed. Whoever planted that bomb fully intended to cause maximum damage and death, if possible. Yet I had only forgiveness in my heart toward them. Only the grace of God could account for my attitude.

In those early days following my release from intensive care, a steady stream of visitors from Antrim and further afield came to sit by my hospital bed and express their sorrow and sympathy over what had happened. Many of them were Protestants. As they talked about their revulsion and anger against those who had planted the bomb, my response was always the same. "Yes, it was a terrible and pointless deed. But I have forgiven them, and I hope that God has forgiven them."

After long months of physiotherapy, I eventually managed to master the art of walking on two artificial legs. I learned to drive a specially adapted car. With my new-found mobility I was able, in a small way, to demonstrate my gratitude for the kindness and concern shown to me by so many Protestants. I volunteered to chauffeur the elderly from the local Nursing Home to their various churches on Sundays—Presbyterian, Methodist, and the Church of Ireland—wherever they wished to go.

One day I heard that Prison Fellowship was asking for car owners to volunteer at their own expense to drive family members who could not afford to pay for transport to visit their relatives in the Magilligan Prison. This prison housed convicted paramilitaries. A friend of mine was aghast when he heard that I had volunteered my services. "Don't you know," he exploded, "that you may well be transporting family members of the same people who planted the bomb under your car?"

Sometimes it seems to take a trauma in our lives to bring us closer to the Lord. My "trauma" came with a bang. Before that, I'm ashamed to admit, though I thought I was a good Christian, I had merely been going through the motions, mechanically performing what I considered to be the duties that God required of me. I did not realize that mere practices cannot make anyone a Christian. I now realize that without my Savior, Jesus Christ, I would be totally lost. He brought me through my accident 20 years ago. His greatness and mercy is just not something that I have read about in the lives of other people. I have also experienced the reality of it in my own life (*Irish Independent*. April 25, 1998).

**New Form of the Kiss of Peace.** William E. McManus of Fort Wayne, suggests that a new form of greeting be tried by Christians to replace the traditional liturgical kiss of peace used in many worship services. Instead of the usual perfunctory handshake, hug, or quick peck on the cheek in the pews, he proposes that the act be held after worship in the church parking lot. McManus urges that every driver would be expected to exchange friendly greetings with every other driver they near, and also cheerfully wave other cars into the narrow exit lane. In addition to cutting down on fender-benders and horn-honking, aggressive pushiness, and outbursts of road-rage, this act of kindness and peace would better convey the way of life that Christ enjoins us to take up. How does it look in your church parking lot after Sunday worship?

■ TOPIC: Life on a Higher Level

■ QUESTIONS: 1. Why did Paul urge his readers to let the realities of heaven fill their thoughts? 2. In what sense have believers died with Christ? 3. What perspective should you have about your life here on earth? 4. How might you live each day for Christ? 5. Why is it important for you to avoid the vices mentioned by Paul?

■ ILLUSTRATIONS:

**A Complete Change.** In his book entitled *An Anthropologist on Mars,* neurologist Oliver Sacks tells about Virgil, a man who had been blind from early childhood. When he was 50, Virgil underwent surgery and was given the gift of sight. But as he and Dr. Sacks found out, having the physical capacity for sight is not the same as seeing.

Virgil's first experiences with sight were confusing. He was able to make out colors and movements, but arranging them into a coherent picture was more difficult. Over time he learned to identify various objects, but his habits—his behaviors—were still those of a blind man. Dr. Sacks asserts, "One must die as a blind person to be born again as a seeing person. It is the interim, the limbo . . . that is so terrible."

To truly see Jesus and His truth means more than observing what He did or said. It means a radical change in the way we think and act. As Paul noted in Colossians 3:10, *[You] have clothed yourselves with the new self, which is being renewed in knowledge according to the image of its creator.*

**No Dumbing Down.** The Third International Mathematics and Science Study issued its report in February, 1998. Despite the fact that Americans increased funding by more than 100 billion dollars per year over the last 15 years, United States students in grades eight and up fared poorly in math. The international study ranked U.S. students 19th out of the 21 participating countries in general math skills. The explanations varied: poorly written textbooks, unqualified teachers, refusal to teach proper skills, and a "dumbing down" of standards.

Paul contended with a similar dumbing down of standards in a culture that wanted to relax its morality. That's why he urged that higher moral standards be maintained by all believers.

**Good for Everyone.** Paul urged his readers to sing praises to God. The admonition of group singing might be important to heed. For centuries, music unified peoples and nations. Sailors sang aboard ships in the 1700s and the 1800s. Soldiers throughout wars sang. Through the 1940s students sang on dates. However, by the 1970s, students no longer sang. Voices were replaced by stereos. Now, technology has further crushed singing. The Walkman has divided America even more by turning music into a solitary and passive experience, reports James E. Shelly, a Cleveland writer. Rather than producing unity, music divides. Few youth even sing, preferring to watch music on MTV.

Paul was right. Sing in order to express your faith in God and to unify the body of Christ.

# WELCOMING OTHERS IN CHRIST

**BACKGROUND SCRIPTURE:** Philemon

**DEVOTIONAL READING:** James 2:1-13

**KEY VERSE:** I pray that the sharing of your faith may become effective when you perceive all the good that we may do for Christ. Philemon 6.

*KING JAMES VERSION*

PHILEMON 4 I thank my God, making mention of thee always in my prayers,

5 Hearing of thy love and faith, which thou hast toward the Lord Jesus, and toward all saints;

6 That the communication of thy faith may become effectual by the acknowledging of every good thing which is in you in Christ Jesus.

7 For we have great joy and consolation in thy love, because the bowels of the saints are refreshed by thee, brother.

8 Wherefore, though I might be much bold in Christ to enjoin thee that which is convenient,

9 Yet for love's sake I rather beseech thee, being such an one as Paul the aged, and now also a prisoner of Jesus Christ.

10 I beseech thee for my son Onesimus, whom I have begotten in my bonds:

11 Which in time past was to thee unprofitable, but now profitable to thee and to me:

12 Whom I have sent again: thou therefore receive him, that is, mine own bowels:

13 Whom I would have retained with me, that in thy stead he might have ministered unto me in the bonds of the gospel:

14 But without thy mind would I do nothing; that thy benefit should not be as it were of necessity, but willingly.

15 For perhaps he therefore departed for a season, that thou shouldest receive him for ever;

16 Not now as a servant, but above a servant, a brother beloved, specially to me, but how much more unto thee, both in the flesh, and in the Lord?

17 If thou count me therefore a partner, receive him as myself.

18 If he hath wronged thee, or oweth thee ought, put that on mine account;

19 I Paul have written it with mine own hand, I will repay it: albeit I do not say to thee how thou owest unto me even thine own self besides.

20 Yea, brother, let me have joy of thee in the Lord:

refresh my bowels in the Lord.

21 Having confidence in thy obedience I wrote unto thee, knowing that thou wilt also do more than I say.

*NEW REVISED STANDARD VERSION*

PHILEMON 4 When I remember you in my prayers, I always thank my God 5 because I hear of your love for all the saints and your faith toward the Lord Jesus. 6 I pray that the sharing of your faith may become effective when you perceive all the good that we may do for Christ. 7 I have indeed received much joy and encouragement from your love, because the hearts of the saints have been refreshed through you, my brother.

8 For this reason, though I am bold enough in Christ to command you to do your duty, 9 yet I would rather appeal to you on the basis of love—and I, Paul, do this as an old man, and now also as a prisoner of Christ Jesus. 10 I am appealing to you for my child, Onesimus, whose father I have become during my imprisonment. 11 Formerly he was useless to you, but now he is indeed useful both to you and to me. 12 I am sending him, that is, my own heart, back to you. 13 I wanted to keep him with me, so that he might be of service to me in your place during my imprisonment for the gospel; 14 but I preferred to do nothing without your consent, in order that your good deed might be voluntary and not something forced. 15 Perhaps this is the reason he was separated from you for a while, so that you might have him back forever, 16 no longer as a slave but more than a slave, a beloved brother—especially to me but how much more to you, both in the flesh and in the Lord.

17 So if you consider me your partner, welcome him as you would welcome me. 18 If he has wronged you in any way, or owes you anything, charge that to my account. 19 I, Paul, am writing this with my own hand: I will repay it. I say nothing about your owing me even your own self. 20 Yes, brother, let me have this benefit from you in the Lord! Refresh my heart in Christ. 21 Confident of your obedience, I am writing to you, knowing that you will do even more than I say.

13

| Monday, Aug. 21 | Philemon 1-7 | *Paul Gives Thanks for Philemon* |
| Tuesday, Aug. 22 | Philemon 8-12 | *Paul Expresses His Love for Onesimus* |
| Wednesday, Aug. 23 | Philemon 13-18 | *Paul Intercedes for Onesimus* |
| Thursday, Aug. 24 | Philemon 19-25 | *Paul's Challenge to Philemon* |
| Friday, Aug. 25 | James 2:1-7 | *Don't Let Fine Clothes Deceive You!* |
| Saturday, Aug. 26 | James 2:8-13 | *Show Mercy, and Love All People* |
| Sunday, Aug. 27 | James 2:14-26 | *Have True Faith; Do Good Works* |

## BACKGROUND

The fourth letter we have in the New Testament from Paul's prison correspondence is his epistle to Philemon. This brief tract is the shortest of Paul's letters preserved in the New Testament. Philemon was a member of the church in Colosse. Apparently a cell group of Christians or the congregation itself met in Philemon's home. Paul intended the house-church as well as Philemon to heed the message that he recorded in his letter, though Philemon was the recipient. The tone throughout the epistle is warm and friendly. Paul mentioned nothing in his letter about the heretical ideas and practices that were threatening the Colossian church.

Philemon had a slave named Onesimus who had escaped and somehow made his way to Rome, where he had come in contact with Paul the prisoner. The fugitive was persuaded to become a Christian, and he started a new life. Onesimus, whose name in Greek means "helpful" or "useful," looked after Paul for a time and became an aid to the elderly apostle in chains.

Paul remembered his duties to others, especially Philemon, a fellow Christian. He sent Onesimus back to Colosse, probably with a co-worker named Tychicus [TICK-ih-huss], who was carrying the epistle to the Colossians and the personal letter to Philemon. Paul's letter to Philemon courteously asked Philemon to welcome Onesimus back as a Christian brother.

Though nothing specifically is stated about slavery, the Letter to Philemon spelled the deathknell of the practice. The prevailing theme of welcoming each other in Christ as fellow believers meant the end of the terrible institution of regarding and treating other human beings as chattel. That's why some call this brief epistle "The Magna Carta of Liberty."

## NOTES ON THE PRINTED TEXT

Paul began his appeal by tactfully building a friendly relationship. The apostle assured Philemon that he kept him in his prayers. Paul had heard about the man's generosity, compassion, and faith. *When I remember you in my prayers, I always thank my God because I hear of your love for all the saints and your faith toward the Lord Jesus* (4-5). Paul also implied that there were still more important opportunities available for Philemon to show his Christian love and faith. *I pray that the sharing of your faith may become effective when you perceive all the good that we may do for Christ* (6).

One particular act of kindness and generosity had come to Paul's attention. Philemon had apparently performed some sort of relief work for his fellow believers. The apostle was impressed and expressed his joy. *I have indeed received much joy and encouragement from your love, because the hearts of the saints have been refreshed through you, my brother* (7).

The acknowledgment of Philemon's kindness paved the way for Paul to request that Philemon welcome back Onesimus. Paul wrote that it was within his authority as an apostle to order Philemon to comply with his request. Yet Paul based his appeal on love, friendship, and his own suffering for Christ's sake. *For this reason, though I am bold enough in Christ to command you to do your duty, yet I would rather appeal to you on the basis of love—and I, Paul, do this as an old man, and now also as a prisoner of Christ Jesus* (8-9).

The close relationship that had developed in prison between Paul and Onesimus was demonstrated by the apostle referring to himself as the converted slave's spiritual father and Onesimus as his child in the faith. *I am appealing to you for my child, Onesimus, whose father I have become during my imprisonment* (10). Paul made a play on words by utilizing Onesimus's name, which means "useful." Though the converted slave had formerly been useless, now he had proven himself to be useful to Paul. Onesimus had lived up to his name. *Formerly he was useless to you, but now he is indeed useful both to you and to me* (11).

The apostle wrote that he was returning Onesimus to Philemon. However, Paul indicated his reluctance, noting that Onesimus had proven quite helpful to him, and that Paul had become attached to Onesimus. The apostle would have preferred to keep Onesimus with him, but this would have been illegal and would also have shown disrespect for Philemon. *I am sending him, that is my own heart, back to you. I wanted to keep him with me . . . during my imprisonment for the gospel; but I preferred to do nothing without your consent, in order that your good deed might be voluntary and not something forced* (12-14).

Paul underscored that the grace of God was evident in the circumstances involving Onesimus. For example, he had left Philemon as a fugitive slave but would return to him as a spiritual brother in Christ. *Perhaps this is the reason he was separated from you for a while, so that you might have him back forever, no longer as a slave but more than a slave, a beloved brother—especially to me but how much more to you, both in the flesh and in the Lord* (15-16).

Paul now detailed his request to Philemon. The apostle urged clemency on Onesimus. *So if you consider me your partner, welcome him as you would welcome me* (17). Paul could not ignore the crime that Onesimus had committed. Roman law was specific. Whoever provided hospitality to a runaway slave was liable to the slave's owner for the value of each day's work that had been lost. Paul promised to act as the guarantor in which he would reimburse the amount of loss incurred by Onesimus's absence. *If he has wronged you in any way, or owes you anything, charge that to my account. I, Paul, am writing this with my own hand: I will repay it* (18-19). The apostle then reminded Philemon that he owed Paul his very soul, for the apostle had led the slave owner to salvation in Christ. *I say nothing about your owing me even your own self* (19).

The imprisoned evangelist was confident that Philemon would respond to his request. Paul thus closed his letter by hinting that he hoped Philemon would give Onesimus his freedom. *Yes, brother, let me have this benefit from you in the Lord! Refresh my heart in Christ. Confident of your obedience, I am writing to you, knowing that you will do even more than I say* (20-21).

## SUGGESTIONS TO TEACHERS

Family members rarely write letters to one another. They might communicate by e-mail or voice mail, but rarely by handwritten, lovingly composed notes. What a contrast this is with Paul's letters! They always bore a personal touch and always conveyed appreciation and concern for his readers. The Letter to Philemon illustrates this truth. The purpose and the wording of this brief epistle exemplify the gracious way fellow believers can communicate with one another.

**1. BOND BETWEEN BELIEVERS IN CHRIST.** Paul felt a close tie with Philemon, for they shared a common bond of faith in Christ. This spiritual relationship meant that they were fellow members of God's family. This remained true, even though they were separated by distance, and perhaps by age, culture, interests, and economic status. Use this truth to comment on how Christians are related to each other as fellow believers, despite their differences. Also mention that such a spiritual tie rules out any form of segregation in churches.

**2. BREACH BETWEEN BELIEVERS.** We don't know what caused the breach between Philemon and Onesimus, but obviously there had been discord in the household. Churches, like families, also have disagreements, sometimes causing a serious falling out between members. Such breaks in the family circle should not be permitted to continue. Reconciliation should take place.

**3. BASIS FOR FAMILY UNITY.** The Letter to Philemon makes it clear that all parties—including Paul, Philemon, and Onesimus—shared a spiritual bond that was stronger than even blood ties. That bond was their common commitment to their Savior. Onesimus's name, which means "helpful" or "useful," symbolized the way that all members of Christ's family should treat one another.

**4. BID FOR RECONCILIATION WITHIN THE FAMILY.** Paul gently and tactfully nudged Philemon to accept Onesimus as a fellow believer in Christ. Such family harmony among Christians is paramount. Take this opportunity to have your class talk about reconciliation within families, both personal households and the church family. What steps should each person take to open up their lives to Christ's healing, whether among members within a congregation or between members of a biological family?

■ **TOPIC:** The Grace of Life

■ **QUESTIONS:** 1. In what way did Philemon show Christian love? 2. How was Philemon's faith evident to Paul? 3. How has becoming a Christian transformed your relationship with your family and friends? 4. In what ways can you show the love of Christ to your employer and coworkers? 5. Whom have you recently had the opportunity to lead to faith in Christ?

■ **ILLUSTRATIONS:**

**Peaceful Colony.** William Penn was awarded land in the New World by King Charles II, and he established a colony known as Penn's woods, or Pennsylvania. Penn, a devout Quaker, took his Christian faith so seriously that he refused to use the power bestowed on him to kill the Native Americans, or Indians, inhabiting the area. No forts were built. No armed troops were organized. Penn insisted on treating the Indians justly. He stated that they were to be regarded as equals.

Whenever differences or tensions arose between the settlers and the Indians, Penn had the disputes resolved by bringing six whites and six Indians together to achieve a peaceful settlement. Other colonies were wracked with bloody attacks by Indians and equally brutal reprisals by the colonists. But Pennsylvania was spared, as long as William Penn's rule of kindness and fairness prevailed. Penn's death brought mourning to the Indians as well as the whites. For a time, the same practices introduced by Penn continued, and no forts or soldiers were to be seen.

As long as the gentle Quakers refused to arm themselves or regard the Indians as threats or foes, peace prevailed. Later, however, the Quakers were outnumbered and outvoted in Pennsylvania. Forts were built and militia were armed. Tragically, the situation changed immediately and with it came armed conflict.

**Lesson from South Africa.** The Truth and Reconciliation Commission established by the Mandela government in South Africa is setting an example for the world in its work with survivors and families of victims of the atrocities of apartheid. Healing has been happening. There was a woman who spent years searching for those who had tortured and murdered her son. When the perpetrators were finally found, brought to trial, and found guilty, the woman was asked by the judge what kind of punishment she wanted them to suffer. "Punishment?" the woman asked, perplexed. "Yes, punishment," the judge said. "We now have the power to punish such people." "Oh, no," she said. "I was searching for these men for a different reason, your honor." "What reason?" the judge asked. "I wanted to know whom to forgive," the woman responded. Finding the truth helped her forgive her son's murderers and uphold her integrity as a human being, rather than seek revenge and contaminate her soul (*The New York Times*, December 14, 1997).

**Two Brothers.** Paul Ray tells the story of two brothers who worked together on the family farm. One was married and had a large family. The other was single.

At the end of the day, the brothers shared everything equally, whether produce or profit.

Then one day the single brother said to himself, "It's not right that we should share the profit and produce equally. I'm alone and my needs are simple." So each night he took a sack of grain from his bin and crept across the field between their houses and dumped it into his brother's bin.

Meanwhile, the married brother said to himself, "It's not right that we should share the produce and profit equally. After all, I'm married and I have my wife and children to look after me in years to come. My brother has no one, and no one to take care of his future." So, each night he took a sack of grain and dumped it into his single brother's bin.

Both brothers were puzzled for years because their supply of grain never dwindled. Then one dark night the two brothers bumped into each other, and it dawned on them what was happening. They dropped their sacks and embraced one another for a long time. The moral of the story is this: "What are you doing tonight?"

---

**FOR YOUTH**

■ TOPIC: A Plea for Acceptance

■ QUESTIONS: 1. How did Paul express his appreciation for Philemon? 2. What appeal did Paul make to Philemon? 3. What is the basis for you forgiving those who have wronged you? 4. How might Christ work through you to remove barriers that exist between you and your fellow believers? 5. How might you exhibit courtesy and respect in your relationships?

■ ILLUSTRATIONS:

**I Forgive. I Forgive.** The *Evangelical Press News* reported that many Americans were moved by the Vietnam-era Pulitzer Prize-winning photo of 9-year-old Phan Thi Kim Phuc (pronounced *fuke*), naked and horribly burned, running from a napalm attack. But for Pastor John Plummer that picture had special significance. In 1972 he was responsible for setting up the air strike on the village of Trang Bang—a strike approved after he was twice assured there were no civilians in the area.

In June 1996 John saw a network news story about Kim Phuc and learned she was not only alive but living in Toronto. Plummer found out she was speaking at the Vietnam Veterans Memorial in Washington, D.C. He invited members of a Vietnam helicopter flight crew to attend the speech with him.

As Kim Phuc addressed the crowd, she said that if she ever met the pilot of the plane she would tell him she forgave him. Though they could not change the past, she hoped they could work together in the future. Plummer was able to get word to Kim Phuc that the man she wanted to meet was there.

"She saw my grief, my pain, my sorrow," Plummer wrote in an article in the *Virginia Advocate*. "She held out her arms to me and embraced me. All I could say was, 'I'm sorry; I'm so sorry,' over and over again. At the same time she was saying, 'It's all right; it's all right; I forgive; I forgive.'" Plummer learned that Kim Phuc became a Christian in 1982. Her faith in Christ enabled her to forgive Plummer for what he had done years ago.

**Reconciled.** Matthew Jack Davis was a private in the Mississippi Infantry that fought at Antietam, Fredericksburg, and Gettysburg. He was captured during the two week Spotsylvania Court House Campaign in northeastern Virginia on May 11 or 12, 1864. He was sent to Fort Delaware, a prisoner of war camp on Pea Patch Island in the Delaware River.

After Lee surrendered, Davis and his fellow soldiers were freed, but they had no money and no transportation to take them back to Mississippi. As they started to walk back, they were refused food and lodging in most cities such as Philadelphia and Wilmington. Hatred for the enemy was too strong. But in Hamburg, Pennsylvania, the three Confederates met 20 discharged Federal soldiers. When introductions were made, the blue-coats took the three men into their camp. There they helped and fed them. The following morning they shared their extra food with the three and gave them a haversack in which to carry the food.

Reconciliation was made. Former enemies could eat and share together, and begin again. Paul urged two former enemies—Philemon and Onesimus—to be reconciled to one another so that harmony and new life could exist.

**Forgiveness.** On September 30, 1997, the French Roman Catholic Church made a belated gesture of contrition. After 57 years of silence, the church repented, apologized, and asked for forgiveness for its role in the deportation of 75,000 Jews during the Nazi occupation of France during World War II. "We beg God's pardon, and we ask the Jewish people to hear our words of repentance," declared Archbishop Olivier de Berranger. Sometimes it is difficult to admit guilt and seek forgiveness. Paul wrote to Philemon to facilitate forgiveness and reconciliation between two estranged parties.